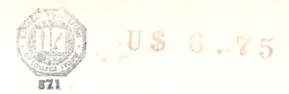

Kant and
the Nineteenth
Century

Contents of *A History of Western Philosophy*

W. T. JONES

California Institute of Technology

Kant and the Nineteenth Century

SECOND EDITION, REVISED

A History of Western Philosophy

Harcourt Brace Jovanovich, Inc.

NEW YORK   CHICAGO   SAN FRANCISCO   ATLANTA

LIST OF COPYRIGHTS AND ACKNOWLEDGMENTS

The author would like to thank the following publishers and copyright holders for permission to use the selections reprinted in this book:

GEORGE ALLEN & UNWIN LTD., for excerpts from *The Phenomenology of Mind* by G. W. F. Hegel, translated by J. B. Baillie.

THE CLARENDON PRESS, OXFORD, for excerpts from *Philosophy of Right* by G. W. F. Hegel, translated by T. M. Knox; from *Theory of Legislation* by Jeremy Bentham, translated by E. Dumont and C. M. Atkinson; from *Encyclopaedia of the Philosophical Sciences*, translated by W. Wallace; from *Essays on Truth and Reality, Appearance and Reality,* and *Collected Essays* by F. H. Bradley. Reprinted by permission of the Clarendon Press, Oxford.

DOUBLEDAY & COMPANY, INC., for excerpts from *The Birth of Tragedy and the Genealogy of Morals* by Friedrich Nietzsche, translated by Francis·Golffing. Copyright © 1956 by Doubleday & Co., Inc. Reprinted by permission of the publisher.

DOVER PUBLICATIONS, INC., for excerpts from *The Will to Believe* by William James.

ALEXANDER DRU for excerpts from *The Journals of Kierkegaard*, translated by Alexander Dru.

E. P. DUTTON & CO., INC., for excerpts from *Essays in Radical Empiricism* and *A Pluralistic Universe* by William James, edited by Ralph Barton Perry. Reprinted by permission of the publishers, E. P. Dutton & Co., Inc.

FABER AND FABER LTD., for an excerpt from "The Love Song of J. Alfred Prufrock" in *Collected Poems 1909–1962* by T. S. Eliot. Reprinted by permission of Faber and Faber Ltd., publishers.

HARCOURT BRACE JOVANOVICH, INC., for an excerpt from "The Love Song of J. Alfred Prufrock," in *The Complete Poems and Plays of T. S. Eliot.*

HARPER & ROW, PUBLISHERS, INC., for excerpts from *The Moral Equivalent of War & Other Essays* by William James, edited by John K. Roth. Reprinted by permission of Harper & Row, Publishers, Inc.

HARVARD UNIVERSITY PRESS for excerpts from *Collected Papers of Charles Sanders Peirce*. Reprinted by permission of the publishers from *Collected Papers of Charles Sanders Peirce*, Vols. I, II, V, VI, and VIII, edited by Charles Hartshorne, Paul Weiss, and Arthur W. Burks (Vol. VIII). Cambridge, Mass.: The Belknap Press of Harvard University Press. Copyright by the President and Fellows of Harvard College as follows: © Vol. I, 1931, 1959; Vol. II, 1932, 1960; Vol. V, 1934, 1962; Vol. VI, 1935, 1963; Vol. VIII, 1958.

ALEXANDER R. JAMES for excerpts from *Pragmatism, The Meaning of Truth,* and *The Varieties of Religious Experience* by William James. *Pragmatism* and *The Meaning of Truth* edited by Ralph Barton Perry.

MACMILLAN & CO. LTD., for excerpts from *Critique of Pure Reason* by Immanuel Kant, translated by Norman Kemp Smith. Reprinted with permission of Macmillan & Co. Ltd. and St. Martin's Press, Inc.

E. S. PEARSON for excerpts from *The Grammar of Science* by Karl Pearson.

SIR ISAAC PITMAN AND SONS LTD., for excerpts from *Karl Marx: Early Writings,* translated and edited by T. B. Bottomore. Originally published by C. A. Watts & Co. Ltd.

PRINCETON UNIVERSITY PRESS for excerpts from *Fear and Trembling* and *The Sickness unto Death* by Søren Kierkegaard, translated by Walter Lowrie, copyright 1941, 1954, Princeton Paperback 1968; from *Either/Or* by Søren Kierkegaard, Vol. II, translated by Walter Lowrie, copyright 1944 © 1959, Princeton Paperback 1971; and from *Concluding Unscientific Postscript* by Søren Kierkegaard, translated by D. F. Swenson and Walter Lowrie, copyright 1941 © 1969, Princeton Paperback 1968, for the American Scandinavian Foundation. Reprinted by permission of Princeton University Press; *Concluding Unscientific Postscript* also by permission of the American Scandinavian Foundation.

RANDOM HOUSE, INC., for excerpts from *The Best Short Stories of Fyodor Dostoyevsky,* translated by David Magarshack. Modern Library, 1955.

HENRY REGNERY COMPANY for excerpts from *Beyond Good and Evil* by Friedrich Nietzsche, translated by M. Cowan.

ROUTLEDGE & KEGAN PAUL LTD., for excerpts from *The World as Will and Idea* by Arthur Schopenhauer, translated by R. B. Haldane and J. Kemp.

THE VIKING PRESS, INC., for excerpts from *The Portable Nietzsche,* translated and edited by Walter Kaufmann. Copyright 1954 by The Viking Press, Inc. Reprinted by permission of The Viking Press, Inc.

GEORGE WEIDENFIELD AND NICOLSON LTD., for excerpts from *Sketch for a Historical Picture of the Progress of the Human Mind* by Marquis de Condorcet, translated by J. Barraclough.

WHITLOCK'S, INC., for excerpts from *Charles S. Peirce's Letters to Lady Welby,* edited by Irwin C. Lieb for the Graduate Philosophy Club of Yale University. Reprinted by permission of Whitlock's, Inc., 15 Broadway, New Haven, Connecticut.

Preface

During the quarter century since A *History of Western Philosophy* was originally planned, it has expanded from one, to two, then to four, and now in this latest revision, to five volumes. The changes incorporated in these revisions reflect what I have learned about the history of philosophy, the nature of the philosophical enterprise itself, and the role that philosophy plays in the general culture. They also reflect a good deal of thought about what characteristics make a textbook useful.

The most noticeable innovation in this revision is the expansion of Volume IV into two separate volumes: IV. *Kant and the Nineteenth Century,* and V. *The Twentieth Century to Wittgenstein and Sartre.* The current division into five volumes conforms to the way courses in the history of philosophy are now organized, and it allows readers to choose the periods on which they wish to concentrate. On the assumption that readers of one volume may not always have access to the others, I have added short summaries of earlier views where these

seemed particularly relevant. Examples are the recapitulation of the main features of Kant's theories at the start of Volume V as a background for the revival
of realism, and a short summary of Aristotle's views as an introduction to Frege's
revolution in logic. On the other hand, because some readers will own more
than one volume, I have added numerous new cross-references from one volume
to another to make it easy to look up fuller accounts of the topics discusssed.

Even more important, the expansion into five volumes has made it possible
for me to add detailed studies of a number of important thinkers whom I
regretfully had to omit from earlier editions. For instance, in Volume IV there
are entirely new chapters on Peirce, James, and Bradley, and Volume V includes
chapters on G. E. Moore, Frege, the *Tractatus,* the Logical Positivists, and
Heidegger. In addition, the chapter on Russell has been completely rewritten
and doubled in length, while the chapters on Husserl, Sartre, and the later
Wittgenstein have also been considerably revised.

There are also a great many changes—some of them major—in my interpretation and evaluation of individual thinkers and their theories. But, despite
all these alterations, my point of view remains basically the same. In revising,
as in originally writing, this history, I have been guided by four principles—
concentration, selectivity, contextualism, and the use of original sources.

An historian of philosophy can either say something, however brief, about
everyone who philosophized, or can give a reasonably consecutive account of
a number of representative thinkers, omitting discussion of many second- and
third-flight philosophers. I have chosen the latter approach, for two reasons. First,
many works based on the first approach are already available, and I see no good
reason for adding to their number. Second, such works are likely to be unintelligible to the beginning student. I still recall my own bewilderment as an under-
graduate in seeking to understand a complicated theory that some expositor had
"boiled down" to a summary. The principle of concentration rests on the thesis
that it is better to fully understand a few theories than to be superficially
acquainted with a great many.

But concentration implies selectivity, and I can hardly hope that even those
who accept the principle of concentration will approve all my selections. There
will probably be no difference of opinion about the great figures of the remote
past. Everyone will surely agree that Plato and Aristotle are the masters of their
age. And perhaps there will be general agreement that Augustine and Thomas
occupy similar positions in the Middle Ages—that Augustine demands more
attention than, say, Boethius, and Thomas more attention than Duns Scotus. But
how is one to choose among philosophers of more recent times? Here one must
try to anticipate the judgment of time. To some extent I have simply avoided
the issue by dealing with more philosophers in the modern period. The result
is that, whereas the first two volumes cover more than two millennia, the last
three focus on hardly more than four hundred years.

Even so, I have been forced to be selective by my determination that here,
as in the earlier periods, I would not mention a philosopher unless I could deal

with his views in some detail. Thus I have repressed a natural desire at least to mention Fichte and Schelling, in order to provide extended analyses of Hegel and Schopenhauer. All these thinkers represent reactions to Kantianism, and although they differ among themselves in many ways, it is better, I believe, to select and concentrate on a few than to attempt to give a complete enumeration. Similarly, I have thought it best to concentrate on one Neo-Hegelian— Bradley— instead of parceling out the available pages among T. H. Green, Bosanquet, and Royce, and I have preferred to focus on G. E. Moore rather than sacrifice a thorough treatment of him in order to mention the many New and Critical Realists who were his contemporaries.

For somewhat different reasons I have resisted an inclination to discuss post-Wittgensteinian developments. In the first place, if one were to move beyond Wittgenstein, there seemed no obvious point of division between what is clearly "past," and so a part of the history of philosophy, and what is clearly "contemporary," and not yet a part of that history. In the second place, as long as a philosopher is alive there is always the danger—at least from the point of view of the historian—that he or she may upset the apple cart by changing his or her mind. I therefore decided that (with the single exception of Sartre) only philosophers who are either dead or no longer active would qualify for inclusion. Accordingly, this edition ends with a discussion of Wittgenstein's *Philosophical Investigations*. So much for the principle of selectivity, or (alternatively) of exclusion.

The third principle underlying the writing of this history is the generally recognized but seldom adopted principle that philosophers are men and women, not disembodied spirits. Some histories of philosophy treat theories as if they were isolated from everything except other philosophical theories. But all the great philosophers have actually been concerned with what may be called "local" problems. To be understood, their theories must be seen as expressions—doubtless at a highly conceptualized level—of the same currents of thought and feeling that were moving the poets and the statesmen, the theologians and the playwrights, and the ordinary people of the age. Otherwise, how could their philosophies ever have been accepted? These philosophers furnished satisfactory answers only because they were alert to the problems that were exercising their contemporaries and because they were harassed by the same doubts. The cultural milieu in which a given philosophy emerges can be ignored only at the risk of making the philosophy seem a detached (and so a meaningless and inconsequential) affair.

In carrying out this principle of contextualism I have begun my account of Greek philosophy by describing the state of affairs in Athens at the end of the Peloponnesian War, and I have drawn on the plays of Euripides and Aristophanes to illustrate the mood of the times. This, I believe, is a necessary setting for Plato, because his central thesis—the theory of forms—was an attempt to answer the scepticism and cynicism of his age. Plato's insistence on the existence of "absolute" standards for conduct and for knowledge is understandable only as a reflection of the social, economic, and political chaos and the moral and religious collapse that occurred at the end of the fifth century.

Similarly, my discussion of medieval philosophy is prefaced with an account of the dissolving Roman Empire, and I have tried to indicate the rich and diversified cultural background within which Christian philosophy developed. In discussing the theories of Augustine and Thomas I have kept in mind that, whereas Augustine expressed the eschatological fervor of a new sect fighting for its life, Thomas embodied the serenity of an imperial and universal religion whose piety had been softened by a new sense of responsibility for "that which is Caesar's."

Finally, in discussing the development of early modern philosophy I have tried to show the many factors—exploration and discovery, the rise of money power, Humanism, the Reformation, and above all the new scientific method—that combined to overthrow the medieval synthesis and to create new problems that philosophy even today is struggling to resolve. Volume IV begins with an account of the change in tone from the Enlightenment to Romanticism, and Volume V with a description of subsequent developments in the first half of this century, all these being illustrated by examples drawn from poetry and the novel. In a word, I have conceived the history of philosophy to be part of the general history of culture and hence to be intelligible only in its cultural context.

The fourth principle is my conviction that in philosophy—or in any discipline, for that matter—nothing takes the place of a direct, patient, and painstaking study of a great and subtle mind. For this reason there is much to be said for the use of a sourcebook. But a sourcebook alone has serious limitations, because its selections are apt to be discontinuous and difficult to follow. The advantage of a text is that it can explicate obscure passages and draw comparisons. Even so, explication and interpretation are not substitutes for the documents themselves. Therefore, each of the volumes in this series stands halfway between textbook and sourcebook and tries to combine the advantages of both: I have set out a philosopher's thought in his own words by a careful selection of key passages and have bound these together with my own comment and criticism. The quoted passages constitute about one third of the contents.

To undertake to give an account of the history of philosophy in its cultural context is a formidable and perhaps presumptuous task for a single expositor. In this undertaking I have received help from a wide variety of sources. In addition to those who commented on the first and second editions, whose names I shall not repeat here, I wish to thank the friends and colleagues who have commented on the new chapters in this revised edition: Russell Abrams, for reading the chapters on Husserl and Heidegger; Jay Atlas, for the chapters on Frege and Russell; Douglass Greenlee, for the chapter on Peirce; Richard Hertz, for the chapters on James and Russell; James A. McGilvray, for the chapters on Peirce, James, and Bradley; Cynthia Schuster, for the chapters on Moore, the *Tractatus,* and Logical Positivism; and Garrett Vander Veer, for the chapter on Bradley. In addition, I am grateful to Robert J. Fogelin and Stephen A.

Erickson, who read all the new material. These readers have saved me from many errors of fact and interpretation; for errors that remain I must be responsible, and I shall be grateful if any that come to notice are pointed out to me.

I am obliged to the many publishers and copyright holders (listed on pages iv–v) through whose cooperation the quotations used in these volumes appear. Since I have followed the style of the various writers and translators I have quoted, there is some variation in spelling, capitalization, and punctuation in the reprinted passages. Full bibliographical notes, keyed to the text by letters rather than numbers, appear at the end of each volume.

For the secretarial work on the manuscript I am indebted to Harriet King, Parker Palmer, Edith Taylor, Joy Hansen, and Valera Hall, who divided the typing, and to Margaret Mulhauser, who once again allowed me to impose on her the onerous tasks of checking references and proofreading successive drafts.

W. T. Jones

Contents

5

6

Introduction

The eighteenth-century *philosophes* were persuaded that they lived in the best of all possible worlds. Because nature seemed to them beneficent—"Whatever is, is right"—and because people seemed rational, they concluded that progress was inevitable. But this optimism soon suffered a series of heavy blows. The French Revolution, which was supposed to mark the overthrow of tyranny, only ushered in a more formidable tyrant—Napoleon. The Industrial Revolution, instead of bringing peace and plenty, resulted in urban overcrowding and misery. And Hume's use of Locke's empirical criterion of meaning proved to have undermined—even more than Hume himself realized—both the concept of nature and the concept of reason. As a result a countermovement began to emerge—a movement hostile to science, sceptical of progress, opposed to prosperity, and increasingly alienated from the long-dominant values of rationality, self-consciousness, objectivity, and detachment. (Chapter 1.)

Some of the complex interactions between formal philosophical theory and the two divergent currents of thought and feeling described above can be seen in the philosophy of Kant. Kant recognized the destructive potential of Hume's critique; one of the main drives that animated his thought was the desire to answer Hume's criticisms of the claims of science and to show that an a priori knowledge of nature is possible. (Chapter 2.) A second main drive of his philosophy, however, was to limit scientific knowledge in order to make a place for feeling, for what he called "faith." (Chapter 3.) Both of these aims were accomplished in a single stroke by what Kant called his "Copernican revolution" in the theory of knowledge. Abandoning the traditional view that minds are the essentially passive contemplators of independently existing objects, Kant held that objects are constructs in which the activity of minds plays an essential part.

Many important consequences followed from this revolution. Indeed, philosophy since Kant has been largely a series of modulations of, and reactions against, his formulations. Kant maintained first that since cognition involves construction, things into which this constructive activity has not entered are literally unknowable, and second that there is a realm of reality that is inaccessible to human minds because they have not participated in its construction. Post-Kantian philosophy has divided into two main streams, depending on which part of this double thesis was accepted and which part rejected. Some philosophers agreed with Kant that knowledge is limited to the spatiotemporal world but rejected his unknowable things-in-themselves as mere vestiges of an outmoded metaphysics; as a result they concentrated their attention on this world and its problems. Other philosophers agreed with Kant that there is a reality independent of human minds but did not want to admit that this reality is unknowable. Accordingly, since these philosophers accepted Kant's contention that reason is limited to the spatiotemporal world, they had to rely on some other mode of access to the reality they believed lay behind the phenomena. The result was a reaffirmation of metaphysics, but in an antirational (or at least arational) form very different from the pre-Kantian rationalistic metaphysics.

Hegel and Schopenhauer represented these two tendencies in nineteenth-century thought. Hegel rejected Kant's things-in-themselves; reality, he argued, is "for" minds. But he greatly expanded the role of mind in the construction of reality (or "experience"). Whereas Kant had limited that role to a few standard syntheses that are common to all human minds everywhere, Hegel held that mind itself undergoes development; it passes through successive stages, each of which includes the lower stages while superseding them. Schopenhauer adopted the other alternative. Kant's spatiotemporal world, he held, is the appearance of an underlying reality that becomes accessible in intuition, that is, when we free ourselves from the constructions of sense perception and of science. Intuition, which is direct, unmediated apprehension, discloses this reality to be a blind, insatiable will from which the only escape is a universal asceticism. (Chapter 4.)

Though Schopenhauer's view had affinities with the Romantic rejection of reason and science, the predominant world view for many decades descended more or less directly from the Enlightenment's optimism, meliorism, and confidence. The difference was that the instrument of progress was no longer "pure" reason; it was now reason informed by the methods of empirical science. Since these scientifically oriented philosophers rejected Kant's things-in-themselves, and since they saw that the industrialization and urbanization of Europe were creating grave economic and social problems, their attention shifted from metaphysics to social philosophy. The British Utilitarians, the Comtians, and the Marxists were all representative of these developments. (Chapter 5.)

But the philosophers of the countermovement, as it has just been called, were not only suspicious of science as a cognitive enterprise; they were also contemptuous of the concentration of attention on the improvement of social conditions and on material welfare. Instead, they concentrated on existential problems—above all, on finding what Kierkegaard called "a focus and a center" for their own lives, something that would give meaning to what they felt to be an otherwise meaningless existence. This search led Kierkegaard himself to reject reason and to repudiate evidence. At best they yield only "approximations," but he demanded absolute certainty. He found this certainty, paradoxically, in the passionate affimation of the "absurdity" that God became incarnate as man and died on the Cross for our sins. Nietzsche's solution to this existential problem was completely antithetical to Kierkegaard's. God is dead, he said. It follows that there can be no absolute values or criteria to guide our choices. The individual who is strong enough to face these truths and to create values for himself is rare. Indeed, he is an overman, sharply distinguished from those who slavishly conform to the ethic of their society or who, like Kierkegaard, make a cowardly leap of faith. (Chapter 6.)

James's reaction was very different, partly because, though like Kierkegaard, he had passed through a religious crisis, his temperament was basically optimistic and confident. If he too could be said to be concerned with "existential" problems, it was with the practical problems of adjustment to life rather than with somehow managing to overcome it. Moreover, James came to philosophy from medicine and psychology instead of from theology or classical philology, and his experience in these fields deeply marked his approach to philosophy. His approach was not that of a cognitivist who seeks to understand the universe: it was that of a therapist who was concerned to help people in quandaries. Thus, though he undertook an epistemological investigation into the nature and limits of knowledge, it was less to lay the basis for a secure science (as with Kant) than to undermine the pretensions of scientism by showing that science, as much as religion, rests on faith. This being the case—and this is what the pragmatic theory of truth really meant to James—people are entitled to believe whatever they deeply want to believe. (Chapter 8.)

Whereas James was content with belief, provided that it satisfies our "needs," the chief need Peirce recognized was that for knowledge, not mere belief. Peirce's main interest was to get his ideas clear, and this presupposed that there is something objective, something independent of ourselves, for us to become progressively more clear about. Peirce was thus a metaphysician, but one who, instead of relying on the Hegelian logic, used the method of science to fix his beliefs. One of the most important characteristics of the universe that Peirce's investigations disclosed is the feature that he called Thirdness. Thirdness is a triadic relation, and the most fundamental of all these relations is that obtaining between a sign, its object, and its interpretant. Thus Peirce replaced the relatively slippery notion of meaning with the more precise conception of the action of a sign. Meanwhile, reflection on the superiority of the method of science as a way of fixing belief led Peirce to tackle the problem of meaning from still another angle. What emerged was a new criterion of meaning: The meaning of any proposition is identical with the "sum of the experimental phenomena predicted by" that proposition. This, and not James's vague criterion of "working," is what pragmatism meant to Peirce. (Chapter 7.)

Like Peirce, and unlike James and Kierkegaard and Nietzsche, Bradley was a cognitivist and a metaphysician. But otherwise he and Peirce had almost nothing in common. Peirce was a scholastic realist who differed from Aristotle and Aquinas chiefly in the fact that, as he said, the method of science was available to him and had not been available to them. Bradley for his part held that the method of science, far from fixing our beliefs securely, yields at best only "appearance," and so must be supplemented and superseded by a special metaphysical method. In this respect Bradley was a follower—indeed, he was one of the last in a long series of followers—of Hegel. But in Bradley's hands Hegelian dialectic, instead of leading to the construction of a vast and imposing metaphysical system, proved to be a destructive weapon. He concluded, on the one hand, that thought "lives" by relations and, on the other hand, that relations are in principle contradictory. It followed that the Absolute, though knowable in degree, is ultimately unknowable. This conclusion seemed to many critics to leave Bradley no options save scepticism or mysticism. And since Bradley seemed to have demonstrated that this conclusion follows inescapably from Kant's view of the relation between mind and its objects, those who disliked the constructivism implicit in Kantianism concluded that a wholly new start was in order. Thus at the turn of the century the stage was set for a pursuit of objectivity along a number of different but converging paths. (Chapter 9.)

Dust as we are, the immortal spirit grows
Like harmony in music; there is a dark
Inscrutable workmanship that reconciles
Discordant elements, makes them cling together
In one society.

WORDSWORTH

Ah, what a dusty answer gets the soul
When hot for certainties in this our life!

GEORGE MEREDITH

CHAPTER 1

The Age of Reason

The Mood of the Enlightenment

If one had to characterize the seventeenth and eighteenth centuries by a single word, that word would be "optimistic." It is not surprising that the Age of Reason—or the Enlightenment, as it is also called—was optimistic. Europe had finally emerged from a long period of superstition and bigotry. The new science was revealing that the universe, appearances to the contrary, is a vast but fundamentally simple mechanism. As a part of this orderly universe man's behavior should be subject to prediction, and hence to control, in the interests of improving his material and social well-being. Great progress had already been made in this respect. There seemed to be no reason why continued, indeed unlimited, progress was not possible.

A characteristic expression of these widely held beliefs is found in Condorcet's[1] *Sketch for a Historical Picture of the Progress of the Human Mind:*

> If man can, with almost complete assurance, predict phenomena when he
> knows their laws, . . . why, then, should it be regarded as a fantastic under-
> taking to sketch, with some pretence to truth, the future destiny of man on
> the basis of his history? The sole foundation for belief in the natural sciences
> is this idea, that the general laws directing the phenomena of the universe,
> known or unknown, are necessary and constant. Why should this principle
> be any less true for the development of the intellectual and moral faculties
> of man than for the other operations of nature? . . .
>
> Our hopes for the future condition of the human race can be subsumed
> under three important heads: the abolition of inequality between nations,
> the progress of equality within each nation, and the true perfection of
> mankind. . . .
>
> Is there on the face of the earth a nation whose inhabitants have been
> debarred by nature herself from the enjoyment of freedom and the exercise
> of reason?
>
> Are those differences which have hitherto been seen in every civilized
> country in respect of the enlightenment, the resources, and the wealth enjoyed
> by the different classes into which it is divided . . . [an inevitable] part of
> civilization itself, or are they due to the present imperfections of the social
> art? . . . In other words, will men approach a condition in which everyone
> will have the knowledge necessary to conduct himself in the ordinary affairs
> of life, according to the light of his own reason, to preserve his mind free
> from prejudice, to understand his rights and to exercise them in accordance
> with his conscience and his creed . . . ?
>
> In answering these . . . questions we shall find in the experience of the
> past, in the observation of the progress that the sciences and civilization have
> already made, in the analysis of the progress of the human mind and of the
> development of its faculties, the strongest reasons for believing that nature
> has set no limit to the realization of our hopes. . . .
>
> The time will therefore come when the sun will shine only on free men
> who know no other master but their reason; when tyrants and slaves, priests
> and their stupid or hypocritical instruments will exist only in works of history
> and on the stage; and when we shall think of them only . . . to learn how
> to recognize and so to destroy, by force of reason, the first seeds of tyranny
> and superstition, should they ever dare to reappear amongst us. . . .
>
> New instruments, machines and looms can add to man's strength and can
> improve at once the quality and the accuracy of his productions, and can
> diminish the time and labour that has to be expended on them. The obstacles
> still in the way of this progress will disappear, accidents will be foreseen
> and prevented, the insanitary conditions . . . will be eliminated. . . .

1 Condorcet (1743–94) was a mathematician who made important contributions to the study of
probability theory. Although he was a strong supporter of the French Revolution, he was
proscribed by the radical Jacobins because he opposed them. He wrote the *Sketch* while in
hiding and died before finishing it.

So not only will the same amount of ground support more people, but everyone will have less work to do, will produce more, and satisfy his wants more fully. . . .

Organic perfectibility or deterioration amongst the various strains in the vegetable and animal kingdom can be regarded as one of the general laws of nature. This law also applies to the human race. No-one can doubt that, as preventitive medicine improves and food and housing become healthier . . . the average length of human life will be increased. . . . It is reasonable to hope that all other diseases may likewise disappear as their distant causes are discovered. Would it be absurd then to suppose that this perfection of the human species might be capable of indefinite progress; that the day will come when death will be due only to extraordinary accidents[;] . . . and that ultimately the average span between birth and decay will have no assignable value? . . .

Finally may we not extend such hopes to the intellectual and moral faculties? . . .

How consoling for the philosopher who laments the errors, the crimes, the injustices which still pollute the earth and of which he is often the victim is this view of the human race, emancipated from its shackles, released from the empire of fate and from that of the enemies of its progress, advancing with a firm and sure step along the path of truth, virtue and happiness![a]

What Condorcet projected in his *Sketch* was a secular, this-worldly heaven: His belief in the inevitability of progress was not an empirical hypothesis, despite the form in which it is cast and the language used to describe it. More akin to religious belief, it was an article of faith, immune to negative empirical evidence because it sustained Condorcet in the trials and defeats he encountered.

The key ideas that underpin Condorcet's optimistic faith are nature and reason. These two concepts were indeed central to almost all the thinking of the eighteenth century. Doubtless, they meant rather different things to different people; yet, because men agreed on what was unnatural and irrational, it is possible to get at the mood of the Enlightenment by examining what the writers of the eighteenth century excluded from nature and reason. Whether they were thinking of time past or of time present, whether of physical nature or of human nature, they excluded the unpredictable and miraculous, especially the possibility of intervention by supernatural forces from outside the closed system of nature. Accordingly, although few Enlightenment thinkers were explicit atheists, they were, at most, very tepid Deists. They envisaged a God who, having created an orderly universe, left it strictly alone.

Opinion varied through a broad spectrum—from that of a relative sceptic like Voltaire, who held that if God did not exist He would have to be invented, to that of Rousseau, who regarded himself as a Christian but who was certainly far from orthodox.

It is not in my power to believe that passive and dead matter can have brought forth living and feeling beings. . . . I believe, therefore, that the world is governed by a wise and powerful will; I see it or rather I feel it, and it is a great thing to know this. But has this same world always existed, or has it been created? Is there one source of all things? Are there two or many? What is their nature? I know not; and what concern is it of mine? . . . I see God everywhere in his works; I feel him within myself; I behold him all around me; but if I try to ponder him himself, if I try to find out where he is, what he is, what is his substance, he escapes me. . . .[b]

Furthermore, most eighteenth-century thinkers, whether sceptics or believers, drew a sharp distinction between the few simple truths of natural religion, on which they held all men could agree, and the complex theological doctrines that divided the various "high" religions into hostile camps.[2] The *philosophes* had nothing but contempt for Christianity, regarded either as a body of formal philosophical beliefs or as an institution wielding political power. Edward Gibbon's[3] attitude, for instance, was coldly supercilious:

A candid but rational inquiry into the progress and establishment of Christianity may be considered as a very essential part of the history of the Roman empire. While that great body was invaded by open violence, or undermined by slow decay, a pure and humble religion gently insinuated itself into the minds of men, grew up in silence and obscurity, derived new vigour from opposition, and finally erected the triumphant banner of the cross on the ruins of the Capitol. . . .

Our curiosity is naturally prompted to inquire by what means the Christian faith obtained so remarkable a victory over the established religions of the earth. To this inquiry, an obvious but satisfactory answer may be returned; that it was owing to the convincing evidence of the doctrine itself, and to the ruling providence of its great Author. But, as truth and reason seldom find so favourable a reception in the world, and as the wisdom of Providence frequently condescends to use the passions of the human heart, and the general circumstances of mankind, as instruments to execute its purpose; we may still be permitted, though with becoming submission, to ask not indeed what were the first, but what were the secondary causes of the rapid growth of the Christian church? . . .

When the promise of eternal happiness was proposed to mankind, on condition of adopting the faith and of observing the precepts of the gospel, it is no wonder that so advantageous an offer should have been accepted by great numbers of every religion, of every rank, and of every province in the Roman empire. The ancient Christians were animated by a contempt for their present existence, and by a just confidence of immortality, of which the doubtful and imperfect faith of modern ages cannot give us any adequate

2 In *The Social Contract*, for instance, Rousseau distinguished between "the religion of man" and the Christianity of his own day. The former, which he identified with the teachings of the Gospels, is "holy, sublime, and true." The latter, he felt, "clouds the true worship of Divinity with vain ceremonies."

3 Gibbon (1737–94) was the author of *Decline and Fall of the Roman Empire*, one of the great monuments of historical scholarship.

notion. In the primitive church, the influence of truth was very powerfully strengthened by an opinion which, however it may deserve respect for its usefulness and antiquity, has not been found agreeable to experience. It was universally believed that the end of the world and the kingdom of Heaven were at hand. The near approach of this wonderful event had been predicted by the apostles; the tradition of it was preserved by their earliest disciples, and those who understood in their literal sense the discourses of Christ himself were obliged to expect the second and glorious coming of the Son of Man in the clouds, before that generation was totally extinguished, which had beheld his humble condition upon earth, and which might still be witness of the calamities of the Jews under Vespasian or Hadrian. The revolution of seventeen centuries has instructed us not to press too closely the mysterious language of prophecy and revelation; but, as long as, for wise purposes, this error was permitted to subsist in the church, it was productive of the most salutary effects on the faith and practice of Christians, who lived in the awful expectation of that moment when the globe itself, and all various race of mankind, should tremble at the appearance of their divine Judge.[c]

Gibbon made it clear that he regarded the triumph of this "pure and humble" religion as a major catastrophe.[4] He believed, however, that the age in which he lived was freeing mankind from this incubus; hence he faced the future with confidence, expecting posterity to build a new world on rational lines, freed from the prejudice, superstition, and ignorance with which the Church had so long bound men's minds.[5]

It is also obvious, even in this short passage, that Gibbon was determined to treat Christianity as a social and cultural phenomenon. Whatever may be thought about its supernatural origin, Christianity has a natural history and is just as much a neutral object of study as are the pagan cults, the barbarian invasions, or the criminal insanity of Caligula. Suppose, for instance, that the "philosophical historian" wishes to inquire about the reliability of a particular document. Does he ask whether the author was a devout Christian? He does indeed; but instead of taking this devotion as a guarantee of the truthfulness of the report, he becomes suspicious of the information that the document contains. For the author was an interested party, and the historian knows enough about human nature to recognize the bias that personal loyalties create. We read of miracles and prodigies. Are we to accept them? On the contrary; we must "conclude that . . . the eyes of the spectators have sometimes been deceived by fraud [and] the understanding of the readers . . . much more frequently . . . insulted by fiction." In every case our rule must be to accept only those claims that are "agreeable to experience." In adopting this criterion, Gibbon applied

---

4 In summarizing his account of the Middle Ages, Gibbon said, "I have described the triumph of barbarism and religion."

5 It was always convenient for the "Protestant and philosophic" historian to talk about the evils of the Catholic Church while intending his readers to understand the evils of religion.

to historical inquiry one of the same criteria that Newton applied to physics. In this sense Gibbon's history was scientific.

Indeed, it is fair to say that the Enlightenment rejected the concept of divine intervention in the world and relegated God to the role of spectator. This it did in order to be able to deal with a closed, completely regular system. Whatever differences existed among eighteenth-century views of the nature of "nature," a common feature of these views was the notion of order.

This theme was clearly sounded by Montesquieu (1689–1755) in the opening lines of his great work on social anthropology: "Laws, in their most general signification, are the necessary relations arising from the nature of things. In this sense all beings have their laws: the Deity His laws, the material world its laws, the intelligences superior to man their laws, the beasts their laws, man his laws." Montesquieu recognized that the study of human nature is more difficult than the study of physical nature, not because it is less subject to laws, but because its laws are more complex.

> The intelligent world is far from being so well governed as the physical. For though the former has also its laws, which of their own nature are invariable, it does not conform to them so exactly as the physical world. This is because, on the one hand, particular intelligent beings are of a finite nature, and consequently liable to error; and on the other, their nature requires them to be free agents. Hence they do not steadily conform to their primitive laws; and even those of their own instituting they frequently infringe.[e]

This passage has a medieval sound, but whereas a medieval theologian would have followed it with a disquisition on sin, grace, and salvation, Montesquieu at once launched into an analysis of the factors that produce this variability in human conduct. Consider, for instance, the conclusion of his famous study of climate: "If it be true that the temper of the mind and the passions of the heart are extremely different in different climates, the laws ought to be in relation both to the variety of those passions and to the variety of those tempers."[f] In other words, there are underlying regularities (in Montesquieu's assumption) that can be discovered in the midst of the superficial diversities of human character and conduct, and these regularities should be taken into account in political science, that is, in the adjustment of constitutions and systems of government to the needs and capacities of different peoples. This empirical and pragmatic interest dominated Montesquieu's whole work. Observation, for instance, showed the following:

> Cold air constringes the extremities of the external fibres of the body; this increases their elasticity. . . . On the contrary, warm air relaxes and lengthens the extremes of the fibres [and so] diminishes their force and elasticity.
>
> People are therefore more vigorous in cold climates . . . ; the blood moves more freely towards the heart, and reciprocally the heart has more power. This [in its turn] must produce various effects; for instance, a greater boldness . . . , a greater sense of superiority . . . ; a greater opinion of security. . . .[g]

It follows that the kind of government suitable for men living in hot climates (despotism) is entirely inappropriate for men living in the temperate zone. Montesquieu buttressed his conclusions with pages of supporting evidence— observations on differing audience reactions in England and Italy to the same operas, conclusions inferred from experiments on a frozen sheep's tongue, and so on. We may smile at some of his evidence and at the facility with which he made sweeping generalizations concerning complex causal relationships, but to do so is to miss his achievement. Montesquieu's thesis was that stable governments depend (at least in part) on adjustment to the psychological makeup of the governed; that psychological traits depend (at least in part) on physiological characteristics; and that physiological characteristics depend (at least in part) on environmental factors like climate. Thus, even though human nature is more complex than physical nature, Montesquieu nevertheless believed that there are laws that determine human conduct. Furthermore, these laws are to be discovered by an essentially empirical method, and, once discovered, the knowledge of them can be utilized to resolve social conflicts and thus to make life better in every respect.

So much for nature. As for reason—the other leading idea of the age—despite considerable diversity of opinion, a similar core of common meaning can be detected in the work of eighteenth-century thinkers. Though these thinkers equated reason with anything from common sense to strict logical deduction on a geometric model, they generally agreed that there exists an innate intellectual power, which is equal, or nearly equal, in all men. They reasoned that all men have what Descartes had called *bon sens*. Consequently, given adequate education, men will be able to solve all the problems that arise in the course of their lives. Reason will demonstrate—reason was already demonstrating in the work of the physicists, in the work of anthropologists like Montesquieu, and in the work of historians like Gibbon—that nature is orderly, that the universe, though a mighty maze, is nonetheless not without a plan. Reason will demonstrate that each man's long-range interests dovetail with those of other men, and thus men can work together in peace and harmony, each pursuing his own good.

Because men are, by and large, capable of running their own affairs, laws can be kept at a minimum. *Laissez-faire* political and economic systems and moral theories based on self-respect, decency, and the dignity of man are the logical outcomes of this line of thought. Americans are familiar with it in the form it took in the organization of the United States; but this spirit of reasonableness, sanity, democracy, and optimism about the capacities of human nature was not confined to one nation. It can, therefore, be illustrated from many sources. Since, however, we shall shortly be concerned with the philosophical theories of Kant, let us examine a little essay of his called, characteristically, *What Is Enlightenment?* [h]

> Enlightenment is man's release from self-imposed tutelage. Tutelage is the inability to use one's natural powers without direction from another. This

tutelage is called "self-imposed" because its cause is not any absence of rational competence but simply a lack of courage and resolution to use one's reason without direction from another. *Sapere aude!*—Dare to reason! Have the courage to use your own minds!—is the motto of enlightenment.

Since Kant took it for granted that reason is an adequate power in most men, he held that bringing it to bear on the solution of social, moral, and other problems was merely a matter of having the courage to use it.

Laziness and cowardice explain why so many men . . . remain under a life-long tutelage and why it is so easy for some men to set themselves up as the guardians of all the rest. . . . If I have a book which understands for me, a pastor who has a conscience for me, a doctor who decides my diet, I need not trouble myself. If I am willing to pay, I need not think. Others will do it for me. . . .

Do we now live in an *enlightened* age? No; but we live in an age of *enlightenment*. Though certainly much is lacking, the obstacles to the general enlightenment are gradually being reduced. Men are releasing themselves from self-imposed tutelage and learning to deal freely with religious and other matters.

This discussion has been primarily devoted to religious enlightenment, because . . . religious tutelage is not only the most harmful but the most degrading of all. But with regard to civil liberties, however, there should be room for every man to extend himself to his full capacities. As the use of reason gradually spreads and develops it will first have an effect on the character so that men become more capable of managing their freedom. Eventually it will have an effect on the principles of government, for rulers will find it to their own advantage to treat men in accordance with their dignity as rational creatures.

To this may be appended a sentence from Kant's essay on *Perpetual Peace:*

The problem of establishing a state . . . is solvable for a race of devils if only they are intelligent. The problem is, given a group of rational beings who require universal laws for their preservation, but each of whom is secretly inclined to exempt himself from them; to organize a constitution in such a way that, although their private purposes conflict, they check each other, with the result that their public conduct is the same as if they had no such evil purposes.[i]

If the political problem can be solved by intellectual analysis and for a race of devils, it can surely be solved for a race of men, who are endowed not only with intellects but with sentiments of benevolence, friendship, and humanity.

Thus Kant, and the whole century along with him, agreed with Pope that "the proper study of mankind is man"—not the particularity and variability of individual men, but the abiding human nature that could be confidently assumed a possible and legitimate object of study. The reason in us that was presently exploring the external universe could turn within and, discovering its own essential nature, fashion a social order that would reflect the rationality of the cosmos.

The Collapse of Confidence

The basic assumption of the Enlightenment was that the universe is rational in all its aspects and in every detail. Because the physical universe is rational, there are a number of "rational principles" at work in it; it therefore has a simple orderly pattern. Because the human intellect is rational, it has the capacity to discover these principles, to understand the pattern. Because the human will is rational, it is capable of acting in the light of this knowledge. Given these beliefs, it is not surprising that the age was optimistic.

But such optimism could not last. Hardly had these beliefs been accepted when they began to be challenged. The application of science to technology, a process that was supposed to result in unlimited improvement of material conditions, actually led to urban slums, in which the lot of the workers was far worse than that of the peasants of "unenlightened" feudal times.[6] The French Revolution, which had promulgated the rights of man and which had been held by its supporters to herald a new age of reason and of democratic freedom, collapsed into a reign of terror. This was followed by an absolutism even more formidable, because it was more efficient, than the regime that the Revolution had overthrown.[7] Far from being rational creatures able to control their destinies, men seemed driven by their hates and fears—moved less by enlightened self-interest or by cool benevolence than by irrational and destructive aggressions against one another and even against themselves.

The type of man who emerged in the nineteenth century was thus very different from the new-model man who had appeared during the Renaissance and who had dominated Europe for two centuries. That man had been self-con-

---

6 See p. 163.
7 To appreciate the disillusionment caused by the failure of the Revolution, it is necessary to understand the inordinate hopes that its outbreak had occasioned. In *A Decade of Revolution* (New York, 1934), pp. 65–66, Crane Brinton quotes some contemporary enthusiasm. For instance, the German historian A. L. Schlozer stated: "One of the greatest nations in the world, the greatest in general culture, has at last thrown off the yoke of tyranny. . . . Without doubt God's angels in heaven have sung a Te Deum." Then, after citing Wordsworth, Goethe, and other literary figures, Brinton adds, "Perhaps most impressive is the description [Henrik] Steffens gives [he was fifteen years old at the time] of how his father . . . gathered his sons about him, and with tears of joy told them that the Bastille had fallen, that a new era had begun, that if they were failures in life they must blame themselves, for henceforth 'poverty would vanish, the lowliest would begin the struggles of life on equal terms with the mightiest, with equal arms, on equal ground.'"

fident and self-assured; though considering himself in harmony with his environment, he also believed himself capable of mastering it if need be. In contrast, the new man of the nineteenth century was uneasy, anxious, alienated, and introspective. He was increasingly unsure of himself—doubtful of the validity of his values, of his ability to communicate in a meaningful way with others, and of his ability even to know himself.

Dostoevsky's short story *Notes from Underground* contains one of the earliest—and also one of the most powerful—portraits of this new, anxious man.[8] The opening of the story consists of a long monologue:

> I am a sick man. . . . I am a spiteful man. No, I am not a pleasant man at all. I believe there is something wrong with my liver. However, I don't know a damn thing about my liver; neither do I know whether there is anything really wrong with me. I am not under medical treatment, and never have been. . . . I refuse medical treatment out of spite. . . . I don't expect I shall be able to explain to you who it is I am actually trying to annoy in this case by my spite; I realise full well that I can't "hurt" the doctors by refusing to be treated by them; I realise better than any one that by all this I am only hurting myself and no one else. Still, the fact remains that if I refuse to be medically treated, it is only out of spite.
>
> . . . .
>
> I assure you, gentlemen, that to be too acutely conscious is a disease, a real, honest-to-goodness disease . . . not only too much consciousness, but any sort of consciousness is a disease. . . . Tell me this: why did it invariably happen that . . . I was not only conscious but also guilty of the most contemptible actions which—well, which, in fact, everybody is guilty of, but which, as though on purpose, I only happened to commit when I was most conscious that they ought not to be committed? . . . I was ashamed (and quite possibly I still am ashamed); it got so far that I felt a sort of secret, abnormal, contemptible delight when, on coming home on one of the foulest nights in Petersburg, I used to realise intensely that again I had been guilty of some particularly dastardly action that day, and that once more it was no earthly use crying over spilt milk; and inwardly, secretly, I used to go on nagging myself, worrying myself, accusing myself, till at last the bitterness I felt turned into a sort of shameful, damnable . . . delight! Yes, into delight. Into delight! I'm certain of it. . . . Good Lord, I have talked a lot, haven't I? But have I explained anything? How is one to explain this feeling of delight? . . .
>
> Let me continue calmly about the people with strong nerves who do not understand the subtleties of the pleasure I have been speaking of. Though

---

8 Fyodor Dostoevsky (1821–81) was educated as an army engineer in Russia, but he soon resigned his commission to concentrate on his writing. In 1849 he was convicted of "taking part in criminal plots" against the Czarist regime; the sentence of death was commuted at the last moment, and he was imprisoned in Siberia for several years. Subsequently, he became an archconservative and reactionary. *Notes from Underground* was published in 1864.

on some occasions these gentlemen may roar at the top of their voices like bulls, . . . they at once capitulate in face of the impossible. The impossible is to them equivalent to a stone wall. What stone wall? Why, the laws of nature, of course, the conclusions of natural science, mathematics. When, for instance, it is proved to you that you are descended from a monkey, then it's no use pulling a long face about it: you just have to accept it. When they prove to you . . . that all the so-called virtues and duties and other vain fancies and prejudices are, as a result of that consideration, of no importance whatever, then you have to accept it whether you like it or not, because twice-two—mathematics. Just try to refute that.

"Good Lord," they'll scream at you, "you can't possibly deny that: twice two *is* four! Never does nature ask you for your opinion. . . . You are obliged to accept her as she is and, consequently, all her results. A stone wall, that is, is a stone wall, . . . etc., etc." But . . . what do I care for the laws of nature and arithmetic if for some reason or other I don't like those laws of twice-two? . . . I shall not reconcile myself to it just because I have to deal with a stone wall and haven't the strength to knock it down.

As though such a stone wall were really the same thing as peace of mind. . . .

You say that science itself will then teach man . . . that he himself is nothing more than a sort of piano-key or organ-stop, and that, in addition, there are the laws of nature in the world; so that whatever he does is not done of his own will at all, but of itself, according to the laws of nature. Consequently, as soon as these laws of nature are discovered, man will no longer have to answer for his actions, . . . [and] everything will be calculated and specified with such an exactness that there will be no more independent actions or adventures in the world.

Then—it is still you who are saying this—new economic relations will be established, . . . so that all sorts of problems will vanish in a twinkling simply because ready-made solutions will be provided for all of them. It is then that the Crystal Palace will be built.[9] . . . Everything will be so splendidly rational. . . .

Quite right, but there's the rub! . . . Reason is only reason, and it can only satisfy the reasoning ability of man, whereas volition is a manifestation of the whole of life, I mean, of the whole of human life, including reason with all its concomitant head-scratchings. And although our life, thus manifested, very often turns out to be a sorry business, it is life none the less and not merely extractions of square roots. . . . What does reason know? Reason only knows what it has succeeded in getting to know . . . , whereas human nature acts as a whole, with everything that is in it, consciously, and unconsciously, and though it may commit all sorts of absurdities, it persists. . . . The whole meaning of human life can be summed up in the one statement that man only exists for the purpose of proving to himself every minute that he is a man and not an organ-stop![j]

---

9 [The Crystal Palace was built in London to house the exhibition of 1851, which was designed to demonstrate the progress of the sciences. Dostoevsky views it here as a symbol of everything he disliked in contemporary culture—AUTHOR.]

This underground man, as Dostoevsky observes, has "all the characteristics of an anti-hero." He and his contemporaries "have lost all touch with life, we are all cripples, every one of us. . . . We are stillborn."[k] What a change from the self-confident optimist of the eighteenth century! Underground man is solitary: "I did have a sort of a friend once, but by that time I was already a tyrant at heart: I wanted to exercise complete authority over him."[l] He is masochistic: "My liver hurts me—well, let it damn well hurt—the more it hurts the better."[m] Underground man lives by feeling; he is profoundly pessimistic: "It is much better to do nothing at all! Better passive awareness!"[n] He is "passionately fond of destruction and chaos"[o]; he is endlessly introspective because he is convinced that no matter how deeply he probes, he can never find his real motive: "I had a noble loophole for every thing."[p] Most of all, underground man actually does not want to find his real motive—he is always hiding from himself: "There are certain things in a man's past which he does not divulge to everybody but, perhaps, only to his friends. Again there are certain things he will not divulge even to his friends; he will divulge them perhaps only to himself. . . . But, finally, there are things which he is afraid to divulge even to himself. . . ."[q]

Because *Notes from Underground* was published in 1864, discussion of it may seem to be out of place in a chapter on the end of the Enlightenment; after all, Kant's *Critique of Pure Reason,* which is examined in the following chapter, was written almost a hundred years earlier. But some of the changes that went into the formation of underground man were already in motion when Kant wrote, and his *Critique* was a response to them.

One of the major changes that led to this shift in values was Hume's discovery that there is no "necessary connection" among matters of fact. In most respects Hume was representative of this age—in his "mitigated" scepticism, his cool benevolence, his contempt for "enthusiasm," his irreligion. But as regards nature and reason—which, as we have seen, were the leading concepts of the Enlightenment and the bases for its optimism—Hume's views were revolutionary, far more revolutionary than he himself realized. Hume regarded reason as merely an instrument for detecting relations among ideas; reason can tell us nothing, he thought, about the real world. We do experience nature—the real world—as ordered. But there is no evidence, Hume maintained, that the order we find there is necessary: There is no rationale in nature to which the rational mind of man conforms. Hume in effect was driving a wedge between reason and nature. In doing so, he opened the way for a shift in beliefs and values that he would have deplored, for a shift to that whole complex of attitudes expressed in *Notes from Underground*—for instance, underground man's conviction that "you can't explain anything by reasoning and consequently it is useless to reason."[r]

Among Hume's contemporaries Kant was almost alone in recognizing the destructive force of this attack on reason. As is evident from *What Is Enlightenment?* Kant was deeply committed to the Enlightenment ideal.[10] Hence he was

10 See pp. 7–8.

deeply disturbed by Hume's argument. He realized that to answer Hume some compromise was necessary and in this compromise he proposed to save as much as he could. Ultimately, however, Kant made many more concessions to anti-rationalism than he realized: His *Critique* was not merely a response to the changes that marked the end of the Enlightenment; it was a working-out of the basic conceptual scheme in terms of which the new underground view of man later came to be expressed.

Kant's philosophy thus constitutes one of the fundamental turning points in the history of Western thought. In studying his theories, and those of the philosophers who followed him, we must look for the complex interactions between formal philosophical speculation and the deeper currents of thought and feeling that were to surface in such literary works as *Notes from Underground.*

CHAPTER 2

Kant: Theory of Knowledge

Immanuel Kant (1724–1804) was born in Königsberg in East Prussia (now incorporated in the Soviet Union) and lived all his life in that provincial city. His parents were lower middle class, industrious, and deeply religious. They were Pietists, members of one of the numerous sects on the Protestant left that held that the Reformation had bogged down in its own form of dogmatism. They believed that true religion was a matter of the inner life and emphasized simplicity and obedience to the moral law. Kant came to dislike the evangelical side of Pietism; he had as little use for "enthusiasm" (hymn-singing and other manifestations of "fervor") as Hume or Gibbon. But in contrast to Hume, whose religious background was not dissimilar, Kant remained all his life a deeply religious man.

Little need be said about the details of Kant's life; as one writer has remarked, it was like the most regular of regular verbs. Kant was educated at the University of Königsberg, where he studied classics and theology, and subsequently physics and philosophy. He had, of course, to earn his own living, and his first job was that of a tutor in a private family. Kant did not like the relationship that this entailed, and by 1755 he was back at the university, where he remained the rest of his active life. His lectures were very popular (it is worth emphasizing this in view of the difficulty of his published works), and without ever leaving Königsberg he became in time the best-known professor in Germany. Distinction brought comfort and security, and though he was full of those little eccentricities that students expect to find in their teachers, he was an excellent conversationalist and a charming host. Kant's principal work, the *Critique of Pure Reason* (1781), is concerned primarily with epistemology and metaphysics, but Kant also wrote on anthropology, esthetics, ethics, and law; early in his career he did original work in astronomy and physics.

The following examination of Kant's philosophy is divided into two main parts: (1) a discussion of his attempt to show how, despite Hume's attack on "necessary connection," real knowledge of matters of fact is possible and (2) an account of the values that he believed lay outside this field of scientific, matter-of-fact knowledge. Kant's version of the nature and limits of scientific knowledge is the concern of the present chapter, which discusses, first, the nature of the problem Kant believed he had inherited from Hume and his general solution to this problem, and, second, Kant's attempted validation of knowledge in mathematics and physics and his criticism of alleged metaphysical knowledge. The next chapter considers Kant's theory of value: first, his ethical theory, including his conception of duty and his solution to the problem of freedom, and, second, his conception of religion.

Kant's Hypothesis

In order to comprehend what Kant sought to do in his *Critique of Pure Reason*, it is necessary to understand that by the middle of the eighteenth century philosophy had got itself into a most embarrassing situation. Descartes' aim had been to put the new physics on a firm philosophical foundation. This meant providing a field in which physical inquiry could be carried on undisturbed by theological scruples and at the same time excluding mechanism from the realm of values (as Hobbes had failed to do). Descartes believed he had accomplished this by dividing reality into two metaphysically distinct substances, matter and mind. But subsequent attempts to straighten out these apparently reasonable assumptions had resulted in the most paradoxical solutions, solutions that, though different in many respects, were alike in unintentionally demolishing the intellectual basis for physical theory.

The Continental Rationalists pressed Descartes' rationalistic bias to its logical conclusion. They aimed at certainty; because they held that mathematical knowledge is certain, they regarded mathematics as the ideal of all knowledge. They quite failed to see that, as Hume pointed out, the indubitable knowledge so obtained consisted merely of implicatory relations holding among propositions. To obtain a knowledge of matters of fact they needed perception, but they had written off perception as mere confused thinking, that is, as no more than degenerate conception. Hence their theories remained only speculation, incapable of being verified or refuted.

Locke and his followers pursued an exactly opposite course, but they ended up with an equally frustrating conclusion. They were less concerned with certainty than with the actual world—the shoes, ships, and sealing wax of experience. They recognized, of course, that we have access to the actual world in sense perception, but they held that what we perceive are ideas caused in us by things outside us. Unfortunately, as Hume pointed out, if we start from the assumption that what people are aware of are their own mental states, this is precisely where we remain: We do not know an external world; we know only our own ideas. Thus, in a curious way, by following very different paths both the rationalists and the empiricists reached the same sceptical dead end: The former were confined to tracing out implicatory relations among ideas; the latter, to recording relations of coexistence and succession among ideas.

Meanwhile, the working scientists, unperturbed by philosophical doubts about the nature of their subject, had been making advance after advance, and the Hobbesian vision of a world that was thoroughly mechanistic seemed about to be fulfilled in detail. Hence Hobbes's challenge to the traditional religious and teleological view of the cosmos was more formidable than ever. It had begun to occur to scientists that they might get on very nicely without the hypothesis of a God; as regards morality, it seemed clear that in a completely deterministic universe obligation could be only a vain and chimerical delusion. It was therefore no longer necessary to protect the infant science of physics from the theologians. Indeed, the shoe was now on the other foot. It looked as if traditional values were becoming subjective illusions in a world of neutral fact.

KANT'S VIEW OF SCIENTIFIC METHOD

It was obvious to Kant, then, that the Cartesian compromise had failed. But exactly where had it gone wrong? It was clear, Kant thought, that Descartes had misunderstood the nature of scientific method, which involves both an empirical factor and a rational factor. Descartes' followers had alternatively emphasized each of these factors, with the disastrous results we have seen. None of his followers understood how the two factors combine in cognition; none succeeded in giving an intelligible account of knowledge. Accordingly, Kant undertook to make a much more rigorous and sophisticated analysis of the nature of scientific method than had yet been undertaken.

He began by emphasizing the striking contrast between natural science before and after Galileo. It seemed to him that everyone agreed that, since Galileo's time, physics had been on "the secure path of a science." This did not mean that every proposition in physics was infallibly certain; it meant that when physicists made conflicting assertions about nature they were able to agree on "a common plan of procedure" for settling their dispute. Formerly, natural science had deserved the appellation "science" only by courtesy; it had been a "merely random groping."

What had brought about this revolutionary change? Kant thought that the essence of scientific method could be grasped by concentrating attention on those novel features, introduced by Galileo and the other early seventeenth-century physicists, that had made physics for the first time an "objective science."

> Natural science . . . enter[ed] upon the highway of science . . . only about a century and a half [ago, when] Bacon, by his ingenious proposals, partly initiated this discovery, partly inspired fresh vigour in those who were already on the way to it. In this case also the discovery can be explained as being the sudden outcome of an intellectual revolution. . . .
>
> When Galileo caused balls, the weights of which he had himself previously determined, to roll down an inclined plane; when Torricelli made the air carry a weight which he had calculated beforehand to be equal to that of a definite volume of water; or in more recent times, when Stahl changed metal into lime, and lime back into metal, by withdrawing something and then restoring it, a light broke upon all students of nature. They learned that reason has insight only into that which it produces after a plan of its own, and that it must not allow itself to be kept, as it were, in nature's leading-strings, but must itself show the way with principles of judgment based upon fixed laws, constraining nature to give answer to questions of reason's own determining. Accidental observations, made in obedience to no previously thought-out plan, can never be made to yield a necessary law, which alone reason is concerned to discover. Reason, holding in one hand its principles, according to which alone concordant appearances can be admitted as equivalent to laws, and in the other hand the experiment which it has devised in conformity with these principles, must approach nature in order to be taught by it. It must not, however, do so in the character of a pupil who listens to everything that the teacher chooses to say, but of an appointed judge who compels the witnesses to answer questions which he has himself formulated. Even physics, therefore, owes the beneficent revolution in its point of view entirely to the happy thought, that while reason must seek in nature, not fictitiously ascribe to it, whatever as not being knowable through reason's own resources has to be learnt, if learnt at all, only from nature, it must adopt as its guide, in so seeking, that which it has itself put into nature. It is thus that the study of nature has entered on the secure path of a science, after having for so many centuries been nothing but a process of merely random groping.
>
> . . . .
>
> The examples of mathematics and natural science, which by a single and sudden revolution have become what they now are, seem to me sufficiently

remarkable to suggest our considering what may have been the essential features in the changed point of view by which they have so greatly benefited. . . . Hitherto it has been assumed that all our knowledge must conform to objects. But all attempts to extend our knowledge of objects by establishing something in regard to them *a priori*, by means of concepts, have, on this assumption, ended in failure. We must therefore make trial whether we may not have more success in the tasks of metaphysics, if we suppose that objects must conform to our knowledge. This would agree better with what is desired, namely, that it should be possible to have knowledge of objects *a priori*, determining something in regard to them prior to their being given. We should then be proceeding precisely on the lines of Copernicus' primary hypothesis. Failing of satisfactory progress in explaining the movements of the heavenly bodies on the supposition that they all revolved round the spectator, he tried whether he might not have better success if he made the spectator to revolve and the stars to remain at rest. A similar experiment can be tried in metaphysics, as regards the *intuition* of objects. If intuition must conform to the constitution of the objects, I do not see how we could know anything of the latter *a priori;* but if the object (as object of the senses) must conform to the constitution of our faculty of intuition, I have no difficulty in conceiving such a possibility. Since I cannot rest in these intuitions if they are to become known, but must relate them as representations to something as their object, and determine this latter through them, either I must assume that the *concepts,* by means of which I obtain this determination, conform to the object, or else I assume that the objects, or what is the same thing, that the *experience* in which alone, as given objects, they can be known, conform to the concepts. In the former case, I am again in the same perplexity as to how I can know anything *a priori* in regard to the objects. In the latter case the outlook is more hopeful. For experience is itself a species of knowledge which involves understanding; and understanding has rules which I must presuppose as being in me prior to objects being given to me, and therefore as being *a priori.* They find expression in *a priori* concepts to which all objects of experience necessarily conform, and with which they must agree. As regards objects which are thought solely through reason, and indeed as necessary, but which can never—at least not in the manner in which reason thinks them—be given in experience, the attempts at thinking them (for they must admit of being thought) will furnish an excellent test of what we are adopting as our new method of thought, namely, that we can know *a priori* of things only what we ourselves put into them.[a]

There are two main points in this passage. First, Kant notes that if (as everyone up to then had held) the test of truth is agreement of the mind with an external object, only particular truths can be known. We can watch a particular body and see that it gravitates; we can watch another and see that it gravitates; and so on. But we can never know that *all* bodies gravitate, because we can never observe all bodies to see whether or not they gravitate. Consequently, agreement of the mind with its objects cannot be the test of truth, at least as far as universal propositions are concerned. Why not, Kant asks, do what a scientist does when one of his hypotheses breaks down? Why not try another hypothesis? This is just what Copernicus did. After men had tried for centuries to work out a satisfactory astronomical theory on the hypothesis that the earth is the center of the planetary system, it occurred to Copernicus to try something else—to put the sun at the center of the system. This hypothesis was successful. And just as only prejudice had so long prevented men from trying the heliocentric hypothesis, so only prejudice had prevented men from trying a new epistemological hypothesis. It may seem "inevitable" that truth consists in the mind's agreement with its objects, but this "inevitability" is only the result of our having got used to thinking in these terms. The actual procedure of the scientist shows how inadequate the old conventional view really is.[1]

This brings us to Kant's second point, which concerns the crucial role that experiment plays in science. To make an experiment is to ask a question; unless we ask questions of nature we do not get answers. If a Gallup pollster silently hands blank pieces of paper to the housewives whose doorbells he rings, he will never find out their preferences in breakfast foods. Similarly, if Galileo had simply waited for bodies to fall in order to report their velocities, we would all still be in ignorance of this matter. In Kant's view, this consideration completely alters the conventional notion of the mind's relation to its objects. It means that the mind is not passive but active, and that Locke's metaphor of the blank tablet is profoundly mischievous.

In other words, examination of the nature of scientific knowledge shows that in scientific thinking truth does not consist merely in the agreement of the mind with an already existing state of affairs, for if this were all there were to it, the mind would never come to know any scientific truth at all. This led Kant to frame a new epistemological hypothesis that would conform with the way the mind actually proceeds when it thinks scientifically.

As will be seen, Kant's new hypothesis was a reversal of the old, rejected hypothesis (corresponding to the Copernican shift from a geocentric to a heliocentric system). It was originally assumed that the mind must agree with its objects; however, this assumption proved not only hopelessly inadequate to account for universal truths but a caricature of the nature of scientific thought. Thus Kant adopted the hypothesis that the mind's objects must agree with the mind. Let us see if this fared better.

DISTINCTION BETWEEN FORM AND CONTENT

Kant's hypothesis will seem absurd if we fail to distinguish between the form of a judgment and its content. Kant did not mean to suggest that in judgments like "Some roses are red" or "There is a centaur in my office," the objects judged about have to agree with the mind. For, obviously, the truth (or falsity) of such

---

1 Kant did not altogether reject a correspondence theory of truth. Rather, he held that it is inadequate as a complete account. See pp. 40–43.

judgments depends on the agreement (or disagreement) of the judgment with an external state of affairs. If there is a centaur in my office, the judgment is true; if there is not, it is false. And the way to find out is to go to the office and look.

But all the judgments we make fall into certain classes, depending on their form. For instance, they assert either that something has such-and-such a property ("This rose is red"), or that something is the cause of something else, or that something has such-and-such a degree of some quality, and so on. There is a kind of putting together that consists in attribution; there is another kind of putting together that consists in causation; and so on.

KNOWLEDGE A COOPERATIVE AFFAIR

Kant's hypothesis did not concern particular judgments (for example, "This rose is red"); rather, it concerned the various types of putting together (for example, attribution). According to his hypothesis, knowledge is a cooperative affair in which both mind and object make a contribution, and mind contributes the relations while objects contribute the relata. But mind does not, according to this hypothesis, contribute the *particular* relations of sense experience—not "on the table," "on the sofa," "on the desk." What it contributes is the spatial relationship common to all these situations, the relationship designated by the term "on"—the relationship of "superposition," if we want another term to describe it. Or take the judgment "This rose is red." What we are judging about here is, of course, something we see—a rose that is red. But an immense quantity of sense data of all kinds—visual, tactile, and olfactory experiences—is constantly streaming in upon us. Nonetheless, we are able to sort out from these data the experience of a rose that is red because, according to this hypothesis, attribution (the relation designated by the term "is") is one of the ways in which the mind organizes and structures the welter of experiences that it encounters.

To put this differently, attribution is one of the types of questions that the mind asks nature and in terms of which, accordingly, nature answers. Thus, all the particular questions (or experiments) that scientists ask take one or the other of certain basic forms. "Who killed President Kennedy?" the Warren Commission asked. This is a particular question, but it has a causation form. Now, if all the questions asked of nature were to have one or the other of certain basic forms, obviously all the answers given by nature would have these same forms, and there would then be some knowledge about nature that is independent of all particular experiences. Or, again, suppose the new hypothesis to be correct and that we know the *types* of judgment, that is, the basic ways in which the mind relates (or organizes) its experiences. We would then have absolutely certain knowledge, not about this particular experience ("This rose is red"), but about the form of all experience (ordered under the form "is"). In other words, it would not be necessary that the particular rose be red; Hume was correct about this—the rose might be white or yellow. But it would be necessary, if Kant's hypothesis is correct, that experience be organized into things-having-properties, for this way of perceiving things proves to be one of the universal forms of human experience. Hence, despite Hume's attack, there does exist a "necessary connection" among matters of fact—not a necessary connection between this particular fact A and that particular fact B, but a necessary connection, or structure, that organizes experience into an "A-is-B" type.

An example may help. Consider the process by which crude oil is refined into various petroleum products—kerosene, gasoline of various octane numbers, and so on. The refining process corresponds, in this analogy, to the standard forms of judgment in terms of which, according to Kant's hypothesis, experience is organized. If we know that such-and-such steps have been built into the refining process, we can say with confidence that gasoline of such-and-such an octane number will issue from the refinery. The "necessary connection" is not found in the crude oil; it is supplied by the refining process.

Similarly, suppose we have a machine for sorting oranges that consists of an inclined plane with holes of various sizes. Oranges rolling down the surface of the plane fall through the holes into boxes underneath. If one of the holes is, say, two and one-half inches in diameter, we can say that no orange in the box under this hole has a diameter greater than two and one-half inches; and the same applies to the other holes. Although there are many things about the oranges that we could not tell without examining them (for example, whether some are rotten or whether some are green), we can know that the oranges in a particular box cannot be larger than such-and-such a size. Here again we have discovered a necessary connection, namely, that between being in a particular box and having a maximum diameter of so many inches. We know this connection prior to measuring any of the oranges, because we know the nature of the sorting principle being employed.[2]

THE GENERAL PROBLEM OF PURE REASON

So far in this chapter Kant's hypothesis has been formulated in laymen's terms. Before we can proceed to Kant's attempt to prove his hypothesis, the argument must be reformulated in the highly technical language he himself used. In Kant's terminology the question is, "How are synthetical a priori judgments possible?" This, according to Kant, is "the general problem of pure reason." We must first understand how this question is related to the distinction, formulated by Kant in his study of the nature of scientific method, between the content of an experience and certain standard forms, or ways, of organizing that experience.

---

2 It must be borne in mind that this is only a mechanical metaphor. In Kant's view, the mind, which orders experience, is not at all *like* the machine, which "orders" oranges. The mind is not static like the machine; it is active. In fact, in Kant's view, it is *not* a thing at all; it is the ordering process itself. The example is intended to show only that if we know the nature of *an ordering principle* we can know a priori the characteristics of order imparted by it to the things it orders.

A judgment, according to Kant, is a movement of thought in which two items are brought together and combined. We judge whenever we say, "This house is large," "That dog is a Sealyham," or "The interior angles of a triangle equal two right angles." The mind brings the items together in judgment because it detects a connection between them. It is this connection that is the warrant, or basis, for the judgment. Now, the most obvious kind of evidence on which we base our judgments is experience: It is sense experience, for instance, that warrants our judging that a particular house is large. Such a judgment Kant called empirical, or "a posteriori." In contrast, there is a kind of judgment that is "independent of all experience." For instance, we do not have to measure the angles of a particular triangle to know that its interior angles equal two right angles; we know this as a result of a geometric proof—it follows from Euclid's definition of the nature of a triangle that the interior angles of any triangle equal two right angles. This kind of judgment Kant called pure, or "a priori." There are two characteristics of a priori judgments that enable us to distinguish them with certainty from a posteriori judgments.

> Experience teaches us that a thing is so and so, but not that it cannot be otherwise. First, then, if we have a proposition which in being thought is thought as *necessary*, it is an *a priori* judgment. . . . Secondly, . . . if, then, a judgment is thought . . . in such manner that no exception is allowed as possible, it is not derived from experience, but is valid absolutely *a priori*. . . . Necessity and strict universality are thus sure criteria of *a priori* knowledge, and are inseparable from each other.[b]

In addition to distinguishing between a posteriori and a priori judgments, Kant distinguished between analytical and synthetical judgments. In an analytical judgment the predicate is covertly contained in the subject and may be obtained by analysis of it. "Roses are flowers" is an example: That roses are flowers is a part of the definition of roses. In a synthetical judgment the predicate is *not* contained in its subject. "Some roses are red" is an example: Red is not a part of the definition of rose.

We thus have two pairs of judgments, a priori–a posteriori and analytical–synthetical. These pairs yield four logically possible classes of judgments, as follows:

	a posteriori	a priori
analytical	1 analytical a posteriori	2 analytical a priori
synthetical	3 synthetical a posteriori	4 synthetical a priori

But the class in the upper left quadrant (class 1) is obviously empty: There can be no analytical a posteriori judgments, since all analytical judgments are universal and necessary. Thus there are three classes of judgment to examine, and the question is, "What *kind* of evidence warrants each of these classes?" There is no problem about class 2. All judgments of this class are warranted by the law of contradiction. Since being a flower is a part of the definition of rose, we would contradict ourselves if we asserted that a rose is not a flower. The knowledge yielded by this type of judgment, it will be seen, is just what Hobbes called knowledge of the agreement and disagreement of names. Similarly, there is no problem about class 3. The warrant for synthetical a posteriori judgments is experience. The judgment "This rose is red" is warranted by the visual experience (under suitable light conditions) of the rose's redness.

But what about class 4? What warrant can there be for synthetical a priori judgments? The "principle," as Kant called it, of this type of judgment cannot be the law of contradiction, for judgments in this quadrant are synthetical—that is, their predicates are not contained covertly in their subjects. Nor can the principle be experience, for "experience teaches us only that a thing is so and so," and judgments in this quadrant, being a priori, assert a universal and necessary connection. Is there any third type of principle, other than experience or the law of contradiction, that might serve as a warrant for synthetical a priori judgments? Hume thought not. He pointed out, first, that there is never any logical impossibility in denying an assertion of a matter of fact (we do not contradict ourselves if we judge, "This rose is not red," whereas we contradict ourselves if we judge, "This rose is not a flower") and, second, that it is impossible to "collect" from any series of particulars, however numerous, universality and necessity. Accordingly, Hume's position, expressed in Kantian language, is this: All judgments are either synthetical a posteriori (judgments about what Hume called matters of fact) or analytical (judgments about what he called relations of ideas). This was the basis for Hume's scepticism regarding causality and inductive inference. He believed he had shown that there was no evidence—and *could be* no evidence—that because *a* had been associated with *b* in the past, it would continue to be associated with *b* in the future.

Kant, of course, wanted to show that there are judgments of the synthetical a priori type—judgments that are both "instructive," like synthetical a posteriori, matter-of-fact judgments, and universal and necessary, like analytical judgments. But, once again, what possible warrant can there be for such judgments? We are left therefore with the following situation regarding the principles of various classes of judgment:[3]

	a posteriori	a priori
analytical	1 null	2 warranted by law of contradiction
synthetical	3 warranted by experience	4 ?

3 Kant's system of classification does not take account of some judgments—for instance, contradictions: "Squares are round" is not analytical, according to Kant's definition, and it is certainly not synthetical.

The fourth quadrant, then, poses "the general problem of pure reason"—that is, "How are synthetical a priori judgments possible?" We shall not progress very far toward an answer until we narrow the question down. Kant pointed out that, rightly or wrongly, philosophers have believed judgments of the kind he called synthetical a priori to occur in three areas, namely, mathematics, natural science, and metaphysics. The general question "How are synthetical a priori judgments possible?" thus divides into three subquestions: (1) "How are synthetical a priori judgments possible in mathematics?" (2) "How are synthetical a priori judgments possible in natural science?" and (3) "Are synthetical a priori judgments possible in metaphysics?" Note the change in phrasing in the third question.

Kant agreed with Hume that synthetical a priori judgments are *not* possible in metaphysics, although he believed that our disposition to ask and to try to answer metaphysical questions points to the fact that reason has a "regulative" use. More will be said about this later in the chapter.

Kant agreed with Hume that mathematical judgments are universal and necessary, but he maintained that they are synthetical rather than analytical.[4] He also agreed with Hume that most judgments in natural science are a posteriori. But—and this is the crucial point, of course—he denied that all are a posteriori. Thus the proposition "Friction causes heat" is a posteriori because it is a generalization of experience. But the proposition "Every event has a cause" is a priori. In Kant's view, the fact that this and certain other basic propositions in physics are a priori means that inductive inference is validated. Hence the empirical proposition "Friction causes heat" is highly probable, not a wild shot in the dark, as Hume's view implied.

Kant's point can be illustrated by the game of guessing what card a dealer is going to turn up next. If, after an ordinary deck of fifty-two cards has been shuffled, we are invited to bet that the first card turned up will be the ace of spades, we would want odds of 52 to 1. Of course, after the first card has been drawn and removed from the deck, the odds would decrease. But suppose that, after each drawing, the card is reinserted in the deck and the deck is reshuffled. Then the odds would remain 52 to 1. Further, if the deck is increased in size, the odds would grow greater. And if it contained an infinite number of cards, we would refuse to bet, for the odds would be infinitely against us. There is no evidence, according to Hume, that the human situation is not like this: Every drawing of a card (every event that takes place) is an isolated occurrence, and we can make no inference from what has happened to what may happen.

But what if the dealer tells us (we shall have to assume that he can be trusted) that he has arranged the cards in a definite order? Then, suppose that the following sequence occurs: ace of spades, ace of hearts, ace of diamonds, ace of clubs, king of spades, king of hearts, king of diamonds, king of clubs, queen

4 Though Hume wavered about the status of geometry, when he held that it is synthetical, he said that it is not a priori; when he allowed that it is a priori, he insisted that it is analytical.

of spades, ... Most of us would probably bet that the next card will be the queen of hearts. If it is, we would probably take lower odds (that is, feel more confident) that the next card will be the queen of diamonds and the next the queen of clubs. In a word, on the assumption that there *is* an order, we begin to form hypotheses about what that order is (for example, that the dealer has arranged the cards in their order of value in bridge). Of course, any hypothesis we frame may be falsified—the next card after the queen of clubs may be the deuce of spades, for the order may be "three times round from the top of the deck, then three times round from the bottom of the deck." Hence, though we can never be *certain* of what the order is, our hypothesis can become increasingly probable, and after a sufficient number of correct predictions we may regard the hypothesis as "certain for all practical purposes." But all this depends, it will be seen, on the deck being well ordered; if it is not, all probabilities at once reduce to zero.

In this example, of course, we must rely without evidence on the honesty of the dealer. According to Kant's hypothesis, our confidence in the orderliness of the physical world rests on firmer grounds. It is derived from the fact that we know that every event necessarily has a cause. We can never be sure, with respect to any particular event *a*, that its cause is *b*. But because we know that there is *some* event that is the cause of *a*, we can become increasingly confident it is *b*.

All this holds only if the proposition that every event has a cause is, as Kant claimed, necessarily true. And that it is true is precisely what Hume denied. The concept "cause," Hume pointed out, cannot be derived analytically from the concept "event." Since it cannot be so derived, we cannot say that every event necessarily has a cause. Hence inductive inference is not validated. Does Kant's reply to Hume merely reaffirm what Hume denied? If so, it is surely a poor answer.

Those who criticize Kant on this score, however, miss his main point. It seemed to him that there is a *prima facie* case in favor of synthetical a priori judgments in mathematics and natural science. The only reason, he thought, for questioning them would be the suspicion aroused by Hume's attack. The situation must have seemed to Kant to be rather like that expressed in the legal maxim "A man is innocent until proved guilty." Suppose that circumstantial evidence suggests that a highly respectable citizen has committed a particularly revolting murder. If the evidence against him is shown to be misleading and incompetent, his reputation should be rehabilitated.

This is precisely the position Kant took with regard to synthetical a priori judgments in mathematics and natural science, and this is why he framed his question as he did. He did not ask *whether* such judgments are possible; he asked *how* they are possible. It did not seem to him that he was assuming the point at issue between himself and Hume, for he thought that Hume was disturbed by his own conclusion and would be delighted to be proved wrong. Although a man might be able to rest in "mitigated" scepticism, no man would *choose* to adopt this position. Hence, Kant thought, it was necessary only to show that Hume's suspicion of these judgments was based upon a mistake, namely, the mistaken belief that the only possible basis for making a connection in a synthetical judgment is experience. To "rehabilitate the reputation" of such a judgment, one had only to find the real connection that is operative.

At this point it will be helpful to translate back from the technical language Kant actually used into the form-and-content language that has been derived from Kant's analysis of scientific method. Kant's hypothesis, as formulated earlier, was that certain standard forms are contributed by the mind, in terms of which the content of experience is organized. These standard forms "sort" the content of experience into standard patterns. Though the materials that are thus organized into patterns are not necessary, the patterns themselves are necessary, for without them the variable contents would be only a chaotic jumble, not the well-ordered content we actually experience. Accordingly, if there are any standard forms, there is a kind of knowledge that is synthetical (because the predicate of the judgment is not contained in the subject) and that is also a priori (because it is contributed to experience by the mind and is therefore universal and necessary for all experience). Thus Kant's hypothesis can be rephrased to mean that there are, after all, judgments in the fourth quadrant, and that these judgments are warranted neither by experience nor by the law of contradiction but by an organizing principle of the mind.

If this hypothesis can be proved, the "problem of pure reason" is solved, and a correct combination of the empirical and rational elements in knowledge will have been found. If the hypothesis is correct, then "all our knowledge begins with experience," as Locke and the other empiricists had insisted. But it does not necessarily follow, as they supposed, "that it all arises out of experience." Indeed, if the hypothesis is correct, *all* knowledge, not just scientific knowledge, contains elements that are not drawn from experience but supplied by the mind itself. Such elements would be a priori in the sense required.

> But though all our knowledge begins with experience, it does not follow that it all arises out of experience. For it may well be that even our empirical knowledge is made up of what we receive through impressions and of what our own faculty of knowledge (sensible impressions serving merely as the occasion) supplies from itself. If our faculty of knowledge makes any such addition, it may be that we are not in a position to distinguish it from the raw material, until with long practice of attention we have become skilled in separating it.
>
> This, then, is a question which at least calls for closer examination, and does not allow of any offhand answer:—whether there is any knowledge that is thus independent of experience and even of all impressions of the senses. Such knowledge is entitled *a priori*, and distinguished from the *empirical*, which has its sources *a posteriori*, that is, in experience.[c]

So far, Kant has not *proved* that there is any necessary synthetical a priori knowledge. His position, in terms of the sorting-machine analogy, is as follows:

We could make a priori judgments about the size of oranges in boxes beneath the machine, providing we knew the dimensions of the holes in the machine's surface. Similarly, assuming that all the objects of knowledge were connected by certain basic types of putting together, we could know a priori several relational characteristics of all objects, providing we were able to discover what these basic types of putting together were. But that this is so remains to be proved.

Let us return to the three central questions that Kant hoped to answer: "How are synthetical a priori judgments possible in mathematics?" "How are they possible in physics?" and "Are they possible in metaphysics?" It will be seen that Kant proposed to answer the first two questions by showing that there are certain basic types of putting together that operate in these fields. As regards the third question, in Kant's view, the answers to the questions about mathematics and physics dispose of the possibility of there being knowledge of metaphysical objects.

The A Priori in Mathematics

Kant dealt with his first question—"How are synthetical a priori judgments possible in mathematics?"—in a section of the *Critique* called the "Transcendental Aesthetic." He called it "aesthetic" because he believed the basis for this kind of knowledge to be immediate, nondiscursive, and sensuous; he called it "transcendental" because he believed that such knowledge is not *in* experience but a necessary condition *for* experience. His first step was to try to show that mathematical knowledge is synthetical.

> *All mathematical judgments, without exception, are synthetic.* This fact, though incontestably certain and in its consequences very important, has hitherto escaped the notice of those who are engaged in the analysis of human reason. . . .
>
> We might, indeed, at first suppose that the proposition $7 + 5 = 12$ is a merely analytic proposition, and follows by the principle of contradiction from the concept of a sum of 7 and 5. But if we look more closely we find that the concept of the sum of 7 and 5 contains nothing save the union of the two numbers into one, and in this no thought is being taken as to what that single number may be which combines both. The concept of 12 is by no means already thought in merely thinking this union of 7 and 5; and I may analyse my concept of such a possible sum as long as I please, still I shall never find the 12 in it. We have to go outside these concepts, and call in the aid of the intuition[5] which corresponds to one of them, our five fingers,

---

5 [By "intuition" Kant meant "immediate and sensuous," as opposed to "discursive and reasoned." This was the point of his calling the whole section the "Transcendental Aesthetic"—AUTHOR.]

for instance, . . . adding to the concept of 7, unit by unit, the five given in intuition. For starting with the number 7, and for the concept of 5 calling in the aid of the fingers of my hand as intuition, I now add one by one to the number 7 the units which I previously took together to form the number 5, and with the aid of that figure [the hand] see the number 12 come into being. That 5 should be added to 7, I have indeed already thought in the concept of a sum = 7 + 5, but not that this sum is equivalent to the number 12. Arithmetical propositions are therefore always synthetic. This is still more evident if we take larger numbers. For it is then obvious that, however we might turn and twist our concepts, we could never, by the mere analysis of them, and without the aid of intuition, discover what [the number is that] is the sum.

Just as little is any fundamental proposition of pure geometry analytic. That the straight line between two points is the shortest, is a synthetic proposition. For my concept of *straight* contains nothing of quantity, but only of quality. The concept of the shortest is wholly an addition, and cannot be derived, through any process of analysis, from the concept of the straight line. Intuition, therefore, must here be called in; only by its aid is the synthesis possible.[d]

Those who agree with Hobbes that mathematical judgments are analytical will, of course, think that the "Transcendental Aesthetic" is a waste of time, for there is no problem, as Kant himself pointed out, about the necessity of analytical judgments. But for those who share Kant's view that mathematical judgments are synthetical, there is indeed a puzzle about how such judgments can be a priori. Hence the hypothesis put forward in the "Transcendental Aesthetic" is worth considering.

BASIS OF MATHEMATICAL CERTAINTY

Let us therefore proceed to the second stage in Kant's argument: Assuming that mathematics is synthetical, how can it be a priori? What, for example, is the basis of certainty in geometry, the science of the properties of space? We must first ask what space is. According to the Newtonian view, space is an absolute reality, independent of ourselves, a big box in which events occur. According to the Leibnizian view, space is not real (the monads are nonspatial) but relational, a structure produced by sense and imagination. Neither of these views, however, wholly satisfied Kant. For one thing, he was much impressed by the curious kind of spatial relationship obtaining between, for instance, right- and left-handed gloves. If space were merely relational, as Leibniz claimed, it would be possible to superimpose one glove on the other, for all the relationships between parts (for example, between thumb and forefinger in each glove) are identical. The gloves ought to be spatially identical, like two vases made from the same mold. The fact that they are not shows there is more to space than the relation of parts.

On the other hand, if space were Newtonian, how could we ever have the a priori knowledge of it claimed in geometry? We could know that in the part of space under inspection here and now triangles have interior angles equal to 180°, but how could we know that this is true, as geometry claims, in all space everywhere? It is the old problem, obviously, of the impossibility of explaining a priori knowledge on the usual assumption that the mind's objects are independent reals and that truth consists in bringing the mind into agreement with them.

Furthermore, Kant noted that although we grasp the difference between right-handed and left-handed gloves as soon as we see them, we are unable to give this difference a rational, discursive formulation. This suggested to Kant that the mind's apprehension of space is sensuous ("aesthetic") rather than intellectual.

Drawing all these considerations together Kant came to the conclusion that space is simply a mode of the mind's apprehension of its world. It is, in fact, one of the ways of putting together whose existence he had already hypothecated to account for our knowledge of objects. It is not a putting together *in judgment*, for (as we have seen) our experience of space is sensuous, not intellectual. But, like the types of putting together that occur in judgment, it is a way of relating and organizing experiences. And because it is contributed by the mind, we can be a priori certain that *all* the mind's objects have spatial characteristics. That is, the mind organizes its experiences spatially, just as, in the sorting-machine analogy, the machine spreads oranges out into different boxes.

Space is not an empirical concept which has been derived from outer experiences. For in order that certain sensations be referred to something outside me (that is, to something in another region of space from that in which I find myself), and similarly in order that I may be able to represent them as outside and alongside one another, and accordingly as not only different but as in different places, the representation of space must be presupposed. The representation of space cannot, therefore, be empirically obtained from the relations of outer appearance. On the contrary, this outer experience is itself possible at all only through that representation.

Space is a necessary *a priori* representation, which underlies all outer intuitions. We can never represent to ourselves the absence of space, though we can quite well think it as empty of objects. It must therefore be regarded as the condition of the possibility of appearances, and not as a determination dependent upon them. . . .

Space is not a discursive or, as we say, general concept of relations of things in general, but a pure intuition. For, in the first place, we can represent to ourselves only one space; and if we speak of diverse spaces, we mean thereby only parts of one and the same unique space. Secondly, these parts cannot precede the one all-embracing space, as being, as it were, constituents out of which it can be composed; on the contrary, they can be thought only as *in* it. Space is essentially one; the manifold in it, and therefore the general concept of spaces, depends solely on [the introduction of] limitations. Hence it follows that an *a priori*, and not an empirical, intuition underlies all concepts of space.[e]

This argument is directed chiefly against the empiricists, who held space to be an empirical concept derived from the perception of things as "outer" (as the concept "red" is derived from the perception of red objects). Kant's point here is that since the experience of "outer" already implies space, space cannot be derived from it. We can think of space without objects in it, but we cannot think of objects that are not in space. Hence our experience of space is prior to, and a condition of, our experience of objects. Kant assumed that, if objects are not a condition of our experience of space, space must be a condition of our experience of objects.

Next, Kant undertook to show that the apriority of space (which he believed himself to have established) validates the claim of geometry to be an a priori and synthetical science. Geometry is the science of space. According to Kant, space is not an independently existing entity but a way in which the human mind organizes its experience. Hence, what the geometrician investigates is not the properties of outer objects but the modes of our faculty of intuition (outer perception). Hence, again, any properties found to characterize a particular region of space (for example, that the space here and now is such that triangles formed in it have interior angles equal to 180°) will characterize space everywhere, for the geometric properties in question are a projection of the human mind. Since they are among the basic ways in which the mind organizes the objects of its experience, all objects that the mind experiences will have these properties.

> Geometry is a science which determines the properties of space synthetically, and yet *a priori*. What, then, must be our representation of space, in order that such knowledge of it may be possible? It must in its origin be intuition; for from a mere concept no propositions can be obtained which go beyond the concept—as happens in geometry. Further, this intuition must be *a priori*, that is, it must be found in us prior to any perception of an object, and must therefore be pure, not empirical, intuition. For geometrical propositions are one and all apodeictic, that is, are bound up with the consciousness of their necessity; for instance, that space has only three dimensions. Such propositions cannot be empirical or, in other words, judgments of experience, nor can they be derived from any such judgments.
>
> How, then, can there exist in the mind an outer intuition which precedes the objects themselves, and in which the concept of these objects can be determined *a priori*? Manifestly, not otherwise than in so far as the intuition has its seat in the subject only, as the formal character of the subject, in virtue of which, in being affected by objects, it obtains *immediate representation*, that is, *intuition*, of them; and only in so far, therefore, as it is merely the form of outer *sense* in general.
>
> Our explanation is thus the only explanation that makes intelligible the *possibility* of geometry, as a body of *a priori* synthetic knowledge.[f]

LIMITATIONS OF KANT'S VIEW

What are we to make of this "transcendental exposition" (or validation) of the synthetical a priori character of geometry? Since Kant's day, our notion of the object of geometric knowledge has radically altered as a result of, first, the development of non-Euclidean geometries and, subsequently, the discovery that there are parts of space (for example, the microspaces within an atom and the macrospaces of the galaxies) of which these other geometries appear to give better accounts than does Euclidean geometry. It looks, indeed, as if the various geometries (including Euclidean geometry) are so many logics rather than sciences of space. Whether or not any of these logics *is* relevant to the description of the spatial properties of bodies thus becomes an empirical, not an a priori, question. It just happens that Euclidean geometry is particularly relevant to ordinary perceptual space and to the problems of constructing buildings, surveying fields, and so on. This is why people thought for so long that it was per se the science of space. But as new kinds of experiences (say, those obtained by looking into high-powered telescopes) were obtained, it was found that the behavior thus observed could be more conveniently accounted for in terms of a non-Euclidean geometry. Thus the applicability of any given geometry is determined by the kind of experience it is applied to.

Where does this leave Kant's transcendental exposition? Though it seems clear that Kant was mistaken in believing that such-and-such specific forms of spatial putting together are a priori, it does not necessarily follow that he was mistaken about space being a form of the mind's apprehension of its world. Space might be a mode of ordering contributed by the mind, and the various geometries might be accounts of the various possible types of such ordering. Thus, to revert to the sorting-machine analogy, we might know a priori that the oranges were ordered (that is, sorted), but we might not know which of several possible sorting principles was being used. To determine the exact type of principle being used would require an empirical study of the machine. Though this type of determination would be much less than Kant wanted to prove (and much less than he thought he had proved), it would be a very important point to have established.

APPEARANCE AND REALITY

If space is a way in which the mind orders things, obviously things are not really (in themselves) spatial; and what they really are we cannot possibly imagine. For we can imagine things only as spread out in space—this is the only form of externality that minds like ours can conceive of.

> Space does not represent any property of things in themselves, nor does it represent them in their relation to one another. That is to say, space does not represent any determination that attaches to the objects themselves, and which remains even when abstraction has been made of all the subjective conditions of intuition. . . .
>
> It is, therefore, solely from the human standpoint that we can speak of

space, of extended things, etc. . . . This predicate can be ascribed to things only in so far as they appear to us, that is, only to objects of sensibility. The constant form of this receptivity, which we term sensibility, is a necessary condition of all the relations in which objects can be intuited as outside us; and if we abstract from these objects, it is a pure intuition, and bears the name of space. Since we cannot treat the special conditions of sensibility as conditions of the possibility of things, but only of their appearances, we can indeed say that space comprehends all things that appear to us as external, but not all things in themselves, by whatever subject they are intuited. . . . For we cannot judge in regard to the intuitions of other thinking beings, whether they are bound by the same conditions as those which limit our intuition and which for us are universally valid. . . . Our exposition therefore establishes the *reality*, that is, the objective validity, of space in respect of whatever can be presented to us outwardly as object, but also at the same time the *ideality* of space in respect of things when they are considered in themselves through reason, that is, without regard to the constitution of our sensibility.[g]

The "Transcendental Aesthetic" also contains an exposition of time, which can be treated more briefly because it is largely parallel to the exposition of space. According to Kant, time, like space, is a "pure form of intuition," that is, a mode of ordering (or of putting together) that is immediate and sensuous, not a matter of judgment. Just as our minds order our experiences spatially, as being above or below, to the right or left, of other experiences, so they order these experiences temporally, as being before, after, or simultaneous with other experiences. There is, of course, a felt difference, immediately recognizable and unmistakable, between time and space—between, for instance, before and after on the one hand and above and below on the other. And this felt difference is perceived by us as the difference between what is inner and what is outer. Whatever we experience as spatial, we hold to be a datum of "outer sense." This is true of the materials of the five senses, all of which have this character of externality. Regarded, however, as states of oneself, these same materials are experienced as having a temporal order, that is, as coming before, after, or simultaneous with other experiences we have. Hence, in contrast to space, "time is nothing but the form of inner sense, that is, of our awareness of ourselves and of our own inner state."

So far in his account of the a priori properties of experience, Kant has not reached anything like the level of ordinary human experience, which consists in a knowledge of objects, that is, of complex and relatively enduring structures. So far, that is, Kant has dealt merely with the spatiotemporal ordering of contents, for example, with experiences of colored patches succeeding one another. Kant's point is that *to have even this very elementary kind of experience* there must be certain synthetical ordering activities of the mind. Obviously, to have an experience of *objects*, still more complex types of putting together must occur. This brings us to the natural sciences, which, unlike mathematics, are concerned with the cognition of physical objects.

The A Priori in Physics

Kant's second question—"How are synthetical a priori judgments possible in physics?"—is discussed in a section of the *Critique* called the "Transcendental Logic." Kant called it "logic" because he was concerned with the kinds of putting together that occur in judgment (in contrast to the immediate, sensuous putting together discussed in the "Aesthetic"); he called it "transcendental" because, once again, he was concerned not with the content of experience but with the conditions that make an experience of objects possible.[6]

As we have seen, Kant did not maintain that *all* judgments in the natural sciences are synthetical a priori (as he held all mathematical judgments to be). But he did think that certain judgments must be synthetical a priori in order to provide an underpinning for the inductive procedures of the sciences.

Furthermore, Kant hoped to do more than merely show that there are *some* a priori elements in our experience of objects. In the "Aesthetic" he was not content merely to establish spatiality; he wanted to establish a particular kind of spatiality (namely, Euclidean spatiality). That is, he wanted to do more than reply to Hume in a general way, by showing how an objective world can exist and inductive inference can be possible. He wanted to show, specifically, that the concept employed in Newtonian physics (the particular kinds of order it presupposes) are a priori.

It is necessary, therefore, to distinguish two questions: (1) Can a case be made for the existence of *some* ordering elements contributed by the mind? (2) Can it be shown that these elements are those presupposed in Newtonian physics? The first question is relatively simple, and the answer seems to be in the affirmative. The second question is much more difficult, and it involved Kant in many complications.

THE TWO ELEMENTS IN JUDGMENT

Let us remind ourselves of what was said earlier about judgment.[7] To think is to judge; knowledge is the end product of judging, and judging is a kind of putting together. According to Kant, two different components are always involved in judging: a direct, sensuous component and a conceptual, structural component. The difference between these components is like the difference between "guidebook" knowledge of a city and direct experience of it. A man could sit at home with his Baedeker, memorizing a map of Rome and learning the names of various buildings and their dimensions. As a result, he might be able to tell us quite a lot about the dome of St. Peter's. But if he has never seen the basilica, if he has never looked at a dome, his knowledge is, in Kant's terminology, "empty."

---

6 The "Transcendental Logic" is in turn divided into two parts: the "Transcendental Analytic" and the "Transcendental Dialectic." The "Analytic" is concerned with what may be called the proper use of logic; the "Dialectic," with its improper use. Here we are concerned with the "Analytic"; for the "Dialectic," see pp. 51–58.

7 See pp. 24–25.

He has acquired a number of concepts ("dome," "lantern," "pendentive," "barrel vault"), but they lack the concrete filling of perception and feeling. At the other extreme is the tourist who rushes through Europe so fast that, though he has "seen" St. Peter's (in the sense of having looked in that direction as his bus sped by), his knowledge of it is, again in Kant's terms, "blind." He lacks the historical and architectural knowledge that would structure, organize, and focus the sensory experience.

Kant's first point then—and surely it is a good one—is that all effective knowledge must contain two elements—an experiential element (a concrete filling of sense data, perceptions, and feelings) and a structural or relational element (a conceptual ordering of the percepts and feelings). This double requirement is what Kant meant to insist on when he said that "thoughts without content are empty, intuitions without concepts are blind. It is just as necessary to make our concepts sensible, that is, to add the object to them in intuition, as to make our intuitions intelligible, that is, to bring them under concepts." [h] Even the most rudimentary kind of judgment, a judgment of identification (for example, "That was a clock striking three") is a case in point. Only when an experience (a noise) is "brought under" a concept ("clock striking") can it be identified, or known for what it is.

This is an extremely important distinction, and Kant was the first philosopher to formulate it unambiguously. Most rationalists, from Plato down to Descartes and his successors, had taken it for granted that cognitive processes form a continuum; they regarded perception as "confused thought"—that is, as the same sort of activity as reasoning, differing only in degree of adequacy. Although the empiricists, of course, had not maintained that perception is confused, neither had they drawn the Kantian distinction between percepts and concepts, for they had tended to treat concepts as fictions, or even (as with the extreme nominalists) as merely words. Hence they too failed to emphasize that there are two indispensable elements in human knowledge. Here, then, is another reason why Kant's theories can be regarded as a watershed in the history of philosophy. On the whole, most nineteenth- and twentieth-century philosophers have accepted Kant's distinction between percepts and concepts, with the limitations that this entails regarding direct, immediate knowledge of the self and its world. Those philosophers who did not nevertheless had to deal with the distinction Kant had drawn; philosophy could not return to its pre-Kantian course.

A PRIORI CONCEPTS

To return to the argument of the "Transcendental Logic": Obviously, most concepts, like the concept "clock striking," are what Kant called empirical. They are derived from experience. That their derivation requires complicated acts of thought is beside the point here. The question for Kant was whether there are any pure a priori concepts, that is, forms of thought (of judging) that correspond to space and time as pervasive forms of sensing.

The "clue" to the discovery of these pure a priori concepts lies in recognizing that all judgments whatsoever fall into one or the other of several types (categorical, hypothetical, affirmative, negative, and so forth). According to Kant, we could not make a judgment of any of these types unless we *understood* the "relationship" being asserted. By "relationship" Kant meant, not the particular relationship in a particular judgment ("All crows are black"), but the generic relationship ("All —— are ——"). To grasp the particular connection between "crow" and "black," sense experience is required, for the concept "crow" is an empirical concept like the concept "clock striking." But before *any* particular empirical judgment of this type can be made, it is necessary to understand the generic relationship "All —— are ——." Hence the concept "All —— are ——" is a pure a priori concept, antecedent to all experience and a condition of there being any specific judgments of this type and therefore any knowledge of this kind.

Kant believed that Aristotelian logic furnished a complete and exhaustive table of all possible types of judgment. Hence from this list he drew up a corresponding list of pure a priori concepts. Kant classified the various possible types of judgment as follows:

I. QUANTITY OF JUDGMENTS	II. QUALITY
Universal	Affirmative
Particular	Negative
Singular	Infinite

III. RELATION	IV. MODALITY
Categorical	Problematic
Hypothetical	Assertoric
Disjunctive	Apodeictic[i]

Since, in Kant's view, each form of judgment is an a priori concept (or "category") by means of which the mind orders its various particular judgings, there is a table of categories that corresponds exactly with the table of types of judgment:

I. OF QUANTITY	II. OF QUALITY
Unity	Reality
Plurality	Negation
Totality	Limitation

III. OF RELATION	IV. OF MODALITY
Of Inherence and Subsistence (*substantia et accidens*)	Possibility–Impossibility
Of Causality and Dependence (cause and effect)	Existence–Nonexistence
Of Community (reciprocity between agent and patient)	Necessity–Contingency[j]

It is important to see that, once Kant had discovered the all-important connection between the types of judgment and the a priori concepts (or forms of synthesis), the actual list of a priori concepts followed automatically, being guaranteed by the authority of Aristotle's logic.

> The same function which gives unity to the various representations *in a judgment* also gives unity to the mere synthesis of various representations *in an intuition;* and this unity, in its most general expression, we entitle the pure concept of the understanding. The same understanding, through the same operations by which in concepts, by means of analytical unity, it produced the logical form of a judgment, also introduces a transcendental content into its representations, by means of the synthetic unity of the manifold in intuition in general. On this account we are entitled to call these representations pure concepts of the understanding, and to regard them as applying *a priori* to objects—a conclusion which general logic is not in a position to establish.
>
> In this manner there arise precisely the same number of pure concepts of the understanding which apply *a priori* to objects of intuition in general, as . . . there have been found to be logical functions in all possible judgments. For these functions specify the understanding completely, and yield an exhaustive inventory of its powers. These concepts we shall, with Aristotle, call *categories*.[k]

THE METAPHYSICAL DEDUCTION

This is what Kant called the "metaphysical deduction" of the categories.[8] In it he purported to show that every judgment the mind makes ("Roses are red," "Crows are black," "Friction causes heat") presupposes one or the other of twelve different synthetical operations ("puttings together"), or categories. It is important to understand that a category is *not* a fixed pigeonhole into which experience is dumped. One of the unfortunately misleading aspects of the sorting-machine analogy is that it suggests this sort of static conception—as, for that matter, does Kant's own term, "category." On the contrary, the categories are transcendental concepts, or rules, that underlie and make possible those actual, empirical syntheses that occur every time we judge. In calling them "transcendental," Kant merely meant they are not empirically observable "puttings together," as are the judgments "Roses are red" and "That was a clock striking three." We can be sure that they occur because, if they did not, the actual judgments we make could not occur.

THE TRANSCENDENTAL DEDUCTION

From the metaphysical deduction, Kant went on to what he called the "transcendental deduction" of the categories. So far he had merely shown that

---

8 By "deduction" Kant meant proof, or justification. The metaphysical deduction corresponds to the "expositions" of space and time—that is, it validates the existence of pure a priori concepts.

pure a priori concepts, or categories, underlie all our acts of judging. The function of the transcendental deduction was to show that these same categories make possible the kind of world we live in, namely, a world in which self knows objects. In other words, to talk about "acts of judging" is to deal in abstractions. It is a *self* that judges, and what it judges about are *objects*. The transcendental deduction is thus an extension of the metaphysical deduction.

The main points of the argument of the transcendental deduction are as follows: (1) All experience, whatever else it involves, is of the succession of a variety of contents. (2) To be experienced at all, these successive data have to be combined, or held together in unity for a consciousness. (3) Unity of experience therefore implies unity of self. (4) This unity of self is as much an object of experience as anything else is. (5) It follows that experience of both the self and its objects rests on prior acts of synthesis, which, because they are the conditions of any experience at all, are not themselves experienced. (6) These prior syntheses are made possible by the categories.

Kant's argument may perhaps be made clearer by reference to Locke's rather facile remark that the mind somehow "collects" certain of its ideas. Among these, according to Locke, are some of our most important ideas, for example, the ideas of substance and causality. In a sense, Kant's transcendental deduction was an attempt to define Locke's "somehow" with precision. Kant saw, as Locke did not, that the concept "collection" undermines the empirical criterion of meaning. Unlike, for example, the idea "red," substance and cause do not have their sources in experience. On the contrary, they make possible the very experience that would explain them.

THE CONDITIONS THAT MAKE EXPERIENCE POSSIBLE

Human experience is an experience of *objects*, or, as they may be called, unified representations. Human experience, that is, does not consist merely in a subjective flow of sense data in a mind that claims all these data as its own. With such a flow, "objects" are to be contrasted: Objects occupy, or have, an *objective* order different from their place in one's individual mental life. But what is implied by the existence of such "objects of representation"?

> We have stated above that appearances are themselves nothing but sensible representations, which, as such and in themselves, must not be taken as objects capable of existing outside our power of representation. What, then, is to be understood when we speak of an object corresponding to, and consequently also distinct from, our knowledge? It is easily seen that this object must be thought only as something in general = x, since outside our knowledge we have nothing which we could set over against this knowledge as corresponding to it.
>
> Now we find that our thought of the relation of all knowledge to its object carries with it an element of necessity; the object is viewed as that which prevents our modes of knowledge from being haphazard or arbitrary, and which determines them *a priori* in some definite fashion. For in so far as they

are to relate to an object, they must necessarily agree with one another, that is, must possess that unity which constitutes the concept of an object.

But it is clear that, since we have to deal only with the manifold of our representations, and since that x (the object) which corresponds to them is nothing to us—being, as it is, something that has to be distinct from all our representations—the unity which the object makes necessary can be nothing else than the formal unity of consciousness in the synthesis of the manifold of representations. It is only when we have thus produced synthetic unity in the manifold of intuition that we are in a position to say that we know the object. But this unity is impossible if the intuition cannot be generated in accordance with a rule by means of such a function of synthesis as makes the reproduction of the manifold *a priori* necessary, and renders possible a concept in which it is united. . . .

All knowledge demands a concept, though that concept may, indeed, be quite imperfect or obscure. But a concept is always, as regards its form, something universal which serves as a rule. The concept of body, for instance, as the unity of the manifold which is thought through it, serves as a rule in our knowledge of outer appearances. But it can be a rule for intuitions only in so far as it represents in any given appearances the necessary reproduction of their manifold, and thereby the synthetic unity in our consciousness of them. The concept of body, in the perception of something outside us, necessitates the representation of extension, and therewith representations of impenetrability, shape, etc.

All necessity, without exception, is grounded in a transcendental condition. There must, therefore, be a transcendental ground of the unity of consciousness in the synthesis of the manifold of all our intuitions, and consequently also of the concepts of objects in general, and so of all objects of experience, a ground without which it would be impossible to think any object for our intuitions; for this object is no more than that something, the concept of which expresses such a necessity of synthesis.[1]

In Kant's view, self and object are not independent entities but reciprocal elements in experience. If we start from object, we are led to self; if we begin with self, we are led to object. The experience of either one involves the experience of the other, and the experience of both depends on the prior occurrence of certain synthetical acts. Kant called these acts "transcendental" because, though never themselves experienced, they have to be presupposed to account for the existence of those empirical unities that are experienced, namely, "self" and "object." They have to be presupposed, that is, to account for the existence of experience as we know it. These synthetical acts depend on, and conform to, the categories.

> There can be in us no modes of knowledge, no connection or unity of one mode of knowledge with another, without that unity of consciousness which precedes all data of intuitions, and by relation to which representation of objects is alone possible. This pure original unchangeable consciousness I shall name *transcendental apperception*. . . .

This transcendental unity of apperception forms out of all possible appearances, which can stand alongside one another in one experience, a connection of all these representations according to laws. For this unity of consciousness would be impossible if the mind in knowledge of the manifold could not become conscious of the identity of function whereby it synthetically combines it in one knowledge. The original and necessary consciousness of the identity of the self is thus at the same time a consciousness of an equally necessary unity of the synthesis of all appearances according to concepts, that is, according to rules, which not only make them necessarily reproducible but also in so doing determine an object for their intuition, that is, the concept of something wherein they are necessarily interconnected. . . .

The *a priori* conditions of a possible experience in general are at the same time conditions of the possibility of objects of experience. Now I maintain that the categories, above cited, are nothing but the conditions of thought in a possible experience, just as space and time are the conditions of intuition for that same experience. They are fundamental concepts by which we think objects in general for appearances, and have therefore *a priori* objective validity. This is exactly what we desired to prove. . . .

That the *laws* of appearances in nature must agree with the understanding and its *a priori* form, that is, with its faculty of *combining* the manifold in general, is no more surprising than that the appearances themselves must agree with the form of *a priori* sensible intuition. For just as appearances do not exist in themselves but only relatively to the subject in which, so far as it has senses, they inhere, so the laws do not exist in the appearances but only relatively to this same being, so far as it has understanding. Things in themselves would necessarily, apart from any understanding that knows them, conform to laws of their own. But appearances are only representations of things which are unknown as regards what they may be in themselves. As mere representations, they are subject to no law of connection save that which the connecting faculty prescribes. Now it is imagination that connects the manifold of sensible intuition; and imagination is dependent for the unity of its intellectual synthesis upon the understanding, and for the manifoldness of its apprehension upon sensibility. All possible perception is thus dependent upon synthesis of apprehension, and this empirical synthesis in turn upon transcendental synthesis, and therefore upon the categories. Consequently, all possible perceptions, and therefore everything that can come to empirical consciousness, that is, all appearances of nature, must, so far as their connection is concerned, be subject to the categories. Nature, considered merely as nature in general, is dependent upon these categories as the original ground of its necessary conformity to law (*natura formaliter spectata*). Pure understanding is not, however, in a position, through mere categories, to prescribe to appearances any *a priori* laws other than those which are involved in a *nature in general*, that is, in the conformity to law of all appearances in space and time. Special laws, as concerning those appearances which are empirically determined, cannot in their specific character be *derived* from the categories, although they are one and all subject to them. To obtain any knowledge whatsoever of these special laws, we must resort to experience; but it is the *a priori* laws that alone can instruct us in regard to experience in general, and as to what it is that can be known as an object of experience.[m]

A DISCUSSION OF KANT'S VIEW OF EXPERIENCE

This passage is undeniably difficult, partly because, like a juggler who has to keep a number of balls in the air at once, Kant found that the various concepts he was discussing—experience, self, and object—all involved one another and hence could not be discussed separately. But part of the difficulty also stems from the fact that—even after three hundred years—we are still so accustomed to thinking about the world in Cartesian and Lockian terms that it is hard for us to adjust to Kant's radically different way of looking at things.

Let us therefore examine a simple experience in terms of a traditional and then a Kantian type of analysis. Suppose that I hear a clock striking three. According to the traditional analysis, my experience is as follows: (1) The clock is an object out there, independent of me. That is, even if there were no "me" over here, the clock would still exist and still strike, unaffected in any way by my nonexistence. (2) I am over here, another independent object. If the clock did not exist I would still be myself, unaffected by its nonexistence—except, of course, that I would not now hear it strike. (3) But the clock does exist; it does strike. I hear it and then judge, "That is a clock striking three." This is the Cartesian and Lockian way of looking at things.

In contrast, Kant makes no metaphysical assumptions about independently existing minds and objects. Instead, he starts from the experience itself and asks, "What conditions make this experience possible?" In terms of the example, what must be the case for me to be able to have the particular experience of a clock striking three? In the first place, I must already have learned, at mother's knee or in school, that clocks strike and that one can tell time in this way. If I were a Zulu or a Bantu and told time by the sun, I might have had no prior acquaintance with clocks. In this event, when the clock strikes three I would not have the experience of hearing the clock strike three. Doubtless, I would hear noises, but I would not be able to judge, "That is a clock striking three." Accordingly, the first condition of my being able to have the experience that I do have is possession of a number of empirical concepts, that is, concepts learned in experience. Though nobody, presumably, would deny that I possess such concepts, the traditional analysis does not bring this out, since it does not focus on the conditions that make experience possible.

According to Kant, of course, a priori concepts as well as empirical concepts are necessary conditions for experience. Furthermore, when these a priori concepts are taken into account, a wholly different notion of the self and its objects emerges. The next stage in Kant's analysis was designed to bring out these points. According to this analysis, when I judge, "That is a clock striking three," I am assigning an objective order to the successive strikes and am attributing them to a clock as their cause. That is, though the strikes have an order and a date in my own experience (having occurred later and earlier than other experiences of mine), they also have a public order and a public date, which I attribute to them. This, indeed, is the way I distinguish them from a dream that I might have about a clock striking. "Dreamed" strikes have an order and a date in my experience, but in recognizing them as having been dreamed I do not assign them an objective order as well.

Hence it is fair to call these three strikes an object whose cause is the clock. Of course, they are only a very simple object, consisting of three auditory sense data. Nonetheless, they are an object—for an object is precisely some set of sense experiences to which a public order and a public date are assigned. Accordingly, Kant's question can be rephrased as follows: "What is necessary for there to be an experience of an object?" In the case of the object "three strikes of a clock," what is necessary in addition to such empirical concepts as "clock" and "strike"?

It is important to see, first, that even the simplest of simple experiences contains diversity. Yet to be *an* experience, this diversity must be collected, or put together into unity. According to Kant's thesis, this putting together involves the categories—that is, nothing less than the categories are necessary to make even the experience of three strikes possible.

So much for "object"; what of "self"? Like its objects, the self is a collection —but it is a collection of desires, memories, expectations, feelings, and attitudes rather than of sense data. Moreover, though the self *is* a collection, it is not *merely* a collection. For if the self unifies the various data (in this case, the strikes) by collecting them into an object (the experience of a clock striking three), what unifies the self into the object (collection) that the self is admitted to be? The self cannot be a mere collection, for a mere collection cannot collect itself.[9] In a word, what is true of the experience of objects is equally true of the experience of self: The experience of even the simplest of simple objects (three strikes) is possible only because of the syntheses that bind the experienced diversity into unity. But the self, too, is an object. Hence the syntheses in question underlie the self just as much as they underlie its objects.

Here, then, is a plurality of noises experienced as "three strikes of a clock." According to Kant's analysis, this experience can occur only under the following conditions. To begin with, I must apprehend all three experiences as being similar.[10] This does not mean that I must identify the noises explicitly as strikes. I may do this, of course; but it is not necessary that I do so in order to experience the strikes as three. It means simply that I must discriminate these noises from other, dissimilar noises. For instance, suppose a car happened to honk its horn between the first and second strikes; I do not count the horn noise in and thus get four. Furthermore, when I get to the second strike, it is necessary, in Kant's terminology, to "reproduce" the first strike.[11] By "reproduce" Kant did not mean consciously recall; he meant merely carry over. That is, I must carry the first strike forward after it is over and combine it with the second. Since the first

---

9 This point was put with devastating force by F. H. Bradley: "Mr. Bain collects that the mind is a collection. Has he ever thought who collects Mr. Bain?"—*Ethical Studies* (Oxford, 1927), p. 39, n. 1.
10 Kant called this the "synthesis of apprehension in imagination."
11 This is the "synthesis of reproduction in imagination."

strike is over and done, it is fair to say that in carrying it over to the second I "reproduce" it. If I could not do this, I would begin over again and never get beyond "one, . . . one, . . . one, . . ." Then, having collected this plurality (or "manifold," as Kant called it) into a unity, I must attribute it to the clock as its cause.[12] Otherwise I might be able to count three strikes, but I would not experience, as I do, three strikes *of* a clock. That is, it is not enough that I merely collect the plurality of noises under the empirical concept "strike." I must order them in accordance with an a priori rule—in this case, a rule that assigns the strikes specific locations in objective time. I must assign the strikes that I hear to a later time than the time that I assign to what is going on in the clock (clapper tapping bell), and this time must be *objectively* later, not merely later in my personal life. Finally, for the three strikes to be unified into one experience of three strikes of a clock, there must be a self that endures at least as long as the three strikes last. If I died and were reborn a different person between the first and second strikes, I would say "one," not "two," when the second strike occurred.

In insisting on the existence of a self that unifies experience, Kant did not mean that we are conscious of the puttings together involved in experiencing an object. It is not that I have to be self-conscious and say, "Now I am hearing the first strike of a clock; now I am hearing the second strike, and I am the same I that heard the first strike"; and so forth. Even if I were self-conscious about my experience, this would be simply *another* and more complicated experience the existence of which depended on prior, nonexperienced mental operations. These "puttings together" (or "transcendental syntheses," as Kant called them) are, in fact, even more obviously the conditions of such an involved, self-conscious experience than they are the conditions of the simple awareness of "three strikes."

As has been said, the three strikes of a clock are an object—doubtless a very rudimentary object as compared with a desk, St. Peter's in Rome, or Mount Everest, but still an object. What are put together in this instance are three identical, or nearly identical, noises. In the case of a desk, a much larger manifold of visual and tactile materials is involved; in the case of Mount Everest, a still vaster assemblage. But the principle is everywhere the same. They are all objects-for-a-self. They all involve a temporal succession of data, recognized, remembered, held together in a unifying experience, and assigned an objective order and date. Furthermore, my experience, taken in its entirety, is a whole in which the striking clock, the desk, St. Peter's, and Mount Everest all have temporal and spatial loci within a unified, one-dimensional time and a unified, three-dimensional space. That is, my experience, as a whole, is one object in the sense that it is a unified structure, or order, of sensory content. My experience is, in fact, a cosmos.

So far we have been considering the knowledge situation from the object

12 This is the "synthesis of recognition in concepts."

side (the strikes); the situation is the same when looked at from the point of view of the self. If the three strikes are, as has been said, an object, they are equally states of a self. And if the object is a synthesis of data of outer sense, the self is a synthesis of data of inner sense.[13] When we look for a self we never find more than various synthesized experiences. The self and its objects are not two distinct substances confronting each other in mutual independence; they are simply two aspects of a complex situation. Looked at from one point of view, experience is a self that knows a world of objects; looked at from the opposite point of view, it is a world of objects known by a self. There is just as much self as there is object and just as much object as there is self. Self and object are correlative concepts.

Instead of hypostatizing self and its objects as independent entities, Kant held that self and objects are both ordered elements in our experience. Experience, to be experience, must be ordered; this was Kant's point. This order presupposes the existence of certain synthesizing activities that are not themselves experienced. Without them, the order that is found in experience, and that is an empirical fact, would not be possible. This empirical self can become as much an object of experience as can a desk or Mount Everest. But the self as object is not the underlying synthetical activities. It as much presupposes those conditions as do the desk and the mountain; it is as much made possible by them as are the desk and the mountain. Experience is an ordered manifold, and "self" and "objects" are names for elements in this manifold. The key to the nature of knowledge, then, is order (or rule, or law); this is what makes experience—including the self and its objects—possible. Without order, there is no experience and hence no self and no objects.

DEDUCTION OF THE CATEGORIES

So far, Kant has shown (providing his argument is correct) that an order of some sort has to be presupposed as the condition of any experience, however rudimentary. Kant next undertook to show that the world as we actually experience it—a world of relatively stable objects—reflects precisely those patterns that he called categories and that he had derived from Aristotle's twelve types of judgment. To follow Kant through the detailed deduction of all twelve categories (the "Analytic of Principles") would require much more space than can be afforded here. Let us therefore examine his procedure by considering his account of the two most important categories, substance and causality.

Kant began his deduction of these two categories with some general remarks applicable to both:

> Experience is an empirical knowledge, that is, a knowledge which determines an object through perceptions. It is a synthesis of perceptions, not

---

13 Here we are considering what Kant called the empirical self. There is also, according to Kant, a transcendental self ("the transcendental unity of apperception"), which underlies and makes possible *both* the empirical self and the objects it experiences.

contained in perception but itself containing in one consciousness the synthetic unity of the manifold of perceptions. This synthetic unity constitutes the essential in any knowledge of *objects* of the senses, that is, in experience as distinguished from mere intuition of sensation of the senses. In experience, however, perceptions come together only in accidental order, so that no necessity determining their connection is or can be revealed in the perceptions themselves. For apprehension is only a placing together of the manifold of empirical intuition; and we can find in it no representation of any necessity which determines the appearances thus combined to have connected existence in space and time. But since experience is a knowledge of objects through perceptions, the relation [involved] in the existence of the manifold has to be represented in experience, not as it comes to be constructed in time but as it exists objectively in time. Since time, however, cannot itself be perceived, the determination of the existence of objects in time can take place only through their relation in time in general, and therefore only through concepts that connect them *a priori*. Since these always carry necessity with them, it follows that experience is only possible through a representation of necessary connection of perceptions.

The three modes of time are *duration, succession,* and *coexistence.*[14] There will, therefore, be three rules of all relations of appearances in time, and these rules will be prior to all experience, and indeed make it possible. By means of these rules the existence of every appearance can be determined in respect of the unity of all time.[n]

This argument starts, once again, from two basic distinctions. First, everyone constantly distinguishes between what is subjective (for example, dreamed strikes of a clock) and what is objective (actual strikes of a clock). Of course, I may on occasion be doubtful (Is that a dagger that I see before me? Am I awake or dreaming?). On occasion I may be mistaken. But everyone makes this fundamental distinction. Furthermore, it is not a distinction between what is inside experience and what is outside experience; it is a distinction *within* experience. Both the dreamed strikes and the actual strikes are segments of the flow of my experience; the mark of objectivity is the regularity and order of those segments to which I assign the status of objects.

Second, we all distinguish, within waking experience, between the order in which we happen to experience things and the order that those things have. For instance, we distinguish between the order in which we learn something and the order of the things we have learned: Many children study American history in school before they study ancient history; as a result, they hear about George Washington before they hear about Julius Caesar. But they do not, on this account, think that Washington lived before Caesar. Rather, they assign each to a single, public, temporal order that is independent of the subjective order in which they experienced it. Again, people may on occasion make mistakes, but

14 [Coexistence is the product of the third category of relation, or "Reciprocity" (see the table of categories, p. 35). It is necessary to pass over detailed discussion of the operation of this category—AUTHOR.]

the fact that mistakes are made itself validates the distinction in principle. And this distinction too is a fundamental one: Human experience would not be human experience without the notion of an order that is indifferent to the order of actual experience.

It follows that whatever is necessary for us to be able to make these distinctions must be the case, even though it may never be possible to verify this "whatever is necessary" directly in experience. To put this differently, the empirical criterion of meaning does not apply to itself. Hume had argued that we should accept nothing that cannot be verified (that is, encountered) in experience. Kant's reply to this, in effect, was that we nonetheless may—indeed must—accept whatever is necessary for us to have experience, even though that itself is never experienced.

THE CATEGORIES OF SUBSTANCE AND CAUSALITY

According to Hume (and Kant), we never experience substances and we never experience necessary connections; we experience only succession. How then do we get the "idea" of stable, enduring entities, objects related causally to other objects? Having looked in vain for objects, Hume concluded that we "feign" them. Kant concluded that they must be attributed to a priori concepts, namely, to relational structures, or patterns—not innate ideas such as Descartes thought God had implanted in us—in terms of which our minds organize our experiences. Specifically, what we bring to experience are the notions of permanence and regular sequence. These are the categories of substance and causality. As for substance,

> . . . our *apprehension* of the manifold of appearance is always successive, and is therefore always changing. Through it alone we can never determine whether this manifold, as object of experience, is coexistent or successive. For such determination we require an underlying ground which exists *at all times*, that is, something *abiding* and *permanent*, of which all change and coexistence are only so many ways (modes of time) in which the permanent exists. And simultaneity and succession being the only relations in time, it follows that only in the permanent are relations of time possible. In other words, the permanent is the *substratum* of the empirical representation of time itself; in it alone is any determination of time possible. . . . If we ascribe succession to time itself, we must think yet another time, in which the sequence would be possible. Only through the permanent does existence in different parts of the time-series acquire a magnitude which can be entitled duration. For in bare succession existence is always vanishing and recommencing, and never has the least magnitude. Without the permanent there is therefore no time-relation. Now time cannot be perceived in itself; the permanent in the appearances is therefore the substratum of all determination of time, and, as likewise follows, is also the condition of the possibility of all synthetic unity of perceptions, that is, of experience. All existence and all change in time have thus to be viewed as simply a mode of the existence

of that which remains and persists. In all appearances the permanent is the object itself, that is, substance as phenomenon; everything, on the other hand, which changes or can change belongs only to the way in which substance or substances exist, and therefore to their determinations. . . .

Permanence is thus a necessary condition under which alone appearances are determinable as things or objects in a possible experience.°

Thus Kant replaced the metaphysical relation of "inherence," which the rationalists venerated and the empiricists ridiculed, with an empirical and temporal relation—endurance through time. A substance is not a mysterious substratum that somehow owns, or has, various attributes. A substance is a complex pattern of sensory materials[15] that are experienced as permanent. And, of course, it is the *pattern* that is permanent, not the individual materials—these are constantly changing. In addition, since substance is one of the ways in which our minds organize our experiences, it follows that there are no transcendental, supersensible substances. The only substances are those stable, relatively permanent complexes that we encounter in experience. Finally, what is necessary is *not* that a particular empirical thing be a substance; what is necessary is simply that our minds order experience substantivally. To ascertain which particular segments, or aspects, of experience are substances and which are not is a purely empirical inquiry. And there is nothing final or definitive about the results of this inquiry. All particular judgments are provisional, and future investigation may well upset present indications about the specific nature of the relatively permanent parts of experience. All we can be sure of is that, however we judge a particular matter in detail, we shall continue to organize our experience substantivally.

This conception of substance is a good example of Kantian compromise. Kant was at one with the empiricists in denying any purely rational concept; he agreed with them that "substance-attribute" must be an observable relation. On the other hand, he held Hume to be mistaken in denying that the concept of substance has any objective validity at all. Substance-attribute is an empirically observable relation precisely because it is the product of a necessary function performed by the human mind in its task of regulating and ordering the world. Like the rationalists, Kant maintained that the necessity attributed to substance is real (not illusory, as the empiricists claimed). But, like the empiricists, he held that it is a mode of human experience (not an obscure force residing in allegedly independent substances-in-themselves, as the rationalists claimed).

Kant's treatment of the problem of causality parallels his treatment of the problem of substance. In his view, not only do we attribute permanence to objects; we also attribute causality to them. That is, we believe objects to be related to one another systematically according to a rule of succession. There is a rule that relates sensory materials to one another so that they are experienced

15 For a possible modification of this view, see the discussion of ambiguities in Kant's conception of the phenomenal object, pp. 48–49.

as a complex of sensory materials enduring together through time to form one object. In addition, there is a rule that relates each of these complexes to another complex so that the former is experienced as following the latter in a regular way—that is, one is experienced as the "effect" of the other.

The apprehension of the manifold of appearance is always successive. The representations of the parts follow upon one another. Whether they also follow one another in the object is a point which calls for further reflection. . . . For instance, the apprehension of the manifold in the appearance of a house which stands before me is successive. The question then arises, whether the manifold of the house is also in itself successive. This, however, is what no one will grant. . . . That which lies in the successive apprehension is here viewed as representation, while the appearance which is given to me, notwithstanding that it is nothing but the sum of these representations, is viewed as their object. . . . The object is *that* in the appearance which contains the condition of this necessary rule of apprehension.

Let us now proceed to our problem. . . . I also note, in an appearance which contains a happening (the preceding state of the perception we may entitle A, and the succeeding B) B can be apprehended only as following upon A; the perception A cannot follow upon B but only precede it. For instance, I see a ship move down stream. My perception of its lower position follows upon the perception of its position higher up in the stream, and it is impossible that in the apprehension of this appearance the ship should first be perceived lower down in the stream and afterwards higher up. The order in which the perceptions succeed one another in apprehension is in this instance determined, and to this order apprehension is bound down. In the previous example of a house my perceptions could begin with the apprehension of the roof and end with the basement, or could begin from below and end above; and I could similarly apprehend the manifold of the empirical intuition either from right to left or from left to right. In the series of these perceptions there was thus no determinate order specifying at what point I must begin in order to connect the manifold empirically. But in the perception of an event there is always a rule that makes the order in which the perceptions (in the apprehension of this appearance) follow upon one another a *necessary* order.

In this case, therefore, we must derive the *subjective succession* of apprehension from the *objective succession* of appearances. Otherwise the order of apprehension is entirely undetermined, and does not distinguish one appearance from another. . . . The objective succession will therefore consist in that order of the manifold of appearance according to which, *in conformity with a rule*, the apprehension of that which happens follows upon the apprehension of that which precedes. Thus only can I be justified in asserting, not merely of my apprehension, but of appearance itself, that a succession is to be met with in it. This is only another way of saying that I cannot arrange the apprehension otherwise than in this very succession. . . .

Let us suppose that there is nothing antecedent to an event, upon which it must follow according to rule. All succession of perception would then be only in the apprehension, that is, would be merely subjective. . . . We should then have only a play of representations, relating to no object. . . .

If, then, we experience that something happens, we in so doing always presuppose that something precedes it, on which it follows according to a rule. Otherwise I should not say of the object that it follows. For mere succession in my apprehension, if there be no rule determining the succession in relation to something that precedes, does not justify me in assuming any succession in the object.ᴾ

Kant's contention, in a word, is that if there were not (1) enduring complexes and (2) succession of these complexes according to a rule, we would not experience *objects*. But we do experience objects. Therefore there must be such rules, even though they can never be directly experienced as distinct elements in the manifold of sense.

Here, as with the concept of substance, Kant proposed a compromise between the empiricists' position and the rationalists' position. He agreed with the empiricists that there is no mysterious transfer of force, no exercise of power, in the causal relation. He agreed with them also that all particular causal judgments are based on observation of actual sequences and are provisional in character. But, according to Kant, although the empiricists were correct in maintaining that there is no necessary connection between particular matters of fact, they were mistaken in concluding that the principle of causality is false. To Kant, this was just the reverse of the mistake made by the rationalists, who concluded that because the principle of causality is necessarily true, the connections between particular events are necessary. According to Kant, the principle of causality is necessarily true, but the source of its necessity (as with substance) is in the structure of our minds.

THE PHENOMENAL OBJECT

We have now reached a point of major dispute in Kantian exegesis. What did Kant mean, in the transcendental deduction, by describing the object of representation as "something in general = x"?[16] There is general agreement about what Kant did not mean. He meant neither the metaphysical substratum of the Scholastics and the rationalists nor the mere lively-expectation-based-on-association of the empiricists. This is clear from his repeated criticisms of both positions. There is also general agreement that the x in the equation involves succession according to a rule. What distinguishes an object (or "thing") from a "mere blind play of representations, even less than a dream," is, as we have seen, the fact that when we experience an object, our representations succeed one another according to a rule, not according to a private fantasy in our own mind.

The parting of the ways in Kantian interpretation comes with the question,

16 See p. 37.

"What exactly are the elements, thus ordered, that succeed one another according to a rule?" The simplest interpretation is that by "representations" Kant meant the raw data of sense experience. According to this view, the desk you and I talk of seeing is not a public object "out there" in a public space. There are, in fact, two desks, or as many desks as there are viewers, for each viewer's sense data are his private subjective experiences. What is objective and public is simply the common order in which the various private sense data occur.

There seems to be no doubt that a great deal of the time Kant did think in terms of this relatively subjectivist point of view. There is also no doubt that he wanted to insist on more objectivity than this view permits. Kant was not particularly concerned by the fact that, according to the subjectivist view, an object is not at all what you and I uncritically suppose it to be. But he was concerned by the fact that, according to the subjectivist view, the object is not what Newtonian science supposes it to be—namely, objectively existing matter in motion.

As has been said, Kant wanted to show not merely that there is some order, or pattern, in experience (succession according to a rule) but that the rules according to which experience is ordered are those presupposed by Newtonian physics. Thus it is not surprising to find that the subjectivist view did not really satisfy him. In fact, he presents in the deduction, along with this view and by no means clearly distinguished from it, a much more complicated view in which the x involves not merely sense-data-according-to-a-rule but what Kant called a "phenomenal object." Because phenomenal objects (Newtonian matter in motion) are spatially and temporally organized, they are, like the sense data, modes of appearance.[17] But they are also supposed, by both common sense and natural science, to be the *causes* of the ordered sense data (which constitute the whole of appearance, according to the subjectivist view). The difficulty with this view is not merely that the phenomenal object complicates the picture and occupies an anomalous place between things-in-themselves and representations. The fundamental difficulty is that, according to Kantian principles, the phenomenal object itself must be a synthesis of representations. But if it is, it cannot be the cause of the representations in question. This would amount to supposing it to be the product of that of which it is the cause.[18]

SUMMARY

This discussion of the categories has brought us to a conclusion that parallels the conclusion drawn earlier about Kant's view of Euclidean geometry. As we

17 See pp. 31–32.
18 This difficulty has been put very effectively by T. D. Weldon in *Kant's Critique of Pure Reason* (Oxford, 1947), p. 25. According to the view in question, "it would appear that there must be perception to give material for synthesis before there can be perception caused by synthesized objects. In other words, something must happen before it happens, which is certainly rather peculiar."

have seen, Kant did not show that such-and-such a type of order (Euclidean for space, Newtonian for things) is a priori, but he did show that *some* order is necessary for there to be any experience at all. This conclusion will not be acceptable to those who insist (as Kant did) on the possibility of a rational knowledge of nature. The great tradition in the West has been strongly rationalistic; it will be a matter of concern to many people, therefore, that even Kant's modified, watered-down rationalism failed. On the other hand, those who accept the pragmatic point of view of modern science will hold that the full deduction was simply so much wasted motion and that it has only an antiquarian interest. The prevalent view today, indeed, is not merely that the Newtonian concepts are not a priori, but that *no* scientific concepts are ever more than provisional and hypothetical in character, and that their function is merely to provide principles for ordering experience.

But rejection of the second stage in Kant's argument (in which he tried to deduce the specific categories) does not mean that the first stage of the deduction (in which he formulated the new relation between the self and its objects) was inconsequential. In the first place, it enabled Kant to provide an intelligible basis for inductive inference and to show that only a dogmatic empiricism need end in scepticism. The root of the trouble was not empiricism; it was the assumption that only what is given in sensation is real. In Kant's view, the starting point of a true empiricism must be the empirical fact that men experience connections between matters of fact, for example, "objects." Since the connections are real, the conditions that make them possible must also be real, even though they are not themselves encountered, or verified, in experience.

Kant understood that it was fatal to assume that in the knowledge situation an independently existing self confronts an independently existing object. For one logical consequence of this assumption is that the self knows only its own states—but, indeed, it cannot know even these. Something is radically wrong with premises that lead to such a conclusion. Here again, according to Kant, the critical starting point must be the fact of experience. Self and its objects can be seen to grow out of, or to be formed in, experience. There must be self (in some sense) for there to be any experience at all; there must be experience for there to be any self at all. But self is not a content, not a thing. It is a form of unity. No wonder, if self is not a thing, that the empiricists could not find it, and that they became sceptical as they searched for it in vain. Having asked themselves the wrong questions, they naturally failed to get the right answers. By pointing out the right questions, Kant provided the basis for a philosophy of science that could be as radically empirical as it liked without contradicting itself the moment it opened its mouth.

In addition to rehabilitating empiricism, the deduction provided a devastating criticism of the pretensions of rationalism: "Concepts without percepts are empty." In Kant's view, the real function of all those concepts by means of which the rationalists had sought to explore and interpret a supersensuous metaphysical reality is to organize the manifold of sense into meaningful and stable patterns.

The concepts of substance, causality, and the rest are meaningless except as synthetical relationships within the spatiotemporal manifold. The very arguments that validate these concepts *for* experience limit them *to* experience. The result of their misapplication beyond experience is "transcendental illusion."

It follows that the answer to Kant's third main question—"Are synthetical a priori judgments possible in metaphysics?"—is negative. This general conclusion is obvious once the nature of the deduction has been grasped. But because metaphysical thinking had such a grip on men's minds in his day, Kant devoted many pages to an exhaustive demonstration of the principal fallacies of rationalistic metaphysics.

Critique of Rationalistic Metaphysics

Kant proposed to show that in each of the three main areas of rationalistic speculation—self, being-in-general, and God—the rationalists were involved in an illegitimate attempt to apply the categories to things-in-themselves.

THE SELF

As regards the self, the subject of study in rationalistic psychology,

> . . . since the proposition "I think" (taken problematically) contains the form of each and every judgment of understanding and accompanies all categories as their vehicle, it is evident that the inferences from it admit only of a transcendental employment of the understanding. . . . We therefore propose to follow it, with a critical eye, through all the predicaments of pure psychology. . . .
>
> (1) In all judgments I am the *determining* subject of that relation which constitutes the judgment. That the "I," the "I" that thinks, can be regarded always as *subject*, and as something which does not belong to thought as a mere predicate, must be granted. It is an apodeictic and indeed *identical* proposition; but it does not mean that I, as *object*, am for myself a *self-subsistent* being or *substance*. . . .
>
> (2) That the "I" of apperception, and therefore the "I" in every act of thought, is *one*, and cannot be resolved into a plurality of subjects, and consequently signifies a logically simple subject, is something already contained in the very concept of thought. . . . But this does not mean that the thinking "I" is a simple *substance*. . . .
>
> The analysis, then, of the consciousness of myself in thought in general, yields nothing whatsoever towards the knowledge of myself as object. The logical exposition of thought in general has been mistaken for a metaphysical determination of the object. . . .
>
> The whole procedure of rational psychology is determined by a paralogism, which is exhibited in the following syllogism:

> *That which cannot be thought otherwise than as subject does not exist otherwise than as subject, and is therefore substance.*
>
> *A thinking being, considered merely as such, cannot be thought otherwise than as subject.*
>
> *Therefore it exists also only as subject, that is, as substance.*

In the major premiss we speak of a being that can be thought in general, in every relation, and therefore also as it may be given in intuition. But in the minor premiss we speak of it only in so far as it regards itself, as subject, simply in relation to thought and the unity of consciousness, and not as likewise in relation to the intuition through which it is given as object to thought. Thus the conclusion is arrived at fallaciously.[q]

This fallacy, called "the fallacy of four terms," occurs, in an obvious way, in the following argument:

All Greeks live in the Balkan peninsula
Kant's argument is Greek to me
_____

Therefore Kant's argument lives in the Balkan peninsula

Since the term "Greek" is used in different senses in the two premises, the argument has four terms, not three. There is only a verbal link between "Kant's argument" and "Balkan peninsula," and hence no conclusion can be drawn.

According to Kant, the rationalists' argument about the self depends on exactly the same sort of ambiguity: "'Thought' is taken in . . . two . . . totally different senses: in the major premiss, as relating to an object in general and therefore to an object as it may be given in intuition; in the minor premiss, only as it consists in relation to self-consciousness. In this latter sense, no object whatsoever is being thought; all that is being represented is simply the relation to self as subject (as the form of thought)."[r] To put this in a slightly different way, the rationalists' argument depends on an ambiguity in the term "self" (or "I"). For there are, according to Kant, two kinds of self: the empirical self and the transcendental self. The rationalists' argument confuses them in the same way that the argument in the example above confuses two different kinds of "Greek." That there are two different kinds of self follows from the basic thesis of the *Critique*—that transcendental conditions, which are not themselves experienced, must nevertheless be presupposed to underlie our experience of objects.

Now, the term "self" can be used to designate one type of entity encountered in experience—for example, the object that is just now sitting at the desk, reading about Mount Everest, and listening to the clock strike three. This is the empirical self; it is no more and no less an object than is any other thing in experience. The categories apply to it; indeed, they are the a priori conditions of experiencing it. But they apply to it with the same sort of purely empirical relevance with which they apply to "desk," "clock striking," or "Everest." The empirical self is just as much an object for scientific study—and in just the same sense—as is any other empirical object. Its behavior follows according to a rule; it no more exercises a mysterious metaphysical energy than does the desk.

On the other hand, there are the transcendental conditions, the synthetical operations, that accompany and make possible all this empirical experience. Because the rationalists did not clearly distinguish these conditions from the empirical self, they designated them by the term "self." Yet, as Kant believed he had demonstrated in the *Critique,* these transcendental syntheses are very different from the empirical self. They are not objects; rather, they are conditions of there being any objects at all—including the empirical self. They are forms, functions of unity. Since the categories apply only to a sensuous content, the notion that these operations are substances and causes is complete nonsense. Hence questions that can arise only in connection with synthesized data ("Is the self divisible or simple?" "Is it permanent or impermanent?") have no meaning when applied to the "I think." No wonder contradictions arise.

It is evident that this argument does two things at once: It demolishes the pretensions of the old rationalistic a priori psychology and lays the basis for a new and thoroughly empirical psychology. There is a third consequence that is even more important: It follows that we never have, and never can have, direct awareness (intuition) of the self. Of the self viewed as the transcendental conditions underlying experience we have no experience at all. This self lies wholly beyond experience. Of the empirical self we do have experience, but, like our experience of every other object, this experience is not direct. It is mediated by space, time, and the categories. During the nineteenth and twentieth centuries, a dispute arose among philosophers over whether or not to accept this conclusion of Kant's. Although some philosophers willingly adjusted to it, most sought to escape from it. For the culture of the past two centuries has been increasingly dominated by a profound feeling of alienation, a sense of being forever at a distance from that with which one longs, deeply and passionately, to be identified. This was one of the consequences to which Kantianism seemed to lead.

BEING-IN-GENERAL

Next, Kant turned his attention to being-in-general, the principal topic of inquiry in the traditional, rationalistic metaphysics. Kant considered four theses of rationalistic metaphysics and showed each of them to be contradicted by an antithesis. He argued that, since *both* thesis and antithesis can be proved, the attempt to know being-in-general is illegitimate and knowledge is limited to the ordered spatiotemporal manifold of experience. The four theses and their antitheses are as follows:

Thesis	*Antithesis*
(1) The world has a beginning in time, and is also limited as regards space.	(1) The world has no beginning, and no limits in space; it is infinite as regards both time and space.

Thesis	*Antithesis*
(2) Every composite substance in the world is made up of simple parts, and nothing anywhere exists save the simple or what is composed of the simple.	(2) No composite thing in the world is made up of simple parts, and there nowhere exists in the world anything simple.
(3) Causality in accordance with laws of nature is not the only causality from which the appearances of the world can one and all be derived. To explain these appearances it is necessary to assume that there is also another causality, that of freedom.	(3) There is no freedom; everything in the world takes place solely in accordance with laws of nature.
(4) There belongs to the world, either as its part or as its cause, a being that is absolutely necessary.	(4) An absolutely necessary being nowhere exists in the world, nor does it exist outside the world as its cause.[s]

The position taken in the antitheses (reflecting the empirical-scientific point of view) has whatever backing is to be derived from sticking close to verifiable facts and "never [taking] leave of the natural order." On the other hand, the position taken in the theses gains powerful support from

> . . . a certain *practical interest* in which every right-thinking man, if he has understanding of what truly concerns him, heartily shares. That the world has a beginning, that my thinking self is of simple and therefore indestructible nature, that it is free in its voluntary actions and raised above the compulsion of nature, and finally that all order in the things constituting the world is due to a primordial being, from which everything derives its unity and purposive connection—these are so many foundation stones of morals and religion. The antithesis robs us of all these supports, or at least appears to do so. . . .
>
> If there is no primordial being distinct from the world, if the world is without beginning and therefore without an Author, if our will is not free, and the soul is divisible and perishable like matter, *moral* ideas and principles lose all validity, and share in the fate of the *transcendental* ideas which served as their theoretical support.[t]

But questions of fact are decided by consideration of facts. Since the questions raised in the theses and antitheses are factual questions (and both the rationalists and the empiricists would have considered them to be such), the empiricists' case is correct—at least in its criticism of the claims of the rationalists to have positive knowledge of first causes, free wills, and so on. The trouble with the empiricists, Kant thought, was that they proceeded to make positive claims as dogmatic in their own way as those of the rationalists.

If the empirical philosopher had no other purpose in propounding his antithesis than to subdue the rashness and presumption of . . . [the rationalist], his principle would be a maxim urging moderation in our pretensions, modesty in our assertions, and yet at the same time the greatest possible extension of our understanding, through the teacher fittingly assigned to us, namely, through experience. If such were our procedure, we should not be cut off from employing intellectual *presuppositions* and *faith* on behalf of our practical interest; only they could never be permitted to assume the title and dignity of science and rational insight. . . .

But when empiricism itself, as frequently happens, becomes dogmatic in its attitude towards ideas, and confidently denies whatever lies beyond the sphere of its intuitive knowledge, it betrays the same lack of modesty; and this is all the more reprehensible owing to the irreparable injury which is thereby caused to the practical interests of reason.[u]

According to Kant, then, it is just as much a mistake to say there is no first cause as to say there is a first cause. All four of the theses and antitheses concern the totality, the whole. But the whole is not, and cannot be, an *object* of experience (for all objects are inside experience). The categories, therefore, do not apply to it. Hence questions about the nature of the whole—for instance, what sort of cause the whole is—are literally nonsense. Cause, as we have seen, is a category; it is a concept that has application only within experience. As long as the empiricists stuck to this, they were on firm ground, for there is no first (or free) cause in experience. Similarly, we can be sure we shall never come to the end of experience. But to infer from these truths that the world as a whole is an infinite, meaningless mechanism is illegitimate—just as illegitimate as it is to argue that the world has, or is, a free cause.

Kant's discussion of first causes and necessary beings in itself casts doubt on the rationalists' claims that a science of God is possible. Kant, however, devoted a special section to a criticism of the traditional arguments for the existence of God.

GOD

According to Kant, there are "only three possible ways of proving the existence of God by means of speculative reason." These are the *ontological*, the *cosmological*, and the *physico-theological* proofs. Kant attempted to show that all these arguments are invalid, and that, accordingly, a science of God (that is, rationalistic theology) is as impossible as is a science of totality or of pure self.

The first alleged proof of the existence of God is the ontological argument.

In all ages men have spoken of an *absolutely necessary* being, and in so doing have endeavoured, not so much to understand whether and how a thing of this kind allows even of being thought, but rather to prove its existence. There is, of course, no difficulty in giving a verbal definition of the concept, namely, that it is something the non-existence of which is impossible. But this yields no insight into the conditions which make it necessary to regard the non-existence of a thing as absolutely unthinkable. . . .

All the alleged examples are, without exception, taken from *judgments*, not from *things* and their existence. But the unconditioned necessity of judgments is not the same as an absolute necessity of things. The absolute necessity of the judgment is only a conditioned necessity of the thing, or of the predicate in the judgment. The [mathematical] proposition does not declare that three angles are absolutely necessary, but that, under the condition that there is a triangle (that is, that a triangle is given), three angles will necessarily be found in it. . . .

If, in an identical proposition, I reject the predicate while retaining the subject, contradiction results; and I therefore say that the former belongs necessarily to the latter. But if we reject subject and predicate alike, there is no contradiction; for nothing is then left that can be contradicted. To posit a triangle, and yet to reject its three angles, is self-contradictory; but there is no contradiction in rejecting the triangle together with its three angles. The same holds true of the concept of an absolutely necessary being. If its existence is rejected, we reject the thing itself with all its predicates; and no question of contradiction can then arise. . . . "God is omnipotent" is a necessary judgment. The omnipotence cannot be rejected if we posit a Deity, that is, an infinite being; for the two concepts are identical. But if we say, "There is no God," neither the omnipotence nor any other of its predicates is given; they are one and all rejected together with the subject, and there is therefore not the least contradiction in such a judgment. . . .

If . . . we admit, as every reasonable person must, that all existential propositions are synthetic, how can we profess to maintain that the predicate of existence cannot be rejected without contradiction? This is a feature which is found only in analytic propositions, and is indeed precisely what constitutes their analytic character. . . .

"Being" is obviously not a real predicate; that is, it is not a concept of something which could be added to the concept of a thing. It is merely the positing of a thing, or of certain determinations, as existing in themselves. Logically, it is merely the copula of a judgment. The proposition, "God is omnipotent," contains two concepts, each of which has its object—God and omnipotence. The small word "is" adds no new predicate, but only serves to posit the predicate *in its relation* to the subject. If, now, we take the subject (God) with all its predicates (among which is omnipotence), and say "God is," or "There is a God," we attach no new predicate to the concept of God, but only posit the subject in itself with all its predicates. . . . A hundred real thalers do not contain the least coin more than a hundred possible thalers. For as the latter signify the concept, and the former the object and the positing of the object, should the former contain more than the latter, my concept would not, in that case, express the whole object, and would not therefore be an adequate concept of it. My financial position is, however, affected very differently by a hundred real thalers than it is by the mere concept of them . . . ; yet the conceived hundred thalers are not themselves in the least increased through thus acquiring existence outside my concept.

By whatever and by however many predicates we may think a thing—even if we completely determine it—we do not make the least addition to the thing when we further declare that this thing *is*. Otherwise, it would not be exactly the same thing that exists, but something more than we had thought in the concept; and we could not, therefore, say that the exact object of my concept exists. . . .

The attempt to establish the existence of a supreme being by means of the famous ontological argument of Descartes is therefore merely so much labour and effort lost; we can no more extend our stock of [theoretical] insight by mere ideas, than a merchant can better his position by adding a few noughts to his cash account.ᵛ

The second argument is the cosmological proof.

It runs thus: If anything exists, an absolutely necessary being must also exist. Now I, at least, exist. Therefore an absolutely necessary being exists. The minor premiss contains an experience, the major premiss the inference from there being any experience at all to the existence of the necessary. . . .

In order to lay a secure foundation for itself, this proof takes its stand on experience, and thereby makes profession of being distinct from the ontological proof, which puts its entire trust in pure *a priori* concepts. But the cosmological proof uses this experience only for a single step in the argument, namely, to conclude the existence of a necessary being. What properties this being may have, the empirical premiss cannot tell us. Reason therefore abandons experience altogether, and endeavours to discover from mere concepts what properties an absolutely necessary being must have. . . . Thus the so-called cosmological proof really owes any cogency which it may have to the ontological proof from mere concepts. . . .

[Moreover] in this cosmological argument there lies hidden a whole nest of dialectical assumptions, which the transcendental critique can easily detect and destroy. . . .

We find, for instance, (1) the transcendental principle whereby from the contingent we infer a cause. This principle is applicable only in the sensible world; outside that world it has no meaning whatsoever. . . . The principle of causality has no meaning and no criterion for its application save only in the sensible world. But in the cosmological proof it is precisely in order to enable us to advance beyond the sensible world that it is employed. (2) The inference to a first cause, from the impossibility of an infinite series of causes, given one after the other, in the sensible world. The principles of the employment of reason do not justify this conclusion even within the world of experience, still less beyond this world in a realm into which this series can never be extended.ʷ

The third proof is the argument from design, which Hume had already submitted to a devastating criticism. Kant called this the "physico-theological" proof.

This proof always deserves to be mentioned with respect. It is the oldest, the clearest, and the best suited to ordinary human reason. . . .

The chief points . . . are as follows: (1) In the world we everywhere find clear signs of an order in accordance with a determinate purpose, carried out with great wisdom; and this in a universe which is indescribably varied in content and unlimited in extent. (2) . . . the diverse things could not of themselves have co-operated, by so great a combination of diverse means, to the fulfilment of determinate final purposes, had they not been chosen and designed for these purposes by an ordering rational principle in conformity with underlying ideas. (3) There exists, therefore, a sublime and wise cause (or more than one) . . . of the world. . . . (4) The unity of this cause may be inferred from the unity of the reciprocal relations existing between the parts of the world, as members of an artfully arranged structure—inferred with certainty in so far as our observation suffices for its verification, and beyond these limits with probability, in accordance with the principles of analogy. . . .

On this method of argument, the purposiveness and harmonious adaptation of so much in nature can suffice to prove the contingency of the form merely, not of the matter, that is, not of the substance in the world. To prove the latter we should have to demonstrate that the things in the world would not of themselves be capable of such order and harmony, in accordance with universal laws, if they were not *in their substance* the product of supreme wisdom. But to prove this we should require quite other grounds of proof than those which are derived from the analogy with human art. The utmost, therefore, that the argument can prove is an *architect* of the world who is always very much hampered by the adaptability of the material in which he works, not a *creator* of the world to whose idea everything is subject. This, however, is altogether inadequate to the lofty purpose which we have before our eyes, namely, the proof of an all-sufficient primordial being.[x]

Thus examination of typical metaphysical assertions about the self, about the universe as a whole, and about God, and of the arguments by which the rationalists sought to sustain them, confirmed for Kant the general conclusion he had reached by a consideration of the nature of the categories as ordering principles— namely, that knowledge is limited to the spatiotemporal realm that the categories order. It therefore seemed to Kant that a science of metaphysics, of a realm of being that transcends the spatiotemporal, is clearly impossible.

Regulative Use of Reason

Are we then to conclude, as the empiricists did, that the concepts of God, self, and totality are vain and chimerical illusions? If we do so, we fly in the face of those practical interests that Kant considered to be the foundations of morality and religion. Moreover, it would be difficult to see how men ever came to accept these concepts in the first place, or why such concepts have survived so long and despite all criticism.

Since Kant held that nothing in nature is "in vain," he believed that these concepts, too, have a use. As a matter of fact, in his critique of rationalistic metaphysics he did not attack the concepts themselves. He merely pointed out that the rationalists misused them. The rationalists went wrong, first, in supposing that self, God, and totality are *objects* like desk or Mount Everest, and, second, in trying to cognize them by means of the categories, which are appropriate only to the interpretation of objects. The question therefore is, "What constitutes a legitimate employment of such concepts as God, self, and totality?"

Whatever the use of these concepts proves to be, it must be within the limits of, or in connection with, experience. Now the function of most concepts is to organize experience. Suppose we are social anthropologists making a statistical survey of a certain community. We set up various classificatory systems—male, female, high-school graduate, college graduate, and so on—and proceed to interpret our data in terms of these concepts. Some concepts, however, instead of functioning in the direct classification of experience, serve as maxims that guide us in the business of classifying. Occam's razor[19] is an example; so is the maxim, just cited, that nothing in nature is in vain. Kant called this function the regulative use of concepts, since concepts thus employed "regulate" our use of concepts in ordinary ways.

> Everything that has its basis in the nature of our powers must be appropriate to, and consistent with their right employment—if only we can guard against a certain misunderstanding and so can discover the proper direction of these powers. We are entitled, therefore, to suppose that transcendental ideas . . . have an excellent, and indeed indispensably necessary, regulative employment, namely, that of directing the understanding towards a certain goal upon which the routes marked out by all its rules converge, as upon their point of intersection. This point is indeed a mere idea, a *focus imaginarius,* from which, since it lies quite outside the bounds of possible experience, the concepts of the understanding do not in reality proceed; none the less it serves to give to these concepts the greatest [possible] unity combined with the greatest [possible] extension. Hence arises the illusion that the lines have their source in a real object lying outside the field of empirically possible knowledge—just as objects reflected in a mirror are seen as behind it. . . .
>
> We may illustrate this by an instance of the employment of reason. . . . At the start we have to assume just as many different powers as there are different effects. For instance, in the human mind we have sensation, consciousness, imagination, memory, wit, power of discrimination, pleasure, desire, etc. Now there is a logical maxim which requires that we should reduce, so far as may be possible, this seeming diversity, by comparing these

19 William of Occam, a fourteenth-century Franciscan, formulated the maxim that entities should not be multiplied beyond necessity—that is, when we are presented with two hypotheses, both of which account for a given fact, we should give preference to the simpler of the two.

with one another and detecting their hidden identity. . . . Though logic is not capable of deciding whether a *fundamental power* actually exists, the idea of such a power is the problem involved in a systematic representation of the multiplicity of powers. The logical principle of reason calls upon us to bring about such unity as completely as possible. . . .

Chemists have sought, step by step, to reduce the different kinds of earths (the material of stones and even of metals) to three, and at last to two; but, not content with this, they are unable to banish the thought that behind these varieties there is but one genus, nay, that there may even be a common principle for the earths and the salts. . . .

The logical principle of genera, which postulates identity, is balanced by another principle, namely, that of *species*, which calls for manifoldness and diversity in things, notwithstanding their agreement as coming under the same genus, and which prescribes to the understanding that it attend to the diversity no less than to the identity. . . .

This law of specification cannot be derived from experience, which can never open to our view any such extensive prospects. Empirical specification soon comes to a stop in the distinction of the manifold, if it be not guided by the antecedent transcendental law of specification, which, as a principle of reason, leads us to seek always for further differences, and to suspect their existence even when the senses are unable to disclose them. . . .

Reason thus prepares the field for the understanding: (1) through a principle of the *homogeneity* of the manifold under higher genera; (2) through a principle of the *variety* of the homogeneous under lower species; and (3) in order to complete the systematic unity, a further law, that of the *affinity* of all concepts—a law which prescribes that we proceed from each species to every other by gradual increase in the diversity. These we may entitle the principles of *homogeneity, specification,* and *continuity* of forms. . . .

The first law . . . keeps us from resting satisfied with an excessive number of different original genera, and bids us pay due regard to homogeneity; the second, in turn, imposes a check upon this tendency towards unity, and insists that before we proceed to apply a universal concept to individuals we distinguish subspecies within it. The third law combines these two laws by prescribing that even amidst the utmost manifoldness we observe homogeneity in the gradual transition from one species to another, and thus recognise a relationship of the different branches, as all springing from the same stem.[y]

GOD, SELF, AND TOTALITY AS REGULATIVE CONCEPTS

Kant next applied the notion of the regulative use of concepts to the ideas of God, self, and totality. That is, he showed how these three ideas function as important regulative maxims in scientific inquiry:

There is a great difference between something being given to my reason as an *object absolutely*, or merely as an *object in the idea*. In the former case our concepts are employed to determine the object; in the latter case there is in fact only a schema for which no object, not even a hypothetical one, is directly given, and which only enables us to represent to ourselves other objects in an indirect manner, namely in their systematic unity, by means of their relation to this idea. Thus I say that the concept of a highest intelligence is a mere idea, that is to say, its objective reality is not to be taken as consisting in its referring directly to an object (for in that sense we should not be able to justify its objective validity). It is only a schema constructed in accordance with the conditions of the greatest possible unity of reason—the schema of the concept of a thing in general, which serves only to secure the greatest possible systematic unity in the empirical employment of our reason. . . . We declare, for instance, that the things of the world must be viewed *as if* they received their existence from a highest intelligence. The idea is thus really only a heuristic, not an ostensive concept. It does not show us how an object is constituted, but how, under its guidance, we should *seek* to determine the constitution and connection of the objects of experience. If, then, it can be shown that the three transcendental ideas (the psychological, the cosmological, and the theological), although they do not directly relate to, or determine, any object corresponding to them, none the less, as rules of the empirical employment of reason, lead us to systematic unity, under the presupposition of such an *object in the idea;* and that they thus contribute to the extension of empirical knowledge, without ever being in a position to run counter to it, we may conclude that it is a necessary maxim of reason to proceed always in accordance with such ideas. This, indeed, is the transcendental deduction of all ideas of speculative reason, not as *constitutive* principles for the extension of our knowledge to more objects than experience can give, but as *regulative* principles of the systematic unity of the manifold of empirical knowledge in general, whereby this empirical knowledge is more adequately secured within its own limits and more effectively improved than would be possible, in the absence of such ideas, through the employment merely of the principles of the understanding.

I shall endeavour to make this clearer. . . .

The first [regulative] idea is the "I" itself, viewed simply as thinking nature or soul . . . ; in a word, the idea of a simple self-subsisting intelligence. Yet [reason] has nothing in view save principles of systematic unity in the explanation of the appearances of the soul. It is endeavouring to represent all determinations as existing in a single subject, all powers, so far as possible, as derived from a single fundamental power, all change as belonging to the states of one and the same permanent being, and all *appearances* in space as completely different from the actions of *thought.* The simplicity and other properties of substance are intended to be only the schema of this regulative principle, and are not presupposed as being the actual ground of the properties of the soul. For these may rest on altogether different grounds, of which we can know nothing. . . .

The second regulative idea of merely speculative reason is the concept of the world in general. . . . The absolute totality of the series of . . . conditions . . . is an idea which can never be completely realised in the empirical employment of reason, but which yet serves as a rule that prescribes how we ought to proceed in dealing with such series, namely, that in explaining appearances, whether in their regressive or in their ascending order, we ought to treat the series *as if* it were in itself infinite, that is, *as if* it proceeded *in indefinitum*. . . . All this shows that the cosmological ideas are nothing but simply regulative principles, and are very far from positing, in the manner of constitutive principles, an actual totality of such series. . . .

The third idea of pure reason, which contains a merely relative supposition of a being that is the sole and sufficient cause of all cosmological series, is the idea of *God*. We have not the slightest ground to assume in an absolute manner (to suppose in itself) the object of this idea. . . . It becomes evident that the idea of such a being, like all speculative ideas, seeks only to formulate the command of reason, that all connection in the world be viewed in accordance with the principles of a systematic unity—*as if* all such connection had its source in one single all-embracing being, as the supreme and all-sufficient cause. It is thus evident that reason has here no other purpose than to prescribe its own formal rule for the extension of its empirical employment, and not any extension *beyond all limits of empirical employment*.[z]

This conception of a regulative principle was one of the most suggestive notions in Kant's philosophy. It enabled him, while sticking to his emphasis on verification and empirical meaning, to do justice (as a Humian empiricist could not) to those deep urgings to transcend experience, to seek a totality, and to find a necessary being that are so persistent a part of the human constitution. One of the strengths of Kant's position, and one of the marks of his greatness, was his refusal to write off any of the really persistent questions. Nothing would be easier than to work out a philosophy that solved these problems by shouting "Nonsense!" at them. But the persistent questions have a way of returning to plague those who ignore them.

The point here is not that Kant was able to give an account of God, self, and totality that would seem correct to everyone but that instead of writing them off as whimsical survivals of an age of superstition, he recognized that an account of them had to be given. Obviously, people who like to think in anthropomorphic or imagistic terms will not be satisfied with Kant's account. Kant's reply to them would have to have been that if one lives at an imagistic level one is not likely to be concerned about the metaphysical and philosophical paradoxes that hypostatization involves.[20] But the fact that one does not recognize difficulties does not mean that difficulties do not exist. As long as these concepts are thought of as constitutive of objects, the difficulties remain; if they are taken as regulative maxims, the difficulties vanish. Those basic urgings directed toward totality and transcendence may not have the kind of object that literal-minded people (and rationalistic philosophers) think of—a nonempirical, supernatural object. Nevertheless, they *do* have an empirical object, not in the sense of being directed toward some particular concrete thing, but in the sense of performing an integral function in ordinary, empirical knowing. Far from being inconsistent with a scientific view of the world, they in fact complement it.

20 For further discussion of this problem, see Vol. V, p. 86.

THINGS-IN-THEMSELVES

The concept of thing-in-itself, or "noumenon," as Kant also called it, is a further complication of his view.[21] As we have seen, in Kant's view, all experience is of a spatiotemporal manifold, and space and time are simply forms of the human mode of perception. They are the basic ways in which our minds perceive things. It seems to follow that things have a nature in their own right, though it also follows that we can never have the remotest idea of what such things are like. Some other type of mind, one not limited to knowledge based on sensuous awareness, might know things as they really are. But we, obviously, cannot.

That we are forever excluded from knowledge of noumena is clearly the conclusion to be drawn from Kant's epistemology. Part of the time Kant understood this. At such times he pointed out that noumena are "unknowable" and "problematic," that they are "merely limiting concepts":

> At the very outset, . . . an ambiguity . . . may occasion serious misapprehension. The understanding, when it entitles an object in a [certain] relation mere phenomenon, at the same time forms, apart from that relation, a representation of an *object in itself*, and so comes to represent itself as also being able to form *concepts* of such objects. And since the understanding yields no concepts additional to the categories, it also supposes that the object in itself must at least be *thought* through these pure concepts, and so is misled into treating the entirely *indeterminate* concept of an intelligible entity, namely, of a something in general outside our sensibility, as being a *determinate* concept of an entity that allows of being known in a certain [purely intelligible] manner by means of the understanding.
>
> If by "noumenon" we mean a thing so far as it is *not an object of our sensible intuition,* and so abstract from our mode of intuiting it, this is a noumenon in the *negative* sense of the term. But if we understand by it an *object* of a *non-sensible intuition,* we thereby presuppose a special mode of intuition, namely, the intellectual, which is not that which we possess, and of which we cannot comprehend even the possibility. This would be "noumenon" in the *positive* sense of the term. . . .
>
> Since, however, such a type of intuition, intellectual intuition, forms no part whatsoever of our faculty of knowledge, it follows that the employment of the categories can never extend further than to the objects of experience. Doubtless, indeed, there are intelligible entities corresponding to the sensible entities; there may also be intelligible entities to which our sensible faculty of intuition has no relation whatsoever; but our concepts of understanding, being mere forms of thought for our sensible intuition, could not in the least apply to them. That, therefore, which we entitle "noumenon" must be understood as being such only in a *negative* sense. . . .
>
> If the objective reality of a concept cannot be in any way known, while yet the concept contains no contradiction and also at the same time is

21 The question of the exact relation between noumena and things-in-themselves, and of whether Kant intended to identify them, has been much debated by Kantian scholars.

connected with other modes of knowledge that involve given concepts which it serves to limit, I entitle that concept problematic. The concept of a *noumenon*—that is, of a thing which is not to be thought as object of the senses but as a thing in itself, solely through a pure understanding—is not in any way contradictory. For we cannot assert of sensibility that it is the sole possible kind of intuition. Further, the concept of a noumenon is necessary, to prevent sensible intuition from being extended to things in themselves, and thus to limit the objective validity of sensible knowledge. The remaining things, to which it does not apply, are entitled noumena, in order to show that this knowledge cannot extend its domain over everything which the understanding thinks. But none the less we are unable to comprehend how such noumena can be possible, and the domain that lies out beyond the sphere of appearances is for us empty. That is to say, we have an understanding which *problematically* extends further, but we have no intuition, indeed not even the concept of a possible intuition, through which objects outside the field of sensibility can be given, and through which the understanding can be employed *assertorically* beyond that field. The concept of a noumenon is thus a merely *limiting concept,* the function of which is to curb the pretensions of sensibility; and it is therefore only of negative employment. At the same time it is no arbitrary invention; it is bound up with the limitation of sensibility, though it cannot affirm anything positive beyond the field of sensibility. . . .

If the concept of a noumenon be taken in a merely problematic sense, it is not only admissible, but as setting limits to sensibility is likewise indispensable.[a]

This interpretation of noumena is consistent with the basic theses of the *Critique*. From this point of view, the concept of noumenon (thing-in-itself) is simply another regulative idea—a *focus imaginarius* for each individual thing (desk, Mount Everest, "I"), just as the concept of totality is a *focus imaginarius* for the pursuit of scientific truth.

Unfortunately, side by side with this view of noumena as regulative principles there is another and much less critical[22] conception. The truth is that Kant often lapsed into thinking of noumena as objects that exercise a causal efficacy in the phenomenal world. This application of the categories of substance and causality is, of course, quite as illegitimate as any of the applications that Kant himself criticized in discussing rationalistic metaphysics. Like everyone else, Kant had begun from the traditional Cartesian substantival dualism; here is a vestigial remnant of that way of thought, from which he had not been wholly able to free himself. Noumenal self and noumenal object (taken as things, not as regulative, or "limiting," concepts) are the two substances of Cartesianism with the new critical conception of the "Analytic" suspended between them.

22 Since Kant called his book a *Critique,* it is convenient to use the term "criticism" (or "the critical philosophy") to refer to his views, especially to those features of his thought that were consistent with the innovative insights of his theory of knowledge.

Facts and Values

As we have seen, one of the two main objects of Kant's philosophy was to justify, in the face of Humian scepticism, the claims of science to have real knowledge of matters of fact. The other main object was to justify traditional religious and moral insights against the scientific view of the world as a purposeless mechanism. Kant believed he had accomplished these two seemingly antithetical aims by his account of the nature of knowledge. According to Kant's interpretation, knowledge is possible just because it consists in recognizing an order projected into a sensuous manifold by certain synthetical mental acts. Knowledge in the scientific sense is *guaranteed* by the fact that it is *limited* to the spatiotemporal manifold. It is necessary only to point out that God and the self are not spatiotemporal in order to see that the conclusions of science have absolutely no relevance, one way or the other, to the moral and religious life. This general formula is discussed in detail in the next chapter. But it is easy to see, even at this point, that it was much more promising than the Cartesian line of attack on this problem. Instead of drawing a distinction on substantival lines, with all the concomitant complications of interaction, parallelism, and so on, Kant drew a distinction between what is within and what is beyond the spatiotemporal manifold.

If the object of moral judgment (the locus to which praise and blame, for instance, are ascribed) is the supposedly substantival self of Cartesianism, then morality is indeed a vain and chimerical illusion, for the existence of such a self is inconsistent with the principles of physics. But if space and time, substance and causality, are forms that the mind introduces into experience, then the self about which moral judgments are made is not a substance and does not act causally in the spatiotemporal world.

In Kant's view, it is true that we cannot *know* such a self, for knowledge is limited to what is within the spatiotemporal manifold. But it also follows, precisely because knowledge is thus confined to the manifold, that we cannot know that such a self does *not* exist. Indeed, we cannot know anything, one way or the other, about such a noumenal self. Thus, if there are any other grounds for believing in its existence, we are warranted in so believing.

> What is the value of the metaphysics that is alleged to be thus purified by criticism and established once for all? On a cursory view of the present work it may seem that its results are merely *negative*, warning us that we must never venture with speculative reason beyond the limits of experience. Such is in fact its primary use. . . . So far . . . as our Critique limits speculative reason, it is indeed *negative;* but since it thereby removes an obstacle which stands in the way of the employment of practical reason, nay threatens to destroy it, it has in reality a *positive* and very important use. At least this is so, immediately we are convinced that there is an absolutely necessary *practical* employment of pure reason—the *moral*—in which it inevitably goes

beyond the limits of sensibility. Though [practical] reason, in thus proceeding, requires no assistance from speculative reason, it must yet be assured against its opposition, that reason may not be brought into conflict with itself. To deny that the service which the Critique renders is *positive* in character, would thus be like saying that the police are of no positive benefit, inasmuch as their main business is merely to prevent the violence of which citizens stand in mutual fear, in order that each may pursue his vocation in peace and security. That space and time are only forms of sensible intuition, and so only conditions of the existence of things as appearances; that, moreover, we have no concepts of understanding, and consequently no elements for the knowledge of things, save in so far as intuition can be given corresponding to these concepts; and that we can therefore have no knowledge of any object as thing in itself, but only in so far as it is an object of sensible intuition, that is, an appearance—all this is proved in the analytical part of the Critique. Thus it does indeed follow that all possible speculative knowledge of reason is limited to mere objects of *experience*. But our further contention must also be duly borne in mind, namely, that though we cannot *know* these objects as things in themselves, we must yet be in position at least to *think* them as things in themselves; otherwise we should be landed in the absurd conclusion that there can be appearance without anything that appears. . . .

The doctrine of morality and the doctrine of nature may each, therefore, make good its position. This, however, is only possible in so far as criticism has previously established our unavoidable ignorance of things in themselves, and has limited all that we can theoretically *know* to mere appearances.

[From what has already been said, it is evident that] even the *assumption*—as made on behalf of the necessary practical employment of my reason—of *God, freedom,* and *immortality* is not permissible unless at the same time speculative reason be deprived of its pretensions to transcendent insight. For in order to arrive at such insight it must make use of principles which, in fact, extend only to objects of possible experience, and which, if also applied to what cannot be an object of experience, always really change this into an appearance, thus rendering all *practical extension* of pure reason impossible. I have therefore found it necessary to deny *knowledge*, in order to make room for *faith*.[b]

There are two main points in this passage: (1) the distinction between "knowing" and "thinking" and (2) the concept of "faith." As regards the first point, at the place where he introduced this distinction, Kant inserted a footnote:

To *know* an object I must be able to prove its possibility, either from its actuality as attested by experience, or *a priori* by means of reason. But I can *think* whatever I please, provided only that I do not contradict myself, that is, provided my concept is a possible thought. This suffices for the possibility of the concept, even though I may not be able to answer for there being, in the sum of all possibilities, an object corresponding to it. But something more is required before I can ascribe to such a concept objective validity, that is, real possibility; the former possibility is merely logical. This something more need not, however, be sought in the theoretical sources of knowledge; it may lie in those that are practical.[c]

An example will show how this distinction is to be understood. I cannot think "round square," for in attempting to do so, I contradict myself. I can, however, think "square," for there is nothing contradictory about the idea of a four-angled figure. Similarly, I can think "chiliagon," for there is nothing contradictory about the idea of a thousand-angled figure. Thus the square and the chiliagon are both logical possibilities. But how do I ascertain whether they are more than mere logical possibilities? One way is by means of experience: I know that the square, at least, is more than a mere logical possibility because I encounter squares in experience. This is what Kant meant by grounding objectivity validity in "the theoretical sources of knowledge."

Kant next applied this line of thought to God, freedom, and immortality. If God, freedom, and immortality are noumena, they are logically possible (according to Kant) because one can think them: There is nothing contradictory in the idea of something that is unknowable because it lies outside all experience. But are God, freedom, and immortality objectively valid as well? Theoretical knowledge (for example, the kind of knowledge obtained in physics) can prove nothing about their objective validity, since such knowledge is limited to phenomena, that is, to occurrences within the spatiotemporal manifold. But there is another way of moving from logical possibility to objective validity, namely, by grounding the latter in the "practical" sources of knowledge. Unless God, freedom, and immortality are objectively real (not mere logical possibilities), the moral life is a vain and chimerical illusion. Thus our own strong feeling about the genuineness of our duties to others is the "practical" ground that warrants our belief in the objective validity of these concepts, just as—at a completely different level, of course—our strong feeling about the genuineness of our percept of a square warrants our belief in the objectivity validity of the concept of four-angled figure.

But what sort of objective validity do God, freedom, and immortality have? In the Western tradition, at least since the time of Aristotle, the objectivity validity ascribed to God has usually been that of a substance exercising causal efficacy in the world. As for the supposed objective validity of the self—in Western thought the self, too, has been conceived of as a substance acting causally on its environment, including its own body. But the whole argument of the *Critique* rules out this way of thinking about God, freedom, and immortality. The objective validity that the *Critique* has shown them to have cannot be substantival or causal, since these concepts are explicitly limited to phenomena.[23] Unfortunately, all language, including both commonsensical language and philosophical language, is a thing-language, a language descriptive of objects interacting causally with other objects. Hence it is difficult to find a way of talking about God, freedom, and immortality that does not suggest them to be things. Perhaps the best way of dealing with this problem is to think of them as values. Kant does not make this suggestion himself, but "value" seems to be a good term to

23 As has already been seen, and as will be seen again, Kant was by no means consistent in staying within this self-imposed restriction. See pp. 64 and 84–88.

represent his view, for values are not commonly regarded as interacting causally, and they are the objects of enjoyings or appreciatings, not of perceivings.

This brings us to the second main point in the passage under examination—the concept of faith. By "faith" Kant did not mean any subjective, private, or whimsical belief that an individual may choose to hold. His position was not at all like that of saying, "Since nobody can ever see the surface of Venus, nothing can prevent my believing that it is chromium-plated and steam-heated." In saying that he "denied knowledge," Kant meant that he was limiting the *area of applicability* of science—limiting it, that is, to the spatiotemporal realm. By "belief" he really meant *another* kind of experience, one just as well grounded and just as public and objective, in its way, as scientific knowledge is in its. He would have expressed his meaning better had he written, "I have found it necessary to limit scientific knowledge in order to make room for an appreciation of values." What Kant actually proposed was to replace the Cartesian dual-substance theory with a dualism of kinds of experience. There is an experience of things in space and time, which he called "knowledge"; there is also an experience or appreciation of values, which he called "faith." Nomenclature apart, this distinction was to have important consequences not just in the history of philosophy but in the whole development of culture in the nineteenth and twentieth centuries.

CHAPTER 3

Kant: Theory of Value

Ethical Theory

Most pre-Kantian moral theories (even those of Christian philosophers) were based on the concept of good. In contrast, Kant's was based on the primacy of right. The first question a Greek philosopher asked himself was, "What is the good?" The next question was, "How shall I attain it?" Since it was generally agreed that "happiness" was the good, there was no need to show people that they *ought* to aim at it. In fact, the only puzzle was why so much of the time people did not aim at it. Philosophers like Plato thought the answer was ignorance. Men acted wrongly not because their wills were bad but, quite simply, because they did not know what would make them happy.

For this reason, Greek ethics had a means-end form, a form that very deeply marked the thought of many Christian philosophers—for instance, St. Thomas. There can be no doubt, however, that Christianity, with its concept of an omnipotent Father who ought to be obeyed in all things, introduced a new emphasis into moral philosophy. Since, in the Christian view, God's commands are rules, the notion of right, or conformity to rule, became important. At the same time, Christian thinkers took up the Stoic emphasis on motivation. These two concepts came together in the notion not merely of punctilious conformity to rule but of conformity because the rule issues from the source it issues from. To conform to the rule because we fear punishment is of no account. And to do so because we hope to be rewarded for obedience, or because conformity is a means to happiness, is to "reduce" morality to the Greek type, though of course with a very different set of prescriptions about how to be happy. From the Christian point of view, then, the morally good motive is a very special—one might almost say a very peculiar—one. To act morally, a man must see that the act is right (that is, commanded) and must do it because he sees that it is right. Thus a Christian ethics is likely to focus on the concept of duty as the exclusive moral motive. A Christian ethics is also likely to emphasize sin, rather than ignorance, as the cause of wrongdoing. Since God's commands are clear, a man who fails to conform must have a perverse or stubborn will.

More than almost any other thinker, Kant identified himself with this emphasis on duty and attempted to give it philosophical formulation. He did not, of course, talk about divine commands—he was concerned with ethics, not theology. As a matter of fact, in a way that shows how much he was a man of the Enlightenment, he made reason, not God, the source of the moral law. Nevertheless, duty is the central concept of Kant's ethical theory. In Kant's view, only a good will is morally valuable; and a good will is simply one that (1) knows what its duty is (that is, knows what reason commands) and (2) does the dutiful act because it is dutiful.

> Nothing can possibly be conceived in the world, or even out of it, which can be called good, without qualification, except a Good Will. Intelligence, wit, judgment, and the other *talents* of the mind, however they may be named, or courage, resolution, perseverance, as qualities of temperament, are undoubtedly good and desirable in many respects; but these gifts of nature may also become extremely bad and mischievous if the will which is to make use of them, and which, therefore, constitutes what is called *character*, is not good. It is the same with the *gifts of fortune*. Power, riches, honour, even health, and the general well-being and contentment with one's condition which is called *happiness*, inspire pride, and often presumption, if there is not a good will to correct the influence of these on the mind, and with this also to rectify the whole principle of acting, and adapt it to its end. The sight of a being who is not adorned with a single feature of a pure and good will, enjoying unbroken prosperity, can never give pleasure to an impartial rational spectator. Thus a good will appears to constitute the indispensable condition even of being worthy of happiness. . . .

A good will is good not because of what it performs or effects, not by its aptness for the attainment of some proposed end, but simply by virtue of the volition, that is, it is good in itself, and considered by itself is to be esteemed much higher than all that can be brought about by it in favour of any inclination, nay, even of the sum-total of all inclinations. Even if it should happen that, owing to special disfavour of fortune, or the niggardly provision of a step-motherly nature, this will should wholly lack power to accomplish its purpose, if with its greatest efforts it should yet achieve nothing, and there should remain only the good will (not, to be sure, a mere wish, but the summoning of all means in our power), then, like a jewel, it would still shine by its own light, as a thing which has its whole value in itself. Its usefulness or fruitlessness can neither add to nor take away anything from this value.[a]

CONCEPT OF GOOD WILL

This notion of a will that is good in itself without regard to what it effects seemed "so strange" to Kant himself that he tried to bolster it up by a complicated argument. Starting from the familiar thesis that "nothing in nature is in vain," Kant argued that reason must, therefore, have *some* function. But this function cannot be the preservation of life or the acquisition of happiness, for both these functions could be better performed (as with insects) by instinct. It follows, according to Kant, that "our existence has a different and far nobler end, for which . . . reason is properly intended." This end can only be cultivation of a "will not merely good as a means to something else but good in itself."

Kant's argument is unlikely to appeal to anyone who is not already convinced on other grounds. And Kant's position will seem to most people unduly narrow. Although he did not argue (as some of his critics have supposed) that a good will is "the sole and complete good," he did maintain that it is "the supreme good and the condition of every other." Are we then to think of a good will as a necessary ingredient in other goods, as eggs are a necessary ingredient in cake? This appears to be a part of what Kant meant. But he also believed that the goodness of a good will can come into competition with other goods. For example, one of the hard facts of life is that we sometimes have to choose between keeping a promise, and thereby doing our duty, and securing a better job that will enable us to provide more adequately for our family. In Kant's view, whenever we face such an alternative we should always choose the good will rather than the other good, no matter what it may be. These two points of view are not inconsistent—we might, for instance, have to choose between scrambling our eggs and using them in a cake. But it seems unreasonable to insist that it is always better to scramble our eggs than to use them in a cake.

Kant's stand here, with its exclusive emphasis on the good will, inevitably raises the question, "What is the basis, or principle, of choice among different values?" The utilitarian solution to this problem, a solution that was popular in Kant's own day, provided an easy criterion: The goodness of every value lies in the pleasure it produces.[1] According to this view, the goodness of a good will resides in the amount of pleasure such a will produces—just as the goodness of a beautiful picture resides, presumably, in the amount of pleasure it produces. There is thus never any *moral* problem, strictly speaking, in choosing among the different acts open to us. There may be a problem about ascertaining which of the acts will be productive of the greater good, but once that is settled, we know what we ought to do.

In insisting that virtue is valuable in its own right and apart from what it accomplishes, Kant was doubtless reacting against this oversimplified view. But though many people would agree that a good will is good "apart from anything further," they might deny that it is the *only* moral value. Like the Utilitarians, Kant oversimplified the problem of choice, but in a reverse way. In Kant's view, choice in effect is never a problem, for a good will is always supreme.

This position is so extreme that some commentators have doubted that Kant actually held it. What Kant was trying to express, they argue, is that although there are all sorts of values, a good will is the unique moral value. In the scale of, say, economic values or esthetic values, a good will might not rate so high, but in the scale of moral value, it is *eo ipso* highest. Hence, whenever we choose as moral beings, we ought to choose a good will.

Sometimes, certainly, Kant came close to saying this, but such a view only transfers the problem to another level: choice between different scales. As esthetic men, one kind of choice is correct; as moral men, another kind of choice is correct. But which kind of choice is better? It will not do to say, "Which *ought* we to choose?" for this is already to adopt the moral point of view. Obviously, we *ought* to choose the moral choice. Are we then to admit that these different scales of value are incommensurate?

We can be sure that Kant would have repudiated such an irrational (or arational) conclusion. But to repudiate a conclusion is unfortunately not to provide a satisfactory alternative. To find such an alternative is obviously essential for those people who hold that values should consist in some kind of single, rational hierarchy, or system. This remains a very difficult problem.

NATURE OF DUTY: CONFORMITY TO LAW IN GENERAL

In any case, whether or not the good will is supreme, in order to understand Kant's position we have to ask what, according to Kant, its structure is. This is equivalent to asking, "What is the nature of duty?" for, as we have seen, Kant held the good will to be one that does its duty.

> *Duty is the necessity of acting from respect for the law.* . . . It is only what is connected with my will as a principle, by no means as an effect—what

1 Utilitarians differed, however, as to whether we are to take account of (1) our own pleasure only, (2) other people's pleasure only, or (3) the greatest total amount of pleasure regardless of how it is distributed.

does not subserve my inclination, but overpowers it, or at least in case of choice excludes it from its calculation—in other words, simply the law of itself, which can be an object of respect, and hence a command. Now an action done from duty must wholly exclude the influence of inclination, and with it every object of the will, so that nothing remains which can determine the will except objectively the *law*, and subjectively *pure respect* for this practical law, and consequently the maxim that I should follow this law even to the thwarting of all my inclinations.

Thus the moral worth of an action does not lie in the effect expected from it, nor in any principle of action which requires to borrow its motive from this expected effect. For all these effects—agreeableness of one's condition, and even the promotion of the happiness of others—could have been also brought about by other causes so that for this there would have been no need of the will of a rational being; whereas it is in this alone that the supreme and unconditional good can be found. The preeminent good which we call moral can therefore consist in nothing else than *the conception of law* in itself, *which certainly is only possible in a rational being*, in so far as this conception, and not the expected effect, determines the will. This is a good which is already present in the person who acts accordingly, and we have not to wait for it to appear first in the result.[b]

Here again Kant believed he was merely stating with precision what everyone believes as a matter of course.

Kant's first point is that, to satisfy the moral requirement, it is not enough that an act of a certain kind be done. I might, for instance, while intending to lie, happen to tell the truth through a slip of the tongue. From a moral point of view I would have told a lie.[2]

Kant's second point is that it is not enough that the act be intended. If I am moved to keep a promise by a sudden feeling of pity for a man whom I have promised to help, my act is still without moral value. In Kant's view, it must be done from a "principle" (or "maxim," or "imperative")—that is, I must have a regular, explicitly formulated, and carefully thought-out rule, and I must perform the act because I see that it is an instance of the rule. Suppose, for instance, that I am the owner of a filling station. I may have the rule "Honesty is the best policy." From this I may have concluded that a reputation for integrity is more valuable than the petty profits that would accrue from refusing to make refunds on faulty repair jobs. Now suppose that a customer asks for a refund. If I give it to him because I like the color of his tie, or because I happen to be in a good mood, I am not acting on principle. Only if I give it to him because I see that the repairs I made on his car were faulty, and that this case comes under my general rule, am I acting on principle.

Kant's third point is that it is not enough to act merely on principle. For an act to have *moral* worth, the principle must be of a particular kind. "Honesty is the best policy," as it happens, is not a principle of the requisite kind; it is

2 Compare Jesus' dictum about the man who commits adultery in his heart.

only a "conditional" principle. Duty, on the other hand, is universally (or, as Kant said, "categorically") binding.

There are two points to be considered here. (1) *Is* duty universally binding? Kant did not try to prove this, for he thought it obvious that whatever is a duty for one man is equally a duty for all other men. (2) *Are* maxims like "Honesty is the best policy" conditional? This seems to be so, for (supposing this were one's maxim) if anyone happened not to want to make a profit, there would be no reason to be honest. Furthermore, "Honesty is the best policy" might not be binding for every situation. It might be a satisfactory principle, for example, for a big business but not for a small one, for dealing with steady customers but not for dealing with tourists just "passing through," and so on. The fact is that it is a means-end type of principle, and no such principle yields a categorical rule unless the end is a universal end.

It seemed to Kant that happiness might be thought just this kind of end.

> There is *one* end . . . which we may with certainty assume that all [men] actually *have* by a natural necessity, and this is *happiness*. . . . [But] the imperative which refers to the choice of means to one's own happiness, *i.e.* the precept of prudence, is still always *hypothetical;* the action is not commanded absolutely, but only as means to another purpose. . . .
>
> The notion of happiness is so indefinite that although every man wishes to attain it, yet he never can say definitely and consistently what it is that he really wishes and wills. The reason of this is that all the elements which belong to the notion of happiness are altogether empirical, *i.e.* they must be borrowed from experience, and nevertheless the idea of happiness requires an absolute whole, a maximum of welfare in my present and all future circumstances. Now it is impossible that the most clear-sighted [man] should frame to himself a definite conception of what he really wills in this. . . . We cannot therefore act on any definite principles to secure happiness, but only on empirical counsels, *ex. gr.* of regimen, frugality, courtesy, reserve, &c., which experience teaches do, on the average, most promote well-being. Hence it follows that the imperatives of prudence do not, strictly speaking, command at all, that is, they cannot present actions objectively as practically *necessary;* that they are rather to be regarded as counsels (*consilia*) than precepts (*praecepta*) of reason.[c]

In Kant's view, that is, "happiness" is not a definite state of affairs, like graduating from college or getting a job. It is a regulative concept that performs the same function with respect to conduct[3] that "totality" performs with respect to theory. Though happiness is in a sense an end, it is not a specific, concrete end to aim at (as a student may plan his courses so as to graduate); rather, it is the ideal in terms of which our pursuit of all such specific, concrete ends is organized.

Assuming, then, that duty is universally binding, what kind of principle guides

3 See pp. 60–62.

us when we act from a sense of duty? What kind of principle operates, that is, when I tell the truth not because it is prudent (the best policy) to do so but because I recognize that it is my duty to do so? The only answer, according to Kant, is that the principle is the "conception of law in general." If I do x for the sake of y, I am acting on a conditional principle; on the other hand, unless I do x in accordance with *some* principle, I am acting merely on whim or impulse. The only possibility, therefore, is that the principle that moves me is just the *idea* of principle. That is, what moves me cannot be the idea of any particular maxim ("An apple a day keeps the doctor away," "A stitch in time saves nine"), for all particular maxims are conditioned on our wanting the end they produce ("health" or "saving"). What moves me must be the idea of law in general.

Since, as Kant pointed out, his argument has

> ... deprived the will of every impulse which could arise to it from obedience to any [particular] law, there remains nothing but the universal conformity of its actions to law in general, which alone is to serve the will as a principle, *i.e.* I am never to act otherwise than *so that I could also will that my maxim should become a universal law*. Here, now, it is the simple conformity to law in general, without assuming any particular law applicable to certain actions, that serves the will as its principle, and must so serve it, if duty is not to be a vain delusion and a chimerical notion.[d]

DIFFICULTIES WITH THIS FORMULATION

Kant believed that he had obtained this conclusion by analyzing the ordinary, commonsense conception of duty as a universally binding requirement. Yet some people may take Kant's analysis as confirming their suspicion that there is something very queer about this whole idea of an absolutely binding duty. This idea of law in general, which the analysis discloses to be what is meant by a sense of duty, is certainly rather odd. Does any such idea as Kant described ever move men to act? And if it does, why is being moved by it supremely valuable?

This line of criticism has nothing to do with the question of whether a good will is good in itself or has only a utilitarian good. It is quite possible to hold that a good will is good in itself and to deny that acting from a sense of duty (as described by Kant) ever occurs or is valuable. One might hold, for instance, that certain *other* motives are what make the good will good.

This, of course, is just what Hume had argued. As a matter of fact, his analysis of the goodness of the good will was in effect a criticism in advance of Kant's conception. Thus, although Hume agreed with Kant that "a good will" is the unique object of moral value, he held its goodness to lie in its benevolence, not in its dutifulness. He did not deny that action from a sense of duty occurs. But he gave a completely different account of it; far from assigning it supreme value, he thought it had only derivative value. Hume's main criticism of the type of position later taken by Kant was that it involved a vicious circle. "No action," he pointed out, "can be virtuous, or morally good, unless there be in human nature some motive to produce it, distinct from the sense of its morality."[e] For suppose it is claimed that the virtue of telling the truth lies in telling it *because it is virtuous* to do so. Unless we insist that telling the truth is virtuous on some other ground (as Kant denied), we are forced to say that the virtue of telling the truth lies in the virtue of telling the truth. Telling the truth per se is not virtuous. What is virtuous is telling-the-truth-because-telling-the-truth-is-virtuous. But this in turn requires correction, and it is easy to see that we become involved in an infinite regress—the virtue of telling the truth lies in the virtue of telling the truth lies in the virtue of telling the truth lies in the virtue. . . . The only way to stop the regress is to admit that something other than the virtue of telling the truth is the ground for the virtue of telling the truth.

> I conclude [Hume wrote] that the first virtuous motive, which bestows a merit on any action, can never be a regard to the virtue of that action, but must be some other natural motive or principle. To suppose, that the mere regard to the virtue of the action, may be the first motive, which produc'd the action, and render'd it virtuous, is to reason in a circle. Before we can have such a regard, the action must be really virtuous; and this virtue must be deriv'd from some virtuous motive. And consequently the virtuous motive must be different from the regard to the virtue of the action. A virtuous motive is requisite to render an action virtuous. An action must be virtuous, before we can have a regard to its virtue. Some virtuous motive, therefore, must be antecedent to that regard.

Hume did not deny, of course, that men sometimes act from what can fairly be described as a sense of duty. But that they do so, he believed, was capable of explanation by the general psychological law of association. Just as I may come to like a certain melody on its own account, even though I originally liked it only because I heard it frequently in the company of someone close to me, so I may come to admire truth-telling on its own account, but actually only because it was originally associated with some other motive. Thus, in the course of time, men have developed all sorts of categorical imperatives ("Tell the truth," "Keep promises," "Repay debts"). A sense of our duty to perform these actions may be our current motive for performing them, just as Kant claimed. But this is possible only because some specific, concrete motive (like benevolence) originally moved us to perform them. The merit of the benevolence motive has simply been transferred by association to the dutiful act. Thus what Kant believed to be so unique about duty (the concept of law in general) is merely the sign that the original maxim has been sloughed off and forgotten.

There are many categorical imperatives for which it is easy to revive the forgotten maxim. Take the imperative "Stop at a red traffic light." This has become so imbedded in our behavior that if we were asked why we ought to do so, we are likely to reply, quite simply, "Because, of course, it is *red*." As soon as we think about it, however, we see that underlying the imperative is a maxim of the form "Violations of red traffic signals are dangerous to life and limb," or "Violations are likely to incur fines." Thus the "categoricalness" of the imperative disappears. Hume contended that the same process that produced this apparently categorical imperative also produced all others (like "Tell the truth" or "Keep promises"). The only difference is that the latter, being even more deeply imbedded in our behavior, have a more compulsive (that is, categorical) tone.

This capacity of the human mind to form categorical imperatives is of immense practical importance. If men lacked this capacity, the act of deciding what to do would require so much thought that life would hopelessly bog down. If every time we saw a red traffic light we had to stop, think of the general maxim, and ask ourselves whether this case comes under the maxim, our journeys would take much longer and the accident rate at intersections would greatly increase. Hume would have said that Kant simply erected this very useful capacity into a transcendent moral principle.

If such a criticism is correct, Kant's first formulation of the categorical imperative—"Act only on that maxim whereby thou canst at the same time will that it should become a universal law"—is seriously defective. Moreover, it is clear (on grounds that have nothing to do with Hume's analysis) that this formula is not an adequate statement of the nature of obligation. In the first place, it is possible to generalize into universal rules all sorts of maxims that no one (and certainly not Kant) would hold to be obligatory. For instance, I could perfectly well hold that every purchaser of a new book should write his name on the flyleaf when he acquires it. Although there is nothing self-contradictory about this maxim, it is also morally neutral. We feel no obligation either to inscribe our names or to abstain from inscribing them.

Kant might have replied that if I act in accordance with this, or any other, particular maxim, I am still not acting morally, even though the maxim can be universalized. To act morally, I must obey "nothing but . . . law in general." That is, the moral motive is "simple conformity to law in general." If this means, as it would seem, that I must ignore the specific character of the rule and act simply from the notion of following a rule because it is a rule, the result will be to justify all sorts of acts that most people would call immoral. For instance, during World War II Hitler laid down the rule that all Jews should be exterminated. Kant's argument would not justify the acts of Germans who exterminated Jews because they were afraid of disobeying Hitler or because they hated Jews or because they hoped to acquire the property of the Jews. But it *would* justify the acts of any Germans who exterminated Jews for the sole reason that they had been ordered to do so.

Or, to return to the maxim, "Every purchaser of a new book should write his name on the flyleaf": According to the present interpretation of Kant's meaning, I act morally not when I inscribe my name from the motive of obeying this particular maxim, but when I inscribe my name from the motive of obeying law in general. Yet the result, as far as *action* is concerned, is the same. I still inscribe my name on the flyleaf of my new book, and this is not an act that anyone would describe as morally good or virtuous. This must be the consequence as long as moral theorists concentrate attention on our acting from a certain motive without regard to the results that our action produces. They will find themselves praising as morally valuable actions that common sense calls indifferent or even wrong.

These considerations show that universalization cannot be a positive criterion of duty. But neither is it a negative criterion: There are many actions that Kant condemned (and that many other people would condemn) whose maxims can be universalized. For example, in Kant's view, it is our duty not to commit suicide. Yet there is nothing self-contradictory about a prospective suicide's willing that everyone else commit suicide. In Kant's view, it is our duty to repay debts. Yet there is nothing logically inconsistent about the position of a defaulter who is ready for everyone to repudiate promises to pay. Universal repudiation would, of course, soon lead to a general abandonment of the credit system. But economic chaos is not a logical impossibility, and Kant's argument cannot be used to appeal to the defaulter unless we admit that the imperative to pay debts is not categorical but prudential.

Thus it cannot be correct to say, as Kant did, that the essence of morality consists in acting in accordance with a categorical imperative. Nevertheless, if the emphasis is put not on the need for logical consistency but on the need for generality, then Kant's point does seem to have moral significance: We all tend to make exceptions to general rules when our own interests are involved. Suppose we have an imperative to the effect that contracts ought to be fulfilled (it does not matter here that the imperative is prudential). Since we know that every violation of a rule tends to weaken it, we are likely to be very stern with prospective violators on the basis of their selfishness and shortsightedness. It is only too easy, however, when *we* are the prospective violators, to shift our ground and emphasize the fact that a single exception "hardly matters at all." Hence, if before we act we always ask ourselves, "Do I want this kind of act to become a general rule?" our answer would have to be in the negative, and we might therefore abstain from making an exception for ourselves. Thus the real point of Kant's formulation seems to be that in morality we are not to count our own "I" differently from the way we count the "I's" of other people.

ANOTHER ACCOUNT OF DUTY: REASON AN END IN ITSELF

So far in his account of duty Kant has described a dutiful, or morally good, act as one whose principle is a universal and categorical imperative. It happens, however, that Kant gave a second formulation of the imperative of duty—"So act as to treat humanity whether in thine own person or that of any other, in every case as an end withal, never as means only." Though Kant believed his two formulations to be equivalent, the second, it will be seen, was much more fruitful.

> Man and generally any rational being *exists* as an end in himself, *not merely as a means* to be arbitrarily used by this or that will, but in all his actions, whether they concern himself or other rational beings, must be always regarded at the same time as an end. All objects of the inclinations have only a conditional worth; for if the inclinations and the wants founded on them did not exist, then their object would be without value. But the inclinations themselves being sources of want are so far from having an absolute worth for which they should be desired, that, on the contrary, it must be the universal wish of every rational being to be wholly free from them. Thus the worth of any object which is *to be acquired* by our action is always conditional. . . . Rational beings . . . are called *persons*, because their very nature points them out as ends in themselves. . . . These, therefore, are not merely subjective ends whose existence has a worth *for us* as an effect of our action, but *objective ends*, that is things whose existence is an end in itself: an end moreover for which no other can be substituted, which they should subserve *merely* as means, for otherwise nothing whatever would possess *absolute worth*; but if all worth were conditioned and therefore contingent, then there would be no supreme practical principle of reason whatever.
>
> If then there is a supreme practical principle or, in respect of the human will, a categorical imperative, it must be one which, being drawn from the conception of that which is necessarily an end for everyone because it is *an end in itself*, constitutes an *objective* principle of will, and can therefore serve as a universal practical law. The foundation of this principle is: *rational nature exists as an end in itself*.[f]

This passage epitomizes the spirit of the Enlightenment—the point of view to which Locke, for instance, gave such notable expression and the view that was one of the driving forces in the American and French revolutions. According to this belief, a human being has an intrinsic value just because he is a human being and quite apart from whatever special advantages may accrue from birth, wealth, beauty, or station in life.

Whereas Locke for the most part emphasized the rights men own as men, Kant emphasized the duties they owe as men. Most of the acts traditionally regarded as duties can be thought of as deriving their obligatory character from one primary obligation—the duty to treat men as ends in themselves. The act of lying—whether private lying or that public lying called, alternatively, propaganda or advertising—is a good example. Even if we lie not for our own selfish advantage but for the good of those to whom we are lying, we do wrong. We suggest to them that they cannot understand the facts and judge for themselves. We treat them as children still under tutelage, not as men; and, intentionally or not, we deny them their just title and their true dignity as rational creatures.

Finally, in demeaning them, we demean ourselves. We have a station in life to maintain; we have our own responsibilities as men and as rational creatures that it would be shameful to repudiate. *Noblesse oblige*—not the nobility of birth, but the nobility of humanity. We have to live up to our end and destiny as men; to do otherwise would be to let the whole race down.

This point of view—at once proud and humble—is well illustrated by a remark Kant made just before his death. He was very old, very ill, very weak, senile, and almost helpless. Yet when his physician entered his room he struggled to his feet to greet him and refused to sit down again until the visitor had taken a chair. "The feeling for humanity," he explained, "has not yet left me."[g] Standing up in the presence of one's doctor, not because he is a doctor, but because he is a man may be a little thing—a small punctilio of manners. But it does not differ in principle from telling him the truth—because he is a man. Between manners and morals, in this view, there is no chasm. Conduct at any level at once expresses and flows from one's understanding of one's status as a man in company with other men. Everyone counts as one—this is the point at which Kant's two formulations come together: My duties to others are no different from my duties to myself, and my rights are identical with theirs.

It would seem that Kant was expressing more here than the attitude of his own century—that he put his finger on, and gave cogent expression to, one of the abiding values of the West. Today, we would doubtless allow (though Kant, of course, would not have agreed) that the code of morals and manners varies from age to age and from place to place. Rising to greet one's guests, for instance, is merely a conventional, outward symbol of the respect one feels. Saluting with a sword or rubbing noses would do just as well. It is the respect that is important, not the gesture by which it is communicated. Or take lying: To tell one's servant to say one is "not at home" to a visitor is morally wrong only in a society that interprets this phrase literally. But in a society that understands it as a polite convention for saying one is tired or busy, it is no more untruthful than saying that the sun rose this morning.

It is important to note, too, that Kant's second formulation escapes the paradox that the virtue of a dutiful act lies in doing it because it is virtuous. For this formulation has uncovered a bona fide end that is realized in morally good (virtuous, dutiful) conduct. This end is the worth, or value, of the human personality. Kant's point, which is surely sound, is that this is a different kind of end from, say, that which moves a man when he tells the truth because he is afraid of being found out and punished. There is no moral worth in telling the truth to escape punishment; there *is* moral worth in telling the truth because one sees that it is his "end and destiny" as a man to do so. Kant's statement that morally good action does not aim at an end is a confused, and confusing, way of expressing what he meant. Nevertheless, Kant's point is a valid one—the end aimed at in morally good action is different from the end aimed at in other acts, and the structure of its maxim is different. The maxim in morally good conduct does not, strictly speaking, have a means-end structure; it has a class-inclusion structure. When we act morally we do not tell the truth as one step in a process aimed at achieving a result beyond itself; we tell it because we see that truth-telling belongs to the class of acts that the *noblesse* of human personality requires of us.

A THIRD ACCOUNT OF DUTY: THE AUTONOMOUS WILL

Kant also gave a third formulation of the categorical imperative: Act in accordance with the principle that "the laws to which you are subject are those of your own giving, though at the same time they are universal." In one sense, everything in nature is subject to laws: the stone as it falls and the animal as it feeds. But a will that acts on principle is subject to laws in a different sense from the stone or the animal. For when men act on principle (for example, when they eat an apple because "An apple a day keeps the doctor away") they know what they are doing, and why. This is the mark of rational behavior. Furthermore, a will that is subject to laws in the sense that it is attached to each of its laws by an interest (for example, health) must be distinguished from a will that is itself a lawgiver. In the former case, the law is derived from the circumstances of the physical or social world (a certain kind of vitamin deficiency is compensated for by eating apples); in the latter case, the will itself gives the law. Hence the latter will can be described as autonomous and free.

> The practical necessity of acting on this principle, *i.e.*, duty, does not rest at all on feelings, impulses, or inclinations, but solely on the relation of rational beings to one another, a relation in which the will of a rational being must always be regarded as *legislative,* since otherwise it could not be conceived as *an end in itself.* Reason then refers every maxim of the will, regarding it as legislating universally, to every other will and also to every action towards oneself; and this not on account of any other practical motive or any future advantage, but from the idea of the *dignity* of a rational being, obeying no law but that which he himself also gives.
>
> Now, morality is the condition under which alone a rational being can be an end in himself, since by this alone it is possible that he should be a legislating member in the kingdom of ends. Thus morality, and humanity as capable of it, is that which alone has dignity.
>
> What then is it which justifies virtue or the morally good disposition, in making such lofty claims? It is nothing less than the privilege it secures to the rational being of participating in the giving of universal laws, by which it qualifies him to be a member of a possible kingdom of ends, a privilege to which he was already destined by his own nature as being an end in himself, and on that account legislating in the kingdom of ends; free as regards all laws of physical nature, and obeying those only which he himself gives, and by which his maxims can belong to a system of universal law, to which at the same time he submits himself. For nothing has any worth except what the law assigns it. . . . *Autonomy* then is the basis of the dignity of human and of every rational nature.

From what has just been said, it is easy to see how it happens that although the conception of duty implies subjection to the law, we yet ascribe a certain *dignity* and sublimity to the person who fulfils all his duties. There is not, indeed, any sublimity in him, so far as he is *subject* to the moral law; but inasmuch as in regard to that very law he is likewise a *legislator,* and on that account alone subject to it, he has sublimity. We have also shown above that neither fear nor inclination, but simply respect for the law, is the spring which can give actions a moral worth. Our own will, so far as we suppose it to act only under the condition that its maxims are potentially universal laws, this ideal will which is possible to us is the proper object of respect; and the dignity of humanity consists just in this capacity of being universally legislative, though with the condition that it is itself subject to this same legislation.

Autonomy of the will is that property of it by which it is a law to itself (independently of any property of the objects of volition). The principle of autonomy then is: Always so to choose that the same volition shall comprehend the maxims of our choice as a universal law. . . . That the principle of autonomy in question is the sole principle of morals can be readily shown by mere analysis of the conceptions of morality. For by this analysis we find that its principle must be a categorical imperative, and that what this commands is neither more nor less than this very autonomy.[h]

Here, again, Kant is emphasizing what was called, in the discussion of the second formulation, the structure of the maxim that moves us to morally good conduct. According to that formulation, in morally good conduct we are moved by respect for personality. This maxim has quite a different structure from that which moves us when we eat an apple by a desire for health; and it seems appropriate to describe this difference in structure by saying that the morally good maxim is autonomous. Respect for personality is respect for ourselves—not, of course, for our private selves, but for the humanity we share with other men. Hence in morally good action the will can be said to be *self*-legislative.

Bearing in mind this concept of self-legislation, or "autonomy," let us return to the first formulation of the imperative. As was pointed out, the major weakness of that formulation was that it seemed to lead to the absurdity of saying, for example, that we have a duty to put our name on the flyleaf of every new book we purchase. This seemed to follow because it seemed that we had to interpret Kant as holding that we act morally either (1) whenever we follow a maxim that can be universalized or (2) whenever we obey the "idea of law in general." In view of the third formulation, however, we can now interpret Kant as meaning that we act morally whenever our motive is respect for ourselves and for other men as persons, or "lawgivers." That is, we act morally, not when we act out of respect for the idea of law in general, but when we act out of respect for men as creatures capable of understanding laws (rules) and of acting on them.

It is obvious that Kant's third formulation makes the notion of a moral imperative more intelligible. But can it still be called categorical? In Kant's view, this question turns on whether we do indeed attribute to personality an absolute and overriding value. "Supposing that there were something *whose existence* has *in itself* an absolute worth, something which, being *an end in itself,* could be a source of definite laws, then in this and this alone would lie the source of a possible categorical imperative, i.e., a practical law."[i] In other words, even an imperative of the form "Do x for the sake of y" would be categorical providing y is an absolutely necessary end. In Kant's view, of course, the absolute worth of personality makes it such a necessary end.

Was Kant correct? Certainly, some people seem to agree with him. For instance, conscientious objectors who refuse to fight under any circumstances because "human life is sacred" are really taking the position, as Kant did, that personality is the supreme value. Similarly, those who oppose capital punishment not on grounds of policy but simply because "it is always wrong to take another's life" are taking this position. Many people, however, would disagree with this view. As regards conscientious objection, they believe that there are circumstances in which we ought to resist. For example, they would hold that, far from it having been our duty to submit to Nazi tyranny rather than kill a single German in World War II, it would have been positively wicked to have submitted. It is not that such people do not value personality; it is simply that they do not attribute an absolutely overriding value to it.

Kant, of course, would have wanted to prove these people mistaken, for he held the supreme value of personality to be absolutely necessary. His argument here depends on the notion of a noumenal self.[4] Now *if* everyone had a noumenal self, and if this self (not the self that is a phenomenal object in space and time, not even the synthetical operations that make this phenomenal self possible) were supremely valuable, then there would be a categorical imperative absolutely binding on all men whether they recognized it or not.

But is there such a self? And if so, is it supremely valuable? Kant offered no evidence to support these contentions. He thought it enough to show merely that such a self is "possible." His position (as with his reply to Hume on the problem of induction)[5] can be summed up as follows: (1) Everyone initially believes the self to have supreme value. (2) This value becomes suspect only because of a puzzlement about its possibility and efficacy. (3) As soon, therefore, as this puzzlement is cleared up the original belief is reinstated.

Unfortunately for Kant, the reply to Hume regarding induction and this argument about the self are not on the same footing. Whatever may be thought about the logic of his reply to Hume, it is not enough merely to show (as Kant proposed to do) that our belief in the self and its value is possible. To begin with, although "everyone" initially believes that induction is possible, it is certainly not the case, as we have just seen, that "everyone" believes that the self is supremely valuable. Kant might have replied that though they do not think

4 See p. 64.
5 See pp. 25–26.

it supremely valuable, they ought to. But this would be to argue in a circle. Kant had hoped to explain "ought" by reference to the value of personality; therefore he could not turn around and use obligation to justify that value. Furthermore, even those who agree with Kant that the self is supremely valuable may not attribute this value, as he did, to the noumenal self. It may well be the empirical self that the conscientious objector values. For it is *that* self, not a timeless noumenal entity, that the conscientious objector refuses to kill. In addition, it is impossible to deduce the value of personality either from the notion of a transcendent unity of apperception or from the notion of the self as a lawgiver. Hence if the "ought" in the sentence, "People ought to recognize the supreme value of the noumenal self" is intended in its *logical* rather than its *moral* sense, the conclusion does not follow. Furthermore, as we have seen, the very notion of a noumenal self—the self that is outside the space-time world but somehow acting causally in it—is inconsistent with the main thesis of the *Critique*, which limits causality to the space-time manifold. Finally, as we have also seen, it is doubtful whether a categorical imperative (in the sense of a universally applicable duty) is required for morality, or indeed even compatible with morality.

The Free Will

Perhaps the most vexing question in Kant's philosophy is the question of free will. Kant held (with many other philosophers) that "ought" implies "can."[6] He also held obligation to be the essence of morality. Hence it was of fundamental importance to him, unless morality was to be admitted a vain and chimerical illusion, to prove "can." The difficulty was that he also believed that everything that happens is infallibly determined by antecedent events in time. If a psychologist knew enough about me and about the "laws" of human nature, he would be able to predict my future behavior as certainly as an astronomer is able to predict a solar or a lunar eclipse. Kant, it is important to note, had absolutely no doubt about this natural necessity. In his view, if we *had* to choose between it and freedom, we would have to abandon the latter, even though it meant abandoning the whole moral view of the world. But how can we avoid choosing? Is it possible to reconcile human freedom and natural necessity?

NOUMENAL CAUSALITY

To resolve this dilemma Kant fell back (as in the problem about an absolutely necessary value inhering in personality) on a positive conception of noumena,

6 Compare, for instance, "we *ought* to conform . . . ; consequently we must *be able* to do so"—*Religion Within the Limits of Reason Alone*, translated by T. M. Greene and H. H. Hudson (Open Court, Chicago, 1934), Bk. II, §1B, p. 55.

in contrast to the merely regulative role assigned them in accordance with the general doctrine of the critical philosophy. Kant admitted that to attribute freedom and natural necessity to the very same self is to become involved in contradictions. But he held that there are two selves, the noumenal self and the empirical self. It is the noumenal self that freely chooses and hence is morally responsible, and it is the empirical self whose behavior is completely determined by antecedent events in time. Thus, according to Kant, the contradiction is removed.

The notion of causality as *physical necessity*, in opposition to the same notion as *freedom*, concerns only the existence of things so far as it is *determinable in time*, and, consequently, as phenomena, in opposition to their causality as things in themselves. Now if we take the attributes of existence of things in time for attributes of things in themselves (which is the common view), then it is impossible to reconcile the necessity of the causal relation with freedom; they are contradictory. For from the former it follows that every event, and consequently every action that takes place at a certain point of time, is a necessary result of what existed in time preceding. Now as time past is no longer in my power, hence every action that I perform must be the necessary result of certain determining grounds *which are not in my power*, that is, at the moment in which I am acting I am never free. . . .

Consequently, if we would save [freedom], no other way remains but to consider that the existence of a thing, so far as it is determinable in time, and therefore its causality, according to the law of physical necessity, belong to *appearance*, and to attribute *freedom to the same being as a thing in itself*. . . . But . . . when we try to explain their combination in one and the same action, great difficulties present themselves. . . .

When I say of a man who commits a theft that, by the physical law of causality, this deed is a necessary result of the determining causes in preceding time, then it was impossible that it could not have happened; how then can the judgment, according to the moral law, make any change, and suppose that it could have been omitted, because the law says that it ought to have been omitted: that is, how can a man be called quite free at the same moment, and with respect to the same action in which he is subject to an inevitable physical necessity? Some try to evade this by saying that the causes that determine his causality are . . . ideas produced by our own faculties, whereby desires are evoked on occasion of circumstances, and hence actions are wrought according to our own pleasure. This is a wretched subterfuge. . . . It does not matter whether the principles which necessarily determine causality by a physical law reside *within* the subject or *without* him, . . . if, as is admitted by these men themselves, these determining ideas have the ground of their existence in time and in the *antecedent state,* and this again in an antecedent, &c. Then it matters not that these are internal; it matters not that they have a psychological and not a mechanical causality. . . . Psychological freedom (if we choose to apply this term to a merely internal chain of ideas in the mind) . . . involves physical necessity, and therefore leaves no room for *transcendental freedom,* which must be conceived as independence on everything empirical. . . . Without this freedom . . . no moral law and no moral imputation are possible. . . .

Now, in order to remove in the supposed case the apparent contradiction between freedom and the mechanism of nature in one and the same action, we must remember . . . that the necessity of nature . . . appertains only to the attributes of the thing that is subject to time-conditions, consequently only to those of the acting subject as a phenomenon; that therefore in this respect the determining principles of every action of the same reside in what belongs to past time, and *is no longer in his power* (in which must be included his own past actions and the character that these may determine for him in his own eyes as a phenomenon). But the very same subject being on the other side conscious of himself as a thing in himself, considers his existence also *in so far as it is not subject to time-conditions*, and regards himself as only determinable by laws which he gives himself through reason; and in this his existence nothing is antecedent to the determination of his will, but every action, and in general every modification of his existence, varying according to his internal sense, even the whole series of his existence as a sensible being, is in the consciousness of his supersensible existence nothing but the result, and never to be regarded as the determining principle, of his causality as a *noumenon*. In this view now the rational being can justly say of every unlawful action that he performs, that he could very well have left it undone; although as appearance it is sufficiently determined in the past, and in this respect is absolutely necessary; for it, with all the past which determines it, belongs to the one single phenomenon of his character which he makes for himself, in consequence of which he imputes the causality of those appearances to himself as a cause independent on sensibility.[j]

This is an extremely difficult passage. Does Kant mean (1) that the particular act (the theft) could have been otherwise or (2) that the whole empirical character, including this act, could have been otherwise? It is hard to see how the former assertion could be considered compatible with the claim that the act was determined by antecedent events in time.[7] The latter assertion is initially more plausible, for it seems to be possible to say, given a man's weak character, both (1) that antecedent events in time (slum upbringing, drunken father, shiftless mother, and so forth) infallibly determined that he would develop into a thief and (2) that he is responsible because there was an initial free act (before birth?) in which he chose the kind of character that would fall victim to this environment. But the second assertion is really not helpful. For even if we can accept the notion of such an initial choice as meaningful, this act cannot be held to initiate a closed series. A man and his character are not isolated events; they are parts

---

7 But compare such an explicit statement as this: "Whatever his previous deportment may have been, whatever natural causes may have been influencing him . . . , his action is yet free and determined by none of these causes; hence it can and must always be judged as an *original* use of his will. . . . However evil a man has been up to the very moment of an impending free act (so that evil has actually become custom or second nature) it was not only his duty to have been better [in the past], it is *now* still his duty to better himself. To do so must be within his power"—*Religion Within the Limits of Reason Alone*, translated by T. M. Greene and H. H. Hudson (Open Court, Chicago, 1934), Bk. I, §4, p. 36.

of a causal nexus—parents' genes, health of mother, and so forth. Hence precisely the same problem raised against the notion of a particular free act (this theft) must be raised against the notion of a free series (this empirical character), for taken as a whole the series is as particular as the act.[k] It is thus a foregone conclusion that, as long as one insists on freedom as a real spontaneity intruding into the natural world, no solution is possible.

This seems so obvious that we may wonder why Kant did not recognize it himself. The main reason is simply that the critical point of view was such a radical departure from the orthodox, traditional way of viewing the world that Kant could not prevent himself from sliding back into that old way of thinking. This is particularly true with respect to the two important concepts, noumena and freedom.

As regards noumena, the critical point of view required that objects (things, substances) and causality be limited to the realm of experience; and part of the time, of course, Kant saw that this was so and insisted on it. Yet he repeatedly lapsed into thinking of noumena as objects, and of the noumenal self as causally efficacious. The simple truth is that use of a thing-language is so habitual that it is very difficult not to reify whatever one tries to think about—including noumena. Thus, running through the whole of Kant's philosophy is a serious ambiguity between what may be called a critical conception of noumena and a conventional conception. This ambiguity becomes entangled in Kant's doctrine of freedom in the following way: In certain parts of the *Critique*, when Kant is discussing free will, he is referring (as we have seen) to a spontaneous cause that effects changes in the course of events. This may be described as the conventional view of freedom, and it fits in with the conventional view of noumena. But in other parts of the *Critique*, when Kant is discussing freedom, he describes the kind of maxim that he believed to be morally good. That is, part of the time he considers freedom to mean acting from a certain motive— namely, respect for men as creatures who are capable of understanding laws. Viewed in *this* way, freedom has nothing to do with spontaneous causality: We are free whenever we act from this motive, regardless of the fact that a psychologist could predict that, under such-and-such circumstances, we would act from it. And this view of freedom fits in with the critical conception of noumena.

How did Kant come to think of freedom in this double, and highly ambiguous, sense? The answer is that when he was thinking in terms of the third formulation of the categorical imperative, he naturally referred to the morally good will as "self-legislative," or "autonomous." And since "autonomy" and "freedom" are, in one sense, synonymous, he was led to call the morally good act free. But of course freedom, especially when predicated of the will, has a second meaning— "being spontaneous." There are, then, two quite different senses in which it is permissible to call the will free: when one is talking about "autonomy"—the unique structure of the morally good maxim—and when one is making an assertion about the relation of that maxim to antecedent events (or rather, about its lack of relation to any antecedent events).

Taken in the second sense, freedom is obviously inconsistent with natural necessity. To say that an act is free in this sense is to assert that it could have been otherwise, and to say that it is determined is to assert that it could not have been otherwise. But taken in the first sense, freedom is not inconsistent with natural necessity: Here we are merely saying that *when* a maxim with such-and-such a structure occurs and a man acts on it, that man is free ("autonomous") and his conduct is morally valuable. To say that the maxim is autonomous (free) is not to make any assertion at all about the circumstances that produce the maxim in question. If we knew enough about the man's past we could doubtless predict that at a particular time he would act in a certain way and from a motive that has this "autonomous" structure.

Kant's solution to the "antinomy" of freedom and natural necessity seems to have consisted in sliding back and forth between freedom as "spontaneous causality" and freedom as "maxim with autonomous structure." In the following passage an attentive reader can catch the shifts as they occur and observe how the conclusion depends on them.

> The *will* is a kind of causality belonging to living beings in so far as they are rational, and *freedom* would be this property of such causality that it can be efficient, independently on foreign causes *determining* it; just as *physical necessity* is the property that the causality of all irrational beings has of being determined to activity by the influence of foreign causes.
>
> The preceding definition of freedom is *negative*, and therefore unfruitful for the discovery of its essence; but it leads to a *positive* conception which is so much the more full and fruitful. Since the conception of causality involves that of laws, according to which, by something that we call cause, something else, namely, the effect, must be produced; . . . hence, although freedom is not a property of the will depending on physical laws, yet it is not for that reason lawless; on the contrary, it must be a causality acting according to immutable laws, but of a peculiar kind; otherwise a free will would be an absurdity. Physical necessity is a heteronomy of the efficient causes, for every effect is possible only according to this law, that something else determines the efficient cause to exert its causality. What else then can freedom of the will be but autonomy, that is the property of the will to be a law to itself? But the proposition: The will is in every action a law to itself, only expresses the principle, to act on no other maxim than that which can also have as an object itself as a universal law. Now this is precisely the formula of the categorical imperative and is the principle of morality, so that a free will and a will subject to moral laws are one and the same.[1]

SUMMARY

We can see, then, that as a result of an ambiguity in the term "freedom" Kant came to think that he had reconciled natural necessity and spontaneous causality and thus had solved the problem over which, as he said, "centuries have labored in vain." Kant, of course, had done nothing of the kind. But he *had* done something much more important. By rigorously limiting knowledge

in the strict sense to the spatiotemporal manifold, he made room for an appreciation of ourselves as moral beings with individual rights and with obligations
to others. Freedom in what may be called the critical sense is thus entirely in
accord with the spirit of the general solution of the problem of pure reason.
It falls within the province of what Kant misleadingly called "faith"—for by
faith he meant, not an ungrounded belief in something that contradicts the
evidence of the sciences, but a sensitivity to, and appreciation of, values.

To put this differently, freedom in the critical sense conforms to the central
theme of Kant's whole philosophy, the theme that knowledge of objects and
appreciation of values (including the value of being a person) are simply modes
of experience too different ever to conflict. Accordingly, if *before* the appearance
of modern physics we had any reason to accept the traditional appreciation of
man as a focus of values, we have the same reason for doing so *after* the appearance of modern physics. As soon as we realize that physics is concerned exclusively with knowledge of objects, and that the traditional view only *seems* to be
making assertions about objects, we see that physics has nothing to say one way
or the other about the traditional view. Just as the motor that runs a phonograph
turntable has nothing to do with the esthetic quality of the symphony we hear
on it (though it may have a great deal to do with how well or how poorly we
hear it), so the state of our cortex has nothing to do with the genuineness of
the value we experience (though it may have a great deal to do with the fact
that we experience it). It is the business of science (and especially of physiological
psychology) to examine the conditions under which such experiences occur. It
might be possible, for instance, to show that only a cortex of such-and-such a
configuration is able to experience the feeling that Kant called "respect." But
this would not mean that the feeling is illusory, or that the animals who experience it are not at the same time members of a "kingdom of ends," a world
of mutual rights and obligations that is as real, in its own dimensions of reality,
as the cortex is in its.

Kant's fundamental thesis is that we are dealing with two kinds of reality and
hence with different criteria of meaning and truth. If we suppose that values are
real in the way that facts are real and try to assess them by the criteria proper
to facts, the values disappear. But the same thing would happen to facts if we
tried to assess them by the criteria proper to values. Of course, it is unlikely that
anyone today would make the second kind of mistake. But this, as a matter of
fact, is exactly what medieval philosophers did, and it explains why they never
developed a competent science. Then, when the new physics appeared on the
scene, men began to make the first kind of identification and to assess values by
the standards of facts. In both cases, the identification was made to seem plausible by that confused mode of thought in which it appeared that both values and
facts are substances, and that therefore the same criteria ought to apply. It was
Kant's analysis of substance in phenomenalistic terms, as a spatiotemporally
organized manifold, that cleared up the confusion and paved the way for the
rehabilitation of the valuational point of view.

This is an important insight. But to make a place for values is not to give an account of them; to show that the criteria of truth and meaning that obtain in the natural sciences do not apply in the field of value is not to show what criteria *do* apply there. It seems clear, even at this point, that Kant's treatment of the field of value was far less adequate than his parallel treatment (in the *Critique of Pure Reason*) of the field of fact. There can hardly be any question, for instance, that his account of moral values (the kinds of value realized in conduct) was seriously one-sided. Although he was not committed to the narrow rigorism (duty for duty's sake) popularly attributed to him, his concentration on "right" to the exclusion of "good" resulted in his neglecting whole ranges of value that are capable of being realized in conduct, and with which moral philosophy should therefore be concerned.

Religion

The limitations of Kant's view of values appear also in his treatment of religion. We have seen that, in Kant's view, the only use theoretical reason can make of the idea of God is as a means to regulate inquiry, not as a means to designate an object. But, according to Kant, the whole meaning of the idea of God is not exhausted in its regulative use. On the contrary, just as the conception of the self as a limit leaves a "place" open for a real self in some other, valuational, non-thing sense, so the conception of God as a limit leaves a place open for a real God in some other sense. But, what other sense? For what kind of God is there a place in the Kantian system? As we shall see, Kant vacillated between a more critical view, in which he held God to be a value, and a less critical view, in which he held God to be a force or power in a more traditional sense. Thus Kant's conception of God reflects the same ambivalence found in his conception of freedom.

A "PRACTICAL" PROOF OF GOD'S EXISTENCE

Kant began his proof by pointing out that it does not follow, just because the existence of God cannot be proved by theoretical reason, that *no* proof of His existence is possible. The traditional proofs, whose inadequacy he had exposed in the *Critique of Pure Reason*, all rested in one way or another on theoretical considerations (such as the allegation that it is logically necessary to think of a first cause). Kant, however, based his own proof on moral considerations, and in doing so he supposed it to be exempt from the fallacies to which the traditional proofs fell victim.

Such a proof requires, first, a distinction between the *supreme* good (virtue) and the *perfect* good (virtue and happiness).

To need happiness, to deserve it, and yet at the same time not to participate in it, cannot be consistent with the perfect volition of a rational being. . . . The distribution of happiness in exact proportion to morality (which is the worth of the person, and his worthiness to be happy) constitutes the *summum bonum* of a possible world; hence this *summum bonum* expresses the whole, the perfect good, in which, however, virtue as the condition is always the supreme good. . . .[m]

The argument proceeds as follows: Nothing we know about the physical world suggests that "virtue is the efficient cause of happiness." Indeed, in the mechanistic universe disclosed by natural science the proposition is false. Even if it should prove to be the case that the state of mind we call virtuous is followed by the state of mind we call happiness, the connection would not be moral. Nevertheless, to promote the *summum bonum* is an obligation imposed on all men. And since "ought implies can," this *summum bonum* must be realizable. Some other (and moral) force must therefore be operative in the universe, a force that will at some future date bring about the distribution of happiness in accordance with virtue.

The possibility of . . . the *summum bonum,* viz. Happiness proportioned to that morality . . . must lead to the supposition of the existence of a cause adequate to this effect; in other words, it must postulate the *existence of God,* as the necessary condition of the possibility of the *summum bonum* (an object of the will which is necessarily connected with the moral legislation of pure reason). We proceed to exhibit this connexion in a convincing manner.

Happiness is the condition of a rational being in the world with whom *everything goes according to his wish and will;* it rests, therefore, on the harmony of physical nature with his whole end, and likewise with the essential determining principle of his will. . . . There is not the least ground, therefore, in the moral law for a necessary connexion between morality and proportionate happiness in a being that belongs to the world. . . . Nevertheless, in the practical problem of pure reason, *i.e.* the necessary pursuit of the *summum bonum,* such a connexion is postulated as necessary: we ought to endeavour to promote the *summum bonum,* which, therefore, must be possible. Accordingly, the existence of a cause of all nature, distinct from nature itself, and containing the principle of this connexion, namely, of the exact harmony of happiness with morality, is also *postulated.* . . . The *summum bonum* is possible in the world only on the supposition of a Supreme Being having a causality corresponding to moral character. Now a being that is capable of acting on the conception of laws is an *intelligence* (a rational being), and the causality of such a being according to this conception of laws is his *will;* therefore the supreme cause of nature, which must be presupposed as a condition of the *summum bonum* is a being which is the cause of nature by *intelligence* and *will,* consequently its author, that is God. . . . Now it was seen to be a duty for us to promote the *summum bonum;* consequently it is not merely allowable, but it is a necessity connected with duty as a requisite, that we should presuppose the possibility of this *summum bonum;*

and as this is possible only on condition of the existence of God, it inseparably connects the supposition of this with duty; that is, it is morally necessary to assume the existence of God.[n]

PROOF OF THE IMMORTALITY OF THE SOUL

Kant believed that his argument also proved the immortality of the soul, for the adjustment of happiness to virtue depends on the attainment of virtue.

> The *perfect accordance* of the [will] with the moral law [i.e., complete virtue] is . . . perfection of which no rational being . . . is capable at any moment of his existence. Since, nevertheless, it is required as practically necessary [i.e., it is a state that ought to exist], it can only be found in a *progress in infinitum* towards that perfect accordance. . . .
>
> Now, this endless progress is only possible on the supposition of an *endless* duration of the *existence* and personality of the same rational being. . . . The *summum bonum*, then, practically is only possible on the supposition of the immortality of the soul; consequently this immortality, being inseparably connected with the moral law, is a postulate of pure practical reason (by which I mean a *theoretical* proposition, not demonstrable as such, but which is an inseparable result of an unconditional *a priori practical* law).[o]

There are two main objections to these proofs. First, they contradict the point on which Kant insisted in his moral theory—namely, that virtue is its own reward. Kant cannot have it both ways: If it is our duty to aim at happiness-in-accordance-with-virtue, it is not our duty to aim solely at virtue—and the moral imperative is no longer categorical but hypothetical. Thus, in his account of the *summum bonum,* Kant equates "worth of the person" and "worthiness to be happy."[8] But this is a play on words. The "worth of personality" on which he insists in his discussion of morality is simply the unique value that attaches to reason (whether in ourselves or in others); it has nothing whatever to do with desert.

Second, even supposing it to be our duty to try to produce a state of affairs in which happiness is distributed in accordance with virtue, Kant's conclusion still does not follow. In order to see that it does not, let us deny the conclusion and see what happens. Does it follow that we have no duties at all? Quite the contrary, as Kant himself was the first to point out.

> This proof . . . does not say: it is as necessary to assume the Being of God as to recognise the validity of the moral law; and consequently he who cannot convince himself of the first, can judge himself free from the obligations of the second. No! there must in such case only be given up the *aiming at* the final purpose in the world, to be brought about by the pursuit of the second (viz. a happiness of rational beings in harmony with the pursuit of moral laws, regarded as the highest good). Every rational being would yet have

8 See p. 9.

> to cognise himself as straitly bound by the precepts of morality, for its laws are formal and command unconditionally without respect to purposes (as the matter of volition). . . . To further [happiness] so far as is in our power . . . is commanded us by the moral law; be the issue of this endeavour what it may. The fulfilling of duty consists in the form of the earnest will, not in the intermediate causes of success.
>
> Suppose then that partly through the weakness of all the speculative arguments so highly extolled, and partly through many irregularities in nature and the world of sense which come before him, a man is persuaded of the proposition, There is no God; he would nevertheless be contemptible in his own eyes if on that account he were to imagine the laws of duty as empty, invalid and inobligatory.[p]

This argument in effect denies the premise of the moral proof of God's existence, yet surely it is in conformity with Kant's basic position. Our duty (so far as we have any duty in this connection) is to help to bring about such-and-such a state of affairs (to do so in our own sphere, as it were). It is immaterial whether in this action we fail to make a perfect and complete distribution. And even if it were true that the existence of an obligation to do something depended on the possibility of successfully bringing about the state of affairs in question, God's existence would not help to make *my* obligation real. Indeed, insofar as Kant's moral proof of the existence of God proves anything at all, it proves not that God must exist as a power capable of producing such-and-such a state of affairs, but that *I* must be capable of producing it.

NATURE OF GOD

There is another difficulty connected with the nature of God. Kant's arguments (supposing them to be valid) prove the existence only of a very limited God—merely an agent who distributes happiness in accordance with merit. But Kant, of course, wished to attribute omniscience, omnipotence, and the other theologically important properties to this God:

> From the principle, thus determined, of the causality of the Original Being we must not think Him merely as Intelligence and as legislative for nature. . . . We shall think this Original Being as *all-knowing:* thus our inmost dispositions (which constitute the proper moral worth of the actions of rational beings of the world) will not be hid from Him. We shall think Him as *all-mighty;* thus He will be able to make the whole of nature accord with this highest purpose. We shall think Him as *all-good,* and at the same time as *just:* because these two properties (which when united constitute *Wisdom*) are the conditions of the causality of a supreme Cause of the world, as highest good, under moral laws. So also all the other transcendental properties, such as *Eternity, Omnipresence,* etc. which are presupposed in reference to such a final purpose, must be thought in Him.[q]

It cannot be said that this argument is convincing. The most it proves is that God is a moral being who has considerable power. But such a being is far from either the God of Christian theology or the God of Christian piety. How, for instance, are we to get from "a principle that distributes happiness in accordance with righteousness" to an "only begotten Son"? According to Kant, since we are not the authors of the former idea, it is

> . . . appropriate to say that this archetype has *come down* to us from heaven and has assumed our humanity. . . . This ideal . . . of moral perfection . . . we can represent to ourselves only as the idea of a person. . . . For man can frame to himself no concept of the degree and strength of a force like that of moral disposition except by picturing it as encompassed by obstacles, and yet, in the face of the fiercest onslaughts, victorious. . . .
>
> We need therefore no [actual] empirical example to make [this] idea . . . our archetype. . . . Moreover, if anyone, in order to acknowledge, for his imitation, a particular individual as such an example of conformity to that idea, demands . . . that this individual should have performed miracles or had them performed for him—he who demands this thereby confesses to his own moral *unbelief*, that is, to his lack of faith in virtue. . . .
>
> Now if it were indeed a fact that such a truly godly-minded man at some particular time had descended, as it were, from heaven to earth and had given men in his own person, through his teachings, his conduct, and his sufferings, as perfect an *example* of a man well-pleasing to God as one can expect to find in external experience (for be it remembered that the *archetype* of such a person is to be sought nowhere but in our own reason), and if he had, through all this, produced immeasurably great good upon earth by effecting a revolution in the human race—even then we should have no cause for supposing him other than a man naturally begotten. . . . This is not, to be sure, absolutely to deny that he might be a man supernaturally begotten. But to suppose this can in no way benefit us practically.[r]

The "as it were" that Kant has slipped in here is significant—it is a mark of how greatly his view fails to satisfy the requirements of the orthodox Christian, who holds that Christ literally descended—that this is a matter of fact, not a manner of speaking. Yet even the rarefied and abstracted God that Kant describes is more than the critical philosophy can really allow. For the attribution of any sort of supernatural agency clearly contradicts the central theses of the *Critique of Pure Reason:* Causality is limited, by the whole procedure of the deduction, to phenomena. But there is no need to discuss this in detail, since there is no essential difference between assigning spontaneous, noumenal causality to the self and assigning it to God.

It is not surprising, in view of these difficulties, that Kant himself was not content with this position. Toward the end of his life, a new view began to emerge in his writings, but he died before fully developing it. Although this view was more consistent with the critical philosophy, it was even further removed from Christian orthodoxy than was the view it was replacing. For the essence of this final view lay in interpreting God not as a causal agent but (like the moral self) as a value. According to this interpretation, God would seem to be the same sort of value we attribute to ourselves as persons, the supreme example of that reason we respect in ourselves. What distinguishes God from man is the difference between right and duty. When we appreciate this value in ourselves, we experience it under the form of a compulsion. To respect it is a duty that, often enough, we fail to live up to. When we think of this value in its own right, as a good to be realized (not as an obligation imposed on us), we call it "God."

IDENTIFICATION OF RELIGION AND MORALITY

As stated above, Kant's view may sound odd. Perhaps it will sound less odd if it is pointed out that Kant in effect made a religion of morality. As we have seen, the language he used in discussing his moral law was essentially religious in tone.[9] We respect the moral law as a supreme value, in comparison with which our own personal wants, desires, and demands are completely trivial and insignificant. Now respect is not far from worship. Indeed, it is probably as near to worship as the mind of the Enlightenment, filled with a sense of man's dignity as a rational being, could come. Respect combines the pride of the classical mind (its sense of the autonomy and value of reason) with the humility of the Christian mind (its sense of man's distance from the realization of his ideal). Insofar as we think of the reason within us as imposing certain acts on the persons we feel ourselves to be, we are thinking in *moral* terms. Insofar as we think of reason, not as it is in us or in connection with the acts it dictates to us, but simply as a supreme value in itself, we are thinking in *religious* terms.

In thus identifying religion and morality, Kant revived a view that not only was congenial to the classical mind but that anticipated a trend that appeared in the nineteenth century. In this view, much dropped out that had been important in the Christian tradition. In fact, it may be said that what dropped out was, historically speaking, the core of Christianity—its religiosity, its belief in a personal *and* transcendent God. All the adherents of Christian doctrine would agree that Christianity is certainly a *moral* religion; but most of them would also insist that it is a moral *religion*.

Mechanism and Teleology

The widespread belief that the universe is purposive—not merely a meaningless machine—must also be considered. Since, as has been pointed out, the idea of real causal efficacy is inconsistent with the critical position,[10] we must ask

9 See, for instance, pp. 70–71.
10 See p. 87.

whether there is any interpretation of purposiveness that is consistent with the main theses of the *Critique of Pure Reason*. Kant devoted the *Critique of Judgment* to this question. Although his reply cannot be explored in detail, its main outlines are easily given.

Kant began by analyzing the concept of purposiveness-without-purpose. This may sound like a paradox, but Kant was actually using the concept descriptively. Some works of art, he believed, are planned to look as if they were not planned. An example is the so-called English style of garden. During the seventeenth and much of the eighteenth centuries, the French style of garden, such as that fashioned by Le Notre at Versailles, was the mode. Plants were forced into unnatural geometrical patterns and masses. For instance, trees were planted in straight rows and trimmed to exactly the same height; lawns were designed to look not like grass but like green carpets. The intent was to make the spectator think how much time, effort, and money had gone into making nature look unnatural. During the eighteenth century, however, taste began to change, and the English style of landscape gardening came into favor. This type of garden was just as carefully studied as Le Notre's, but the effect was entirely different. Trees and plants were set out to look as if they had grown up where their seeds happened to fall. Paths wandered artlessly back and forth (instead of being cut through woods on a rigid pattern) and brought one out at a view that the landscape artist intended one to enjoy. The emphasis was on naturalness, but it was designed naturalness. Here, then, is an example of purposiveness-without-purpose.

Kant believed purposiveness-without-purpose to be the essential factor in all esthetic experience. But surely he was mistaken, for witness our enjoyment of the French style of landscape gardening. The most that can be said is that purposiveness-without-purpose is *one* of the factors involved in *some* types of beauty. In esthetics, as in the field of morality, Kant tried to generalize a local (geographically and temporally) preference into a universal explanation.

Kant's primary interest in purposiveness-without-purpose, however, lay not in esthetics but in its supposed relevance to the problems of teleology in the natural world. According to Kant, some natural objects, namely, those objects called "organisms," have the same sort of structure as art objects; they must, therefore, be cognized by means of the same sort of concept. Kant did not mean, of course, that an organism has exactly the *same* structure as an object of art; he meant simply that in both organisms and art objects a means-end relationship among parts, and between parts and their whole, exists. This is why their parts are called "organs." This is *empirically* quite a different kind of relationship from a mechanical one. And this difference is reflected in the kind of question we ask when we set out to understand an organism. When we study an organism we do not look *behind* to the antecedent events in time that determined the state of affairs that now exists; we look *ahead* to the end that the current state of affairs is serving. Thus we ask, "What is the function of such-and-such a gland?" And when we have found, for example, that the gland regulates the organism's size, we feel we understand it—it is explained. According to Kant, all this takes place at a purely empirical level. That is, we do not have to suppose that someone actually *designed* the gland with this purpose in mind.

Purposiveness in organisms is an "as if" concept. We say that a gland functions *as if* God (or someone else) had planned it that way. The concept of purposiveness is thus descriptive and methodological; it designates a characteristic and empirically verifiable relation among parts. Hence we can say that every organism exemplifies purposiveness (a structure of such-and-such a kind) without purpose (no supernatural intellect that actually planned it that way). Thus the organism is like the English style of garden (of course, the garden actually was planned, but it *claims* not to be). For in both the organism and the garden we are judging about an actually existent relationship of parts. Nature, it may be said, is what art tries to be.

There is a difference, it should be noted, between the concept of purposiveness as applied to organisms and the concept as applied to the world in general. In the latter case, "purposiveness" is simply a regulative maxim ("Nothing in nature is in vain") that leads us to act as if every occurrence, however whimsical it may seem to be, has a cause. But with respect to organisms, the concept of purposiveness is more than a merely regulative maxim. Organisms *may* be explicable in mechanistic terms, but not for minds constituted like ours. We inevitably introduce purposive concepts, like the concept of function, if we want to understand organisms. This does not mean, of course, that there is any either-or condition to the situation. "Purposiveness" and "mechanism" are not rival hypotheses about the causes of the objects in question. For, in Kant's view, causality is not a transference of power but a pattern of regularity—a lawfulness in the sequence of events in the manifold. Hence, to say that organisms may be explicable in mechanistic terms is to say merely that it may be possible to find a formula for the pattern of regularity that is deducible from the laws of motion. To say that organisms are explicable in purposive terms is to assert merely that as a matter of fact we use means-end concepts.

There is, then, no conflict between mechanism and purposiveness-without-purpose, for neither is an assertion about what "really" produces a given state of affairs.[11] They are simply alternative descriptions of the state of affairs in question. Thus, for instance, I might describe a certain picture by saying that the artist used such-and-such a palette, such-and-such kinds of brushes, such-and-such a technique of laying on paint, and so on. There is no conflict between this and saying that the picture is "a Crucifixion in the manner of Tintoretto." Note that in the latter statement I am not attributing the canvas to Tintoretto. I am simply giving an alternative description of the canvas, perfectly adequate for anyone acquainted with the manner of Tintoretto. I am not saying that Tintoretto was the painter who "really" produced this canvas; I am saying merely

---

11 The point is that the *Critique of Pure Reason* had ruled out questions about "real" causality (that is, noumenal efficacy).

that the canvas is *as if* Tintoretto had painted it. That is, had he painted it, he would have used a palette like this and a technique like this, and the outcome would have been much the same.

Though purposiveness-without-purpose is a methodological concept of some importance, it may not be clear at first sight what bearing it has on the moral and religious considerations that led Kant to introduce it. According to Kant, the argument shows (1) that questions about whether or not the world "really" has an intelligent author are based on a misunderstanding and cannot be answered one way or the other; (2) that, given minds constituted like ours, we must inevitably think of the world as if it had such an author—that is, as if it had meaning and purpose; and (3) that, far from contradicting the presuppositions of the natural sciences, this "as-if purposiveness" actually supplements them and makes a complete and harmonious world view possible.

This position is obviously a long way from the view of providence that the orthodox Christian understands. Kant's reply to this implied criticism would doubtless have been that the orthodox Christian does not really *understand* what he is demanding of philosophy, and that when one tries to come to grips with the orthodox Christian's idea, it collapses into confusion and anthropomorphism.

Summary

It should now be clear why Kant's theories have often been regarded as difficult. But, despite the great complications encountered in analyzing the details of the various deductions, the basic ideas of the Kantian philosophy are easily grasped. Kant undertook to make a new analysis of the nature of knowledge that would not only show its proper limitations (as the empiricists had undertaken to do) but that would also validate knowledge within its own proper field (as the empiricists had notoriously failed to do). The main feature of this new analysis was the due weight given both to the empirical factor (Galileo's "observe") *and* to the universal and necessary factor (Galileo's "demonstrate"), which none of Kant's predecessors had known how to combine effectively. The main reason for Kant's success in this respect was his grasp of the role of experiment—his recognition, that is, that the answers one gets depend on the questions one asks. The result of Kant's recognition of the mind's role as a "questioner" of nature was a wholly new conception of the nature of the self and its objects, a conception that has had important implications in almost every field of inquiry, from physics and psychology to ethics and art criticism.

The main points in this new view of the nature of self and its objects are: (1) Self and not-self are not metaphysically distinct "ultimates" but "constructs" within the field of experience. (2) Experience is a spatiotemporal manifold in which distinctions are made, including the distinction between self and not-self.

(3) The natural sciences are limited to describing and generalizing about this spatiotemporal manifold and the various "objects" distinguished within it, including self (the science of psychology) and not-self (physics, chemistry, and so on). (4) Experience—the spatiotemporal manifold—is dependent on "transcendental" conditions. Because they are "transcendental," these conditions are not *in* experience (in the sense that red and blue, hot and cold, sweet and sour, are in experience). Hence, despite Hume's failure to find them, there is no evidence for denying their existence. Hume was simply looking for the wrong things in the wrong place. (5) Though these transcendental conditions are not *in* experience and hence cannot be objects of scientific cognition, we know *that* they exist, for they are the necessary conditions of experience. We can argue from what *is* known in experience to what must be true for there to be this knowledge in experience. (6) These transcendental conditions, which are nothing but the basic types of "questions" the mind asks of nature, validate the sciences in their own field and at the same time limit them to this field. (7) Since "God, freedom, and immortality" fall outside this field, the sciences can say nothing one way or the other about them. (8) It follows that God and the free immortal self are neither substantival nor causally efficacious, for substance and causality are concepts relevant only within the experiential field. (9) Nevertheless, God and the free immortal self are real, for their reality is guaranteed by the facts of moral experience.

These, then, are the main points that Kant undertook to establish. It is certainly true, as has already been noted, that he did not prove all he wanted to prove or all he thought he had proved. But the questions a philosopher asks are no less important than the answers he finds for them. The ways in which Kant framed his questions have become, for better or for worse, a part of the fabric of modern culture. Every great philosopher leaves his mark on the subsequent development of thought, not only by his theories, but by the way he formulates his problems. This was true of Plato and Aristotle; ever since their time philosophers have wrestled with the problems they defined. In the remaining chapters of this book we shall see that this was also true of Kant. It is a measure of his stature as a philosopher.

CHAPTER 4

Reactions Against Kantianism: Hegel and Schopenhauer

As we have seen, the Age of Reason was sustained by three basic assumptions: (1) that there is a rational order of eternal truths, (2) that man has a mind capable of understanding these truths, and (3) that he has a will capable of acting in accordance with them. According to the men of the Age of Reason, every science —not only physics and chemistry, but economics, politics, and ethics as well— begins from propositions whose truth is immediately recognizable. The business of each science is to formulate all the theorems that can be derived from its special set of principles; the business of rational men everywhere is to apply this whole body of truths in the ordinary affairs of daily life. "We hold these truths to be self-evident . . . ," said the founding fathers. "Let us sit down in a cool hour," added Bishop Butler, and find ways to apply the truths we all recognize to be the problems of practical life.[1]

---

1 Butler, who died in 1752, naturally did not have the founding fathers' self-evident truths specifically in mind.

During the nineteenth century all three of these basic propositions were attacked from a variety of points of view, and before long there came to be widespread scepticism about them—about the existence of such eternal truths; about the power of the human intellect to know them, even if they did exist; and about the capacity of the will to find a "cool hour," or to act rationally and in accordance with its long-range interests, even supposing that these interests could be discovered.

Taken as a whole, then, nineteenth-century philosophy can be characterized as a series of attempts to deal with the problems created by the collapse of the world view of the Age of Reason. Of the many solutions proposed, none came to dominate Western culture. Indeed, one of the chief characteristics of the nineteenth and twentieth centuries, as compared with earlier ages, is the diversity of world views.

The philosophers who followed Kant found his position an unsatisfactory form of fence-sitting, and most of them climbed down from the fence to one side or the other. As we have seen, Kant believed that there are things-in-themselves, but he denied that we can ever know them. Depending on their underlying values, post-Kantian philosophers either maintained that we do after all have access to things-in-themselves or denied that there are things-in-themselves and limited reality to the space-time manifold and to what Kant called the empirical self. In general, these philosophers also concluded that reason plays either a much larger or a much smaller role—both in cognition and in the moral life—than Kant had allowed. Yet none of these philosophers was untouched by Kant: Those who reaffirmed that knowledge of a transempirical reality is possible did not return to a pre-Kantian type of rationalism; those who limited reality to the space-time manifold did not return directly to Hume.

Why did post-Kantian philosophers accept Kant's distinctions rather than simply revert to earlier theories? In the first place, Kant's influence was too powerful. Everyone had to take account of his views; in fact, for a long time to come everyone thought not only in his terms but also largely in his vocabulary. Even those philosophers who reached conclusions very remote from Kant's were nevertheless Kantian in the sense that they started out from a basically Kantian orientation and merely found reasons for developing his thought in a different direction and with a different emphasis. In the second place, the whole mood of Western culture had changed since Kant's time—indeed, it had been changing even while Kant wrote. These changes in values and outlook greatly affected the course of philosophical speculation.

Romanticism

The new complex of attitudes can be brought under the rubric of "Romanticism." But this is only another of those broad terms (like "Renaissance" and "Reformation") that trap the unwary. For people tend to think that such terms name simple, self-identical entities—that there is a distinct little nugget of "Romanticism," for example, that attaches itself to poems, pictures, and manners during a certain well-defined period. Romanticism is a very complex phenomenon; hence no more than one aspect of it can be considered here, and that only very inadequately. Indeed, it will be necessary to limit discussion to Romanticism as a reaction against the mood of the Enlightenment—in particular, against its conception of knowledge.

Certainly, the spirit of the Enlightenment was open to criticism. Some people were annoyed by its irreligion; others by its complacency; others again by what they felt to be its narrowness and artificiality; and still others by its conviction that by stressing order, rule, and measure, both in the universe at large and in man in particular, everything can be neatly pigeonholed and labeled. To such minds, the universe seemed bigger, richer, more varied and exciting, and more of a unity than the thinkers of the Age of Reason had allowed.

HOSTILITY TO REASON

The focus of the Romantic attack was naturally against "reason," which the Romantics evaluated as "a false secondary power by which we multiply distinctions." To the Romantic mind, the distinctions that reason makes are artificial, imposed, and man-made; they divide, and in dividing destroy, the living whole of reality—"We murder to dissect." How, then, *are* we to get in touch with the real? By divesting ourselves, insofar as we can, of the whole apparatus of learning and scholarship and by becoming like children or simple, uneducated men; by attending to nature rather than to the works of man; by becoming passive and letting nature work upon us; by contemplation and communion, rather than by ratiocination and scientific method.

When Wordsworth was asked by a friend why he "wasted" his time in dreamy reverie and in contemplation of nature, he replied,

> Nor less I deem that there are Powers
> Which of themselves our minds impress;
> That we can feed this mind of ours
> In a wise passiveness.[a]

Inviting his sister to join him in a walk in the woods on a lovely spring day, he pointed out,

> One moment now may give us more
> Than years of toiling reason:
> Our minds shall drink at every pore
> The spirit of the season. . . .
> And bring no book: for this one day
> We'll give to idleness.[b]

And in *The Tables Turned:*

> Books! 'tis a dull and endless strife:
> Come, hear the woodland linnet,
> How sweet his music! on my life,
> There's more of wisdom in it. . . .
>
> One impulse from a vernal wood
> May teach you more of man,
> Of moral evil and of good,
> Than all the sages can. . . .
>
> Enough of Science and of Art;
> Close up those barren leaves;
> Come forth, and bring with you a heart
> That watches and receives.

Keats, too, expressed this feeling:

> O thou whose only book has been the light
> Of supreme darkness, which thou feddest on
> Night after night, when Phoebus was away!
> To thee the Spring shall be a triple morn.
> O fret not after knowledge. I have none,
> And yet my song comes native with the warmth.
> O fret not after knowledge! I have none,
> And yet the evening listens. He who saddens
> At thought of idleness cannot be idle,
> And he's awake who thinks himself asleep.[c]

The notion that only a difference of degree, rather than a difference of kind, exists between mind-awake and mind-asleep, and that, on the whole, our truest insights into the nature of reality come during the latter rather than the former state, is characteristic of Romanticism.

> Our life is twofold: Sleep hath its own world,
> A boundary between the things misnamed
> Death and existence: Sleep hath its own world,
> And a wide realm of wild reality,
> And dreams in their development have breath,
> And tears, and tortures, and the touch of joy;
> They leave a weight upon our waking thoughts,
> They take a weight from off our waking toils,
> They do divide our being; they become
> A portion of ourselves as of our time. . . .
> They make us what we were not—what they will,
> And shake us with the vision that's gone by,
> The dread of vanish'd shadows—Are they so?

> Is not the past all shadow? What are they?
> Creations of the mind?—The mind can make
> Substance, and people planets of its own
> With beings brighter than have been, and give
> A breath to forms which can outlive all flesh.[d]

And just as we are nearer to the truth about the universe when we dream than when we are awake, so we are nearer to it as children than as adults:

> Dear Child! dear Girl! that walkest with me here,
> If thou appear untouched by solemn thought,
> Thy nature is not therefore less divine:
> Thou liest in Abraham's bosom all the year;
> And worship'st at the Temple's inner shrine,
> God being with thee when we know it not.[e]

And as infants we are even nearer:

> Thou, whose exterior semblance doth belie
>   Thy soul's immensity:
> Thou best Philosopher. . . .
>   Mighty Prophet! Seer blest!
>   On whom those truths do rest,
> Which we are toiling all our lives to find . . . ,
> Thou little Child, yet glorious in the might
> Of heaven-born freedom on thy being's height. . . .
> Trailing clouds of glory do we come
>   From God who is our home:
> Heaven lies about us in our infancy!
> Shades of the prison-house begin to close
>   Upon the growing Boy
> But He beholds the light, and whence it flows,
>   He sees it in his joy;
> The Youth, who daily farther from the east
>   Must travel, still is Nature's Priest,
>   And by the vision splendid
>   Is on his way attended;
> At length the Man perceives it die away,
> And fade into the light of common day.[f]

The logical terminus of this line of thought is that animals, even more than humankind, are the best philosophers:

> Poor little Foal of an oppressed Race!
> I love the languid patience of thy face . . .
> Do prophetic Fears anticipate,
> Meek child of Misery! thy future fate? . . .

Or is thy sad heart thrill'd with filial pain
To see thy wretched Mother's shorten'd chain? . . .
Poor Ass! thy master should have learnt to show
Pity—best taught by fellowship of woe! . . .
Innocent Foal . . .
I hail thee Brother—spite of the fool's scorn! . . .
Yea! and more musically sweet to me
Thy dissonant harsh bray of joy would be,
Than warbled melodies that soothe to rest
The aching of pale Fashion's vacant breast![g]

CONCEPTION OF REALITY

What, then, is the reality disclosed in "the drowsy numbness" of intoxication, in the innocence of childhood, "on the viewless wings of poesy," in silent communion with nature, or in the rapt contemplation of a beautiful work of art? Naturally what each poet found was colored by his individual temperament, but among the Romantics there was considerable unanimity. They were impressed by the largeness of reality, an immensity that baffled the methods of science and that made the whole human enterprise, on which the preceding age had set such store, petty and trivial.

Wisdom and Spirit of the universe!
Thou Soul that art the eternity of thought,
That givest to forms and images a breath
And everlasting motion, not in vain
By day or starlight thus from my first dawn
Of childhood didst thou intertwine for me
The passions that build up our human soul;
Not with the mean and vulgar works of man,
But with high objects, with enduring things—
With life and nature, purifying thus
The elements of feeling and of thought.[h]

If the gentler aspects of nature moved Wordsworth, the more turbulent touched Shelley's muse: "the wild West wind, destroyer and preserver," the dizzy ravines and wild waterfalls "where woods and winds contend," and the whole tremendous spectacle of the Alps.

The everlasting universe of things
Flows through the mind, and rolls its rapid waves,
Now dark—now glittering—now reflecting gloom—
Now lending splendour, where from secret springs
The source of human thought its tribute brings
Of waters. . . .
Some say that gleams of a remoter world
Visit the soul in sleep,—that death is slumber,
And that its shapes the busy thoughts outnumber

Of those who wake and live.—I look on high;
Has some unknown omnipotence unfurled
The veil of life and death? or do I lie
In dream, and does the mightier world of sleep
Spread far around and inaccessibly
Its circles? . . .
The wilderness has a mysterious tongue
Which teaches awful doubt, or faith so mild,
So solemn, so serene, that man may be,
But for such faith with nature reconciled;
Thou hast a voice, great Mountain, to repeal
Large codes of fraud and woe; not understood
By all, but which the wise, and great, and good
Interpret, or make felt, or deeply feel.[i]

There was, then, an ambivalence in the Romantic mood. On the one hand, the Romantics believed that their finiteness as men separated them from the immensity of the real:

Roll on, thou deep and dark blue Ocean, roll!
Ten thousand fleets sweep over thee in vain;
Man marks the earth with ruin, his control
Stops with the shore; upon the watery plain
The wrecks are all thy deed, nor doth remain
A shadow of man's ravage, save his own,
When, for a moment, like a drop of rain,
He sinks into thy depths with bubbling groan,
Without a grave, unknell'd, uncoffin'd, and unknown.

On the other hand, they felt an affinity with this great, sublime, and transcendent immensity:

And I have loved thee, Ocean! and my joy
Of youthful sports was on thy breast to be
Borne like thy bubbles, onward. From a boy
I wanton'd with thy breakers—they to me
Were a delight; and if the freshening sea
Made them a terror—'twas a pleasing fear,
For I was as it were a child of thee,
And trusted to thy billows far and near,
And laid my hand upon thy mane—as I do here.[j]

Thus the Romantics rejected two of the cardinal theses of the Enlightenment. The Enlightenment thinkers had perceived man as unique—as different from all the rest of nature because he alone possesses reason. Because the Romantics downgraded reason, they were disposed to think of man as a part of nature, as dependent on nature not only for bodily sustenance but also for his highest thoughts and noblest aspirations:

> The anchor of my purest thoughts, the nurse,
> The guide, the guardian of my heart, and soul
> Of all my moral being.[k]

In addition, because the Romantics disliked sharp distinctions of any kind, they rejected the Enlightenment view of the universe as made up of a large number of separate entities (selves, things) and viewed the universe as one continuous living and dynamic being. For example, in Goethe's *Faust* the Earth Spirit exclaims,

> In the floods of life, in the storm of work,
> In ebb and flow,
> In warp and weft,
> Cradle and grave,
> An eternal sea,
> A changing patchwork,
> A glowing life,
> At the whirring loom of Time I weave
> The living clothes of the Deity.[l]

REACTION TO KANTIANISM

The Romantic mind, as sketched here, would obviously have been both attracted to and repelled by Kantianism. The Romantics believed that Kant was correct in recognizing the limitations of rational knowledge and in pointing out the existence of a vast realm of true reality behind the phenomenal world. But no sooner had Kant opened up these vistas of immensity than he slammed the door in men's faces, maintaining that we can know nothing about that real world—only *that* it exists. To the Romantics, this was intolerable. From their point of view, Kantianism, by showing the radical incompetence of science—its inability to reach any knowledge of things-in-themselves—merely prepared the way for the development of a new metaphysics. Kant's position, in fact, depended on a delicate—one might almost say precarious—balance of antithetical forces; it could be maintained only by a mind sensitive to all these forces and at the same time capable of exercising great self-restraint with respect to its own preferences. Though Kant was unable to maintain this balance consistently, for him balance was at least an ideal. For the Romantics, in contrast, balance was an ideal no longer. The Romantic mind valued unity far more than balance, and identity and commitment far more than any neutral and objective weighing of evidence.

The two philosophers to be considered next—Hegel and Schopenhauer—were deeply influenced by this Romantic mood. Both were persuaded that reality is immense and complex—too complex to be exhaustively explained by the neat conceptual schemes of eighteenth-century rationalism. Both were strongly responsive to the movement and change that the Romantic poets emphasized. Hence for both of them Kant was still too much of an eighteenth-century rationalist. They appreciated the fact that he had conceded the existence of a realm of wide reality beyond the space-time manifold (the world to which he had confined Newtonian physics). But they reacted strongly against the sharp distinction that he had drawn between phenomena and noumena and rejected Kant's agnosticism in this respect. But here Hegel and Schopenhauer themselves parted company.

There are two logically possible arguments open to those who, in opposition to Kant, claim that the mind has access to noumena.[2] On the one hand, it is possible to argue that the "ideas of pure reason" are not merely regulative (as Kant had claimed[3]) but, like the categories, constitutive; and that, furthermore, they are constitutive of things as they are, not of things as they appear. On the other hand, it is possible to agree with Kant that the intellect is limited to things as they appear, and to maintain that the world of things as they really are is nevertheless accessible to us in intuition.

Hegel is the outstanding representative of the first type of criticism; Schopenhauer's philosophy illustrates the second type. Both these views are discussed in some detail below, for each reflects a movement of thought that exerted a powerful influence in many directions throughout the nineteenth century and even into our own day.

Hegel

G. W. F. Hegel, born in 1770, was the son of a minor official in Stuttgart in southern Germany. Though his family was poor, he managed to get a university education. He served for a number of years as a private tutor and later as a newspaper editor and as the principal of a school. Hegel was slow in securing a professorship, chiefly because he published very little until he was thirty-seven. Eventually, however, he was appointed to a chair at Heidelberg and, a year later, to one at Berlin. As he grew older, Hegel became conservative: He prized order above freedom and became deeply suspicious of "reform." Hegel found the

---

2 Of course, it is also possible to reject noumena and to maintain that reality is limited to the space-time manifold. See pp. 160–62.

3 According to Kant, it will be recalled, substance, causality, and the other categories are constitutive of, and limited to, the spatiotemporal manifold—that is, they provide an a priori order for experience. Concepts like God, self, and totality, on the other hand, are methodological aids. Rather than defining objects, they "regulate" our empirical inquiries. See pp. 58–62.

atmosphere of the kingdom of Prussia congenial, possibly because he received the official approval and support of the state. Once established in Berlin, his fame spread and something approaching a Hegelian cult developed.

Hegel is one of the most difficult of philosophers to study, partly, but by no means merely, because of the intrinsic difficulty of his theories. He wrote in an almost deliberately obfuscating manner and was able to complete only bits and pieces of the vast "system" that he envisioned. Hegel considered *The Phenomenology of the Spirit* (published in 1807) to be no more than a preface to the system he proposed—yet *The Phenomenology* is over seven hundred fifty pages in length and has a preface of its own of sixty-five pages. In 1817 he published an outline of the whole system, the *Encyclopaedia of the Philosophical Sciences*, which went through several revisions during his lifetime. The rest of his publications consist of the *Logic* (in two versions), the only completed part of the system, and the notes from his lectures on various subjects—philosophy of history, philosophy of art, history of philosophy—that were recorded by students and published after his death. It is not surprising that there is no agreement regarding the nature of Hegel's views. The discussion presented below relies chiefly on *The Phenomenology* and aims at bringing out only the main features of this great work.

Hegel's View of Reason

A good starting point for this discussion is Hegel's belief that the universe is rational. This, of course, is a conviction he shared with many other philosophers, in particular, the thinkers of the Age of Reason. But, as will be seen, Hegel's view of the nature of reason, and thus of the rationality of the universe, differed in important respects from theirs. However, on one point at least he did agree with them. According to Hegel, to say that the universe is rational is to say that no matter how far apart men may start out, given patience and good will, they can reach agreement regarding the truth. Indeed, to seek agreement is one aspect of being human. Those who refuse to do so "trample the roots of humanity underfoot": "The nature of humanity is to impel men to agree with one another, and its very existence lies simply in the explicit realization of a community of conscious life. What is anti-human, the condition of mere animals, consists in keeping within the sphere of feeling pure and simple, and in being able to communicate only by way of feeling-states."[m]

Hegel's point may be illustrated by a trivial example: Suppose that Mr. A looks at a colored patch and calls it red. Mr. B, looking at the patch, replies, "Oh, no; that's blue." So far A and B are in contradiction—a situation in which men too often find themselves. Perhaps A and B continue to insist dogmatically on their original assertions; but, if they are willing to "return upon and recon-sider" [n] the colored patch that they have observed, they may agree that the color is royal purple—a bluish red or (if one prefers) a reddish blue. Thus A and B may come to see that they were in contradiction only because each was empha-sizing one shade in the color and ignoring the other—each, while affirming his part of the truth, denied the part of the truth that the other was affirming.

A more complex example is that of the dispute over United States policy in Southeast Asia. Some people hold that the aim of United States policy is to protect weak states from subversion by Communist aggression; others maintain that this policy is a vicious neocolonial conspiracy. Those who accept Hegel's view that the universe is rational would have to hold that here too there is a formula, however difficult it may prove to work it out, that reconciles the conflicting interpretations of United States policy. Now, it is a truism that United States policy looks different from different points of view. A Vietnamese villager whose home has been destroyed by American bombers will look at the situation differently from an American marine who has been wounded by a guerrilla sniper. It is also a truism that some perspectives are more limited than others: Presum-ably, the military staff in Saigon has a more complete view of the course of the war than does the wounded marine. But it is not immediately evident that, as Hegel claims, *all* partial perspectives can be harmonized into a simple all-in-clusive perspective.

Yet this is Hegel's claim: (1) Every particular assertion (for example, "This color is red") is only *partially* true, because it is always made from a limited point of view. (2) Every particular assertion *is* nevertheless partially true (the color really is red, when seen under certain lighting conditions or in juxtaposition with that other color). (3) Because every particular assertion ("The color is red") is only partially true, it tends to generate a compensatory assertion ("The color is blue"). (4) These conflicting assertions are reconcilable in a more inclusive assertion ("The color is royal purple"). (5) This more inclusive assertion in turn proves to be partial and thus requires correction by a still more adequate formula-tion.

MINDS AND THEIR OBJECTS

So far Hegel probably sounds like many another philosopher—like Plato, for instance. Plato, too, distinguished between what the world looks like to "common sense" and what it really is for "critical reason," and Plato also held that there is a "profound and fruitful process" by which one rises from the former level to the latter. [o] But whereas Plato believed that the truth consists in eternal and unchanging forms that lie outside the mind illumined by them, Hegel accepted Kant's "Copernican" revolution, his replacement of the notion of mind and its objects as completely independent entities with the radically different notion of mind and its objects as functionally related and as emerging together in experience. Indeed, Hegel carried this insight much farther than Kant had done:

In my view—a view which the developed exposition of the system itself can alone justify—everything depends on grasping and expressing the ultimate truth not as Substance but as Subject as well.
. . . .
In general, in virtue of the principle that . . . substance is implicitly and in itself subject, all content makes its reflection into itself in its own special way. The subsistence or substance of anything that exists is its self-identity; for its want of identity, or oneness with itself, would be its dissolution. But self-identity is pure abstraction; and this is just thinking. When I say Quality, I state simple determinateness; by means of its quality one existence is distinguished from another or is an "existence"; it is for itself, something on its own account, or subsists with itself because of its simple characteristic. But by doing so it is essentially Thought.

Here we find contained the principle that Being is Thought. . . .

Owing to the nature which being thus has, and so far as what is has this nature from the point of view of knowledge, this thinking is not an activity which treats the content as something alien and external; it is not reflection into self away from the content. . . . Rather, since knowledge sees the content go back into its own proper inner nature, the activity of knowledge is absorbed in that content—for it (the activity) is the immanent self of the content—and is also at the same time returned into itself, for this activity is pure self-identity in otherness. In this way the knowing activity is the artful device which, while seeming to refrain from activity, looks on and watches how specific determinateness with its concrete life, just where it believes it is working out its own self-preservation and its own private interest, is, in point of fact, doing the very opposite, is doing what brings about its own dissolution and makes itself a moment in the whole.[p]

Hegel's point in the first sentence is simply that he intends to replace the old metaphysics, which took it for granted that substance was the prime metaphysical concept, with a new metaphysics based on the notion of thought, or of consciousness. For philosophers adhering to the old metaphysics there had been a question about whether only one substance exists or several; and in the latter case, how such substances are related. But there had been general agreement about what a substance is: It is a self-identical and enduring entity that does not itself change but that possesses changing properties, or attributes. It is independent—it is that which stands alone. It is self-subsistent. And so on. Thus, when Descartes discovered his self in the course of methodological doubt, he assumed it to be "a thing which thinks." Hegel's position, in contrast, is much more psychologically acute and much less bound by prior metaphysical commitments. For surely, when we introspect we do not find a thing-self, as Hume had pointed out. But neither do we find only impressions and ideas, as Hume had claimed. What we do find is not easy to describe—the obscurities of the quoted passage testify to this. The difficulty results in part from the fact that Hegel is largely breaking new ground; but it also results from the fact that the only language available to him (and for that matter to us) is so saturated with substantival thinking that one inevitably falls into paradox when using it to talk about what is not a substance but an activity.

THE NATURE OF EXPERIENCE

Perhaps it will be helpful to rephrase Hegel's view of thought in language slightly different from his. Let us start with ordinary, everyday experience. What I find in experience is, first of all, "things"—desks, tables, chairs. Sometimes I am also aware of myself, but even when I am not I know perfectly well that the experience I am having is mine. Now, what I have called "things" Hegel calls "content." And to say that I experience content as mine is to say that I experience it as not-me. It is, as Hegel points out in the passage just quoted, experienced as "other," as over there, as what one is not. Furthermore, I do not experience self in the same sense that I experience "other." To be aware of self is not to be aware of *another* bit of content; it is to be aware of whatever content I happen to be aware of as other. Self-awareness is simply awareness of the object as more sharply distinguished than it once was, as more emphatically not *me* but other-than-me.

An example may be helpful. At the theater I may be "wholly absorbed" in *Hamlet*. Nevertheless, I do not sheerly identify with Hamlet; I "know," even if I am not consciously aware of it, that the Hamlet I see is not a prince of Denmark, but an actor, and that I am in my seat watching him out there on the stage. Hegel's point is that there must be this basic distinction for there to *be* experience at all. There is no experience without some awareness, however faint, that it *is* experience. To understand this point clearly, let us consider another Hegelian distinction, the distinction between an object as it is "in itself" and the object as it is "for" someone, say, for an observer. For example, I may distinguish between my desk as it is in itself and my desk as it is for me, that is, as an object of my experience. But this distinction is not made by the desk as well as by me; it can be made only by conscious beings, by minds. Indeed, the making of this distinction is precisely what "being conscious," or "having a mind," consists in.

Hence, if we accept Hegel's "ultimate truth" that consciousness, not substance, is the prime metaphysical concept, we give a very different account of reality from that given by the traditional metaphysics, which had been dominated by the concept of substance. In the Hegelian view, the notions of independence and unchanging self-subsistence disappear: The mind is not independent, because it can never get away from its other (or content). And if it were to free itself from its other, it would dissolve—for its "being" consists in experiencing content. Nor is the mind unchanging; on the contrary, it is changing all the time—developing, expanding, correcting, and revising itself and its experience.

Although it is possible to speak of the "self-identity" of the mind, or consciousness, this self-identity is very different from the self-identity that traditional metaphysics attributed to substance. The self-identity of substance is the sheer, unbroken self-identity of continuous being. The self-identity of consciousness is awareness of the other in a special, and enlightened, way. And the self-identity of consciousness, unlike the self-identity of substance, is a matter of degree, ranging all the way from the "bare" self-consciousness of the infant, who is marginally aware of, say, becoming warm (and hence of not being *identical* with warmth), to the more complex self-consciousness of a sophisticated and intro-spective adult. At every level, therefore, self-consciousness (self-identity) is the reciprocal, or reflection, of the degree of structure, order, complexity, and variety of the "other." The self of the baby is minimal, because its experience is ele-mentary; the self of the adult is richer, because its experience is more complex. A man who has seen *Hamlet* has a richer self than he had before he saw *Hamlet*, for he is now the-man-who-has-seen-*Hamlet*, that is, the man who has "absorbed" the play, who has compared himself with, and distinguished himself from, the protagonist.

J. Alfred Prufrock learns something about himself by comparing himself with, and distinguishing himself from, Hamlet:

> No! I am not Prince Hamlet, nor was meant to be;
> Am an attendant lord, one that will do
> To swell a progress, start a scene or two,
> Advise the prince; no doubt, an easy tool. . . .[q]

Considered from Hegel's point of view, Prufrock is more of a self after he makes this discovery than before he makes it. He becomes more of a self as the objects from which he distinguishes himself become more various and richly diverse, and as the distinctions that he draws become more subtle and refined.

To summarize: Self and object are not distinct, unchanging entities that face each other across a metaphysical and epistemological chasm; self and object are structures that arise within experience. There is no object without self, and there is no self without object. This doctrine should be familiar, for it is the doctrine of Kant. It is also Kantian to "demote" substance, as Hegel did, from its meta-physical primacy. For Kant had already pointed out that reality does not consist in substances; on the contrary, substance is simply one of the twelve categories by means of which the human mind organizes its experiences.

THE EVOLUTION OF MIND

Kant not only maintained that there are but twelve structuring categories; he also took it for granted that all twelve categories are used by all minds every-where—by the infant as well as the adult, by the caveman as well as the eight-eenth-century *philosophe*. Although Hegel recognized that Kant had taken an immensely important step in shifting the philosophical focus from substance to subject, he held that Kant had not made effective use of this shift, that Kant's use of the concept of subject was vitiated by a culture-bound and time-bound (ahistorical) approach.[4] This "correction" of Kant's doctrine was possible because, in the quarter century between the publication of the *Critique of Pure Reason* and *The Phenomenology*, the notion of time change—that is, of evolution in the broadest sense—had entered, and was already deeply affecting, the European climate of opinion. Kant's conception of mind was largely static; Hegel's was developmental. Moreover, Hegel took account not only of the evolution of the individual mind from infancy to adulthood but also of the evolution of the mind from earliest times down to his own day. Indeed, he thought that these two evolutionary developments were parallel: Ontogeny recapitulates phylogeny. Hence, whereas Kant's metaphysical deduction of the twelve categories was a relatively simple procedure (Kant took them over at one fell swoop from Aristotle's logic[5]), Hegel's exposition of the changing and unfolding types, or levels, of consciousness occupies the whole of *The Phenomenology* and is (or at least purports to be) an empirical inquiry, rather than a strictly logical one.

The differences between Kant and Hegel in this respect are reflected in the contrasting metaphors they employ. A favorite Kantian metaphor is that of a judge in court. According to Kant, the mind is like a judge, who is not involved in the dispute being heard before him; the mind attends to the evidence presented to it and renders a verdict between the rival claims; it decides for one and against the other. Hegel's typical metaphor, in contrast, is that of a bud developing into a blossom:

> The bud disappears when the blossom breaks through, and we might say that the former is refuted by the latter; in the same way when the fruit comes, the blossom may be explained to be a false form of the plant's existence, for the fruit appears as its true nature in place of the blossom. These stages are not merely differentiated; they supplant one another as being incompatible with one another. But the ceaseless activity of their own inherent nature makes them at the same time moments[6] of an organic unity, where they not merely do not contradict one another, but where one is as necessary as the other; and this equal necessity of all moments constitutes alone and thereby the life of the whole.[r]

In Hegel's view, mind is not a judge disinterestedly contemplating a realm of already existent objects; it is an inner force creating and shaping the outer, observable forms. Specifically, at the level of both the individual and the race, mind creates the various esthetic, social, and political forms that, taken together, constitute a given culture at a particular time. This is what he means, in the passage just quoted, by calling mind "the life of the whole."

4 Though Hegel did not use these terms himself, the fact that his criticism of Kant can easily be stated in these terms is an example of Hegel's influence on twentieth-century thought.
5 See p. 35.
6 ["Moment" is a bad translation, since it suggests a very short time interval; Hegel's meaning would be rendered more clearly by a term like "aspect," or "feature," or even "part"—AUTHOR.]

Thus Hegel applied the general doctrine that contradictions are only apparent (because they result from taking a limited view of a complex object) to the notion of there being developmental stages through which consciousness passes. In the evolutionary process nothing is lost. As we have seen, the two conflicting assertions "That color is blue" and "That color is red" are not denied by the assertion "That color is royal purple"; they are incorporated in it as one-sided versions of it. Similarly, each successively higher level of consciousness (whether in the individual or in the race) incorporates all earlier, more elementary levels. Thus Hegel concluded that the higher the level of consciousness, the richer and more "concrete" the content of that consciousness. Accordingly, he rejected both the traditional rationalism and all forms of intuitionism.

CRITICISM OF THE TRADITIONAL RATIONALISM

The traditional rationalism, or *raisonnement,* as Hegel termed it, reflects a level of consciousness at which concepts are assumed to function like the pigeon-holes into which the postman tosses each day's accumulation of letters and packages. *Raisonnement* holds that science consists in classifying; science dumps everything, willy-nilly, into one or another of its pigeonholes. *Raisonnement,* that is, ignores the nuances that make each thing an individual. "If we say 'all animals,'" Hegel sarcastically observed, "that does not pass for zoology."[s] Indeed, it is barely the beginning of zoology. Animal species differ structurally; it is the business of zoology to discover the differences and similarities of structure. Furthermore, individual members of each species—as well as the species themselves—differ from one another. Accordingly, not only do we oversimplify (and thereby falsify) when we lump all species—giraffe, whale, gibbon—together in the single pigeonhole "animal"; we also oversimplify when we ignore individual differences among gibbons. Thus the weakness of *raisonnement* is its "formalism." It "adopts a negative attitude towards the content apprehended."[t] At this level of thought, instead of accommodating ourselves to differences in the content before us, we seek to force this content into conformity with our own more or less arbitrarily chosen concepts. A study of nature that relies on abstract universals

> . . . has no right to the name of science. For we see it there reduced to a lifeless schema, to nothing better than a mere shadow, and scientific organization to a synoptic table. This formalism . . . thinks it has comprehended and expressed the nature and life of a given form when it proclaims a determination of the schema to be its predicate. The predicate may be subjectivity or objectivity, or again magnetism, electricity, and so on, contraction or expansion, East or West, and such like. . . .
>
> The instrument for producing this monotonous formalism is no more difficult to handle than the palette of a painter, on which lie only two colours, say, red and green, the former for colouring the surface when we want a historical piece, the latter when we want a bit of landscape. . . . What results

from the use of this method . . . is . . . like a skeleton with tickets stuck all over it, or like the rows of boxes kept shut and labeled in a grocer's stall; and [it] is as intelligible as either the one or the other. It has lost hold of the living nature of concrete fact; just as in the former case we have merely dry bones with flesh and blood all gone, and in the latter, there is shut away in those boxes something equally lifeless too. We have already remarked that the final outcome of this style of thinking is, at the same time, to paint entirely in one kind of colour; for it turns with contempt from the distinctions in the schematic table, looks on them as belonging to the activity of mere reflection, and lets them drop out of sight in the void of the Absolute, and there reinstates pure identity, pure formless whiteness. Such uniformity of colouring in the schema with its lifeless determinations, this absolute identity, and the transition from one to the other—these are the one as well as the other, the expression of inert lifeless understanding, and equally an external process of knowledge.[u]

CRITICISM OF INTUITIONISM

So much for the traditional rationalism, with its abstract universals. Hegel was equally critical of intuitionism, which, in its pursuit of the immediacy of feeling, ignores the inevitably mediate character of experience. In this respect Hegel's view differed markedly from the typical Romantic attitude, as expressed, for instance, in *Faust*. When Gretchen asks Faust whether he believes in God, Faust replies,

> Who can name him? . . .
> Then call it what you will—
> Happiness! Heart! Love! God!
> I have no name for it!
> Feeling is all;
> Name is mere sound and reek
> Clouding Heaven's light.[v]

From Hegel's point of view, this reply of Faust's represents a level of consciousness that seeks to "run together" what *raisonnement* "has divided asunder." Rightly seeing the emptiness of abstract concepts, this mind mistakenly wants to abandon concepts altogether and to give itself up to sheer immediacy. Thus it corrects *raisonnement,* but it does so at the cost of an equal oversimplification. It wants to

> . . . restore the *feeling* of existence. What it wants from philosophy is not so much insight as edification. The beautiful, the holy, the eternal, religion, love—these are the bait required to awaken the desire to bite: not the notion, but ecstasy, not the march of cold necessity in the subject-matter, but ferment and enthusiasm—these are to be the ways by which the wealth of the concrete substance is to be stored and increasingly extended. . . .

The man who only seeks edification, who wants to envelop in mist the manifold diversity of his earthly existence and thought, and craves after the vague enjoyment of this vague and indeterminate Divinity . . . will easily find for himself the means to procure something he can rave over and puff himself up withal. But philosophy must beware of wishing to be edifying.

Still less must this kind of contentment, which holds science in contempt, take upon itself to claim that raving obscurantism of this sort is something higher than science. These apocalyptic utterances pretend to occupy the very centre and the deepest depths; they look askance at all definiteness and preciseness of meaning.

. . . .

To consider any specific fact as it is in the Absolute, consists here [that is, at this level of consciousness] in nothing else than saying about it that, while it is now doubtless spoken of as something specific, yet in the Absolute, in the abstract identity A = A, there is no such thing at all, for everything is there all one. To pit this single assertion, that "in the Absolute all is one," against the organized whole of determinate and complete knowledge, or of knowledge which at least aims at and demands complete development—to give out its Absolute as the night in which, as we say, all cows are black—that is the very *naïveté* of emptiness of knowledge.ᵂ

Thus, although intuitionism starts from an exactly opposite set of assumptions from those of rationalism, it ends in a formalism of its own, because it too neglects the concreteness, richness, and variety of actual experience.

Hegel's View of Scientific Knowledge

Hegel contrasted these two deficient modes of cognition—traditional rationalism and intuitionism—with a higher level of consciousness that, in accordance with the Hegelian pattern, incorporates them while transcending them. Although Hegel called this higher level "science," it must not be confused with the quantitative mathematical knowledge aimed at in the physical sciences. Rather, it is that "organized whole of determinate and complete knowledge" referred to at the end of the passage just quoted. Because scientific knowledge is conceptual and mediate it differs from the inarticulate feelings of intuitionism. And it differs from *raisonnement* because its concepts, being concrete instead of abstract, are adequate to the real diversity and richness of experience.

Hegel's term for the concrete universal of true science is *Begriff*, which translators formerly rendered in English as "notion" and which they now tend to translate as "concept." The former translation is somewhat inept, but it has the advantage of reminding us that Hegel's *Begriff* differs from an ordinary concept. A *Begriff*, in fact, is a concept that, instead of being imposed from outside, is generated within the content and therefore adequately reflects its uniqueness. Here the metaphor of bud-blossom-fruit is relevant. That is, Hegel's thought is dominated by the idea of life, of an energy that is self-generative and that expresses itself in successively unfolding forms. If we can imagine for a moment that a plant is conscious, we can certainly think of it as becoming increasingly self-conscious as it grows and advances from bud to flower to fruit; and we may think of the fruit as the plant's concept ("notion") of itself, that is, as the plant's understanding of itself as consisting in a succession of forms that have culminated in this fruit. Such a concept of what it is to be a fruit is obviously very different from the externally imposed concept of fruit that a botanist might employ. For the *notion* of fruit is not merely the abstract concept of fruit; it also includes the feeling of being fruit. On the other hand, the notion is conceptual and is hence not "mere" feeling. At the level of the notion feeling becomes "determinate" knowledge; the feeling of being fruit is transcended, but included, in the fruit's articulate self-knowledge of itself as the fulfillment of bud and flower.

Science can become an organic system only by the inherent life of the notion. In science the determinateness, which was [at the level of *raisonnement*] taken from the schema and stuck on to existing facts in external fashion, is the self-directing inner soul of the concrete content. The movement of what is partly consists in becoming another to itself, and thus developing explicitly into its own immanent content; partly, again, it takes this evolved content, this existence it assumes, back into itself, i.e., makes *itself* into a moment,[7] and reduces itself to simple determinateness. In the first stage of the process negativity lies in the function of distinguishing and establishing existence; in this latter return into self, negativity consists in the bringing about of determinate simplicity. It is in this way that the content shows its specific characteristic not to be received from something else, and stuck on externally; the content gives itself this determinate characteristic, appoints itself of its own initiative to the rank of a moment and to a place in the whole. . . .

Instead of making its way into the inherent content of the matter in hand, understanding[8] always . . . assumes a position above the particular existence about which it is speaking. . . . True scientific knowledge, on the contrary, demands abandonment to the very life of the object, or, which means the same thing, claims to have before it the inner necessity controlling the object, and to express this only. Steeping itself in its object, . . . being sunk into the material in hand, and following the course that such material takes, true knowledge returns back into itself, yet not before the content in its fullness is taken into itself, is reduced to . . . the level of being one aspect of an existing entity, and passes over into its higher truth. By this process the whole as such, surveying its entire content, itself emerges out of the wealth wherein its process of reflection seemed to be lost.[x]

7 [See note 6, p. 114—AUTHOR.]
8 [This is another term for the level of consciousness that Hegel called *raisonnement*. It derives from the Kantian distinction between *Verstand* (understanding) and *Vernunft* (reason)—AUTHOR.]

CONSEQUENCES OF THIS VIEW

Several important consequences follow. (1) It is impossible to get at the truth by examining the situation as of some (any) particular time. The only way to get at the truth is by an historical, or genetic, approach in which the evolution up to a particular stage is shown to be the "necessary" outcome of a series of conflicts and discrepancies, and their successive corrections. Thus we do not understand any stage in the life of a plant—say, the flower stage—unless we realize that this stage supersedes (but at the same time incorporates) an earlier bud stage.

(2) "Negation" is not to be feared. It is, in fact, the sign that the formulation so far achieved is one-sided and inadequate; hence it supplies the power that makes possible the advance of mind to higher levels. For instance, if no one says, "Oh no, that color is blue," I am likely to rest contentedly in my initial belief that the color is simply and sheerly red. But if someone contradicts me by calling the color blue, I am moved to advance to a more concrete concept— royal purple. This is what Hegel means, in the passage just quoted, by saying that "negativity consists in the bringing about of determinate simplicity." At the level of science each item is located in a context of related items. Concrete universals ("notions") are more adequate than abstract universals because the context in terms of which a particular item is located is more highly structured and hence more precise. For instance, a mind that is capable of distinguishing only between red and not-red is less capable of locating the exact nuance of this particular color than is a mind that can also distinguish old rose, magenta, royal purple, Prussian blue, and so on. And it is negation that leads the mind from the simple contradiction between red and not-red to these more refined color distinctions. Thus a man's attitude toward contradiction is a mark of what level of consciousness he has attained.

(3) Just as the seemingly "fixed and stable existence" of any object in our experience "carries the process of its own dissolution within itself," so the seemingly fixed and stable self-identity of any particular self—say, mine—carries its own dissolution within it. In the case of the self, too, there is a "process of dissolution" that refines and distinguishes—renders the self "determinate"—by means of negation and mediation. For example, at some point it may occur to me that I am like Hamlet in being indecisive. But then I think, "No, I am not a prince; I am only an attendant lord. Well, I am not *just* an attendant lord, for I *know* that I am one, whereas the typical attendant lord does not think of himself in this way."

But it is a mistake to use language that suggests that there are two separate processes of mediation, one by means of which the objects that I encounter within experience become more determinate and a second by means of which the self that I encounter there becomes more determinate. On the contrary, there is a single process. To distinguish a color as a relatively determinate royal purple rather than as merely an indeterminate red is at the same time, and in the same process, to become more determinate myself. I am now a self that is capable, as I once was not, of discriminating among reds and of distinguishing royal purple. Similarly, to render indecision more determinate by distinguishing a noble, Hamlet-like indecision from merely ordinary, run-of-the-mill indecision is at the same time to become more determinate myself, for I now perceive my own indecision more clearly. As we have seen,[9] in Hegel's view self and its objects are reciprocally related structures that emerge together in experience. A particular self—say, mine, at the level of consciousness that I have now reached—is as determinate as that self's objects are; and a self's objects are as determinate as that self is.

Common sense and philosophical realism, of course, describe the situation very differently. For instance, if I change my assessment of a man's character after I come to know him better, in the view of common sense and realistic philosophy I am contrasting an initial impression of mine with the facts that I have discovered about the man's character. In Hegel's view, this is a loose way of speaking. The correct comparison is not between what is in my experience (my initial impression) and what is outside my experience (the facts of the man's "true" character); the comparison is *within* my experience. My initial impression is not metaphysically different *in kind* from "knowing him better." "Knowing him better" is simply a later, and presumably more reliable, version of my "initial impression." It too is subject to correction as I get to know the man still better.

But we should not conclude that Hegel was a relativist. In his view, all the different types of mentality, all the different levels of consciousness, fall into a single objective order, or hierarchy. And all the different versions are ultimately incorporated and transcended in something that is not a version but the whole itself:

> The truth is the whole. The whole, however, is merely the essential nature reaching its completeness through the process of its own development. Of the Absolute it must be said that it is essentially a result, that only at the end is it what it is in very truth; and just in that consists its nature, which is to be actual, subject, or self-becoming, self-development.
> . . . .
> That the truth is only realized in the form of system, that substance is essentially subject, is expressed in the idea which represents the Absolute as Spirit (*Geist*)—the grandest conception of all. . . . Spirit is alone Reality. It is the inner being of the world, that which essentially is, and is *per se;* it assumes objective, determinate form, and enters into relations with itself— it is externality (otherness), and exists for self; yet, in this determination,

9 See p. 112. Note that this discussion of Hegel's theory is an application of his own doctrine of the transformation (incorporation and transcendence) of earlier stages in later stages. We began our study of Hegel with a preliminary account of his view of self-consciousness. We then passed on to a consideration of the role that negativity and mediation play in the development of the self and its objects. As a result, the initial version of Hegel's view of self-consciousness has been transformed (incorporated and transcended) in the present, relatively more determinate version.

and in its otherness, it is still one with itself—it is self-contained and self-complete, in itself and for itself at once.[y]

Thus, in Hegel's view, the old dualistic distinction between the self and its objects—which Kant had abandoned at the level of phenomena but which he had retained at the level of noumena, is transformed (incorporated but transcended) in a new monism, the monism of Spirit. But what is Spirit? Our best clue to what it is, is our own experience. And the best analogy is the bud-blossom-fruit sequence. Spirit is a living process; it is propelled by the energy of negation and mediation, in which both selves and their objects are continuously emerging, undergoing development, and being replaced by higher forms of themselves.

> The living substance is that being which is truly subject, or, what is the same thing, is truly realized and actual (*wirklich*) solely in the process of positing itself, or in mediating with its own self its transitions from one state or position, to the opposite. . . . True reality is merely this process of reinstating self-identity, of reflecting into its own self in and from its other. . . . It is the process of its own becoming, the circle which presupposes its end as its purpose, and has its end for its beginning; it becomes concrete and actual only by being carried out, and by the end it involves.[z]

SUMMARY OF THE DOCTRINE OF *THE PHENOMENOLOGY*

This long analysis of the doctrine of *The Phenomenology* is summarized below in a passage from its Introduction, in which many of the themes discussed so far are touched on. Since this Introduction, like everything else Hegel wrote, is difficult to read, a brief synopsis may be helpful. The Introduction begins with an attack on the presuppositions of "criticism," an attack not only on the specific assumptions of Kant in his *Critique* but on the presuppositions of any philosopher who holds (as Locke, for instance, did) that before we try to philosophize we must investigate the powers and limits of the mind. Hegel notes that, since such a philosopher uses the mind in his critical inquiries, he assumes the point at issue: The mind must be at least adequate enough to undertake criticism. But Hegel himself escapes this contradiction by asserting that the criteria for evaluating our judgments emerge in experience and that they are constantly being revised in the course of further experience. This "emerging and being revised" is, of course, nothing but the process of mediation that we have already encountered. To launch the mind on this project is to enter the pathway that leads to science. And science is not simply the knowledge that will be found at the end of the pathway; it is the process in its entirety, in which all earlier stages are included and transformed. Science, indeed, is the completely determinate, *total* system of knowledge. Furthermore, because it is the whole, it is not just knowledge about reality (that is, not a "version of" it); it is that reality itself. In the Absolute, in other words, the distinction between knowledge and reality is transcended.

It is natural to suppose that, before philosophy enters upon its subject proper—namely, the actual knowledge of what truly is—it is necessary to come first to an understanding concerning knowledge, which is looked upon as the instrument by which to take possession of the Absolute, or as the means through which to get a sight of it. . . .

For if knowledge is the instrument by which to get possession of absolute Reality, the suggestion immediately occurs that the application of an instrument to anything does *not* leave it as it is for itself, but rather entails . . . a moulding and alteration of it. Or again, if knowledge is . . . a kind of passive medium through which the light of the truth reaches us, then, here too, we do not receive it as it is in itself, but as it is through and in this medium. In either case we employ a means which immediately brings about the very opposite of its own end; or, rather, the absurdity lies in making use of any means at all. It seems indeed open to us to find in the knowledge of the way in which the *instrument* operates, a remedy for this parlous state; for thereby it becomes possible to remove from the result the part which, in our idea of the Absolute received through that instrument, belongs to the instrument, and thus to get the truth in its purity. But this improvement would, as a matter of fact, only bring us back to the point where we were before. . . . If the Absolute were only to be brought on the whole nearer to us by this agency, without any change being wrought in it, like a bird caught by a lime stick, it would certainly scorn a trick of that sort if it were not in its very nature, and did it not wish to be, beside us from the start. . . . Or, again, if the examination of knowledge, which we represent as a medium, makes us acquainted with the law of its refraction, it is likewise useless to eliminate this refraction from the result. For knowledge is not the divergence of the ray, but the ray itself by which the truth comes in contact with us; and if this be removed, the bare direction or the empty place would alone be indicated.

. . . .

[A] critical examination into the reality of knowing does not seem able to be effected without some presupposition which is laid down as an ultimate criterion. For an examination consists in applying an accepted standard, and, on the final agreement or disagreement wherewith of what is tested, deciding whether the latter is right or wrong; and the standard in general, and so science, were this the criterion, is thereby accepted as the essence or inherently real (*Ansich*). But, here, where science first appears on the scene, neither science nor any sort of standard has justified itself as the essence or ultimate reality; and without this no examination seems able to be instituted.

This contradiction and the removal of it will become more definite if, to begin with, we call to mind the abstract determinations of knowledge and of truth as they are found in consciousness. Consciousness, we find, *distinguishes* from itself something, to which at the same time it *relates* itself; or, to use the current expression, there is something *for* consciousness; and the determinate form of this process of relating, or of there being something for a consciousness, is knowledge. But from this being for another we distinguish being in itself or *per se;* what is related to knowledge is likewise distinguished from it, and posited as also existing outside this relation; the aspect of being *per se* or in itself is called Truth. . . .

If now our inquiry deals with the truth of knowledge, it appears that we are inquiring what knowledge is in itself. But in this inquiry knowledge is *our* object, it is *for us;* and the essential nature (*Ansich*) of knowledge, were this to come to light, would be rather its being *for us;* what we should assert to be its essence would rather be, not the truth of knowledge, but only our knowledge of it. The essence or the criterion would lie in us; and that which was to be compared with this standard, and on which a decision was to be passed as a result of this comparison, would not necessarily have to recognize that criterion.

But the nature of the object which we are examining surmounts this separation, or semblance of separation, and presupposition. Consciousness furnishes its own criterion in itself, and the inquiry will thereby be a comparison of itself with its own self; for the distinction, just made, falls inside itself. . . . The essential fact . . . to be borne in mind throughout the whole inquiry is that both these moments, notion and object, "being for another" and "being in itself," themselves fall within that knowledge which we are examining. . . .

The object, it is true, appears only to be in such wise for consciousness as consciousness knows it. Consciousness does not seem able to get, so to say, behind it as it is, not for consciousness, but in itself, and consequently seems also unable to test knowledge by it. But just because consciousness has, in general, knowledge of an object, there is already present the distinction that the inherent nature, what the object is in itself, is one thing to consciousness, while knowledge, or the being of the object *for* consciousness, is another moment. Upon this distinction, which is present as a fact, the examination turns. Should both, when thus compared, not correspond, consciousness seems bound to alter its knowledge, in order to make it fit the object. But in the alteration of the knowledge, the object itself also, in point of fact, is altered; for the knowledge which existed was essentially a knowledge of the object; with change in the knowledge, the object also becomes different, since it belongs essentially to this knowledge. Hence consciousness comes to find that what formerly to it was the essence is not what is *per se,* or what was *per se* was only *per se for consciousness.* Since, then, in the case of its object consciousness finds its knowledge not corresponding with this object, the object likewise fails to hold out; or the standard for examining is altered when that, whose criterion this standard was to be, does not hold its ground in the course of the examination; and the examination is not only an examination of knowledge, but also of the criterion used in the process.

This dialectic process which consciousness executes on itself—on its knowledge as well as on its object—in the sense that out of it the new and true object arises, is precisely what is termed Experience. . . .

In this treatment of the course of experience, there is an element in virtue of which it does not seem to be in agreement with what is ordinarily understood by experience. The transition from the first object and the knowledge of it to the other object, in regard to which we say we have had experience, was so stated that the knowledge of the first object, the existence *for consciousness* of the first *ens per se*, is itself to be the second object. But it usually seems that we learn by experience the untruth of our first notion by appealing to some other object which we may happen to find casually and externally; so that, in general, what we have is merely the bare and simple apprehension of what is in and for itself. On the view above given, however, the new object is seen to have come about by a transformation or conversion of consciousness itself. This way of looking at the matter is *our* doing, what *we* contribute; by its means the series of experiences through which consciousness passes is lifted into a scientifically constituted sequence. . . . Since what at first appears as object is reduced, when it passes into consciousness, to what knowledge takes it to be, and the implicit nature, the real in itself, becomes what this entity *per se* is *for consciousness;* this latter is the new object, whereupon there appears also a new mode or embodiment of consciousness, of which the essence is something other than that of the preceding mode. It is this circumstance which carries forward the whole succession of the modes or attitudes of consciousness in their own necessity. . . .

In virtue of that necessity this pathway to science is itself *eo ipso* science, and is, moreover, as regards its content, Science of the Experience of Consciousness. . . .

In pressing forward to its true form of existence, consciousness will come to a point at which it lays aside its semblance of being hampered with what is foreign to it, with what is only for it and exists as an other; it will reach a position where appearance becomes identified with essence, where, in consequence, its exposition coincides with just this very point, this very stage of the science proper of mind. And, finally, when it grasps this its own essence, it will connote the nature of absolute knowledge itself.[a]

The System as a Whole: The Triadic Pattern

This, then, is Hegel's intention: "To bring philosophy nearer to the form of science—that goal where it can lay aside the name of *love* of knowledge and be actual *knowledge*—that is what I have set before me."[b] He proposed to bring consciousness up to a level at which the various bits and pieces of information that men have gleaned over the millenia are displayed in their true, systematic, determinate, and necessary relationships. Hegel, of course, regarded *The Phenomenology* as merely the preface to this awesome undertaking, as no more than a prospectus. The "toil" of working out the detail was left to a series of works that were to follow it in due course.

This undertaking was, needless to say, a failure. In the first place, Hegel never completed it. In the second place, the parts he finished certainly fall far short of displaying the necessary and determinate relations that Hegel held science to consist in. For these reasons the system is both less interesting and less important than his more programmatic work, *The Phenomenology*, and Hegel's detailed working-out of his vision has had far less influence on the history of philosophy and of culture than the vision itself. Nevertheless, in order to gain a balanced view of Hegel's philosophy, we must at least sample the system. And sample it is all we can do: Fragmentary though it is, it is too vast to be dealt with adequately in anything less than a long book.

As Hegel points out in *The Phenomenology*, thought advances toward truth by negation. Every assertion ("That color is red") is negated by some other assertion ("No, it is blue"), and these two are then reconciled in a third assertion ("Rather, it is royal purple"). Naturally, the thought that is working out the system also moves in this way; hence the system itself will consist of "triads," all of which will be "collected," ultimately, into an immense, all-inclusive "triad"—Idea-Nature-Spirit.

Further, each of the main subdivisions is composed of "subtriads," each of which displays the same pattern of "triplicity." And these subtriads are themselves systematically related, for each of the syntheses that reconciles two "conflicting" assertions is itself negated by a subsequent assertion, and the new conflict is then reconciled at a higher level. Finally, this triadic movement is not simply linear. It is not merely that an individual synthesis becomes the basis for a new advance; rather, a whole *group* of triads is negated by another group, and this conflict is then reconciled by a third group. Since the synthesis in turn becomes the basis for a new advance, the process results in syntheses of groups of groups of concepts. Taken as a whole, then, the system is an elaborate structure composed of triads, subtriads, and sub-subtriads, all related to one another "dialectically"—that is, each higher level reconciles (incorporates and transcends) discrepancies that are discovered at the next lower level.

A diagram may help:

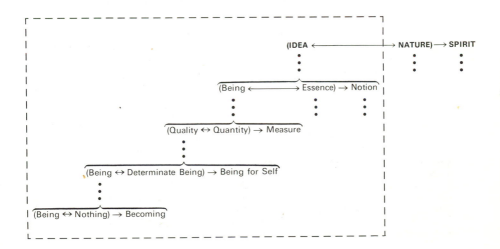

The box indicates the part of the whole "system" that is covered in the *Logic*.[10] A double arrow represents a conflict between two concepts; a single arrow indicates the concept that reconciles the two concepts within the parentheses. A dotted line represents an advance to a higher level, at which point the conflict breaks out again, requiring a new reconciliation. The diagram, of course, shows only a very small segment of the total system; even within the *Logic* the subtriads under Essence and Notion are omitted, and none of the subtriads in the domains of Nature and Spirit is indicated. But the diagram is not intended to be a synopsis; it is designed merely to give a clue as to how the system as a whole "works."

THE *LOGIC*

Let us now look more closely at a few representative segments, beginning with the *Logic*. The main triad of the *Logic* (represented in the diagram at the fourth level from the bottom) is Being-Essence-Notion. Each of these concepts is itself the synthesis of a subordinate triad. Being, for instance, is the synthesis of Quality-Quantity-Measure; Quality, the synthesis of a more subordinate triad, Being-Determinate Being-Being for Self; and Being, the synthesis of a still more subordinate triad, Being-Nothing-Becoming.[11]

BASIC TRIAD: BEING-NOTHING-BECOMING

An examination of the basic triad, Being-Nothing-Becoming, will illustrate the nature of the triadic movement. Let us start with Hegel's own account of this movement.

> Pure BEING makes the beginning: because it is on one hand pure thought, and on the other immediacy itself, simple and indeterminate; and the first beginning cannot be mediated by anything, or be further determined. . . .
>
> When thinking is to begin, we have nothing but thought in its merest indeterminateness: for we cannot determine unless there is both one and another; and in the beginning there is yet no other. The indeterminate, as we here have it, is the blank we begin with, not a featurelessness reached

10 The *Logic* was the only portion of the system that Hegel was able to publish in detail. There are two versions: the *Science of Logic* (1813–16) and the shorter *Encyclopaedia of the Philosophical Sciences* (1817).

11 It should be noted that Hegel used the term "Being" to designate the theses of three different triads. Since the "Being" that is the thesis of the first triad is not the same as the "Being" that is the thesis of the final triad, some philosophers accuse Hegel either of deliberate obfuscation or of extreme carelessness. But of course Hegel held that, though the concepts are different, they are *also* the same. Each time "Being" appears in a triad it has gained an "enriched" and deepened meaning as a result of the various qualifications, conditions, and significations that have been added to it on the way.

by abstraction, not the elimination of all character, but the original feature-lessness which precedes all definite character and is the very first of all. And this we call Being. It is not to be felt, or perceived by sense, or pictured in imagination: it is only and merely thought, and as such it forms the beginning. Essence also is indeterminate, but in another sense: it has traversed the process of mediation and contains implicit the determination it has absorbed. . . .

But this mere Being, as it is mere abstraction, is therefore the absolutely negative: which, in a similarly immediate aspect, is just NOTHING. . . .

Nothing, if it be thus immediate and equal to itself, is also conversely the same as Being is. The truth of Being and of Nothing is accordingly the unity of the two: and this unity is BECOMING.

The proposition that Being and Nothing is the same seems so paradoxical to the imagination or understanding, that it is perhaps taken for a joke. And indeed it is one of the hardest things thought expects itself to do: for Being and Nothing exhibit the fundamental contrast in all its immediacy,—that is, without the one term being invested with any attribute which would involve its connexion with the other. This attribute however, as the above paragraph points out, is implicit in them—the attribute which is just the same in both. . . . It is as correct however to say that Being and Nothing are altogether different, as to assert their unity. The one is *not* what the other is. But since the distinction has not at this point assumed definite shape (Being and Nothing are still the immediate), it is, in the way that they have it, something unutterable, which we merely *mean*. . . .

It may perhaps be said that nobody can form a notion of the unity of Being and Nought. . . . To say that we have no such conception can only mean, that in none of these images do we recognise the notion in question, and that we are not aware that they exemplify it. The readiest example of it is Becoming. Every one has a mental idea of Becoming, and will even allow that it is *one* idea: he will further allow that, when it is analysed, it involves the attribute of Being, and also what is the very reverse of Being, viz. Nothing: and that these two attributes lie undivided in the one idea: so that Becoming is the unity of Being and Nothing. . . .

It remains to note that such phrases as 'Being and Nothing are the same,' or 'The unity of Being and Nothing'—like all other such unities, that of subject and object, and others—give rise to reasonable objection. They misrepresent the facts, by giving an exclusive prominence to the unity, and leaving the difference which undoubtedly exists in it (because it is Being and Nothing, for example, the unity of which is declared) without any express mention or notice. It accordingly seems as if the diversity had been unduly put out of court and neglected. The fact is, no speculative principle can be correctly expressed by any such propositional form, for the unity has to be conceived *in* the diversity, which is all the while present and explicit. 'To become' is the true expression for the resultant of 'To be' and 'Not to be'; it is the unity of the two; but not only is it the unity, it is also inherent unrest,—the unity, which is no mere reference-to-self and therefore without movement, but which, through the diversity of Being and Nothing that is in it, is at war within itself.[c]

Being, according to Hegel, is the most primitive and least determinate, that is, vaguest, of all concepts. When we say merely that something "is," we are asserting the bare minimum that can be said if anything is said at all. We are not saying that the subject being judged about is a substance—or a quality, or a self, or an object, or a cause, or an effect; we are saying merely that it is. Contrariwise, when we make any assertion whatever, however complex or refined, we are also implicitly asserting that the subject being judged about "is." This is why the system, which is to progress continuously from the abstract and indeterminate to the determinate and concrete, begins with "Being."

But as soon as the first concept of the system is formulated, conflict breaks out: The minimum that is asserted when "isness" is claimed is so minimal that it amounts to nothing. Nothing has been said about the item in question. Thus Being "passes over" into its opposite—Nothing. On the basis of traditional Aristotelian logic, we would have to remain at this point, plunged in contradiction until the dispute could be adjudicated by an outside observer, who would decide whether it is correct to assert "Being" or whether it is correct to assert "Nothing." But, as was brought out in the discussion of *The Phenomenology*,[12] Hegel held that no finite assertion is sheerly true or sheerly false. Every assertion contains *some* truth, for unless the person making the assertion is "anti-human," he has detected something that is the case—however one-sided, fragmentary, and partial his perception of it may be. Hence, according to Hegel, what is called for is not a legal verdict that decides *between* conflicting assertions; what is called for is a formula, or concept, that reconciles the assertions by expressing what is true in both without also asserting what is false and one-sided in each. Thus, in the present case, Being and Nothing are reconciled by means of the concept "Becoming."

Becoming reconciles Being and Nothing by incorporating them. Being passes into Nothing: What is this but the concept of decease? Nothing passes into Being: What is this but the concept of origination? Taken together, this double passage yields the concept of Becoming. Notice that Being and Nothing are included in Becoming. They are held in suspension in the concept, not "devoured" by it. A being that merely is, does not become; a nothing that merely is not, does not become. Becoming is both an is and an is-not.

This is the model for all scientific thinking—according to Hegel's view of science. The system (which, taken in its entirety, *is* science) is the continuously expanding and increasingly determinate body of knowledge that results from resolving conflicts into ever larger wholes that incorporate and transcend them. It is impossible to trace this development in detail, as Hegel worked it out in his *Logic*. But we can at least consider the main triad, in which the whole nature of Thought (taken by Hegel as a subjective process occurring in individual minds) is supposedly brought together and synthesized.

12 See p. 110.

MAIN TRIAD: BEING-ESSENCE-NOTION

The same functional relationship obtains among Being-Essence-Notion as among Being-Nothing-Becoming. Let us now try to see how Essence conflicts with Being, and how Notion is the larger whole that includes both. Each of these main concepts, like each of its subconcepts, represents a level of consciousness; it is a way of looking at, or judging about, the world. That is, each is a "category" under which and in terms of which experience is organized. The main category of Being represents what may be called the naïve, or immediate, way of looking at the world. It consists in taking things at their face value, at what they claim to be. (This is true, of course, of all the subconcepts under the main concept Being. All these subconcepts give expression to the impression the world makes on the naïve observer—that things are, that they originate, that they pass away, and so forth.) In contrast to this view of the world is a more critical and sophisticated attitude that recognizes that things are not just what they claim to be. This way of thinking distinguishes, for instance, between substance and accident, between a thing and its properties, between matter and form. All these distinctions are subconcepts under the main concept Essence; each involves distinguishing between what a thing "really" is ("in itself") and what it appears to be ("for" some mind). Essence is that which, though not directly present to us, is mediated by what is directly present. Thus, if Being is immediate, Essence is mediate. And Notion is the synthesis in which these opposites are at once retained and transcended. The nature of this relationship may be indicated by calling Notion *self*-mediate.

The following comparison may be helpful: A high-school graduate who expects to be admitted to a college on the basis of his own estimate of his abilities and without having submitted (in triplicate) birth certificate, health certificate, transcript of record, and numerous other documents, is very naïve. He is operating at the level of Being. A dean of admissions who believes in the infallibility of the Scholastic Aptitude Test, and who never admits a candidate who falls below the minimum score set by his institution, is operating at the level of Essence. He distinguishes between appearance (the candidate's claims) and reality (the test scores), but he fails to see that the test scores themselves must be tested. To operate at the level of Notion would be (in terms of the analogy) to use the tests while recognizing that they are instruments, not absolutes—to use them, that is, but to check them against what the candidate says about himself, against the impression he makes in an interview, and so on.

In a word, at the level of Essence various sceptical doubts arise—for example, "Can we know the really real?" "Are we in contact only with appearance?" —that never occur to a mind thinking at the level of Being. At the level of Notion all these doubts are resolved, because we see that the distinctions on which they are based are made by Thought itself and are only distinctions within Thought.

At the level of Notion we do not, however, lapse back into the naïve confidence we had at the level of Being. We experience at this level neither dogmatic, uncritical certainty nor dogmatic, uncritical doubt. Rather, we feel a sceptical kind of confidence. If the tests are not infallible, they are at least reasonably reliable. Let us therefore use them; they are on the average better than an impressionistic gamble. But let us also be constantly alert to improve them as we use them.

As another example, compare (1) the freedom of arbitrariness ("Do what you will"), (2) the will restrained by rules and laws, and (3) the will that chooses the rules it follows—that does what it wills but wills to be lawful. The latter, which Kant called the self-legislative will, corresponds to Hegel's self-mediate Notion.

The concept of Notion[13] is derived in the following way. One of the subcategories of Essence is cause-and-effect. According to Hegel, we start out by thinking of an effect as different from its cause, but we soon see that the effect is in a sense identical with its cause, though at the same time different from it. That is, the concept of cause-and-effect "collapses" into the concept of reciprocity.

As an example, consider the relation between philosophical theory and the general culture. We operate at the level of *raisonnement* if we believe that we have to choose, for instance, between saying either (1) that a change in the general culture (such as the emergence of the Romantic style) caused a change in philosophical theory (such as the abandonment of Kant's sharp distinction between phenomena and noumena) or (2) that this change in philosophical theory caused the change in taste. Hegel denied that we are ever confronted with such a simple choice. He held that it is true (but one-sided) to say that philosophical changes cause changes in the general culture, and that it is also true (but equally one-sided) to say that changes in the general culture bring about changes in philosophical theory. He held, in short, that in such a situation A is the cause of B *and* B is the cause of A. This is the concept of reciprocity—a category that includes, while it transcends, the lower category of cause-and-effect.

Reciprocity "passes over" into Notion in the following way:

> We must not let the two sides [A is the cause of B; B is the cause of A] rest in their state of mere given facts, but recognise them . . . for factors of a third and higher, which is the notion and nothing else. To make, for example, the manners of the Spartans the cause of their constitution and their constitution conversely the cause of their manners, may no doubt be in a way correct. But, as we have comprehended neither the manners nor the constitution of the nation, the result of such reflections can never be final or satisfactory. The satisfactory point will be reached only when these two, as well as all other, special aspects of Spartan life and Spartan history are seen to be founded in this notion.[d]

13 See p. 117.

Just as all the subcategories of Essence show the character of mediation and all the subcategories of Being the character of immediacy, so all the subcategories of Notion show the character of self-mediation. It is impossible, however, to follow through the whole dialectical movement as worked out by Hegel. We must be content with the fact that it terminates in the category "Absolute Idea," which incorporates (while it transcends) *all* the distinctions and subcategories included in the *Logic*. It is therefore obviously the "richest" and most determinate of all categories and thus contrasts most markedly with the initial category of Being, the most barren and least determinate category. By the same token, Absolute Idea is the most self-mediate of all categories. In fact, since it includes all the others, it is the only category that is fully *self*-mediate. All the others are mediated by a category in some sense other than themselves.

FINAL TRIAD: IDEA-NATURE-SPIRIT

We have now reached the end of the *Logic* (admittedly by a series of gigantic jumps, which inevitably give a distorted impression of the terrain traversed). But from the point of view of the Hegelian system, logic taken as a whole is only the basis for a final, all-inclusive triad, Idea-Nature-Spirit. This final triad repeats on a more massive scale the movement that is supposed to be effected in the first, most elementary synthesis. Just as Nothing and Being are at once the same and different, and Becoming is their synthesis, so Idea passes over into Nature and Nature into Idea, and Spirit is *their* synthesis.

Let us see if Hegel's meaning can be made at all clear. So far discussion has centered on concepts and categories, and it has been tacitly assumed that these are the "ideas" of a mind thinking about an objective, independent world. Taken as Idea, thought has an other, an object; this other is Nature. At this stage, thought and its other are opposed and in contradiction. This, Hegel believed, is the contrast with which, ever since Descartes, philosophy had been confronted—the contrast between knowing subject and object known. In Hegel's view, this contradiction exists only at a rather low level of consciousness. Just as the dean of admissions can advance to a level of thought at which he becomes properly critical of test scores, so philosophers can arrive at a level of thought at which thought and its object are identical (and at the same time different). Idea and Nature are transcended, but not lost, in Spirit. Spirit, in a word, is Thought in the full sense; it is thought knowing itself not merely as thought, but as thought-of-object.

This elucidation may itself require elucidation. Let us consider it in less Hegelian terms. How, we may ask, is it possible to hold (as Hegel did) that thought *is* its object? Is there any difference more obvious or more fundamental than the difference between my idea about a particular thing (say, *Hamlet*) and the thing (*Hamlet*) about which I am thinking? Here am I reflecting on *Hamlet*, and I am thinking about an "object." But what *is* my present object except my (and, of course, other people's) earlier thoughts about (or "versions of")

Hamlet? I am thinking, for instance, about my "impressions" of the play when I last saw it or read it. And at every stage this process repeats itself: It is always a part of myself that I am engaged in thinking about.

This may suggest that Hegel was a "subjective idealist" of the kind Berkeley ought logically to have been. It would seem, that is, that in Hegel's view the world is *my* idea. But this overlooks the doctrine of *The Phenomenology*—namely, that "I" am transcended as well as "my object." [14] Or, to put this into the terminology of the *Logic*, the question of whether other knowers really exist or whether they are only ideas of mine is but a sceptical doubt that occurs at the level of Essence. Just as the distinction between knower and known is transcended in the Absolute, so the distinction between this knower and that one, between me and thee, is transcended.

Why did Hegel claim that reality is of the nature of thought? Because he believed that reality—the all-inclusive whole—*is* that dialectical movement into opposition and transcendence that we have been examining. And this dialectical movement is fairly called "thought," because (according to Hegel) it is precisely what is occurring in men when they think. My thought, *qua* mine, is simply one phase in this larger movement. In fact, nature as *my* object and Nature as the totality of otherness are both simply that "passage into opposition" that characterizes Thought. And just as I transcend my object in knowing it, so Thought transcends its object (in which I am of course included). This transcendence (the synthesis of Idea and Nature) is Spirit.

Thus Nature, the second main section of the Hegelian system, is the otherness of Idea. What natural science offers us is merely one version of reality. What it holds to be ultimate fact—the externality, objectivity, and factuality of the world it investigates—is merely one phase, or level, in the life of consciousness. This interpretation of nature gave Hegel a novel solution to the old problem of the place of values in a world of fact. Descartes had attempted to solve this problem by a substantival dualism; Kant by a cognitive dualism. As a thoroughgoing monist, Hegel could not have allowed that any form of dualism is ultimate. Since there is only one world, facts and values are the same—yet, of course, they are also different. The perspective from which the world seems to consist in facts-spread-out-in-space-and-time is a rather limited sort of perspective; that from which the world seems to be values-organized-teleologically includes the "lower" one while transcending it. But it, too, is only one perspective. It is important to understand that these perspectives, or versions, are not just *different;* they are related to each other dialectically. [15] Since the scientific perspective is included in the valuational perspective, it cannot possibly be superior to it. The latter does not deny the limited truth contained in the former; it illumines it and makes us understand it better, just as a second or third reading of *Hamlet*

14 See pp. 113–15.
15 See p. 110. "Science" is an ambiguous term in Hegel's vocabulary. Generally speaking, when he criticizes science as inadequate, he is referring to the natural science of his own day; when he looks forward to "true" science, he is equating science with philosophical knowledge.

makes us understand the play better. Hence, instead of our having to make a place for value in a world of fact, facts have to find a place for themselves in a world that is more truly understood in terms of purposes and values. Hegel thus believed that philosophers are quite justified in criticizing and correcting the basic concepts of science, for (in his view) philosophy represents a higher level of consciousness than science.

As has been said, Hegel's attempt to put science in its place was not very successful. Unfortunately, this failure has brought his whole view into unnecessary disrepute—unnecessary because it is possible to distinguish between (1) the detailed relationships Hegel supposed himself to be deriving by means of his dialectic and (2) the underlying thesis about the nature of thought and its objects. The latter point may prove to need correction, but it is not necessarily involved in the collapse of the triads that constitute Hegel's "philosophy of nature."

Let us pass on from Nature to Spirit. Spirit (which, as we have seen, is the synthesis of the main triad of the whole system) is itself divided into a subtriad, and this in turn is divided into series of subtriads in accordance with the now familiar Hegelian method. It is impossible to pursue all the ramifications of these triadic developments, but the broad outlines of Spirit may be indicated. According to Hegel, at the level of Spirit we are studying mind—not the abstraction of a concrete thought thinking an other (Logic) nor the opposite abstraction of the other that is being thought about (Nature), but the synthesis of both.

First, in a group of categories called "Subjective Spirit," Hegel considered the inner aspects of concrete mind—a field that today would be called psychology. He held that these categories, taken together, are all deficient and one-sided because they are too "immediate." Accordingly, they are negated by another set of categories—those of Objective Spirit. These in turn overcompensate for the immediacy of Subjective Spirit by an equally one-sided emphasis on mediacy. That is, the categories of Objective Spirit are also concerned with mind, but they are concerned not with mind as it looks to itself on the inside (introspection) but, and exclusively, with mind as it is in its external relations to other minds. In a word, these categories are concerned with what today would be called sociology, ethics, and politics.

The conflict between Subjective Spirit and Objective Spirit is resolved in a new synthesis—Absolute Spirit. The subcategories of this new group are concerned with the highest levels and manifestations of mind—art, religion, and philosophy. In philosophy, especially, we are supposed to have reached a level of consciousness in which knowledge is absolutely articulate and determinate. This is the self-knowledge of a self that has passed out of the finitude in which it is limited by, and contrasted with, an other; but it is not the empty self-knowledge of Aristotle's god, who knows no other and no diversity. To grasp what Hegel means, put Aristotle's god into the world, or rather, let him *be* the world, and let him know himself in all this diversity and totality. His knowledge would then be as complete as that of a transcendent god, and his nature would be as various and complex as that of an immanent god.

This absolute self-knowledge, to which the final triads of the Hegelian system are devoted, is perhaps too esoteric a doctrine for us. Let us return to the somewhat "lower" ground of the categories of Objective Spirit and briefly examine Hegel's social and political theory.

Social Philosophy

In Hegel's view, social philosophy is a purely theoretical undertaking. It is the systematic exposition, that is, the triadic derivation, of the various concepts relevant to this field. Hegel sought to show that such concepts as property, contract, right, police, marriage and the family, and the state form triads, each of which consists in a stage of immediacy followed by a stage of mediacy and a synthesis of the two in a third stage of self-mediation. Since "freedom" is the last category deduced in Subjective Spirit, it becomes the lowest of the present movement. Thus, according to Hegel's system, social philosophy is concerned throughout with human freedom. Each new triad of this section reveals a progressively determinate, and hence more adequate, conception of freedom.

In the first stage of the progression freedom is conceived of in the character of immediacy. This, according to Hegel, is the concept of personality, and at this level the moral problem appears merely as the problem of maintaining certain abstract rights conceived of as belonging to us as persons. Though the general imperative of right can be stated positively ("Be a person and respect others as persons"), Hegel held its negative form to be more fundamental—"Do not infringe personality and what personality entails." At this level, that is, the distinction between persons and things-that-are-not-persons is regarded as fundamental. The former are ends, just as we are. The latter are not ends and hence can be treated as means. Whatever destiny and soul they may acquire is derived from the fact that someone "puts his will into them" and thereby makes them his. Over whatever things a person has appropriated in this way he has an "absolute right"—at this level and subject to the reservation that all such abstract rights are modified at a higher level of thought. Property relations at the level of abstract right are governed by contract, to which (accordingly) Hegel devoted another section of Objective Spirit. This leads to a definition of "wrong" as the violation of contract.

All these concepts are relatively immediate and are negated by a new set of concepts that are relatively mediate. Thus the distinction between persons and things, which seems so important at the level of immediacy, is true as far as it goes; but it is an oversimplification and must be corrected (made more determinate) by distinguishing between inner and outer. So far, that is, we have been considering a level of consciousness that conceives of personality in a simple, uncomplicated way—moral goodness consists in keeping contracts (as between persons); moral badness in violating them. Hegel then proceeded to the negative stage, in which personality is seen to be not simple but complex, and not merely complex but often divided. At this stage will is seen to issue not merely in acts that are lawful or unlawful, but in *motivated* acts. And when we take motives into account we see that acts may be morally bad and legal, or morally good and illegal. Here we reach the level of Morality, in distinction from the lower level of Abstract Right.

In Hegel's view, it is wrongdoing that brings forcefully to our attention the difference between inner and outer. We would not feel an act to be *wrong* if we did not identify ourselves with the law we are breaking. But we also obviously identify ourselves with the breaking of it; otherwise we would not break it. Hence the self, which originally presented a solid front to the world, must admit itself divided. It finds in itself two loyalties—a loyalty to a lower and more immediate end and a loyalty to a higher and less immediate end. When this happens, we have advanced to the "moral standpoint."

The synthesis of Morality and Abstract Right is what Hegel called the Ethical Life. Although Hegel's reasoning here is obscure he seems to be arguing (1) that the notion of right is negated by the notion of good, (2) that these apparently opposing principles have to be brought into harmony in any really adequate account of the moral life, and (3) that the way to do this is to see that our finite, individual will and its private good are transcended in the larger will and larger good of the society of which we are organs. At any rate, this synthesis has brought us from a level of consciousness at which thought about conduct is limited to individuals and their relations to other individuals (for example, contract) to a level at which individuals are seen to be only parts, and at which their true good, and the truly moral (that is, "ethical") life, consists in sharing loyally and fully in the good of the whole.

Political Theory

At this point in the development of the system we pass from ethical theory to political theory. That is, Ethical Life, the synthesis we have just examined, consists in a series of triads that once again traverse the movement from immediacy through mediacy to self-mediation; but this time the concepts involved are concepts in what today would be called political theory. Hegel begins with the Family, finds its negation to be Civil Society, and finally achieves another synthesis, the State. In order to indicate how Hegel conceived of and handled the problems of society, a part of his account of the Family, which (it will be noted) consists in its turn of a subtriad, is quoted below.

> The family, as the immediate substantiality of mind, is specifically charac-
> terized by love, which is mind's feeling of its own unity. Hence in a family,

one's frame of mind is to have self-consciousness of one's individuality within this unity as the absolute essence of oneself, with the result that one is in it not as an independent person but as a member.

. . . .

The family is completed in these three phases:

(a) *Marriage*, the form assumed by the concept of the family in its immediate phase;

(b) *Family Property and Capital* (the external embodiment of the concept) and attention to these;

(c) *The Education of Children and the Dissolution of the Family*.

Marriage, as the immediate type of ethical relationship, contains first, the moment of physical life; and since marriage is a *substantial* tie, the life involved in it is life in its totality, i.e. as the actuality of the race and its life-process. But, secondly, in self-consciousness the natural sexual union—a union purely inward or implicit and for that very reason *existent* as purely external—is changed into a union on the level of mind, into self-conscious love.

On the subjective side, marriage may have a more obvious source in the particular inclination of the two persons who are entering upon the marriage tie, or in the foresight and contrivance of the parents, and so forth. But its objective source lies in the free consent of the persons, especially in their consent to make themselves one person, to renounce their natural and individual personality to this unity of one with the other. From this point of view, their union is a self-restriction, but in fact it is their liberation, because in it they attain their substantive self-consciousness.

The ethical aspect of marriage consists in the parties' consciousness of this unity as their substantive aim, and so in their love, trust and common sharing of their entire existence as individuals. When the parties are in this frame of mind and their union is actual, their physical passion sinks to the level of a physical moment, destined to vanish in its very satisfaction. On the other hand, the spiritual bond of union secures its rights as the substance of marriage and thus rises, inherently indissoluble, to a plane above the contingency of passion and the transience of particular caprice.

. . . .

In essence marriage is monogamy because it is personality—immediate exclusive individuality—which enters into this tie and surrenders itself to it; and hence the tie's truth and inwardness (i.e. the subjective form of its substantiality) proceeds only from the mutual, whole-hearted, surrender of this personality.

Further, marriage results from the free surrender by both sexes of their personality—a personality in every possible way unique in each of the parties. Consequently, it ought not to be entered by two people identical in stock who are already acquainted and perfectly known to one another; for individuals in the same circle of relationship have no special personality of their own in contrast with that of others in the same circle. On the contrary, the parties should be drawn from separate families and their personalities should be different in origin. Since the very conception of marriage is that it is a

freely undertaken ethical transaction, not a tie directly grounded in the
physical organism and its desires, it follows that the marriage of blood-
relations runs counter to this conception and so also to genuine natural
feeling.[e]

As the thesis of a triad, the Family is "immediate," in contrast to the
mediateness of Civil Society. In calling the family immediate, Hegel apparently
had in mind the fact that it lacks the formal, organizational structure of a larger
group like a trade union or a town meeting. In addition, the Family is dependent
on the larger groups of which it is a part. This dependence (and incompleteness)
is the basis for Hegel's passage to Civil Society, the Family's "other." Here, in
the concept of Civil Society, we have arrived at the level of thought that
characterized eighteenth-century political theorizing: Every citizen is a distinct,
individual entity who enters into a compact with other individuals for benefits
he expects to gain thereby. Instead of one good (the family's), there are a plurality
of goods (those of all the citizens). Instead of natural and unconscious relations,
there is an explicit and formal organization. But these relations are conceived,
at the level of Civil Society, to be merely external links that bring together a
number of men, each of whom is a complete and autonomous individual.

What Hegel called a Civil Society most people would simply call a state.
But Hegel reserved the latter term for the superior type of organization that syn-
thesizes (incorporates and transcends) both those intimate (immediate) relations
that are found in the family and those abstract mediate relations that are found
in Civil Society. Thus the State completes the triad. Naturally, the transition to
the State is not abrupt.

Civil Society anticipates in primitive form the kind of organization and
relationships that are fully articulated only in the State. For instance, consider
what happens when citizens become interested in organizations like the Red Cross
or the League of Women Voters. When, as people say, they have put enough
of themselves into the organization, they identify themselves with its fortunes
and find in its successes satisfaction that has nothing to do with private gain
or profit. Thus, even in Civil Society, even in the "externality of the will,"
organizations develop in which this externality is absorbed—organizations in
which individuals find their good in that of the larger whole of which they feel
a part. In this way, we reach the State, which is the supreme type of social order.

It might be supposed that the logic of Hegel's dialectic would have led him
to sweep past the State to incorporate it in a still larger society, of which states
themselves would be organs, and which would include, eventually, the whole
human race. Why, then, did Hegel stop with the State? Hegel could have replied
that he was not writing prophesy; he was developing a system based on the
situation as it existed in his own time, and the national territorial state was the
largest political unit then in existence. But this answer is not satisfactory. To
begin with, in the 1820's there were no "states" in Hegel's special sense of the
term. Indeed, if he had confined himself to description based on the political

situation as it existed in his day he would have had to limit himself to civil societies. However, Hegel was not really doing descriptive political science. Because he found the Prussia of his day congenial, he tended to idealize it, and idealizing it meant (he believed) identifying it with the State. Finally, if Hegel was going to import ideals into what purported to be a systematic exposition of the actual, there were better ideals to introduce. The national territorial unit was an inadequate type of political organization. Every such unit was then, and still is, limited in just the same way as the Family (though to a lesser degree). It would seem that, just as men have to go outside their families to find their true good, so they have to go outside the State. Economic and political developments since Hegel's death have doubtless made this fact more obvious than it was in his day. Nevertheless, his own dialectic as well as the plain facts of life at that time should have shown him that he could not stop with the State. Indeed, Dante had argued more than four centuries earlier that there must be a single human society, because—to put his case in Hegelian terms—security could not tolerate an "other."

Hegel did not merely contend that the State is complete; he also argued that it is the "true" individual. The State, that is, is not merely a collection of independent individuals; its members are related to it as organs are related to the organism of which they are parts. Just as the stomach's significance lies in the contribution it makes to the life of the body, and just as husband and wife lose their personal identities in their marriage,[16] so the citizens of a Civil Society lose their independence in the unity of the State. Hegel did not hold merely that some citizens do, as a matter of fact, identify with the State, just as some individuals identify themselves with their family; he also held that they *ought* to do so, and that if they do not they should be forced to do so, for their own good.

This brings us to the question of consent, which is a central problem for political theories that take the concepts of individual freedom and *laissez faire* seriously—that is, for political theories at the level of *raisonnement*. This question can best be approached via a late eighteenth-century criticism that anticipated much of Hegel's view (without, of course, the apparatus of the system).

Rousseau (1712–78) was temperamentally out of tune with the Enlightenment, the age during which he lived. He held that as long as sovereignty rests in a *plurality* of distinct wills it is necessary either to wait for unanimity (in which case the state will break down through inability to act) or to permit the majority to compel the minority. But does not the latter alternative destroy the moral basis of the state? Rousseau thought that it did, and to get around this difficulty he formulated the doctrine of what he called the "general will."

The "general will" is to be contrasted with the "will of all," or the merely coincidental agreement of a group of individualists. A group of wills is general

---

16 See p. 136. The State differs from the Family in that, whereas the latter's unity is a spontaneous and unconscious development, the former's is the result of deliberate and self-conscious legislation.

when each individual will aims at the common good. It is possible, of course, that the general will and the will of all might result in the same action, for it might just happen that each individualist sees that the way to obtain his private end is to agree to the action in question. But Rousseau held that agreement is much more likely to occur when everyone is trying to decide whether or not a proposed action (for example, an increase in the income tax) is for the good of all, rather than when everyone is trying to decide whether such an action is to his own advantage.

And quite apart from this practical advantage, Rousseau maintained that the general will, unlike the will of all, is a true consensus. It is what everyone really wants—the minority as well as the majority. Hence, even though the minority has to go along with the majority, it is not being compelled to do so. Hence, finally, the moral basis of the state is not destroyed. Suppose ten per cent of the voters think that lowering the tax exemption will increase the revenue and thereby promote the common good, while ninety per cent think that raising the surtax will promote the common good. Obviously, on democratic principles, the surtax will be raised; but those who lost (who voted against raising the surtax) and those who won all want, and get, exactly the same thing. For they do not differ about the *end;* they differ only about the *means.* And since they all get the end they want (promotion of the common good) they are all free, and no one is compelled. There are obviously many difficulties with this view. For one thing, it assumes that what the majority thinks is for the common good always really is for the common good—a view that is optimistic to say the least.

Hegel's theory is hardly more than a reformulation of the general-will doctrine in his own terminology, a reformulation designed to answer this and other objections. When the relations among citizens come to be self-mediate (instead of merely immediate or merely mediate), the result is the sort of political organization that Hegel called the State. It is also what Rousseau called the general will. This follows because at the level of the State the citizens, who formerly perceived themselves as separate and autonomous individuals, have come to see that they are but the organs of the one true individual, the State. Accordingly, what the State wills is also willed by them, as its organs; there is no problem of consent, for there is no compulsion. What appears to be compulsion (what *is* compulsion at lower levels of political organization) is only the process of inducing a man to choose what he really wants, in distinction from what he mistakenly believes he wants. Compulsion is exercised only against his finite, transitory will, which, truly *understood,* is absorbed, and transcended, in the State's will. The citizen is not being forced against his will, because his real will is what the State wants for him. But why is what the State wants what he really wants? Because what the State wants is his true good. And why is what the State wants his true good? Because he is a part of, an organ of, this larger organism. Its good is his—and not merely in the sense that the individual's good is his family's, for here the transcendence, or absorption, is only partial. The father has goods of his own, not identical with those of his son. In the State the absorption of the citizen is complete; nothing survives that is good for him in isolation.

Of course, this is at best only an ideal, for in no actual state, in Hegel's day or in ours, has such complete absorption and transcendence of individual wills been achieved. (Totalitarian regimes, of course, have gone a long way toward repressing dissent and individual differences, but this is not what Hegel had in mind.) The problem is that the larger the political unit, and the more economic, social, and cultural diversity included in it, the less likely that individual differences will be transcended. Realizing this, Rousseau argued in favor of very small communities on the model of the Greek city-state. But Hegel thought in terms of large, "modern" political units; and, as was pointed out earlier, he ought to have thought in terms of still larger ones. Hence the doctrine of the general will, whatever its theoretical value, does not seem particularly relevant to the actual conditions of modern political life.

Evaluation of Hegel's Philosophy

The history of commentary on Hegel's philosophy is itself an illustration of Hegelian dialectic. It has developed by a process that can fairly be called negation. During most of the nineteenth century commentators were chiefly impressed by Hegel's system, which seemed to answer a deep need in nineteenth-century society. As the world was becoming more and more complex, as more and more diversity in belief and in behavior came to light, it was obvious that the old absolutes were being exploded—not only the absolute proposed by the Church but that put forward by the eighteenth-century philosophers. To many people Hegel's system seemed to offer a new and viable absolute; that is, it seemed to claim that a complete account of the universe is possible, an account in which all the diversity is included but in which it is transcended in a final unity.[17] For such people the *Logic*, the only completed part of the system, was Hegel's most important work.

More recently, however, the system has been de-emphasized, and *The Phenomenology* is now considered the core of Hegel's theory. Today critics are inclined to think of the system as merely a sort of classificatory scheme by means of which Hegel provisionally arranged the various topics on which he chose to lecture.[18] From this point of view, the system has hardly more metaphysical significance than does a professor's decision about how to arrange the books in his library.

---

17 This claim to provide certainty and totality also explains to a large extent the appeal of other systems launched in the nineteenth century—Marxism, for instance, and Haeckel's "monistic cosmology." See pp. 184–86 and 199–200.

18 See Walter Kaufmann, *Hegel* (Doubleday, New York, 1965), pp. 225–53.

Evidence to support both these interpretations can be found in Hegel's work. On the one hand, Hegel certainly knew that the system he was working out was the result of his own thought, that is, a thought process occurring in a particular, individual mind. And he knew that he occupied a particular locus in space and time—the universe, Hegel was aware, existed before he was born and would continue to exist after he died. Social, political, and cultural developments would occur in the future, the nature of which he explicitly disclaimed the ability or the desire to predict. Hegel left it to later philosophers to systematize these developments, just as he himself was systematizing knowledge as of the 1820's.

On the other hand, Hegel repeatedly equated his system with scientific knowledge, which he defined as necessary and completely determinate. He did not deny, of course, that the system had emerged at a particular point in time; but he felt that its emergence in this form and at this time was itself a "moment" (phase) in a cosmic system.

> Our epoch is a birth-time, and a period of transition. The spirit of man has broken with the old order of things hitherto prevailing, and with old ways of thinking. . . . it is here as in the case of the birth of a child; after a long period of nutrition in silence, the continuity of the graduate growth in size, of quantitative change, is suddenly cut short by the first breath drawn—there is a break in the process, a qualitative change—and the child is born. In like manner the spirit of the time, growing slowly and quietly ripe for the new form it is to assume, disintegrates one fragment after another of the structure of its previous world. . . . This gradual crumbling to pieces . . . is interrupted by the sunrise, which, in a flash and at a single stroke, brings to view the form and structure of the new world.[f]

Viewed in this way, the system that Hegel worked out is much more than a convenient classificatory scheme. This system (with a small "s") reflects the articulations of the System (with a capital "S") that generated it. And the System, taken as a whole, is a cosmic process in which Mind generates its other, Nature, and then reabsorbs it. For instance, in the Introduction to the *Logic* Hegel states that this work is "the account of God as he is in his eternal essence before the creation of nature and any finite spirit." Here Hegel sounds like Plotinus, for whom the universe was a sequence of emanations issuing from, and returning to, the Absolute. Thus Hegel's own thought, as he was thinking out the system, was the Absolute thinking in him; he is a part of the process he describes.

Hegel's concept of the *Weltgeist*—a term that is variously translated as "world spirit" or "universal mind"—fits in with this interpretation of his philosophy. Hegel seems to have held that individual minds, insofar as they succeed in thinking scientifically, are incorporated in the universal mind. That is, as individual minds come to think scientifically, they undergo a development that exactly recapitulates the development of the universal mind. In so doing, they become "moments" in this mind.

> The task of conducting the individual mind from its unscientific standpoint to that of science had to be undertaken in its general sense; we had to contemplate the formative development of the universal individual, of self-conscious spirit. As to the relation between these two [the particular and general individual], every moment as it gains concrete form and its own proper shape and appearance, finds a place in the life of the universal individual. The particular individual is incomplete mind. . . .[g]

Thus evidence to support both interpretations of Hegel's position can be found. But which is the "true" Hegel? Readers of Hegel will know the answer to this question: Both interpretations are correct with regard to what they assert; both are false with regard to what they deny. Each negates the other precisely because each is a limited and one-sided truth. What is required, then, is a more determinate version of Hegel's position, one that incorporates (while transcending) these two interpretations. And this more adequate interpretation will eventually need to be incorporated in a still more adequate interpretation. And so on.

But how do we know that more and more determinate interpretations are possible? Perhaps Hegel simply and flatly contradicted himself. This question can be generalized as follows: In Hegel's view, all conflicts and discrepancies are amenable to harmonization—but what is the evidence that reality is through-and-through rational, in the Hegelian sense of "rational"? What is the guarantee that all those partial "versions of" can eventually be reconciled in something that is no longer a version of reality but is reality itself? Hegel would doubtless have replied with another question: What exactly are you asking for when you demand a "guarantee" that the universe is rational? Reason can guarantee specific truths, but what sort of guarantee can be given for reason other than the evidence it provides for specific truths? This is what Hegel's remark, quoted earlier, about "anti-human" means.[19] Men must have faith in the rationality of the universe; to lack this faith is not to be a man. Thus the business of philosophy is not to offer guarantees of men's deepest convictions; rather, it is to systematize and clarify these beliefs.

Very well. We may agree that it is not the business of philosophy to prove that the universe is rational; however, it is the business of philosophy to examine what "being rational" entails. Unfortunately, Hegel never made this clear. Although he constantly asserted that rationality involves necessity, he never gave a formal account of what (in his view) necessity is, and the parts of the system that he worked out in detail suggest that his idea of necessity was unfortunately very "indeterminate."

Hegel's system purports to make sense of the actual situation (the state of knowledge as of the 1820's) by showing that all accumulated data about history, anthropology, physics, and psychology—all the bits and pieces of theory and

19 See p. 109.

of fact—are systematically interrelated and in harmony. But in "demonstrating" this harmony, Hegel played fast and loose with the actual facts. Indeed, instead of making sense of the actual by uncovering the systematic interrelations among data, the system became a covert criterion by which Hegel decided what is "really" actual and eliminated what did not fit. As we have seen, Hegel tended to gloss over the actual facts about the Prussian state of 1820 and to interpret it in the light of his ideal of what the "State" ought to be. A similar confusion can be seen in his discussion of the Family. Hegel took it for granted that marriage is (that is, "ought to be") monogamous. But he never showed—indeed, he never could have shown—monogamy to be necessary.[20] If Hegel had been a professor in Salt Lake City in the 1870's, instead of in Berlin in the 1820's, he would doubtless have held that polygamy is "necessary."

This criticism of Hegel is not intended to suggest that it was a mistake for him to aim at systematizing knowledge of, for instance, sociology. Quite the contrary. A sociology that is drowned in data is not much better off than one lost in the clouds. But such a system should grow out of an empirical study of actual behavior and should derive its concepts from that study. This, of course, is exactly what Hegel repeatedly stated in *The Phenomenology*.[21] Thought, he pointed out, should not start with a ready-made set of abstract ideas. For this reason Hegel had nothing but contempt for *raisonnement*. The level of "notion" is more adequate than that of *raisonnement* precisely because it reflects the concrete life of the actual object of thought. All this is admirable, of course. But as the system was worked out in detail, it became a Procrustean bed into which the empirical materials were forced. This is true even though in Hegel's day psychology and sociology hardly existed as empirical sciences and there were precious few data to systematize.

Since Hegel's death, as data have accumulated at an exponential rate and as the difficulty of systematizing them has enormously increased, the artificiality of Hegel's specific system has become more obvious. Hegel, it must be allowed, gravely underestimated the problem of synthesis. Despite his frequent reference to the richness and variety of the actual, he was a monist at heart. This preference for monism over pluralism is also reflected in his failure to take account of the diversity of wills that exist in any large-scale political organization. Just as it may be that the only way to achieve unanimity in the state is by repression, so it may be that the only way to achieve an overall, all-inclusive scientific system is by an arbitrary forcing of the data into the theory. These were costs that Hegel would have regarded as too high to pay, but a persistent ambiguity in his terminology saved him from seeing and having to face this difficult choice.

This ambiguity appears in his use of the term *wirklich*, which Hegel repeatedly equated with the rational. *Wirklich* can be translated as "actual," in which

20 It might be possible to show that a statistically significant correlation holds between monogamy and certain parent-child relations that Hegel considered desirable. But this is quite another thing, of course.
21 See p. 115.

event the assertion that it is the rational is palpably false. Much of what is actual, far from being rational, is arbitrary—as Hegel well knew. However, *wirklich* can also be translated as "real." In this event the assertion is a tautology. The question of what kind of relation exists between the rational-real and the actual thus remains to be dealt with; but because Hegel shifted between this and the other meaning of *wirklich*, it seemed to him that he had answered it satisfactorily.

There are, then, serious difficulties with the Hegelian system, and these difficulties persist whether we interpret it as a simple classificatory system or as a cosmic drama. Let us therefore return to what was called, earlier, the "vision" of *The Phenomenology*. *The Phenomenology* was prophetic in that it set out what were to become central themes of twentieth-century culture. First, it brought into prominence the concept of mediation, with all that it implies about the inevitable distance between knower and known, between the self and its objects, including the self itself. This concept fits in with one of the major concerns of our time, as reflected in Dostoevsky's description of underground man—the impossibility of attaining complete self-knowledge, the alienation of the individual both from himself and from his society.

Second, *The Phenomenology* put forward the view that there are a variety of types of consciousness, each of which is reflected in a different version of reality. It is true that most people today would be sceptical of Hegel's claim that all this variety constitutes a hierarchy culminating in a special type of consciousness that, far from being merely another version, is itself truth and reality. But Hegel's recognition that each type of consciousness is reflected in the social, political, and economic institutions—as well as in the philosophy, science, art, and religion—of a given epoch, has influenced men's thinking in profound ways and may be said to be one of the marks that distinguishes us and our time from every other. To mention examples that range from the momentous to the trivial: It laid the basis for the intellectual revolutions launched by Marx and Freud; it also made possible the division of this history of philosophy into a series of volumes organized around the notion of distinctive types of "minds."

Schopenhauer

Arthur Schopenhauer (1788–1860) was born in Danzig, into a family of wealthy merchants—persons of culture and of an emotional instability that he seems to have inherited, or at least absorbed. The family business for which he was destined bored him, and he soon abandoned it for a literary career. Schopenhauer was vain and snobbish ("Common people certainly look like men; I have never seen any creatures that resembled men so closely"); he was also a brilliant conversationalist, a gourmet, and a man of sensitive taste in music and the other arts. Though he never married, he was attractive to women and had a number of amorous adventures in the fashion of the times. "I have taught what sainthood is," he declared with complacency, "but I myself am no saint."

The World as Idea

Schopenhauer's chief work, *The World as Will and Idea*, was published in 1818, when he was thirty. The title reflects his dual theory that the world is both idea and will. The world inevitably appears to us, given the sort of sensory makeup with which we are endowed, as idea; but in its essence, as we learn through intuition, it is will.

As regards appearance, in Schopenhauer's view what I experience in perception (and in all the modes of knowledge based on, or derived from, perception) is nothing but a series of changes produced in my body. An object out there (for instance, the sun) causes a change in my eye. The brightness that I experience is not "out there" in the sun; it is here, in my eye. Why, then, do I attribute what is an effect here in me (brightness) to the cause out there (sun)? The explanation, according to Schopenhauer, is that in perception two processes occur: By an ordinary causal process the object "out there" causes a change in a sense organ; then, by a curious kind of reverse process, this effect is referred back to its cause. Perception is thus a double process, from object to sense organ and from sense organ back to object. Since the second process is normally unconscious, I mistake the effect for its cause. What I am aware of when I say, "I see the sun," is a brightness-in-the-eye, but because of the unconscious reversing that refers the effect back to its cause, I believe myself to be aware of the sun (the cause of the brightness-in-the-eye).

And, of course, my eye, insofar as it is an object of perception, is as much an effect as is the sun itself. Hence Schopenhauer's view may be described as follows: An unknown x out there (sun as it really is) produces a change in an unknown y (my body as it really is), and this change is experienced as "bright, hot." Schopenhauer's position is thus much more complex than Berkeley's, which it otherwise resembles. Whereas Berkeley had dispensed with the unknown x and y and had held the whole process of perception to be merely a succession of sense data ("ideas"), Schopenhauer held that beneath the sense data are real entities the nature and relations of which are quite different from those reported by the sense data, and which are known in a totally different way.[22]

From this account of perception, Schopenhauer concluded (1) that in knowledge based on perception we never discover what things really are and (2) that we nevertheless know that such objects exist, for they are the causes of what

22 See p. 148.

we perceive. Thus perception cannot possibly give me any information about what the sun is in itself. It yields information regarding only the sorts of effects that the sun has on sense organs like mine.

This reverse passage from effect to cause is what Schopenhauer called "understanding," or knowledge. Although there are great differences in the degree of acuteness with which men make this passage, it is basically the same process, he believed, in stupid men and in clever ones. Stupidity, indeed, is simply a deficiency in the capacity to make the correct passage from effect to cause. A stupid man sees a movement on a dark night, and instead of referring it to its proper cause (a branch blowing in the wind), he refers it to a ghost walking. There is no difference in kind, Schopenhauer held, between such "thinking" and the thought of a man like Newton. The latter's thought process, like that of the former, is an immediate, unconscious passage from effect ("apple lands on head") to cause ("gravity"). Of course, in a great scientific discovery the passage is incomparably more acute, but it is "just like perception, an operation of the understanding, an immediate intuition, and as such is the work of an instant, an *apperçu*, a flash of insight."

It also follows that there is no difference in kind between the human and the animal intellect. In animals the passage is simply less acute than it is in even a stupid human intellect. Schopenhauer believed that animals are incapable of reasoning, and that this latter faculty does distinguish men from them. But this distinction is nothing to man's credit, for reason is very much a secondary power and more of a liability than an asset.

The essential characteristic of reason is that it is conceptual—it "serves to take up the objective connections which are immediately known by the understanding [and] makes them permanent for thought." h After Newton saw the nature of gravity in a single flash of direct insight, he was able to write it down in conceptual form—in words and in mathematical formulas. Reason thus has some use, Schopenhauer rather grudgingly admitted. It makes communication possible, and by enabling us to store up experience (by recording it) it makes long-range, planned activities possible. Without it, the complex economic and social relationships of modern civilization would be impossible. But these gains, Schopenhauer held, are more than offset by the damage that reasoning does. For with reason, "doubt, error, care, and sorrow" enter into human life.

As to the "error" that reason is supposed to introduce, Schopenhauer held that conceptual thinking falsifies the uniqueness and continuity of reality. The concept "green," for instance, is a pigeonhole into which we toss higgledy-piggledy a large number of items, each of which is a distinct shade, a unique tone. The concept "blue" is handled in an equally arbitrary way. We believe not only that all the various shades of blue are identically blue, but that blue is never green and that green is never blue. This is the second mistake reason makes. Not only does it identify things that are really different; it sharply separates things that are in varying degrees similar. Or, putting both mistakes together, it may be said that reason tries to impose distinctions in kind on a reality that is a continuum of differences in degree. This is the trouble with the classification of colors into "green" and "blue." Colors actually form a continuum of tones, and between two colors, one of which we call blue and the other green, there may be no more difference than between two other colors, both of which we call green.

Schopenhauer's position is thus a radical kind of nominalism: There is no common property that is named by a term like "blue." Carried to its logical conclusion, this means that the type of communication modern science holds as ideal—that is, communication by means of mathematical concepts—is hopelessly inadequate. It is doubtless useful in constructing buildings, bombs, and bridges, and in other activities in which rough approximations can be tolerated. In Schopenhauer's view, the fact that a building thirty stories high requires foundations of such-and-such a size is a useful but basically trivial thing to know. This kind of knowledge tells us nothing about the texture of the material of which the building is constructed, its color, its feel, or its beauty—all these things must be experienced directly in perception.

Reason, Schopenhauer held, is as practically incompetent and as morally bad as it is cognitively inadequate. In the field of practice, concepts throw our aim off. Thinking too precisely on an event, weighing the pros and cons, we lose our power of decision and fumble when we come to act. Thus the general who tries to plan a campaign in advance (that is, to act conceptually) will be at a disadvantage, as will the man who tries to apply the "science of mechanics" to the game of billiards. Similarly, in manners and in social intercourse, "all that is attractive, gracious, charming in behavior, all affectionateness and friendliness, must not proceed from concepts for if it does 'we feel intention and are put out of tune.'"[i] The same is true for virtue and holiness; they proceed not from reflection but from character. All that reasoning does in the moral sphere is to make lying and dissimulation possible.

As will be seen, Schopenhauer's position is closely related to Wordsworth's ("We murder to dissect") and to the general Romantic emphasis on feeling, immediacy, and intuition. Schopenhauer attacked everything that the Enlightenment held to be valuable and true. The very form of his argument—its lack of logical organization, its exaggeration, and its passion—is typically Romantic.

The World as Will

This brings us to the second point in Schopenhauer's theory—the fact that the world is will. So far we have seen merely that perception does not give us knowledge of the real world and that science is at an even further remove from reality: Science, as the conceptualization of perception, falsifies the latter's immediacy. Fortunately, however, man is not limited to perception and the sciences. He has an intuition of the inner nature of reality (of the unknown x's and y's that are the causes of perception), and this intuition discloses their inner nature to be will. Schopenhauer's starting point was the self—the central focus, in one way or another, of modern philosophy from Descartes to Kant. As we have seen, perception yields only appearance—not the sun as it really is but the sun as it affects my body, and my body is simply another perceptual object. But though we *perceive* ourselves as bodies, existing in various spatiotemporal relations with other bodies (for example, the sun), we *intuit* ourselves as will, and this self-knowledge becomes the basis for a further exploration of the world in intuition. Not only are we "really" will, but, according to Schopenhauer, the whole world is will: All those "things" that cause sensations in our bodies, and whose nature is forever hidden from perception and the sciences, are really in their inner nature "will," like ourselves. The passage in which Schopenhauer expounded this central thesis of his philosophy will serve to illustrate his method:

> The meaning for which we seek . . . would never be found if the investigator himself were nothing more than the pure knowing subject (a winged cherub without a body). But . . . his knowledge, which is the necessary supporter of the whole world as idea, is yet always given through the medium of a body. . . . His body is, for the pure knowing subject, an idea like every other idea, an object among objects. [Nevertheless he also experiences] its movements and actions . . . in an entirely different way. . . . The answer to the riddle is given to the subject of knowledge who appears as an individual, and the answer is *will.* This and this alone gives him the key to his own existence, reveals to him the significance, shows him the inner mechanism of his being, of his action, of his movements. The body is given in two entirely different ways to the subject of knowledge. . . . It is given as an idea in intelligent perception. . . . And it is also given in quite a different way as that which is immediately known to every one, and is signified by the word *will.* . . . The act of will and the movement of the body are not two different things objectively known, which the bond of causality unites; . . . they are one and the same, but they are given in entirely different ways,—immediately, and again in perception. . . . The action of the body is nothing but the act of the will objectified, *i.e.,* passed into perception. . . . The whole body is nothing but objectified will, *i.e.,* will become idea.[j]

This view is not without grave difficulties. According to Schopenhauer, body and will are the same thing experienced in different ways. Hunger, for instance, is "objectified" as teeth, throat, and bowels. But how can Schopenhauer "know" that the perceptual experience of body and the intuitive experience of will are experiences of the same thing (the self) and not experiences of two different things (body, will)? An example will point up the problem. When we put on distorting spectacles, we believe we are experiencing the same landscape that we experience without the spectacles. But there is a well-defined operation (taking off and putting on the glasses) by which we get from one experience to the other. Without such an operation we could never know that there was a correspondence. This is just what Schopenhauer's theory lacks: There is no well-defined operation that "connects" perception and intuition—they are completely different modes of experience.

Further, even if we could know that will and body are the same, what grounds are there for saying that the experience we call "will" is more real than the experience we call "body"? The spectacles are "distorting" because our experience when we wear them fails to agree with other people's experience. But perception as such can be called "distorting" only on the basis of a preference for one kind of experience over another. Here, then, Schopenhauer reveals a typical Romantic preference for the inner, the unmediated, the continuous, and the dynamic.

Passing over the hidden value-judgment on which rests the contention that I am "really" will, let us consider the next part of Schopenhauer's thesis, namely, that everything else is also "really" will. Schopenhauer sought to prove this thesis by an argument from analogy—indeed, this would seem to be the only possible form of proof. But such an argument is weak at best and becomes progressively weaker as the points of similarity become fewer. Thus I may say other men are surely will, because they are so much like me; and the same may be said, perhaps, for animals. But what about such inanimate objects as plants, trees, stones, the iron ore or coal buried deep in the earth, and the sun and the planets? Schopenhauer realized that this is not a proof in the ordinary sense. It is not an appeal to empirical evidence, as in the sciences. Rather, it is an appeal to an insight that Schopenhauer believed all men share, if only obscurely. Thus the truth that the world is will is proved by "raising" it from the level of immediate consciousness to the level of abstract knowledge.

When we read a poem we sometimes feel, "That is just what I have been trying to say!" We think that we and the poet have experienced the same sentiment, but that whereas our experience of it was vague, his was clear. It would seem that Schopenhauer intuited something—the fact that the world is will—and gave an account of this intuition that he believed all other men would come to accept as an adequate version of their own intuitions. When they read *The World as Will and Idea* they will say (he believed), "This is what I have all along obscurely felt about the world!"

It follows that anyone in whom *The World as Will and Idea* does not evoke this sense of recognition stands outside the whole affair. Perhaps this sounds like radical subjectivity, but we must remember that Schopenhauer thought everyone *would* recognize a community of feeling, and that this feeling was an insight into a real and objective state of affairs. In his affirmation of a public reality he agreed with the rationalists and stood against any sort of solipsism or scepticism. But here, of course, his kinship with rationalism ended. He was not interested, as the rationalists were, in a detailed, systematic knowledge of reality. Indeed, in his view, systematic knowledge is quite impossible: There is nothing to know about reality except that it is will—it has no articulate structure like

Spinoza's substance or Thomas' God. It is just blind struggle. But even if there were something to know about it, from Schopenhauer's point of view knowledge of it would be inconsequential. Conduct, not theory, certifies the truth;[23] theories about conduct are *ex post facto,* and their variety merely indicates the range of verbalisms by which different men rationalize what happens. What matters is not what we know but how we feel and what we do. A Romantic philosophy does not interest itself in epistemology or in metaphysics as formal, systematic disciplines. It is characteristic, therefore, that in Schopenhauer's philosophy the former was replaced by an examination of art, and the latter by a study of the religious attitude.

The Nature of Art

According to Schopenhauer, art has two functions. First, esthetic experience yields a more adequate vision of the world as it really is than does science. Second, the peculiar nature of the esthetic object often allows us to adopt toward this vision the kind of attitude that Schopenhauer regarded as moral. Hence esthetics has both a cognitive and an ethical function and leads eventually into religion.

THE COGNITIVE FUNCTION OF ART

In order to understand what Schopenhauer regarded as the cognitive function of art, let us look briefly at his account of architecture and sculpture. In both arts we experience the play of light and shadows on surfaces. This, Schopenhauer thought, gives us a truer insight into the nature of light than does the physical theory of light. The equations that the physicist uses give us merely a summary— and an artificial one at that—of the *perception* of light. But when we look at light *esthetically* (and one of the functions of any art object is to put us into the esthetic attitude), we grasp its inner nature. Of course, we cannot *say* what it is (that is, we cannot say it conceptually); but we *know* what it is. The statue (or the building) in its plastic handling of light "says" (non-conceptually) what light is; and if it is a fine work of art it will give an esthetically sensitive observer a complete knowledge of the nature of light. In Schopenhauer's view, there is only one reason for translating this complete knowledge into concepts. Though we lose almost all in the translation, the small particles of meaning that we catch in our crude conceptual net may prove to have pragmatic value.

Architecture also enables us to know gravity. In our esthetic appreciation of the vaulting of a Gothic cathedral, for instance, we come to know the inner nature of gravity. In contrast, Newton's inverse-square law gives us only the outer husks of meaning.

23 See pp. 156–57.

But what is the relation between light and gravity on the one hand and will on the other? Do we experience will when we experience gravity and light esthetically? If so, why do we call them "light" and "gravity," instead of "will"? Schopenhauer replied that will "manifests" itself at various levels and in various degrees of adequacy. Gravity and light are both very low, or unconscious, levels of manifestation. In gravity, for instance, there is a tension of opposites—the buttresses push against the vaulting, the vaulting bears down on the walls, and so on. In the progression from inanimate objects to plants, to animals, and finally to man successively higher manifestations of will occur. This holds, of course, only when we look at the objects in question esthetically—a scientific perception of man is no more revealing of the nature of will than is a scientific perception of gravity. But an esthetic experience of man is far more revealing of the nature of will than is an esthetic experience of gravity. For man really is a more complete expression of will than gravity, and if we can only adopt an esthetic attitude toward man, we shall see that this is the case.

This is what a painting (if it is a work of art) does. If we look at a man, most of us remain at the level of perception; if we look at a *portrait* of a man, we *may* remain at the level of perception, but we may also rise, with the painter's assistance, to an esthetic contemplation of man's inner nature as will. The difference between the artist and the ordinary man lies in the former's capacity to move into the esthetic attitude on his own, by looking at some natural object; most of us, on the other hand, depend on the "lead" the artist gives by the way he organizes the pigments on his canvas. The same is true of the poet. Few people have ever been put into the esthetic attitude by looking at a young ass. But Coleridge apparently was. Accordingly, his verses may put a sensitive reader into a similar attitude.

THE ESTHETIC ATTITUDE

So far the cognitive function of art has been under consideration. The moral function of art results directly from the nature of the esthetic attitude. We can best understand this nature by contrasting it with our usual practical attitude. Because we are, of course, "really" will, the will in us projects itself into every aspect of our phenomenal life—it drives us into activity. This is true even of the cognitive attitude, which, Schopenhauer believed, is anything but the calm, dispassionate contemplation that the rationalists supposed it to be. "Knowledge is completely subject to the will. . . . Only through [its] relations [to his body] is the object *interesting* to the individual, *i.e.*, related to the will. Therefore the knowledge which is subject to the will knows nothing further of objects than their relations." [k] This is most obviously true at the level of perception, for we attend only to what interests us or to what we hope to make use of. But it is equally true of science, for science, as has been said, is merely the systematization of perceptually experienced relationships. Hence the sciences are all equally rooted in, and geared to, the demands of the will.

It must be remembered that (according to Schopenhauer) will, though it may be conscious at the human level of manifestation, is essentially blind, and its struggles are pointless. Since it is not going anywhere in particular, it never gets anywhere. It merely desires, without knowing what it wants or why. Hence its satisfactions are ephemeral. A reflection of this general frustration appears in our fluctuation between unsatisfied craving and ennui. Until we attain what we want, we are unhappy; as soon as we possess it, we are bored. Our restless will has passed on to some other desire. Like Faust, we are always seeking, and never finding, the moment to which we can say, "Stay, thou art so fair!"

Obviously, the best thing that could happen to us would be somehow to break free from this fruitless, meaningless servitude to the will, so that we no longer desire at all. As Byron wrote,

> My blood is all meridian; were it not,
>   I had not left my clime, nor should I be,
> In spite of tortures ne'er to be forgot,
>   A slave again of love,—at least of thee.

> 'Tis vain to struggle—let me perish young—
>   Live as I lived, and love as I have loved;
> To dust if I return, from dust I sprung,
>   And then, at least, my heart can ne'er be moved.[1]

Doubtless the only final rest from will is in death, as Byron shortly found at Missolonghi. But meanwhile, Schopenhauer believed, a temporary surcease is possible in esthetic contemplation. The function of the esthetic object is, as we have seen, to throw us into the esthetic attitude, and what distinguishes this attitude from all others is precisely that it is *not* practical. In it we are not getting and spending and otherwise laying waste our powers. We are not identifying, classifying, organizing, pigeonholing, and systematizing for the sake of one or the other of our will's fleeting desires. On the contrary, as long as we are submerged in the object's beauty, these pressures relax their grip and we are free.

> If, raised by the power of the mind, a man relinquishes the common way of looking at things, gives up tracing . . . their relations to each other, the final goal of which is always a relation to his own will; if he thus ceases to consider the where, the when, the why, and the whither of things, and looks simply and solely at the *what*; if, further, he does not allow abstract thought, the concepts of the reason, to take possession of his consciousness, but, instead of all this, . . . lets his whole consciousness be filled with the quiet contemplation of the natural object actually present, whether a landscape, a tree, a mountain, a building, or whatever it may be; inasmuch as he *loses* himself in this object (to use a pregnant German idiom), i.e., forgets even his individuality, his will, and only continues to exist as the pure subject, the clear mirror of the object, so that it is as if the object alone were there, without any one to perceive it, . . . then . . . he who is sunk in this perception is no longer

individual, for in such perception the individual has lost himself; but he is *pure*, will-less, painless, timeless *subject of knowledge.*[m]

This is virtually identical with the attitude expressed by Keats in his *Ode on a Grecian Urn:*

Thou still unravish'd bride of quietness,
    Thou foster-child of silence and slow time,
Sylvan historian, who canst thus express
    A flowery tale more sweetly than our rhyme:
What leaf-fring'd legend haunts about thy shape
    Of deities or mortals, or of both,
        In Tempe or the dales of Arcady?
    What men or gods are these? What maidens loth?
What mad pursuit? What struggle to escape?
        What pipes and timbrels? What wild ecstasy?

Heard melodies are sweet, but those unheard
    Are sweeter; therefore, ye soft pipes, play on;
Not to the sensual ear, but, more endear'd,
    Pipe to the spirit ditties of no tone:
Fair youth, beneath the trees, thou canst not leave
    Thy song, nor ever can those trees be bare;
        Bold Lover, never, never canst thou kiss,
Though winning near the goal—yet, do not grieve;
    She cannot fade, though thou hast not thy bliss,
        For ever wilt thou love, and she be fair! . . .

O Attic shape! Fair attitude! with brede
    Of marble men and maidens overwrought,
With forest branches and the trodden weed;
    Thou, silent form, dost tease us out of thought
As doth eternity: Cold Pastoral!
    When old age shall this generation waste,
        Thou shalt remain, in midst of other woe
Than ours, a friend to man, to whom thou say'st,
    "Beauty is truth, truth beauty,"—that is all
        Ye know on earth, and all ye need to know.

The function of art, then, is to "tease us out of thought" and to project us into a realm where pursuit is frozen and desire is stilled. Unfortunately, this relief is only temporary;[24] the pressure exerted by the will is strong, and we soon relapse into the senseless round of passion and frustration.

24 Schopenhauer's view excludes a good many objects commonly regarded as works of art. Paintings of the nude body and of fruits and flowers, if they arouse desire, only intensify the practical attitude. The same is true for paintings of subjects that fill us with loathing. Of course, the artist is not always responsible. Do what he may, vulgar people may misread the work of art. This is another limitation on the moral function of art: It is confined to a cultivated elite.

It might be thought that the logical solution would be suicide. But this is not true, according to Schopenhauer. To commit suicide is not to defeat the will; it is to allow the will to triumph over us. The notion that suicide is the way out of our misery is based on the illusion that this phenomenal self of ours, and its phenomenal life, is real. But life (objects in space and time and in causal relations with their environment) is merely the *appearance* of will; all the events of an individual life, including its beginning and its end, are merely incidents in this phenomenal flow. Hence, in killing ourselves we do not kill will; we merely eliminate one little segment of appearance.

> Will is the thing-in-itself, the inner content, the essence of the world. Life, the visible world, the phenomenon, is only the mirror of the will. . . . It is true we see the individual come into being and pass away; but the individual is only phenomenal. . . . Birth and death belong merely to the phenomenon of will, this to life. . . . The form of this phenomenon is time, space, and causality, and by means of these individuation, which carries with it that the individual must come into being and pass away. But this no more affects the will to live, of whose manifestation the individual is, as it were, only a particular example or specimen, than the death of an individual injures the whole of nature. . . . The man who has comprehended and retained this point of view may well console himself, when contemplating his own death and that of his friends, by turning his eyes to the immortal life of Nature, which he himself is. . . .
>
> Above all things, we must distinctly recognise that the form of the phenomenon of will, the form of life or reality, is really only the *present*, not the future nor the past. The latter are only in the conception, exist only in the connection of knowledge. . . . Our own past, the most recent part of it, and even yesterday, is now no more than an empty dream of the fancy, and such is the past of all those millions [who lived in thousands of years that are past]. What was? What is? The will, of which life is the mirror, and knowledge free from will, which beholds it clearly in that mirror. . . .
>
> Therefore, if a man fears death as his annihilation, it is just as if he were to think that the sun cries out at evening, "Woe is me! for I go down into eternal night." . . . Life is assured to the will to live; the form of life is an endless present, no matter how the individuals, the phenomena of the Idea, arise and pass away in time, like fleeting dreams. Thus even already suicide appears to us as a vain and therefore a foolish action.[n]

But the realization that life is appearance and that the multiplicity of selves, and their private interests, is illusion points the way to a solution. Knowledge that the objects of desire are illusion, that the distinctions and honors we prize, the goals we aim at, the self on which we insist, are illusions, acts as a quieter of the will, in the same way that art does, but permanently. In this kind of knowledge, indeed, "the will suppresses itself." This, and not suicide, is the real denial of the will.

Moral Theory

This marks the transition from esthetics to ethics. Schopenhauer related the various types of conduct—from the undiluted egoism of Hobbes' "war of all against all" to the sainthood of the Christian and Hindu religions—to the successive degrees of man's realization of the truth about the world. The first advance from Hobbesian egoism occurs when a man comes to see that his is not the only will in the world and that other men are, like himself, foci of desire. At this stage pure egoism is replaced by fellow-feeling and a sense of justice and equality. The just man still asserts his own will, but unlike the egoist he does not deny the rights of others to assert their wills. In other words, this is the level of the *laissez-faire* philosophy of the Enlightenment.

The next step is the realization that all these foci of desire are manifestations of one underlying will—that is, that differences between us are only phenomenal and that we are all basically one. This stage, Schopenhauer believed, was reached by the ancient Hindus. In their religion the identity of all the real was asserted. "This thou art," the Hindu was taught to say, as all the beings in the world, living and lifeless, passed successively before him. Doubtless the Hindus expressed this truth—"the fruit of the highest human knowledge and wisdom"—in a mythological language, but "never has a myth entered, and never will one enter, more closely into the philosophical truth which is attainable to so few than this primitive doctrine of the noblest and most ancient nation." How inferior, then, is the Christian religion! How ridiculous to seek to convert the Hindus! "In India our religions will never take root. The ancient wisdom of the human race will not be displaced by what happened in Galilee. On the contrary, Indian philosophy streams back to Europe, and will produce a fundamental change in our knowledge and thought."°

Here, where sympathy and pity replace justice, we attain to sainthood and renunciation. At this level, when a man

> . . . no longer makes the egotistical distinction between his person and that of others, but takes as much interest in the sufferings of other individuals as in his own, and therefore is not only benevolent in the highest degree, but even ready to sacrifice his own individuality whenever such a sacrifice will save a number of other persons, then it clearly follows that such a man, who recognises in all beings his own inmost and true self, must also regard the infinite suffering of all suffering beings as his own, and take on himself the pain of the whole world. . . . Knowledge of the whole, of the nature of the thing-in-itself which has been described, becomes a *quieter* of all and every volition. The will now turns away from life; it now shudders at the pleasures in which it recognises the assertion of life. Man now attains to the state of voluntary renunciation, resignation, true indifference, and perfect will-lessness. . . .
>
> The phenomenon by which this change is marked, is the transition from virtue to asceticism. . . . There arises within him a horror of the nature of

which his own phenomenal existence is an expression, the will to live, the kernel and inner nature of that world which is recognised as full of misery. He therefore disowns this nature which appears in him, and is already expressed through his body, and his action gives the lie to his phenomenal existence, and appears in open contradiction to it. . . . His body, healthy and strong, expresses through the genitals, the sexual impulse; but he denies the will and gives the lie to the body; he desires no sensual gratification under any condition. Voluntary and complete chastity is the first step in asceticism or the denial of the will to live. . . . Nature, always true and naïve, declares that if this maxim became universal, the human race would die out; and I think I may assume, in accordance with what was said . . . about the connection of all manifestations of will, that with its highest manifestation, the weaker reflection of it would also pass away, as the twilight vanishes along with the full light. With the entire abolition of knowledge, the rest of the world would of itself vanish into nothing; for without a subject there is no object.P

It is not easy to see the difference between individual suicide and the race suicide that Schopenhauer recommended. Nor is there any reason to suppose that the great universal will that Schopenhauer hypothecated, with all its grades of manifestation, would vanish if man himself disappeared. But it serves no purpose to press Schopenhauer's position too closely, since, in his own view, he was communicating an insight that transcends conceptual analysis. And he was aware, of course, that this insight has affinities not only with the Vedas but with Christian mysticism.

What I have here described with feeble tongue and only in general terms, is no philosophical fable, invented by myself, and only of to-day; no, it was the enviable life of so many saints and beautiful souls among Christians, and still more among Hindus and Buddhists, and also among the believers of other religions. However different were the dogmas impressed on their reason, the same inward, direct, intuitive knowledge, from which alone all virtue and holiness proceed, expressed itself in precisely the same way in the conduct of life. For here also the great distinction between intuitive and abstract knowledge shows itself. . . . There is a wide gulf between the two, which can only be crossed by the aid of philosophy, as regards the knowledge of the nature of the world. Intuitively or *in concreto*, every man is really conscious of all philosophical truths, but to bring them to abstract knowledge, to reflection, is the work of philosophy, which neither ought nor is able to do more than this.

Thus it may be that the inner nature of holiness, self-renunciation, mortification of our own will, asceticism, is here for the first time expressed abstractly, and free from all mythical elements, as *denial of the will to live*, appearing after the complete knowledge of its own nature has become a quieter of all volition. On the other hand, it has been known directly and realised in practice by saints and ascetics, who had all the same inward knowledge, though they used very different language with regard to it, according to the dogmas which their reason had accepted, and in consequence of which an Indian, a Christian, or a Lama saint must each give a very different account of his conduct, which is, however, of no importance as regards the fact. A saint may be full of the absurdest superstition, or, on the contrary, he may be a philosopher, it is all the same. His conduct alone certifies that he is a saint, for, in a moral regard, it proceeds from knowledge of the world and its nature, which is not abstractly but intuitively and directly apprehended, and is only expressed by him in any dogma of the satisfaction of his reason. . . . To repeat the whole nature of the world abstractly, universally, and distinctly in concepts, and thus to store up, as it were, a reflected image of it in permanent concepts always at the command of the reason; this and nothing else is philosophy.q

The Paradoxical Role of Philosophy

Thus, according to Schopenhauer, philosophy is a bridge between intuition (which is true, but unfortunately incommunicable) and abstract conceptual knowledge (which is communicable, but false). But, in his own account as well as in his own usage, philosophy is conceptual and abstract. How, then, is it distinguished from that abstract conceptual knowledge that Schopenhauer depreciated? And, if "conduct alone certifies sainthood," why go beyond the mystic's intuitive state? Salvation comes not through communicating the truth that we feel, but through living the life that this feeling causes us to live.

In any case, of course, we *cannot* communicate successfully. Hence, if we are to choose among communications, why prefer the philosophical to the mythological? There seems every reason to argue, on Schopenhauer's own premises, that the latter is less false and less inadequate than the former.

Apparently, however, Schopenhauer was correct in pointing out that the philosophical enterprise *begins* from experiences (or, in his terminology, intuitions) that seem important to the philosopher. He was also correct in noting that linguistic conventions often disguise experiential similarities and that it is the task of philosophical analysis to articulate these experiences into a system of abstract concepts. This, as a matter of fact, is just what most philosophers have attempted to do. Thus, to give but one example, Augustine sought to give a rational account of those experiences of sin, frustration, and hope that climaxed in the voice that spoke to him from the sunlight in a garden at Milan. Philosophy is necessarily rationalistic in the sense that it attempts to find some logical structure into which the experiences can be incorporated.

Here we reach the central paradox of Schopenhauer's position. His view of the nature of the real that intuition is supposed to know made a *rational* account of experience impossible. Schopenhauer, of course, happened to be interested less in giving an account of experience than in *feeling* and in getting into a right relation with the reality he felt. In this sense, he and all the other Romantics have a far stronger affinity with the mystical mind than with the strictly philosophical or theological mind. From the point of view of the historian of philosophy, however, Schopenhauer's views are important, for his dislike of system, his distrust of reason, his exaltation of feeling, and his emphasis on practice are all expressive of what proved to be one of the major themes of the nineteenth century.

Hegel and Schopenhauer

In this discussion of Hegel and Schopenhauer the differences between the two philosophers have been emphasized. That there are differences is obvious; in fact, in some respects their views are antithetical. Thus, whereas Hegel claimed that reason is a valid instrument for the cognition of reality, Schopenhauer limited reason to the phenomenal world. In other respects, however, their views are curiously parallel. For example, neither was willing to accept Kant's exclusion of the possibility of metaphysical knowledge: Both wanted to know ultimate reality. Further, Hegel and Schopenhauer were in much closer agreement about the nature of this ultimate reality than might appear at first sight. Both held that it is continuous rather than discrete, and that its nature transcends the capacity of "ordinary" logic. They differed, indeed, chiefly because Hegel believed he had discovered a new logic capable of dealing with this continuous real. It is interesting to note that before he hit upon this new logic, Hegel himself passed through a phase in which he believed thought to be basically inadequate to its object. Thus in an early note in *The Phenomenology* he remarked, "Philosophy must end in religion, because philosophy is thought, and thought always involves finitude and opposition, e.g., the oppositions of subject and object, and of the mind that thinks to matter that does not think. Its business, therefore, is to show the finitude of all that is finite, and through reason to demand its complement or completion in the infinite." [r]

Because Schopenhauer did not conceive of any logic except the "either-or" Aristotelian logic, and because he believed that it was incompetent, he wound up with intuitionism. What enabled Hegel to remain a rationalist was his belief that the principle of identity-in-difference makes possible the reconciliation of opposites in a higher synthesis.

But though Hegel remained a rationalist, his rationalism was very different from the rationalism of the Enlightenment. Hegel was far from unresponsive to the mood of the times, as expressed in the poetry of Goethe, Shelley, Wordsworth, and Byron. Like the Romantics, he had a strong sense of the unity of things. Like them, he believed that the "finite" is incomplete and partial and that it gains its significance from a "larger-than" that is experienced in, while it constantly transcends, the here and now. Thus, just as Schopenhauer held that in intuition we come to see the unity of being ("This thou art"), so Hegel held that all individual thoughts and thinkers are contained in an absolute thought. This is a radical shift from the Enlightenment's insistence on the distinctness and separateness of things. Every individual person, it held, is complete in himself and valuable in his own right; every individual science is an independent system derived from its own set of first principles. Hence, where the Enlightenment had advocated *laissez faire* in politics and economics, both Schopenhauer and Hegel regarded this as merely a rather low level in the development of moral and political ideals.

Schopenhauer, of course, made a direct attack on rationalism, but Hegel's surrender of finite reason (which was what the Enlightenment had understood by reason) in favor of an absolute reason (of which the Enlightenment did not even dream) was equally a sign of the uneasiness that marked the new century, of an awareness that all was not well in the best of all possible worlds. It is true, of course, that Hegel believed he was refurbishing the rationalistic ideal, but (as some of his followers were to point out) a transcendent thought is unknowable by finite means; an absolute reason is, from our human point of view, suprarational. Hence Hegelianism was deeply influenced by Romanticism. As much as Schopenhauer's intuitionism, it was a quest for a new kind of certainty.

CHAPTER 5

Science, Scientism, and Social Philosophy

The Heritage of Kant

Most of the nineteenth-century philosophers considered in this chapter began, like Hegel and Schopenhauer, from an essentially Kantian position. But because their interests and outlook were very different—not only from Kant's but also from Hegel's and from Schopenhauer's—they came up with very different conclusions. Unlike Hegel, these thinkers were for the most part either indifferent or even hostile to the idea of system. Unlike Schopenhauer, they felt no urge to penetrate to a transcendent reality beyond this world. Temperamentally they were secularists—it was in this world, not in the next, they held, that man lived and moved and had his being. Thus these philosophers fixed their attention on what Kant had called the spatiotemporal manifold; they differed from Kant, however, in rigorously limiting reality to this manifold. They emphasized the Kantian thesis that the manifold consists in events that are completely amenable to scientific treatment, but they ignored Kant's argument that this characteristic of the manifold is made possible only by means of "transcendental syntheses." Thus they can be called "phenomenalists," for they rejected the notion of noumena (things-in-themselves) and identified reality with what Kant had called phenomena.

Accordingly, these philosophers were far more antimetaphysical than Kant had been. Although Kant had denied that any knowledge of metaphysical entities is possible, he had nevertheless held that the inclination to pursue metaphysical inquiries is a "natural disposition" of great significance in human life. The secularistic bias of these post-Kantian thinkers led them to write metaphysics off as a massive delusion. They naturally included religion in this assessment—though some of them were quite prepared to use the religious aspirations of the masses as an instrument of power politics. Indeed, because they took their phenomenalism very seriously, these thinkers tended to treat all ideas—not merely religious ones—as ideology; that is, they held that the important question to ask about ideas is not whether they are true or false but how they affect conduct and policy. These philosophers also maintained that all the ideas entertained by any group of people at a given time are elements in their world view and can be predicted from other features of the group's culture. One of the consequences of this position is the general derogation of theory, for in this view theories—including philosophical speculation—become mere ideology. The obvious implications of this position for these thinkers' own theories were either ignored or dealt with only very inadequately by them.

These new trends in philosophy can be said to have followed more or less directly from these philosophers' limited but genuinely Kantian starting point. Other elements in their views, however, were quite different from Kant's. For example, all these philosophers were profoundly influenced by the great shift from an essentially static view of the universe, a view that had predominated in the eighteenth century, to a conception of the universe as evolving through time. As was pointed out in the preceding chapter, this new emphasis affected Hegel's revision of Kant's doctrine, and it was to have an increasing impact on philosophy as the century advanced. One of the consequences of this shift, it will be seen, was a new interest in history and in philosophies of history.

Another way in which this group of nineteenth-century thinkers differed from Kant was in their attitude toward ethics. Kant had valued not what men actually achieve but the motive from which they act—that is, purity of will. The philosophers who followed Kant were much more practically oriented. They recognized that Europe faced major economic and social problems as a result of the failure of institutional structures to adjust to the immense changes that were occurring in men's values and expectations and in their ways of living. Hence all these philosophers were in some measure reformers, and some of them were revolutionaries. In a word, the focus of attention was shifting from the traditional problems of epistemology and ethics to social philosophy, with much less emphasis on the formal elaboration of theory than on the application of theory to concrete problems.

Finally, all these thinkers were convinced that scientific knowledge, which they conceived of in the broadest sense as an empirical method, could be brought to bear on the solution of grave social problems. These thinkers shared Condorcet's optimistic conviction that unlimited progress is possible, for they accepted Bacon's dicta that "knowledge is power" and that this power should be used for the "improvement of man's estate." But they differed greatly from Bacon in their conception of the kind of knowledge that results in power. Here their phenomenalism, their interest in development, and their conception of ideology came together. For all these thinkers, the view that ideas are ideology suggested that men's minds as well as their bodies, their thoughts as well as their actions, could be studied scientifically; the emphasis on development suggested that the old geometric model of explanation could be replaced by a new genetic model; the interest in social problems resulted in an application of science to the study of society. Thus the sciences of sociology and, somewhat later, psychology were born. The formulation of the theory of evolution naturally greatly accelerated all these tendencies. It not only gave additional support to the genetic model of explanation; it also seemed to show that man is a part of nature and is thus subject to its laws. Indeed, the new triumphs of biology led to a rather facile belief in science and its "iron laws," and to an assumption on the part of some thinkers that science provides simple, straightforward answers to all philosophical problems. This point of view, which may be described as "scientism," became increasingly dominant in the second half of the nineteenth century.

It will be useful, before turning to study these social philosophers themselves, to consider some of the political and economic changes that formed the social context of their thought and to which their views were a response.

Revolution and Reaction

When Hegel died in the late autumn of 1831, agitation over the Reform Bill, then before the British Parliament, was at its height. In order to understand why social philosophy increasingly preoccupied men of the new century a word must be said about the developments of which the Reform Bill was a part. The Enlightenment's strong sense of humanity and of the rights of man had been a driving force in the French Revolution, which began as an attempt to put into practice the theory that there are eternal, rational principles that all men can come to know and live by. The chaos of the Revolution itself and of the Napoleonic wars that followed put the movement for reform on ice for almost a quarter of a century. And in 1815, with the restoration of peace after Waterloo, the scene was complicated by new factors that had emerged during the interim.

For one thing, the excesses of the revolutionary mob had alarmed conservatives everywhere—especially the rulers of the European states. The conservatives' notion of peace was the restoration of the *status quo,* and their immediate reaction—the lesson they had learned during the eventful quarter century preceding—was to try to bottle up the forces that had released the Revolution and that in turn had been nourished by it. The result was the formation among the victorious powers (Britain excepted) of a Holy Alliance to repress any suggestion of liberalism.

Meanwhile, pressure for reform had been mounting among the masses. Before the French Revolution, agitation for reform had come largely from above: The *philosophes* had sought not so much to rouse the downtrodden peasant as to provide for him what these enlightened gentlemen deemed to be his due. As industry developed, partly because of the stimulus of the long period of war, an increasingly articulate urban proletariat emerged. This new group knew what it wanted and became unwilling to accept the leadership of its upper-class sponsors.

The application of the new science to production—the development of technology—had begun in a small way in England early in the eighteenth century. Machines were introduced to do the work of men's hands, and steam became the major source of industrial power. The factory replaced the home as the manufacturing center. Weaving, for instance, which had been farmed out to families in their cottages, was replaced by power-driven looms in the factory. As a consequence, the population of many small towns expanded at an enormous rate. For example, between 1800 and 1831, Leeds, Sheffield, and Birmingham more than doubled in population, and Manchester and Liverpool were not far behind. Landlords naturally got fantastic rentals for jerry-built houses. Houses without water or sewage facilities and built for £65–70 rented for £12 per annum; the owner's investment was thus returned in five years. These high rentals resulted in appalling overcrowding; families often occupied a single room, and in Manchester as late as 1845 twenty-seven cases were reported of as many as seven people trying to sleep in a single bed.

Work conditions corresponded. In 1840 the workday still averaged twelve to thirteen hours, excluding time for meals; and occasional holidays had to be made up. Children entered the factories when they were nine years old and were expected to do labor of the hardest kind. Nearly as many children as adults were employed in the mines—167,000 compared with 191,000. Pay was pathetically low, and owners managed to reduce their labor costs still further by such devices as "truck" (payment in commodities) and arbitrary fines for breakage and bad work.

It is not surprising that liberal-minded people were shocked by such conditions or that the laboring class itself began to agitate for "reform." The House of Commons was regarded—and rightly—as the key to the situation. In 1830 the Commons still represented the landowners, the men who had ruled old, agrarian England. The large, new towns were almost totally without representation, and in numerous "rotten boroughs" a mere handful of electors controlled a seat. The struggle over the redistribution of seats in the Commons reflected the larger conflict between the old, dominant class and the new classes that the Industrial Revolution was producing. The passage of the Reform Bill of 1832[1] was a great victory for the middle and lower classes. Although these classes did not become permanent allies, their success in this opening battle meant that the ensuing struggle would take place within the framework of due process, rather than, as on the Continent, in a series of civil disturbances. In continental Europe, repression instead of parliamentary compromise was the order of the day, and dissent had no outlet. Eventually, as in 1848, it welled up in outbreaks of open violence that called forth even more vigorous repression. The result was alternating moods of hope and despair, of hatred and fear, and these moods were reflected in the philosophical theories of the thinkers discussed below.

The Utilitarians

Jeremy Bentham, James Mill, and his son, John Stuart Mill, were the leaders of the Utilitarians, a group of thinkers who dominated British philosophy during most of the century. They were the inheritors of Hume's empiricism and of his psychological associationism, but their interests lay primarily in social theory rather than in epistemology.

"GREATEST HAPPINESS" PRINCIPLE

It was significant of the changing temper of the times and of the influence of Hume that, whereas Locke had sought to base his social philosophy on a number of "eternal verities," the Utilitarians rested theirs on one basic principle, and they believed this principle could be proved by empirical means. Bentham's[2] version of this principle was the starting point for all subsequent Utilitarian theorizing:

> The end and aim of a legislator should be the HAPPINESS of the people. In matters of legislation, GENERAL UTILITY should be his guiding principle. The science of legislation consists, therefore, in determining what makes for the good of the particular community whose interests are at stake, while its

---

1 The Reform Bill disenfranchised fifty-six rotten boroughs. By this and other means, a total of 146 seats were provided for distribution: London got ten; Liverpool, Manchester, Birmingham, and Newcastle, two each; and a large number of other towns, one each. The franchise was made uniform, but a fairly high property qualification was retained.

2 Jeremy Bentham (1748–1832) was the son of a well-to-do attorney. He studied law but never practiced it, for he was more interested in legal theory than in a career at the bar. He wrote extensively on legal and economic subjects and devoted much time to an elaborate scheme for prison reform.

art consists in contriving some means of realization. . . . To apply [this principle] with complete efficiency, that is, to make it the very foundation of a system of reasoning, three conditions must be fulfilled.

First, we must attach to the word *Utility* a clear and precise connotation. . . .

Second, we must assert the supreme and undivided sovereignty of this principle by rigorously discarding every other. . . . No exception to its applicability can, in any circumstances, be allowed.

Thirdly, we must discover some calculus or process of "moral arithmetic" by means of which we may arrive at uniform results.

Nature has placed mankind under the governance of two sovereign masters, *Pleasure* and *Pain.* To them . . . we refer all our decisions, every resolve that we make in life. The man who affects to have withdrawn himself from their despotic sway does not know what he is talking about. To seek pleasure and to shun pain is his sole aim, even at the moment when he is denying himself the greatest enjoyment or courting penalties the most severe. . . . To these two motives the *principle of utility* subjects everything. . . .

The *Principle of Utility,* accordingly, consists in taking as our starting-point, in every process of ordered reasoning, the calculus or comparative estimate of pains and pleasures, and in not allowing any other to intervene.

I am an adherent of the *Principle of Utility* when I measure my approval or disapproval of any act, public or private, by its tendency to produce pains and pleasures. . . . And it must always be understood that I use these words *Pain* and *Pleasure* in their ordinary signification, without having recourse to arbitrary definitions for the purpose of ruling out certain forms of pleasure. . . .

An adherent to the *Principle of Utility* holds virtue to be a good thing by reason only of the pleasures which result from the practice of it: he esteems vice to be a bad thing by reason only of the pains which follow in its train. Moral good is *good* only on account of its tendency to secure physical benefits: moral evil is *evil* only on account of its tendency to induce physical mischief. . . .

The diffusion of Pleasures and the avoidance of Pains are the only ends which a legislator should have in view. It behoves him, then, to acquire a just and precise appreciation of their respective values. Seeing that Pleasures and Pains are the *instruments* he has to work with, he ought to make a very careful study of their magnitude and strength, which, indeed, from another point of view, constitute their value.

Now, if we examine the *value* of a pleasure, considered by itself and in relation to a single individual, we shall find that it depends on four circumstances: (1) *Its Intensity;* (2) *its Duration;* (3) *its Certainty;* (4) *its Proximity.*

The value of a pain depends upon like considerations.

But, in dealing with Pains and Pleasures, it is not enough to assess their value as though they were, necessarily, isolated and independent. Pains and pleasures may have as *consequences* other pains and pleasures. If, therefore, we wish to estimate the *tendency* of any act from which pain or pleasure directly results, we must take into account two other circumstances: These are (5) *its Fecundity* or *Productiveness;* (6) *its Purity. A productive pleasure* is one which is likely to be followed by other pleasures of the same kind. A *productive pain* is one which is likely to be followed by other pains of the same kind. A *pure pleasure* is one which is not likely to produce pain. A *pure pain* is one which is not likely to produce pleasure.

When the calculation is to be made in relation to a number of individuals, yet another circumstance is to be taken into account—(7) *its Extent*. That is, the number of persons who are likely to be affected by this particular pleasure or pain, as the case may be.

Suppose we wish to take exact account of the value of a certain action. We must follow, in detail, the various operations which have just been indicated. These provide the elements of a moral calculus, and Legislation may thus become a mere matter of Arithmetic. The *evil*, or *pain*, inflicted is the expenditure; the *good*, or *pleasure*, engendered is the income.[a]

MILL'S APPLICATION OF THE PRINCIPLE

John Stuart Mill's[3] *Essay on Liberty* is a typical application of the greatest happiness principle. Instead of arguing, as an eighteenth-century rationalist might have done, that liberty is a self-evident right, he tried to show that the greatest good for the greatest number is promoted by allowing citizens to criticize their government, to worship as they please, to choose their own mode of life, and to think and to act as they choose.

The object of this Essay is to assert one very simple principle, as entitled to govern absolutely the dealing of society with the individual in the way of compulsion and control. . . . That principle is, that the sole end for which mankind are warranted, individually or collectively, in interfering with the liberty of action of any of their number, is self-protection. . . . Over himself, over his own body and mind, the individual is sovereign. . . .

It is proper to state that I forego any advantage which could be derived to my argument from the idea of abstract right, as a thing independent of utility. I regard utility as the ultimate appeal on all ethical questions; but it must be utility in the largest sense, grounded on the permanent interests of a man as a progressive being. . . . In all things which regard the external relations of the individual, he is *de jure* amenable to those whose interests are concerned, and, if need be, to society as their protector. . . .

But there is a sphere of action in which society, as distinguished from the individual, has, if any, only an indirect interest; comprehending all that portion of a person's life and conduct which affects only himself. . . . This, then, is the appropriate region of human liberty. It comprises, first, the inward

3 J. S. Mill (1806–73) was educated on a plan worked out by his father and by Bentham. By the age of three he had begun learning Greek; by the time he was eight he had read Xenophon, Herodotus, and Plato. In 1822 he entered India House as a junior clerk and rose rapidly to head of the office, a position equivalent to that of a modern permanent undersecretary of a leading ministry. He wrote voluminously on logic, economics, parliamentary reform, and women's rights (he was one of the founders of the first women's suffrage society) and served briefly as a member of Parliament.

domain of consciousness; . . . liberty of thought and feeling; absolute freedom of opinion and sentiment on all subjects; . . . liberty of tastes and pursuits; of framing the plan of our life to suit our own character; of doing what we like . . . without impediment from our fellow-creatures, so long as what we do does not harm them, even though they should think our conduct foolish, perverse, or wrong. . . .[b]

The difference between basing a defense of liberty on an abstract consideration of right (or on a Kantian categorical imperative) and basing it on a utilitarian calculation of consequences comes out very clearly in Mill's argument in favor of liberty of thought. Opponents of liberty will argue, Mill says, that they are at least justified in repressing false opinions. Mill replies:

We can never be sure that the opinion we are endeavouring to stifle is a false opinion; and if we were sure, stifling it would be an evil still.

First: the opinion which it is attempted to suppress by authority may possibly be true. Those who desire to suppress it, of course deny its truth; but they are not infallible. . . . To refuse a hearing to an opinion, because they are sure that it is false, is to assume that *their* certainty is the same as *absolute* certainty. . . . Ages are no more infallible than individuals; every age having held many opinions which subsequent ages have deemed not only false but absurd; and it is as certain that many opinions now general will be rejected by future ages, as it is that many, once general, are rejected by the present.

There is the greatest difference between presuming an opinion to be true, because, with every opportunity for contesting it, it has not been refuted, and assuming its truth for the purpose of not permitting its refutation. Complete liberty of contradicting and disproving our opinion is the very condition which justifies us in assuming its truth for purposes of action; and on no other terms can a being with human faculties have any rational assurance of being right.

Let us now pass to the second division of the argument, and dismissing the supposition that any of the received opinions may be false, let us assume them to be true, and examine into the worth of the manner in which they are likely to be held, when their truth is not freely and openly canvassed. . . .

Both teachers and learners go to sleep at their post, as soon as there is no enemy in the field. . . . There are many truths of which the full meaning *cannot* be realised until personal experience has brought it home. But much more of the meaning even of these would have been understood, and what was understood would have been far more deeply impressed on the mind, if the man had been accustomed to hear it argued *pro* and *con* by people who did understand it. The fatal tendency of mankind to leave off thinking about a thing when it is no longer doubtful, is the cause of half their errors.[c]

Mill realized that it was not enough to protect freedom of thought from arbitrary and tyrannical governments. Even in parliamentary democracies liberty is always in danger, both because of the tendency of the majority to pass laws that infringe the rights of minorities and also, indirectly but no less harmfully, because of the pressure of public opinion toward conformity. The truth is that though Mill certainly prized liberty, he prized "individuality" and "spiritual development" even more. In fact, liberty was valuable to Mill chiefly because he believed it to be the only social mode in which these ends could be realized: "Individuality is the same thing with development, and it is only the cultivation of individuality which produces, or can produce, well-developed human beings."[d]

It follows that Mill had no sympathy for the Hegelian notion of the state as the "true" individual, of which all the finite citizens are but organs. From Mill's point of view, to talk in this way is to put metaphysical jargon to work in the service of tyranny. Mill's assumption of the basic autonomy of the finite individual can be seen in the very way in which he poses the question, "What are the *limits* of justifiable restriction?"

But those who share Mill's antipathy to the Hegelian ideal of transcending finite individuality in that larger self, the state, must admit that the finite individual is not so completely self-subsistent as Mill held him to be. Consider Mill's contention that restraint is warranted only in the case of "actions where the interest of others is menaced." Given the interlocking and organic nature of society, is there any action that does not have an impact, large or small, on *some* circle of others?

Mill's discussion of "applications" of the utility principle to concrete policy issues reveals serious difficulties of this kind. For instance, to the question of whether the sale of poisons ought to be limited, Mill replies:

> It is one of the undisputed functions of government to take precautions against crime before it has been committed, as well as to detect and punish it afterwards. The preventive function of government, however, is far more liable to be abused, to the prejudice of liberty, than the punitory function. . . . If poisons were never bought or used for any purpose except the commission of murder it would be right to prohibit their manufacture and sale. They may, however, be wanted not only for innocent but for useful purposes, and restrictions cannot be imposed in the one case without operating in the other. . . . Such a precaution, for example, as that of labelling the drug with some word expressive of its dangerous character, may be enforced without violation of liberty: the buyer cannot wish not to know that the thing he possesses has poisonous qualities.[e]

Similar considerations led Mill to maintain that "fornication, for example, must be tolerated, and so must gambling; but should a person be free to be a pimp, or to keep a gambling house? . . . There are arguments on both sides."[f] The trouble is that there are *always* arguments on both sides. Would Mill have wanted to treat cigarettes as poisons, on the ground that inhalation of cigarette smoke is presumably conducive to lung cancer? What about smog? A strict application of the utility principle is likely to lead to more restrictions on liberty, not fewer. Alternatively, had Mill continued to insist on the maximum possible liberty, he would have found himself in the awkward position of advocating policies that, far from maximizing happiness and well-being, actually produce more social harm than good. In the conditions of modern life, an argument like Mill's, which begins by emphasizing the right of every individual to fashion his own destiny unrestrained by police or public opinion, is likely to end by defending the oppression of the individual by other (for example, economic) forces. Thus, in the course of the century since Mill wrote, *laissez-faire* individualism has become a conservative rather than a radical doctrine.

CRITICISM OF THE "GREATEST HAPPINESS" PRINCIPLE

Mill's *Essay on Liberty* illustrates the way in which the Utilitarians applied the greatest happiness principle to the solution of social problems. It can hardly be denied that this principle is more practicable than either the Enlightenment's belief in intuition of self-evident truths or Hegel's elaborate dialectic. Taken simply as a rule-of-thumb reminder that the social order exists for everyone and that what is relevant in the consideration of social change is the well-being of individual citizens rather than logical symmetry, the principle is very valuable. But its advocates demanded a great deal more of it; indeed, they regarded it as that final authority for which, as has been seen, the whole century was searching. That the principle was unfit for such an exalted role will be clear from a study of Bentham's formulation of it.

Bentham accepted Locke's view that everyone aims at his own pleasure and that the essence of social control consists in making certain that socially desirable acts are sufficiently "weighted" with pleasurable consequences to induce men to do them. But whereas Locke believed that the ultimate weighting of social acts is done by God (in the form of promises of heavenly bliss and threats of hellish tortures), Bentham assigned this function to a human legislator. This raised problems that Locke's theory did not have to face. For example, there is no reason to suppose that the legislator is exempt from the universal egoism that (in Bentham's view) causes everyone to seek his own private pleasure. Bentham never asked himself how it comes about that the legislator desires to promote the common good by a suitable arrangement of sanctions.

But, even if Bentham be allowed an altruistic legislator, his theory is still involved in serious difficulties, for the principle by which the legislator is supposed to operate is far from having the "clear and precise connotation" that Bentham attributed to it. To begin with, quantum of good and range of distribution are quite distinct variables in the Utilitarian equation. As between act A and act B, two possible acts open to us in a given case, A may produce the greatest quantum of good, but with a very narrow distribution; B may produce a lesser quantum, but with a much wider distribution. As Utilitarians, which should we choose? The greatest happiness principle does not tell us. "Greatest good" is thus an ambiguous term in its formula. It may mean either (1) largest quantum or (2) widest distribution.

Furthermore, the principle focuses on results, that is, on a future state of affairs. But the future is (1) uncertain (and the more remote, the more uncertain) and (2) indefinitely extensive. We cannot calculate the good and bad consequences of A and B for the *whole* future; if we were to try, we would never act. And there comes a point at which probabilities fade off into guesses. Where do we draw the line? The principle does not tell us. Nor could Bentham have replied that we should stop at the point at which consideration becomes "useless." Unless the greatest happiness principle is redefined, an appeal to it here is circular.

Finally, it seems clear that pleasures cannot be measured with accuracy and hence are not comparable. It is doubtless possible to say that the pleasure of contemplating one's favorite heroine on the movie screen is more intense than the pleasure of reading this account of Utilitarianism, but one cannot say that the former pleasure is twice (or ten times, or a hundred times) more pleasurable. Yet, if Bentham's greatest happiness principle is really to work (if intensity is to be weighed against, say, duration, purity, and extent), intensity must be capable of exact measurement.

The fact is, as Hume had pointed out, that pleasures differ qualitatively rather than quantitatively. Psychologically speaking, it is an oversimplification to talk about pleasure as if it were a qualitatively constant feeling that attaches itself in varying amounts to different activities. For surely the pleasure of eating lobster and the pleasure of eating oysters are not so much quantitatively different as qualitatively different. Hence measurement of the quantity of pleasures is not merely difficult; it is impossible.

UTILITARIAN MORAL THEORY

These criticisms have been confined to pointing out that the Utilitarians were mistaken in supposing that their principle provides a completely satisfactory decision-making instrument. But those who attribute an intrinsic value to motives will find still another deficiency in Utilitarianism: The theory can assign to motives no more than an extrinsic value. Many people, for instance, hold that although it is good to contribute to charities like the Community Chest, it is morally worthless or even contemptible to do so from a motive like publicity-seeking. It is only morally valuable to contribute from a motive like benevolence. Utilitarianism cannot account for this kind of distinction. The only possible utilitarian ground for valuing the benevolence motive above the publicity motive would be the propensity of the former to be more productive of charitable giving than the latter. That benevolence actually has this propensity is debatable; but even if it did, this fact does not seem to be the basis for our preference for it.

Another weakness of Bentham's version of Utilitarianism is its narrow conception of good. Here the question is not whether men always *do* aim at their own pleasure, but whether, if they did always aim at it, they would be leading as fully moral a life as possible. Mill saw the limitations of Bentham's position, and in his essay *Utilitarianism* he tried to correct it. The good, Mill held, cannot be defined simply as a quantity of pleasure, for some pleasures are superior to others. The morally sensitive Utilitarian must therefore aim at producing the greatest possible number of superior pleasures in as wide a distribution as possible. If men were given the choice between being a pig and being Socrates, who, Mill asked, would choose the former? No one, he thought. But since the pig wallowing innocently in his sty obviously has a greater quantum of pleasure than did Socrates brooding in an Athenian jail, the strict Benthamite would have to prefer piggery to philosophy. The fact that he would choose philosophy proves (Mill argued) that utility must take account of the fact that some pleasures (in this case, the pleasure of knowledge) are qualitatively preferable to others (the pleasure of a full stomach).

Mill, it will be seen, did not doubt that "pleasure" is quantifiable. He merely held that pleasures vary not only quantitatively (pleasure A is more intense or more durable than pleasure B) but morally (pleasure A is "higher" than pleasure B). But in thus improving on Bentham's position ethically, Mill introduced a second factor, moral superiority, without giving any criterion for comparison. Suppose pleasure A is more intense than pleasure B, but that B is "higher" than A. How are we to choose between them?

Here again Utilitarianism has run into a problem of incommensurate values. In his essay *On Liberty* Mill failed to face up to this difficulty because he mistakenly believed that maximization of utility leads to the same policy decisions as those reached by consideration of the value of freedom. But, as has been pointed out, liberty and utility are unfortunately often in conflict. It would appear, then, that self-consciousness and the "higher" kinds of knowledge, like liberty, may be incommensurate with the maximization of pleasure.

Let us examine Mill's proof that pleasure (as he understood it, and including the qualitative distinctions just noted) is the supreme end for man.

> Questions about ends are . . . questions what things are desirable. The utilitarian doctrine is, that happiness is desirable, and the only thing desirable, as an end; all other things being only desirable as means to that end. What ought to be required of this doctrine—what conditions is it requisite that the doctrine should fulfil—to make good its claim to be believed?
>
> The only proof capable of being given that an object is visible, is that people actually see it. The only proof that a sound is audible, is that people hear it: and so of the other sources of our experience. In like manner, I apprehend, the sole evidence it is possible to produce that anything is desirable, is that people do actually desire it. . . . This being a fact, we have not only all the proof which the case admits of, but all which it is possible to require, that happiness is a good: that each person's happiness is a good to that person, and the general happiness, therefore, a good to the aggregate of all persons.[g]

Even if we agree that pleasure is the only thing men do desire, does it follow that pleasure is the only thing men ought to desire? Surely not. Mill's confusion here results from his mistaken belief that "visible" and "desirable" are analogous concepts. Since "visible" means "capable of being seen," the fact that people actually see an object is certain proof that it is visible. But "desirable" does not mean "capable of being desired"; it means "worth desiring." And the fact that I desire something no more implies that it is worth desiring than does the fact that I see something prove that it is worth seeing. Doubtless Mill would never have fallen into this confusion of facts (what I do desire) with values (what I ought to desire) if he had not been dominated by the utilitarian ambition to fashion a "scientific" theory of value.

SUMMARY

Utilitarianism (especially in the form of Bentham's moral calculus) is in fact a good example of the deleterious effect that results from treating the natural sciences as the ideal of knowledge per se, and from trying to impose on value-judgments the same criteria that hold in science. The calculus appealed to the Utilitarians, not only because it was useful, but because it seemed to make a science of morality. It claimed, that is, to yield precise, measurable, and objectively valid results. But it is only a pseudoscience, for (as is clearly shown by Mill's correction of Bentham's position) nuances of judgments about taste and morals escape between its quantified categories.

But if, instead of examining Utilitarianism at the theoretical level, we consider it at the level of practice—that is, if we consider the impact it had on social legislation—its influence was great and, on the whole, benign. The Utilitarians were, indeed, not so much theorists as reformers; their theories were designed to be judged by their efficacy as instruments of reform as well as by criteria of logical consistency. In their pragmatism and empiricism, the Utilitarians were spokesmen for the coming age, and they were far in advance of, say, Hegel, who was almost an exact contemporary of Bentham. Yet in one respect Hegel was in advance of Bentham. For in his conception of dialectic Hegel caught a glimpse of the idea of process, one of the leading motifs of nineteenth-century thought. Bentham, in contrast, had virtually no sense of history—no sense, that is, of the slow growth and unfolding of institutions in the course of which they carry their past into their present.

When Bentham looked at existing institutions, he was filled with disgust. In his view, the common law was a hopeless hodgepodge, a confused jungle of precedents dating back to remote antiquity. Let us then do away with all this rubbish, he argued, and provide judges with a single, complete, simple, and above all convenient code of laws. And let us do the same for every other department of life. Everything must be reorganized and put on a rational basis. This rather naïve belief in the possibility of a neat package, this notion that the universe is basically simple and that the mind can fathom its simplicities and use the knowledge of them as a model for conduct, shows how close the Benthamites were to the Age of Reason. It is this duality of view—this Janus-like posture in which they faced both toward the past and toward the future—that makes the Utilitarians so interesting to historians of culture.

Comte

Like the Utilitarians, Comte[4] saw that the development of science had given man great powers to improve his lot and to create a satisfactory environment for himself. He also saw, as they did, that science had created vast social problems that had not existed in earlier and simpler times. Like the Utilitarians, he noted the disparity between the high level of knowledge of physical nature and the almost total lack of application of the new methods to the study of man. Like the Utilitarians, he thought the solution was to create a science of man and to utilize it to solve all the menacing social problems that had followed in the wake of the Industrial Revolution. To develop and to apply such a science seemed to Comte a relatively easy task; he would have been amazed had he known that men are still calling upon science to solve the problems that science helped to create.

THE ADMINISTRATIVE POINT OF VIEW

One reason why Comte was optimistic about the development of a scientific sociology was that, like the Utilitarians, he shared the Enlightenment's sense of human rationality and of the orderliness of the universe. But he had lost the Enlightenment's conviction that all (or, at least, most) men are rational and capable of acting on the basis of a long-range, intelligent analysis. He thought that in most men emotion is dominant and that only a few men—an elite—are capable of sitting down in a cool hour and using scientific method to ascertain *the* answers. Hence his is the administrative point of view *par excellence:* Although the social world looks like a mighty maze to the layman, to the administrator it falls into a relatively simple pattern. The whole problem, therefore, is to enable the administrator to put his scientific knowledge to work in improving the condition of society.

But how is the administrator to induce citizens to adopt his programs? Given the inferior intellects of the majority of citizens, Comte did not think it practicable to rely on each individual's recognition that conformity is, in the long run, most likely to promote his own self-interest. Rather, Comte advocated a

---

4 Auguste Comte (1798–1857) was the son of a French tax collector. He suffered most of his life from poverty and ill health, to which was added an unhappy marriage. For the last nine years of his life, however, Comte was supported by a subsidy raised by public subscription.

highly organized and tightly controlled society of the kind that "economic planning" has made familiar in our time; within this framework, conformity would be assured by appeals to emotion and sentiment. Though this is a thorough rejection of *laissez faire*, there is less difference between Comte's position and that of the Benthamites than might be supposed. Bentham could believe in more *laissez* and less *faire* because, men being simple pleasure-machines, the administrator's job becomes simply one of adding and subtracting suitable units of pleasure. Comte had to argue for less *laissez* and more *faire* because he rejected this simple conception of motivation. Hence, instead of depending on citizens to make the pleasure-pain calculus that Bentham believed them capable of, Comte invented an elaborate religion, with a new calendar of saints, new festivals, and a new cult, designed to move men to adopt the socially acceptable conduct that the administrators wished them to follow.[5]

Thus Comte belongs to the Platonic tradition, both in the sense that he held there is a definite set of answers and in the sense that he believed only relatively few people capable of discerning and acting on them. But whereas Plato believed that these answers are eternal forms cognized by pure acts of reason, Comte held them to be empirical connections ascertainable by methods similar to those used in the natural sciences.

PRIMACY OF CONCEPT OF PROCESS

Another important element in Comte's philosophy is his emphasis on process. During the whole of the period from Hobbes and Descartes through Kant, philosophers had thought of cognition as the analysis of a static reality. This was true because all these thinkers—even the empiricists and the nominalists—were dominated by a belief in the geometric ideal and by the conviction that there is an eternal order of eternal truths.

In Hegel, however, the new point of view had begun to emerge. Hegel's whole dialectical method resulted from a belief that reality is dynamic, not static, and that it therefore requires an analysis different from anything that earlier thinkers had believed appropriate. But Hegel had also held that the real is rational. Comte abandoned this rationalistic dictum and concentrated his attention on the actual, dynamic social process, which he tried to make sense of by showing that it conforms to "law." This law was derived not from reflection

---

5 This calendar was divided into thirteen months, each named for a great man—for example, Homer, Aristotle, Charlemagne, Gutenberg, and Shakespeare. To every day in the year a "saint" was assigned. The saints were arranged systematically under their appropriate months—Fielding, Voltaire, Goethe, Molière, and Lope de Vega, for instance, were all assigned days in the month of Shakespeare. Comte also set out in detail the forms of worship, the symbols ("a woman of the age of thirty with her son in her arms"), and the banners (green and white) to be carried in processions. The intention was to rouse men's feelings for "humanity"—to make them aware of their unity and thus to counteract the selfish motives that normally lead to divisive action and conflicts of all kinds. Comte described all this in exhaustive detail in *The Catechism of the Positive Religion.*

on the nature of what a rational-real must be, but from a supposedly "scientific" and empirical study of the historical process itself. In other words, Comte attempted to apply to the study of man the empirical methods of the natural sciences.

THE LAW OF THREE STAGES

Comte's major generalization about human history was formulated in what he called the "law of three stages." According to this law, every branch of knowledge evolves through three distinct phases. In the first stage, or *theological* phase, causal explanation is based on the idea of volition. This level was reached in physics when, for instance, thunder and lightning were attributed to Zeus's desire to frighten lesser gods and men. The second stage, or *metaphysical* phase, marks a distinct advance. Crude anthropomorphism is replaced by causal explanation based on abstract concepts. This was the level reached in physics when causes were "taken to be abstract forces, veritable entities (that is, personified abstractions) inherent in all beings"—when, that is, men believed that entelechies and vital forces caused stones to seek the center of the earth and acorns to grow up into oaks. The third and final stage, or *scientific* phase, is reached when the attempt to explain is abandoned for the attempt to describe. This stage was reached in physics when Galileo said it was his "purpose merely to investigate . . . some of the properties of accelerated motion, whatever the cause of this acceleration may be."

Note that Comte has radically transformed Kant's account of metaphysics. He agreed with Kant, of course, that metaphysical knowledge is impossible; he also agreed that metaphysics is a "natural disposition." But he denied that this disposition has the intrinsic value that Kant attributed to it. Metaphysical thinking, according to Comte, occurs only at an immature stage in the development of the human mind, and it is destined to die out. The fact that Comte treated metaphysics entirely in an historical context and refused to evaluate it except as relative to that context is typical of the new emphasis on historicity, relativism, and development. Note also that Comte's third stage reflects the phenomenalistic outlook that was coming to the fore. At the third stage men finally understand the world as it really is. That is, according to Comte, reality is identical with Kant's spatiotemporal manifold. Explanation is impossible, because there is nothing to explain; there are only temporal relations of coexistence and succession. The sole business of science is to formulate generalizations regarding the relations actually observed to exist among events.

Is the law of three stages really a law? It is certainly not itself an instance of third-phase thinking (as Comte supposed it to be). That the physical sciences have passed, roughly speaking, through a developmental sequence of the kind Comte described seems to be the case. But this is very scanty evidence on which to formulate a universal historical law. It is, rather, as if Newton had concluded from a few observations of apples in his orchard that gravity is a universal law.

Here it can be seen, even more plainly than with the Utilitarians, that the attempt to take over the criteria and techniques of the physical sciences is likely to result, at the level of social study, in pseudoscience.

It should also be noted that Comte confusedly identified facts and values. Because he held that the scientific level of explanation is the latest reached (a statement of fact), he assumed that it is the best (a statement of value). The assumption, commonly made by thinkers who emphasize process and development, that "later equals better" corresponds to the old rationalistic assumption that "more real equals better."

It was easy for Comte to make this assumption, since, like the Utilitarians, he was interested less in theory—whether theory of knowledge or theory of value—than in practice. Using natural science as his model, he proposed to advance the study of society to the scientific level of thought, which natural science had already reached. In its theological stage, sociology had explained social events by reference to the will of God, and it had justified political authority by divine-right doctrines. In its metaphysical stage (in which, Comte believed, it had bogged down), it explained social events in terms of fictitious abstractions like "state of nature" and "social contract." But positivism, as Comte called his view,[6] would be a real science of society—a social physics, as it were. This scientific sociology would be divided into two main branches: social statics, concerned with describing the laws of order, and social dynamics, concerned with describing the laws of progress.

Comte believed that men had only to look around them to see the need of developing this new social physics, the instrument by which administrators and bureaucrats would bring order out of chaos. To Comte, the chaos—moral, social, political, and intellectual—of the nineteenth century had resulted from the fact that, although the ideas that formerly ordered society had been destroyed, social physics was not yet sufficiently developed to supply new ideas. The old military-feudal social organization, which was simply a reflection of the theological level of thinking, had been outmoded since the sixteenth century. Science had destroyed the theological spirit, while industry had destroyed the feudal-military spirit. To Comte, the view that survived was hopelessly retrograde—holders of this view wished to revert to a type of social organization that was wholly incompatible with the industrialized and urbanized society they also wished to retain. Here, of course, Comte was referring to the type of reactionary politics that had animated the Holy Alliance and that was still stubbornly opposing change both at home and abroad.

ATTACK ON LIBERALISM AND DEMOCRACY

But Comte had equally little use for the liberal opinion that was also at large in the world, busily urging reform. For Comte, liberalism was merely a reflection

6 This should not be confused with Logical Positivism, a movement that developed about one hundred years later, partly in an attempt to carry out Russell's program of philosophical reform. See p. 205 and Vol. V, Ch. 7.

of the second, or metaphysical, level of thought, and its insistence on democracy, liberty, equality, and fraternity made it very dangerous. It was true, he thought, that this "metaphysical polity" had been useful in demolishing the old feudal-military polity and in exploding the myth of divine right by insisting on the "rights of man." But it was totally incapable of formulating any positive conceptions to take the place of those it had destroyed. Every so-called liberal principle was in fact only a "dogma" created by trying to erect a particular criticism of the theological level of thought into a positive doctrine. An example is the "dogma of the sovereignty of the people." Because it "condemns all subordination of inferiors to superiors," it results in anarchy if retained as a positive doctrine. Another example is the "dogma of liberty of conscience." This is

> . . . the mere abstract expression (such as is common in metaphysics) of the temporary state of unbounded liberty in which the human mind was left by the decay of the theological philosophy, and which must last till the social advent of the positive philosophy. . . .
>
> Indispensable and salutary as it has been, this dogma . . . constitutes an obstacle to reorganization. . . . We ignore the deepest necessities of human reason when we would protract that scepticism which is produced by the passage from one mode of belief to another, and which is, in our need of fixed points of conviction, a kind of morbid perturbation which cannot be prolonged beyond the corresponding crisis without serious danger. To be always examining and never deciding would be regarded as something like madness in private conduct. . . . There are very few persons who consider themselves fit to sit in judgment on the astronomical, physical, and chemical ideas which are destined to enter into social circulation; and everybody is willing that those ideas should direct corresponding operations. . . . Can it be supposed that the most important and the most delicate conceptions, and those which by their complexity are accessible to only a small number of highly-prepared understandings, are to be abandoned to the arbitrary and variable decisions of the least competent minds? [h]

It was therefore natural that Comte would be critical of British (and American) parliamentary democracy. The features that some people regard as the strengths of this type of organization—its endless debate and compromise, its dislike of having to make a clean-cut decision, its preference for dealing with specific grievances instead of committing itself to grand principles or large programs—all these infuriated Comte's administrative mind. How much one sympathizes with his criticisms will depend, not so much on whether one thinks that Comte himself supplied "the" answers, as on what one holds to be the chance of developing a true science of society. Obviously, as the conditions of modern life have grown more complex, the need for expert knowledge has increased. The incompetence of ordinary citizens and of their ordinary, elected representatives to resolve the complicated economic and social problems that face modern societies is too notorious to require illustration. On the other hand, it is notoriously dangerous to turn political power over to experts. In the first place, a pseudo-science that is held to be infallible (and that thus becomes doctrinaire) could be disastrous, even though its proponents had the best intentions in the world. In the second place, even granting that a true social science is possible, one must ask whether the superior knowledge of the social scientist is accompanied by a higher order of morality that makes it safe to trust him with the power that knowledge brings. There is little in the history of the century that has elapsed since Comte's death to give us much confidence on either of these scores; there is much to make us realize that the dual problem of acquiring expert knowledge and applying it effectively is one of the critical questions for modern man.

Marx

In many respects Marx's[7] philosophical position is similar to those of the other thinkers whose views are examined in this chapter. Like them, he was deeply concerned about social problems and believed that "science" could guide the continued progress of man by supplying the correct answers to all social questions. Like them, too, he had a phenomenalistic outlook. For Marx, reality was coextensive with Kant's spatiotemporal manifold: There is no transcendent realm beyond the world encountered in experience. Theology and metaphysics, which claim to provide information about such a transcendent world, are only ideologies, by-products of social forces and thus without cognitive reference. In these respects Marx belongs, like the Benthamites and the positivists, to that empirical and scientific tradition that combined Condorcet's optimistic belief in the inevitability of "progress" with the belief that human nature as well as the physical universe conforms to simple "laws" that can be discovered by science.

On the other hand, Marx was much more deeply influenced by Hegel than was any of these other thinkers. Like Hegel, he was a systematizer in the grand manner, and he too held that the key to system is dialectic. And, like Hegel, Marx was responsive to the notion of development, a notion that was becoming a major element in the nineteenth-century climate of opinion, with a concomitant focusing of attention on the philosophy of history. Finally, for Marx as well as for Hegel, "alienation" was a central concept.

ALIENATION

The notion of alienation appears in Hegel's thought as the negative phase of the dialectic—the phase of "otherness," of opposition, of conflict, of media-

---

7 Karl Marx (1818–83) was born in Trier, in the Rhineland, of well-to-do Jewish parents who became Christians when Marx was a child. He was a student at the University of Berlin shortly after Hegel's death, while the latter's influence was still strong. Marx's radical opinions made an academic career impossible; he was tried for treason for his part in the abortive German revolution of 1848–49, and, though acquitted, he was exiled. He spent the remainder of his life in England, where he supported himself by acting as a correspondent for various newspapers, among them, the New York *Tribune*.

tion. By uncovering a discrepancy, it is the driving force for progress and advance to a higher level—it is the Nothing that negates Being at the very start of the Hegelian system. At a later level it is Civil Society, which replaces the "immediacy" of the Family. More generally, and in terms of the admission-procedures analogy discussed earlier,[8] it is the phase of reliance on "objective" tests and formal procedures, which results from having come to distrust the policy of accepting students on the basis of the immediate impression they make in a face-to-face interview. Hegel not only thought of this phase of alienation, of criticism and negativity, as the impetus to advance; he also believed that alienation is finally overcome in a synthesis that includes it while transcending it. For instance, Civil Society is transcended in the State (a political organization modeled on the Prussian monarchy of Hegel's day), which supposedly incorporates the best features both of the Family and of Civil Society. This generally optimistic attitude places Hegel, however much he differed from the Enlightenment thinkers in other respects, in the mainstream of eighteenth-century rationalism.

The Enlightenment philosophers had simply not experienced alienation as a problem, for they had found the world they lived in to be basically congenial. Increasingly, however, in the course of the nineteenth century alienation came to be regarded as an inevitable part of the human condition. It is not surprising that, as the nineteenth century advanced, man came to feel more and more alone and a stranger in the world. Urbanization, with the anonymity it entails; the rootlessness of modern life; mass production, with its separation of the producer from the product and from any sense of fulfillment he might experience; and above all, perhaps, an increasingly secularistic attitude that seemed to leave no place for God or for gods—all these factors contributed to man's feeling of alienation.

The Romantic poets, who wanted to be at one with nature, often felt estranged from it: It seemed to them that the universe had been depersonalized, deanimated, and demythologized by a mechanistic science. This mood was expressed by Keats:

> There was an awful rainbow once in heaven:
> We know her woof, her texture; she is given
> In the dull catalogue of common things.
> Philosophy will clip an Angel's wings,
> Conquer all mysteries by rule and line,
> Empty the haunted air, and gnomed mine—
> Unweave a rainbow. . . .[i]

This sense that man is alone in an indifferent or even hostile universe, this sense of being estranged not only from nature but from other men and even from oneself, deepened as the century advanced. Dostoevsky's underground man is

8 See p. 129.

a powerful example of this sense of alienation. The thinkers discussed in the next chapter typify the way in which this mood profoundly altered the tonality of philosophical theory. For Kierkegaard and later nineteenth-century thinkers, alienation was an inevitable feature of the human condition, from which man is redeemed, if at all, only by grace.

Hegel and Marx, however, were transitional figures in this respect: Although they experienced alienation as a serious problem, they held it to be only a phase in the unfolding of human history; it could and would be overcome. Though both interpreted alienation in historical terms, Hegel thought of it primarily cognitively—as a stage in the development of the spirit toward increasingly full and articulated self-consciousness. Marx interpreted it in socioeconomic and psychological terms. The alienation that concerned him was the estrangement of the worker in an industrial and capitalistic society, an estrangement both from himself and from his fellow men:

> From political economy itself we have shown that the worker sinks to the level of a commodity, and to a most miserable commodity; that the misery of the worker increases with the power and volume of his production; that the necessary result of competition is the accumulation of capital in a few hands, and thus a restoration of monopoly in a more terrible form; and finally that the distinction between capitalist and landlord, and between agricultural labourer and industrial worker, must disappear, and the whole of society divide into the two classes of property owners and *propertyless* workers.
>
> Thus we have now to grasp the real connexion between this whole system of alienation—private property, acquisitiveness, the separation of labour, capital and land, exchange and competition, value and the devaluation of man, monopoly and competition—and the system of *money.*
>
> We shall begin from a *contemporary* economic fact. The worker becomes poorer the more wealth he produces and the more his production increases in power and extent. The worker becomes an ever cheaper commodity the more goods he creates. The *devaluation* of the human world increases in direct relation with the *increase in value* of the world of things. Labour does not only create goods; it also produces itself and the worker as a *commodity,* and indeed in the same proportion as it produces goods.
>
> This fact simply implies that the object produced by labour, its product, now stands opposed to it as an *alien being,* as a *power independent* of the producer. The product of labour is labour which has been embodied in an object and turned into a physical thing; this product is an objectification of labour. . . . The performance of work [is] a *vitiation* of the worker, objectification [is] a loss and *servitude to the object,* and appropriation [is] *alienation.*
>
> So much does the performance of work appear as vitiation that the worker is vitiated to the point of starvation. So much does objectification appear as loss of the object that the worker is deprived of the most essential things not only of life but also of work. . . . So much does the appropriation of the object appear as alienation that the more objects the worker produces the fewer he can possess and the more he falls under the domination of his product, of capital.

All of these consequences follow from the fact that the worker is related to the *product of his labour* as to an *alien* object. . . . The more the worker expends himself in work the more powerful becomes the world of objects which he creates in face of himself, the poorer he becomes in his inner life, and the less he belongs to himself. . . . The worker puts his life into the object, and his life then belongs no longer to himself but to the object. The greater his activity, therefore, the less he possesses. What is embodied in the product of his labour is no longer his own. The greater this product is, therefore, the more he is diminished. The *alienation* of the worker in his product means not only that his labour becomes an object, assumes an *external* existence, but that it exists independently, *outside himself,* and alien to him, and that it stands opposed to him as an autonomous power. The life which he has given to the object sets itself against him as an alien and hostile force.

What constitutes the alienation of labour? First, that the work is *external* to the worker, that it is not part of his nature; and that, consequently, he does not fulfil himself in his work, but denies himself, has a feeling of misery rather than well-being, does not develop freely his mental and physical energies but is physically exhausted and mentally debased. . . . Finally, the external character of work for the worker is shown by the fact that it is not his own work but work for someone else, that in work he does not belong to himself but to another person.[j]

SURPLUS VALUE AND THE EXPLOITATION OF THE WORKERS

The clue to understanding the causes of alienation was the discovery of *surplus value.* Locke had worked out a defense of property based on the distinction between what exists simply in the state of nature (for example, trees growing in a forest) and what man has "removed" from that state by "mixing his labor with it" (trees chopped down and cut into logs). According to Locke, I am justified in appropriating for my own use, to dispose of as I will, whatever I have mixed my labor with. Locke, of course, had in mind very simple societies (for example, nut and berry gatherers); Marx realized that the argument had a very different effect when applied to a society in which many men contribute their labor to machines that a few men own. Under such an economic system, the workers do not retain the surplus value that is produced when they mix their labor with the raw materials of nature; on the contrary, the surplus value accrues to the owners of the machines. As it was stated by Marx's friend and collaborator, Friedrich Engels,[9]

> . . . the appropriation of unpaid labor is the basis of the capitalist mode of production, and of the exploitation of the worker that occurs under it; even

9 Engels (1820–95), Marx's collaborator for forty years, was born in Prussia but lived most of his later life in England. According to his own modest assessment, he "had a certain independent share in laying the foundations of the theory, and, more particularly in its elaboration. But the greater part of its leading basic principles . . . belong to Marx. What I contributed . . . Marx could very well have done without me. What Marx accomplished, I would not have achieved"—*Ludwig Feuerbach and the End of Classical German Philosophy* (Feuer 224).

> if the capitalist buys the labor power of his laborer at its full value as a commodity on the market he yet extracts more value from it than he paid for, and in the ultimate analysis this surplus value forms those sums of value from which are heaped up the constantly increasing masses of capital in the hands of the possessing classes.[k]

The concept of surplus value thus raises a difficult economic question. Fortunately, it is not necessary to evaluate this question in order to understand the main steps in Marx's and Engels' argument: As a result of the industrialization of Europe a fundamental incompatibility had developed between the modes of production on the one hand and the modes of appropriation on the other:

> In the medieval stage of evolution of the production of commodities, the question as to the owner of the product of labor could not arise. The individual producer, as a rule, had, from raw materials belonging to himself . . . , produced it with his own tools. . . . It belonged wholly to him, as a matter of course. His property in the product was, therefore, based *upon his own labor.* . . .
>
> Then came the concentration of the means of production and of the producers in large workshops and manufactories, their transformation into actual socialized means of production and socialized producers. But the socialized producers and means of production and their products were still treated, after this change, just as they had been before, i.e., as the means of production and the products of individuals. Hitherto the owner of the instruments of labor had himself appropriated the product, because, as a rule, it was his own product. . . . Now the owner of the instruments of labor always appropriated to himself the product, although it was no longer *his* product, but exclusively the product of the *labor of others.* . . .
>
> This contradiction, which gives to the new mode of production its capitalistic character, *contains the germ of the whole of the social antagonisms of today.* . . .
>
> The contradiction between socialized production and capitalistic appropriation manifested itself as the antagonism of proletariat and bourgeoisie.[1]

There is thus a grave disparity between the means of production, which have long since been socialized, and property, which remains in private hands and which resists socialization. To remove this disparity, property must be socialized. In a word, since capitalism is responsible for the alienation of the worker (by expropriating his product and by objectifying his relation to it), capitalism must be destroyed. The solution of existing problems "can only consist in the practical recognition of the social nature of the modern force of production, and therefore in the harmonizing of the modes of production, appropriation, and exchange with the socialized character of the means of production. And this can only come about by society openly and directly taking possession of the productive forces. . . ."[m]

What will life be like when this happens? Marx makes it seem idyllic:

> In communist society, where nobody has one exclusive sphere of activity but each can become accomplished in any branch he wishes, society regulates the general production and thus makes it possible for me to do one thing today and another tomorrow, to hunt in the morning, fish in the afternoon, rear cattle in the evening, criticize after dinner, just as I have a mind, without ever becoming hunter, fisherman, shepherd or critic.[n]

This is certainly a utopian outlook, and Marx did not for long believe that it would be possible to escape division of labor in industrial societies merely by changing the modes of appropriation. The main and persistent note, however, is freedom—specifically, the freedom to become a person, a full human being. In a Communist society every man will not only have an existence that is "fully sufficient materially"; he will also have "an existence guaranteeing the free development and exercise" of his "physical and mental faculties."

Communist freedom, then, is the opposite of alienation and objectification. Instead of being treated by other men as an object, and instead of perceiving himself as an object, a mere thing, every man becomes a center of life, creating himself by and through his free choices.

> The extraneous objective forces that have hitherto governed history pass under the control of man himself. Only from that time will man himself, more and more consciously, make his own history—only from that time will the social causes set in movement by him have, in the main and in a constantly growing measure, the results intended by him. It is the ascent of man from the kingdom of necessity to the kingdom of freedom.[o]

The high value that Marx attributes here to human personality is of course common to many thinkers—for instance, to the philosophers of the Enlightenment and to Mill and the Utilitarians. But the language in which this value is stated and the particular quality and flavor given it are different. Marx emphasizes subjectivity, freedom, and self-consciousness; he stresses *making* a life by one's own choices, as distinct from merely *being* a thing. These emphases stem directly from Hegel's theory and ultimately from Kant's contrast between inner and outer experience and from his conception of the self as the synthesizer, the "transcendental unity" whose activity makes experience possible. This conception of "subjectivity" as the goal toward which individuals and societies should aim, despite all the circumstances that increasingly produce "objectivity," was to become one of the central structural and organizing ideas of the nineteenth century, and it was to be adopted by thinkers who in other respects were hostile to Marx and to Marxism.

In discussing their theories of the alienation and exploitation of the worker, Marx and Engels alternate between playing the role of propagandists and playing the role of scientists. In their role as propagandists they urge the workers to unite, and they denounce the crimes of the capitalists: The existing regime must be overthrown, and the purpose of their writings is to mobilize the forces necessary to accomplish this. In their role as scientists they do not incite; rather, they describe and generalize. From this point of view it is not necessary to mobilize the workers: The overthrow of capitalism will not be "brought about"; it will inevitably occur, as a result of economic forces, laws that individuals are powerless to control.

THEORY OF SOCIAL CAUSATION

The propagandistic and scientific points of view are obviously not easy to reconcile. Let us begin discussion of them with Marx's and Engels' theories of social causation and historical determinism. These theories have had perhaps even greater influence than their economic doctrines and deserve examination on their own merits, independent of the concept of surplus value. One of the simplest statements of this theory is contained in the *Manifesto of the Communist Party*, which Marx and Engels wrote in 1847 in anticipation of the revolutionary movement that broke out the following year. The fundamental thesis of the *Manifesto* is stated in the opening sentence: "The history of all hitherto existing society is the history of class struggles." This is expanded by Engels (in a preface written in 1888, after Marx's death) into the assertion

> . . . that in every historical epoch, the prevailing mode of economic production and exchange, and the social organization necessarily following from it, form the basis upon which is built up, and from which alone can be explained, the political and intellectual history of that epoch; that consequently the whole history of mankind . . . has been a history of class struggles, contests between exploiting and exploited, ruling and oppressed classes; that the history of these class struggles forms a series of evolutions in which a stage has [now] been reached where the exploited and oppressed class—the proletariat—cannot attain its emancipation from the sway of the exploiting and ruling class—the bourgeoisie—without at the same time, and once and for all, emancipating society at large from all exploitation, oppression, class distinctions and class struggles.

What evidence did Marx and Engels adduce to support the thesis that the whole history of European society is but the reflection of "a series of revolutions in the modes of production and exchange"? Although they considered chiefly political factors, they held that alterations in esthetic and literary taste, in philosophical theory, and indeed in every department of life reflect these same underlying economic changes.

> Does it require deep intuition to comprehend that man's ideas, views, and conceptions, in one word, man's consciousness, changes with every change in the conditions of his material existence, in his social relations, and in his social life?
>
> What else does the history of ideas prove than that intellectual production changes in character in proportion as material production is changed? The ruling ideas of each age have ever been the ideas of its ruling class.[p]

Thus the feudal nobility, whose power rested on the prevailing type of economic organization, created a culture—artistic, architectural, literary, and philosophical—that was the expression of the feudal social structure. And this society, together with its various cultural idiosyncrasies, collapsed when the modes of production and exchange that had made possible the dominance of a military aristocracy were replaced by modes of production and exchange that were incompatible with feudal property relations. The social organization of the Middle Ages had therefore to give way to a new type of social structure. The first steps in this development occurred with the discovery and colonization of America and the expansion of trade into the Indian and Chinese markets. The guild system of manufacture was unable to supply these growing markets and was eventually replaced by a new organization of production (by division of labor in a single workshop) that was, relatively speaking, much more competent. And this in turn was revolutionized by the invention of machinery and the application of steam power. The result of all these economic changes was the emergence of a new dominant class. The burghers, who in feudal times had been oppressed in a manner indistinguishable from serfs, came to be first an "armed and self-governing" class in their free cities, then a "counterpoise" to the old nobility on the side of the new national monarchies, and finally the ruling class in the modern type of constitutional government.

This shift in the focus of power did not, however, abolish oppression and exploitation; it merely created a more efficient form of exploitation: "For exploitation, veiled by religious and political illusions [there has been] substituted naked, shameless, direct and brutal exploitation."

According to Marx, this bourgeois class proceeded to create a new (and very inferior) culture in its own image. Both moral and esthetic standards were determined by monetary considerations, and much touted political values like "freedom" and "individuality" merely reflected the absence of restriction and control that permitted the bourgeoisie to exploit the workers. These "fine, brave words" meant only a free market in which the capitalist hoped to buy labor cheaply and to sell goods dearly. Freedom and *laissez faire* meant freedom for the capitalist to exploit the worker.

But, according to Marx, this bourgeois class and its institutions are doomed by the very dialectic that enabled them to overthrow feudalism. Just as the feudal nobility was unable to control the economic forces it called up, so the bourgeoisie is confronted with the fact that the property relations underlying bourgeois society are incompatible with modern conditions of production. "The bourgeoisie is unfit . . . to rule because it is incompetent to assure an existence to its slave within his slavery, because it cannot help letting him sink into such a state that it has to feed him, instead of being fed by him. Society can no longer live under this bourgeoisie, in other words, its existence is no longer compatible with society."[q]

Because it is based on private ownership and private profits, bourgeois economy falls inevitably into periodic crises of "overproduction." The desire to make high profits reduces wages and hence cuts down the purchasing power of the public and creates surpluses. These crises are resolved only by opening up new markets or by more thoroughly exploiting old ones. But the new markets eventually become new centers of production themselves, and there is a limit to the absorption of goods by old markets. Thus an era of ever increasing stress develops.

Meanwhile, and again quite inevitably, the bourgeoisie has created the social class that will soon seize the opportunity presented by these recurring crises. For the conditions of modern production have first called into existence the proletariat and then collected it in urban centers where it gains strength and knowledge from this concentration in great masses. What is a proletarian? From the point of view of the capitalist owner, he is merely a soulless appendage to the machine. But the proletarians are gradually becoming aware of themselves and of their destiny. They are coming to realize that the old sanctions of law, morality, and religion, which formerly reconciled them to their lot, are "merely so many bourgeois prejudices behind which lurk just as many bourgeois interests." They are coming to realize the truth of dialectical materialism—namely, that the present conditions of ownership are not "eternally right" but merely a particular stage in social history; that every dominant class has always gained the upper hand by securing the "conditions of appropriation"; and that they can rise only by following the example of their present masters and "destroying the whole superincumbent strata of official society."

But the triumph of the proletariat will not merely bring about the rise of one more new class to repeat in its turn the old story of exploitation and oppression. On the contrary, as soon as the dictatorship of the proletariat has accomplished its purpose and destroyed the last vestiges of the old capitalistic society, the class type of society will disappear. Political power will also disappear, for political power is merely the organization of one class for the suppression of others.

Obviously, this new classless society will develop a culture radically different from anything yet known. For however much earlier societies have differed from one another, they have all had one common feature—class structure.

> No wonder, then, that the social consciousness of past ages, despite all the multiplicity and variety it displays, moves within certain common forms, or general ideas, which cannot completely vanish except with the total disappearance of class antagonisms.
>
> The Communist revolution is the most radical rupture with traditional property relations; no wonder that its development involves the most radical rupture with traditional ideas.[r]

PHILOSOPHY OF HISTORY

Before Marx's day and, as a matter of fact, for a long time afterwards, history was conceived of chiefly in political terms, as the product of decisions made by kings and statesmen to sign a treaty or not to sign it, to go to war or to remain at peace. Marx at once enlarged the scope of history and altered its scale by reducing the great personalities to a very minor role as compared with the economic forces that operated in the society that these men and their biographers supposed them to be guiding. How sympathetic this view is to what has been called the Romantic mood should be obvious. To Marx, Schopenhauer's real will was doubtless a merely anthropomorphic concept. But Marx and Schopenhauer were at least in agreement that the behavior of such individuals is determined by larger-than-individual, and less-than-rational, forces, and that the accounts that the individuals themselves offer of their behavior are inaccurate rationalizations of these underlying and impersonal causes.

There is little doubt that men's conduct is less rational and less enlightened than eighteenth-century thinkers had supposed, and it is important for historians and sociologists to take cognizance of this fact and to seek the nonrational factors that enter into the determination of conduct. But are economic causes more fundamental than other causes? If, for instance, economic factors determine esthetic taste, then esthetic taste (preference for silk over cotton, and so on) determines economic trends. The truth seems to be that a culture constitutes a very complex, interlocking set of relationships that can hardly be surveyed all at once. Hence one must adopt, every time one looks at a given culture, some point of view. From each of these points of view one set of relations necessarily occupies the foreground, and the other sets recede into the background. Because his interest in social reform and his sympathy for the plight of the alienated workers made economic conditions particularly important to Marx, economic relations remained consistently in the foreground of his thought; then, because he noted their prominence without noting the reason for it, he developed a theory of social causation to explain the supposed fact. It is as if a physician interested in the history of medicine first assumed that medical developments were always the basic factors in cultural movement and then tried to work out a medical dialectic to show why.

This serious oversimplification in his view of social causation was hidden from Marx by the ambiguity of his language—especially, the lack of precision in the key terms "production" and "exchange." In different contexts they have different meanings. Sometimes they refer in the most narrow way to purely technological changes—development of the wheel, application of steam, and so forth; sometimes they broaden to include "ideas" and "ideals." The broader meanings are more adequate to the complexity of the facts; the narrower meanings satisfy demands for an elegantly simple and "scientific" formula. Because he failed to notice the shifts from one meaning to another, Marx believed he had found a simple formula adequate to the facts.

That Marx's philosophy of history owes much to Hegel is obvious. It differs from Hegel's, of course, in the all-important fact that the spiritual dialectic (development of consciousness) has been replaced by a materialistic dialectic (changes in modes of production and exchange). The main difference, however, is one of tone. Hegel's favorite metaphor was the unfolding of bud into blossom into flower. According to Hegel, "world historical" figures, like Napoleon, may effect revolutionary changes, but the modal type of change, as it were, is gradual and natural, almost easy. In Marx's view, the modal type of change is revolutionary. Change is not a synthesis in which lower forms are incorporated and transcended in a higher form. Change involves the destruction of one class by another. In his belief that violence and conflict are fundamental realities Marx is far closer to Schopenhauer and to later thinkers like Nietzsche and the survival-of-the-fittest philosophers than he is to the Enlightenment and its rationalist descendants.

One major consequence of shifting to a materialistic dialectic is a transformation in the status of ideas and theories. For Hegel, ideas were the generating causes of all other changes. It was the recognition of some discrepancy or contradiction that led men to move on to a more inclusive and more comprehensive view of themselves and of the world. For Marx, ideas and theories were not causes but epiphenomena, passive by-products of the economic forces that are the real determinants of change. From this ideological way of thinking about theory, it is fair to say that theory has never quite recovered.

Marx's view of religion is a good introduction to his conception of the ideological character of thought in general.

> *Man makes religion;* religion does not make man. Religion is indeed man's self-consciousness and self-awareness so long as he has not found himself or has lost himself again. But *man* is not an abstract being, squatting outside the world. Man is *the human world*, the state, society. This state, this society, produce religion which is an *inverted world consciousness*, because they are an *inverted world*. . . .
>
> *Religious* suffering is at the same time an *expression* of real suffering and a *protest* against real suffering. Religion is the sigh of the oppressed creature, the sentiment of a heartless world, and the soul of soulless conditions. It is the *opium* of the people.
>
> The abolition of religion as the *illusory* happiness of men, is a demand for their *real* happiness. The call to abandon their illusions about their condition is a *call to abandon a condition which requires illusions*. The criticism of religion is, therefore, *the embryonic criticism of this vale of tears* of which religion is the halo.
>
> Criticism has plucked the imaginary flowers from the chain, not in order that men shall bear the chain without . . . consolation but so that he shall cast off the chain and pluck the living flower. The criticism of religion disillusions man so that he will think, act and fashion his reality as a man who has lost his illusions and regained his reason; so that he will revolve about himself as his own true sun. Religion is only the illusory sun about which man revolves so long as he does not revolve about himself. . . .
>
> Luther . . . shattered the faith in authority by restoring the authority of faith. He transformed the priests into laymen by turning laymen into priests. He liberated man from external religiosity by making religiosity the innermost

essence of man. He liberated the body from its chains because he fettered the heart with chains.

But if Protestantism was not the solution it did at least pose the problem correctly. It was no longer a question, thereafter, of the layman's struggle against the priest outside himself, but of his struggle against his *own internal priest,* against his own *priestly nature.*[s]

Thus, though religions claim to be making assertions, for instance, about God, the language of religion is not cognitive; it is only expressive. Religions do not report what is true of the world; they express our inner feelings, tensions, and anxieties. Specifically, they express our despair at "the alienation of man from himself and from nature." Furthermore, religions express this despair in forms that exactly correspond to the other institutions of a culture at any given time. For instance, the objectification and alienation that infect economic and social institutions are reflected in religious beliefs and practices. "Objectification is the practice of alienation. Just as man, so long as he is engrossed in religion, can only objectify his essence by an *alien* and fantastic being; so under the sway of egoistic need, he can only affirm himself and produce objects in practice by subordinating his products and his own activity to the domination of an alien entity, . . . namely money."[t] It follows that the different religions of men living in different places and in different ages "are nothing more than *stages in the development of the human mind—*snake skins which have been cast off by history, and *man* is the snake who clothed himself in them. . . ."[u]

What is true of religion is true of philosophy, and of theory in general. Changes in political theory, or in the legal system, for instance, "are not explained by the so-called general progress of the human mind." They express and reflect "the material conditions of life."

> The mode of production in material life determines the general character of the social, political and spiritual processes of life. It is not the consciousness of men that determines their existence, but, on the contrary, their social existence determines their consciousness. . . . With [any] change of the economic foundation the entire immense superstructure is more or less rapidly transformed. In considering such transformations the distinction should always be made between the material transformation of the economic conditions of production, which can be determined with the precision of natural science, and the legal, political, religious, aesthetic, or philosophic—in short, ideological forms in which men become conscious of this conflict and fight it out.[v]

Thus in the eighteenth century a philosophical theory had emerged that was appropriate for that age. According to this theory,

> . . . superstition, injustice, privilege, oppression were to be superseded by eternal truth, eternal Right, equality based on Nature and the inalienable rights of man.

> We know today that this kingdom of reason was nothing more than the idealized kingdom of the bourgeoisie; that this eternal Right found its realization in bourgeois justice; that this equality reduced itself to bourgeois equality before the law; that bourgeois property was proclaimed as one of the essential rights of man. . . . The great thinkers of the eighteenth century could, no more than their predecessors, go beyond the limits imposed upon them by their epoch.[w]

But what about the great thinkers of the nineteenth century? Did Marx believe that he had succeeded in going beyond the limits imposed by *his* epoch? It is impossible to find in his writings an unambiguous answer. Part of the time—or perhaps it is fairer to say, "all of the time with a part of his mind"—Marx holds that his theory is an exception. It is somehow (but how, exactly?) immune to the cultural relativism that infects all other theories. It is no mere ideology; it is *true*. For instance, the conflict between what religion claims to be and what Marx says it is not merely an ideological dispute reflecting the differing class interests of the contestants. It is a conflict between false claims and scientifically proven assertions: "It is the *task of history,* therefore, once the *other-world of truth* has vanished, to establish the *truth of this world.* The immediate *task of philosophy,* which is in the service of history, is to unmask human self-alienation in its *secular form* now that it has been unmasked in its *sacred form.*"[x]

On the other hand, in the same work Marx suggests that his theory will undermine religion, not because it is true and religion is false, but because it is a more powerful ideology.

> Material force can only be overthrown by material force; but theory itself becomes a material force when it has seized the masses. Theory is capable of seizing the masses when it demonstrates *ad hominem,* and it demonstrates *ad hominem,* as soon as it becomes radical. To be radical is to grasp things by the root. But for man the root is man himself. What proves beyond doubt the radicalism of German theory, and thus its practical energy, is that it begins from the resolute *positive* abolition of religion.[y]

The fact is that Marx alternated between two quite different epistemological positions. One is a kind of scientific realism. According to this view, the truth is defined in terms of correspondence between ideas (or theories) and facts, and the empirical method of the natural sciences is the best—indeed, the only really reliable—method for discovering and checking these correspondences. The other position is radically pragmatic. From its point of view, the truth is what works, and the test of the truth of a particular theory about society or about history is whether it achieves the desired overthrow of capitalism.

In the following passage, for instance, the correspondence theory is rejected on the grounds that it is open to a sceptical attack that the pragmatic test survives:

Our agnostic admits that all our knowledge is based upon the information imparted to us by our senses. But, he adds, how do we know that our senses give us correct representations of the objects we perceive through them? . . . Now, this line of reasoning seems undoubtedly hard to meet by mere argumentation. But before there was argumentation, there was action. *Im Anfang war die Tat.*[10] And human action had solved the difficulty long before human ingenuity invented it. The proof of the pudding is in the eating. From the moment we turn to our own use these objects, according to the qualities we perceive in them, we put to an infallible test the correctness or otherwise of our sense perceptions. If these perceptions have been wrong, then our estimate of the use to which an object can be turned must also be wrong, and our attempt must fail.[z]

In the *Theses on Feuerbach* Marx's pragmatism is even more explicitly stated:

The chief defect of all hitherto existing materialism . . . is that the object, reality, sensuousness, is conceived only in the form of the *object* or *contemplation,* but not as *human sensuous activity, practice,* not subjectively. . . .

The question whether objective truth can be attributed to human thinking is not a question of theory but is a practical question. In practice man must prove the truth, i.e., the reality and power, the "this-sidedness" of his thinking. The dispute over the reality or non-reality of thinking which is isolated from practice is a purely scholastic question.

The materialist doctrine that men are products of circumstances and upbringing, and that, therefore, changed men are products of other circumstances and changed upbringings, forgets that circumstances are changed precisely by men, and that the educator must himself be educated. . . .

The coincidence of the changing of circumstances and of human activity can only be conceived and rationally understood as revolutionizing practice.

The philosophers have *interpreted* the world, in various ways; the point, however, is to *change* it.[a]

This attack on what Dewey later called spectator theories of knowledge[11] not only undermines epistemological theories of the classical type, whether idealistic or realistic; it also undermines Marx's own claim to have formulated the "correct" version of materialism. From the pragmatic point of view stated in the *Theses*, dialectical materialism is only another form of scientism, a rather naïve version of the traditional metaphysics that differs from it only in relying on an allegedly scientific method instead of on perception or reason. Thus in the *Theses* Marx is far more revolutionary—in an intellectual sense—than in his economic theory, for he is attacking a fundamental belief in Western thought, the notion that the objects of human experience are separate entities "out there," that they are complete in themselves and independent of us and our activity.

10 [A quotation from Goethe's *Faust:* "In the beginning was the deed"—AUTHOR.]
11 See Vol. V, pp. 48–49.

Yet here, at his most revolutionary, Marx is developing but one phase of the Kantian heritage, for it was Kant who, more than anyone else, broke down the sharp dualistic distinction between mind and its objects that earlier theory had imposed.

Evolution

As has been frequently pointed out, in the nineteenth century the concept of development was in the air. Darwin[12] felt this interest and focused it on a specific biological problem; in doing so he collected an immense amount of concrete evidence and thus "proved" (doubtless only in a limited area, but this was overlooked by adherents and opponents alike) what had earlier been only a philosophical hypothesis. This gave great impetus to the use of the concept of development as a general methodological tool.

The view that Darwin attacked—that the various species of animals are direct creations of the Deity and are thus eternal and unchanging—was of hoary antiquity, buttressed both by a formidable array of theological arguments and by several important philosophical concepts, such as the doctrines of universals, of essences, and of teleology. Criticism of this view, unlike most intrascientific arguments, therefore touched a great number of very sensitive spots in lay opinion.

ARTIFICIAL SELECTION

Darwin's main thesis, moreover, was so simple that almost anyone could understand it. He pointed out what every animal breeder already knew, that it is possible to select and perpetuate certain strains in domestic animals by breeding to whatever individual differences the owner chooses.

Suppose an owner of collies fancies dogs with longer and narrower skulls. He need only eliminate from every litter the puppies with short, broad skulls and breed those with long, narrow skulls. Since the characteristics of parents tend to be inherited, in each new generation the desired characteristics will appear more frequently. Moreover, as long as the process of elimination is continued, standards of selection will rise; the narrow skulls of one generation

12 Charles Darwin (1809–82) was the son of a well-to-do country doctor and the grandson of Erasmus Darwin and Josiah Wedgwood. After an abortive start toward a medical career, he decided rather unenthusiastically on the church. Before he had progressed very far, he had an opportunity to go on a scientific expedition in Southern waters. Darwin spent five years on this cruise aboard H.M.S. *Beagle* and returned in 1838 an enthusiastic student of natural history. For more than twenty years he slowly worked at his theory of evolution and accumulated evidence to support it. It was only at his friends' insistence that he brought himself to publish it in 1859.

will get narrower and more "aristocratic" in the next. If this characteristic catches the public eye, an economic factor enters the picture, for breeders will not raise dogs they cannot sell. If the public fancies narrow-skulled collies, there is no point in wasting feed on broad-skulled ones. Hence a new variant of the collie may emerge, and if several features (long coat, bushy tail) are jointly selected in this way, a new "species" will soon appear. "Who will believe that animals closely resembling the Italian greyhound, the bloodhound, the bull-dog, pug-dog, or Blenheim spaniel, etc.—so unlike all wild Canidae—ever existed freely in a state of nature?" [b] Though this canine diversity is in part the product of crossing "a few aboriginal species," it results in the main from the selection of certain characteristics from "an immense amount of inherited variation."

NATURAL SELECTION

Though in Darwin's time man's capacity to select and thus produce new variants and species was common knowledge among breeders of domestic animals, no one had ever thought about it in just this connection. Yet, if this process occurs in the case of domestic animals, why may it not occur in the case of wild animals?

> Altogether at least a score of pigeons might be chosen which, if shown to an ornithologist, and he were told they were wild birds, would certainly be ranked by him as well-defined species. Moreover, I do not believe that any ornithologist would place the English carrier, the short-faced tumbler, the runt, the barb, pouter, and fantail in the same genus. . . .
>
> Great as are the differences between the breeds of the pigeons, I am fully convinced that . . . all are descended from the rock-pigeon (*Columba livia*).[13c]

May there not then be a principle of *natural* selection that operates exactly like the breeder's conscious plan, to perpetuate certain characteristics and to eliminate others? Darwin believed he could show there is such a principle.

The first point to note, according to Darwin, is that there is a "universal struggle for existence."

> We behold the face of nature bright with gladness, we often see super-abundance of food; we do not see or we forget that the birds which are idly singing round us mostly live on insects or seeds, and are thus constantly destroying life; or we forget how largely these songsters, or their eggs, or their nestlings, are destroyed by birds and beasts of prey; we do not always bear in mind, that, though food may be now superabundant, it is not so at all seasons of each recurring year.

13 [The sentences quoted are followed by several pages of supporting evidence, themselves but a brief abstract of the material Darwin had at hand; he constantly remarked on the "limitations of space," which compelled him to report his data at what he felt was "insufficient length"— AUTHOR.]

A struggle for existence inevitably follows from the high rate at which all organic beings tend to increase.[14] . . . As more individuals are produced than can possibly survive, there must in every case be a struggle for existence, either one individual with another of the same species, or with the individuals of distinct species, or with the physical conditions of life. It is the doctrine of Malthus[15] applied with manifold force to the whole animal and vegetable kingdom; for in this case there can be no artificial increase of food, and no prudential restraint from marriage.[d]

Obviously, in this kind of competition, any individual difference that makes one member of a species (or one species) even slightly fitter to survive will tend to be perpetuated. This individual will live a little longer and will thus have more offspring, and these offspring will tend to inherit the characteristic in question. Individual members of the species who lack this property will tend to die sooner and so have fewer offspring. Therefore, in the course of time, a variant of the species will emerge characterized by the property that was originally an individual difference in an occasional member of the species. When enough variants are produced in this way a new species in effect evolves. The struggle for survival is thus a principle of natural selection that operates in precisely the same way as deliberate human selection operates in the breeding of domestic animals.

In order to make it clear how, as I believe, natural selection acts, I must beg permission to give one or two imaginary illustrations. Let us take the case of a wolf, which preys on various animals, securing some by craft, some by strength, some by fleetness; and let us suppose that the fleetest prey, a deer for instance, had from any change in the country increased in numbers, or that other prey had decreased in numbers, during that season of the year when the wolf was hardest pressed for food. Under such circumstances the swiftest and slimmest wolves have the best chance of surviving, and so be

14 [Darwin noted that the elephant is the slowest breeder of all known animals; yet if every elephant born lived out its normal life span and produced an average number of offspring, there would be alive, after a period of seven hundred forty to seven hundred fifty years, nearly 19,000,000 elephants descended from the first pair. T. H. Morgan, in *The Scientific Basis of Evolution* (Norton, New York, 1932), p. 121, gives even more impressive figures of fecundity: "It is said that a salmon may produce 28,361,000 eggs . . . ; the queen bee may lay in three years 5,000,000 eggs. The American oyster produces from 15,000,000 to 114,000,000 eggs at each spawning and may spawn four or five times a year. . . . According to Punnett, a rotifer (Hydatina) lays about thirty eggs measuring 0.01 cm. At the end of a year, after sixty-five generations (if all lived), the total mass of material produced would make a sphere larger than the confines of 'the known universe'"—AUTHOR.]

15 [Malthus (1766–1834) was the author of an *Essay on Population* (1798), in which he argued that, but for war, pestilence, and famine, human population would increase at a much greater rate than means of subsistence. This gave Darwin the hint he needed: "In October 1838, I happened to read for amusement Malthus on Population, and being well prepared to appreciate the struggle for existence which everywhere goes on, from long continued observation of the habits of plants and animals, it at once struck me that under these circumstances favourable variations would tend to be preserved and unfavourable ones to be destroyed. The result of this would be a new species. Here then I had a theory by which to work"—AUTHOR.]

preserved or selected, provided always that they retained strength to master their prey at this or some other period of the year, when they were compelled to prey on other animals. I can see no more reason to doubt that this would be the result, than that man should be able to improve the fleetness of his greyhounds by careful and methodical selection, or by the kind of unconscious selection which results from each man trying to keep the best dogs without any thought of modifying the breed. I may add that, according to Mr. Pierce, there are two varieties of the wolf inhabiting the Catskill Mountains, in the United States, one with a light greyhound-like form, which pursues deer, and the other more bulky, with shorter legs, which more frequently attacks the shepherd's flocks.[e]

THE TREE OF LIFE

It is quite impossible in a few extracts to give any idea of the voluminous and impressive evidence, drawn from all manner of sources, including experimental studies of his own, with which Darwin supported his hypothesis. We shall have to content ourselves with Darwin's description of the Tree of Life, the image that sums up his whole theory. According to Darwin, the species do not constitute separate classes frozen in eternal independence and connected only in the will of the deity who created them. Rather, they are comparable to a great tree:

> The green and budding twigs may represent existing species; and those produced during former years may represent the long succession of extinct species. At each period of growth all the growing twigs have tried to branch out on all sides, and to overtop and kill the surrounding twigs and branches, in the same manner as species and groups of species have at all times overmastered other species in the great battle for life. The limbs divided into great branches, and these into lesser and lesser branches, were themselves once, when the tree was young, budding twigs; and this connection of the former and present buds by ramifying branches may well represent the classification of all extinct and living species in groups subordinate to groups. Of the many twigs which flourished when the tree was a mere bush, only two or three, now grown into great branches, yet survive and bear the other branches; so with the species which lived during long-past geological periods, very few now have living and modified descendants. From the first growth of the tree, many a limb and branch has decayed and dropped off; and these fallen branches of various sizes may represent those whole orders, families and genera which have now no living representatives, and which are known to us only in a fossil state. As we here and there see a thin, straggling branch springing from a fork low down on a tree, and which by some chance has been favored and is still alive on its summit, so we occasionally see an animal like the Ornithorhynchus or Lepidosiren, which in some small degree connects by its affinities two large branches of life, and which has apparently been saved from fatal competition by having inhabited a protected station. As buds give rise by growth to fresh buds, and these, if vigorous, branch out and overtop on all sides many a feebler branch, so by generation I believe

it has been with the great Tree of Life, which fills with its dead and broken branches the crust of the earth, and covers the surface with its ever-branching and beautiful ramifications.[f]

This metaphor became, in effect, the guide for the next generation of natural scientists. They were natural historians who sought in the "record of the rocks" those "missing links" that would reveal, as it were, the structure of the Tree of Life, whose surface of leaves and buds is all that we actually see. This work has now been largely done, and the attention of the biological sciences has turned chiefly to the study of those "variations" whose causes Darwin himself did not explain but simply assumed to be the basis on which the process of natural selection operates. The focus of interest has therefore shifted from paleontology to genetics, from the study of fossils to experimental work in laboratories. It has been shown, for instance, that Darwin was wrong in supposing that variations are always slight and that evolution consequently proceeds very slowly by the accumulation of many small differences. And "natural selection," on which Darwin concentrated his attention as the active principle involved, has lost its central importance. It is now held that many structures either are not adaptive or are adaptive only at the end of a process of development, the earlier stages of which had no selective advantage. From this view the doctrine of "natural selection" reduces merely to the truism that whatever new types emerge must be able to survive. What now interests biologists is the mode of origin of the new types.

DARWIN'S INFLUENCE

Though no one today is a Darwinian in the strict sense, Darwin's theory made an immense contribution to the biological sciences. By pointing to the importance of variation, Darwin indicated the crucial area for further study, and, by offering an account in terms of a purely objective, nonteleological concept, he showed that biology could be as much of a science as physics. Far more important than the details of Darwin's explanation of the origin of species was the fact that he thought species had an empirical, rather than divine, origin—an origin of which it is possible to give a scientific account. Darwin's image of the Tree of Life inspired biologists to see their subject as a *unified* field of study, and his example gave them the courage to think about it as a *neutral* field of study, untrammeled by extrascientific conceptions.[16]

16 In *Science and Christian Tradition*, Thomas Huxley (who was known as "Darwin's bulldog") described the vexations scientists experienced: "I had set out on a journey, with no other purpose than that of exploring a certain province of natural knowledge which it was my right and duty to pursue; and yet I found that, whatever route I took, before long I came to a tall and formidable-looking fence. Confident as I might be in the existence of an ancient and indefeasible right of way, before me stood the thorny barrier with its comminatory notice board—'No thoroughfare—By order, Moses.' There seemed no way over; nor did the prospect of creeping round, as I saw some do, attract me. True there was no longer any cause to fear the spring guns and man-traps set by the former lords of the manor; but one is apt to get very dirty going on all-fours. The only alternatives were to give up my journey—which I was not minded to do—or to break the fence down and go through it."

Important as Darwinism has been in biology, its impact in other fields, where Darwin himself did not dream of applying it, has been even more consequential. This history of philosophy is an example of that wider influence, for it is based on the assumption that modern men cannot understand themselves unless they know something of their past. Such a notion would hardly have occurred to the thinkers of the Enlightenment, and it certainly would not have seemed to them a truism, as it does to us today. This, of course, is not merely a matter of "taking an interest" in history, in the narrow sense of the human past; it is, rather, a basic methodological orientation. The fact is that it has now become natural to explain things—all sorts of things—genetically. Men no longer think of things simply as occurring at a specific point in time. They think of things, rather, as enduring through time and they want to know how they develop *through* time.[17] Darwinism was certainly not the exclusive cause of this change in point of view. As a matter of fact, it was in some respects a reflection of changes that were already under way. But its success in dealing with its own specific problem and the influence it had on the course of the biological and social sciences and of philosophy were powerful factors in the further development of this new climate of opinion.

Darwinism made its first immediate impact on the public, however, in connection with the old controversy between science and religion, and it brought this controversy to a new intensity. The very aspects of the theory of natural selection that stimulated the biological scientists were deeply offensive to the conventional religious mind. Actually, there was nothing in the view—as Darwin tried to point out[18]—that was incompatible with the religious outlook. The new physics had raised a much more serious and fundamental problem than had the theory of natural selection. But evolution brought the problem home as an abstract science could never do. After stating his conclusion, "I believe that animals are descended from at most only four or five progenitors, and plants from an equal or lesser number," Darwin went on to say that "argument from analogy" would lead him "one step further"—to the conclusion that "all the organic beings which have ever lived on this earth may be descended from some one primordial form." If this be true, "much light will be thrown on the origin of man and his history." [g]

---

17 "To regard all things in their historical setting appears, indeed, to be an instructive [sic] procedure of the modern mind. We do it without thinking, because we can scarcely think at all without doing it. The modern climate of opinion is such that we cannot seemingly understand our world unless we regard it as a going concern. . . . What is peculiar to the modern mind is the disposition and the determination to regard ideas and concepts, the truth of things as well as the things themselves, as changing entities. . . . Historical-mindedness is so much a preconception of modern thought that we can identify a particular thing only by pointing to the various things it successively was before it became that particular thing it will presently cease to be"—C. Becker, *The Heavenly City of the Eighteenth-Century Philosophers* (Yale University Press, 1932), p. 19.

18 "I see no good reason why the views given in this volume should shock the religious feelings of any one." And he was glad to add in subsequent editions that "a celebrated author and divine" had assured him that it is "just as noble a conception of the Deity to believe He created a few original forms capable of self-development . . . , as to believe that He required a fresh act of creation" for each separate species—*Origin of Species*, p. 496.

The reaction was instantaneous and violent. A meeting of the British Association in June 1860 was almost broken up by a discussion of the new book. Samuel Wilberforce, Bishop of Oxford, attacked it bitterly, ridiculing Darwin's "proofs" and describing the theory as a mere "hypothesis raised most unphilosophically to the dignity of a causal." Unfortunately for Wilberforce, he was not content to attack the theory; he then turned to Huxley, who was sitting near him, and inquired sarcastically whether it was through his grandfather or his grandmother that he claimed descent from a monkey. This gave Huxley, who was a clever debater, the opening he needed: He would much rather, Huxley replied, have a monkey for an ancestor than a man who, like Wilberforce, "prostituted the gifts of culture and of eloquence to the service of prejudice and falsehood." Ladies fainted, the audience burst into protest or applause, and over it all an Admiral of the Royal Navy waved a Bible, affirming its inspired and literal truth and denouncing his old friend Darwin and all his works.[h]

While bishops ranted and scientists in retaliation elevated Darwinism to the level of dogma,[19] the theory began slowly and certainly to operate upon men's minds. Attention, at least of laymen, focused on one or the other of two main points. One was the conviction that the outcome of this struggle is "progress"—bigger, better, newer forms. This was the leading impression that the theory had made on Darwin himself: "There is grandeur in this view . . . that, while this planet has gone cycling on according to the fixed law of gravity, from so simple a beginning endless forms most beautiful and most wonderful have been, and are being evolved."[i] And of course this point of view comports with the aspects of nineteenth-century thought that have been the theme of this chapter—its emphasis on the idea of development, its belief in the value of a scientific approach to the study of man and his problems, and its generally empirical and optimistic outlook.

The other main point in Darwinism on which lay opinion focused was the discovery that nature is a struggle for survival, a savage competition in which the weak and the helpless go to the wall. This aspect of Darwinism powerfully reinforced the contrasting strain in nineteenth-century thought—hostility to science on the grounds that it is responsible not only for the secularization of life (through its mechanistic world view) but also for the alienation of the industrial workers (through its mass-production technology). Some of the thinkers who represent this counter-revolution, or resistance movement, against the predominantly scientific culture of the nineteenth century are examined in the next chapter. This chapter will be brought to a close by considering a few thinkers who are representative of the former, more positive, response to Darwinism.

19 As Samuel Butler (who had no love of bishops) caustically noted, "Science is being daily more and more personified and anthropomorphized into a god. By and by they will say that science took our nature upon him, and sent down his only begotten son, Charles Darwin, or Huxley, into the world so that those who believe in him, etc.; and they will burn people for saying that science, after all, is only an expression for our ignorance of our own ignorance."

Scientific Philosophy

The philosophers of science who were the immediate heirs of evolutionary theory fall into two main groups: those who were old-fashioned metaphysicians (without, however, recognizing it) and those who were openly and admittedly positivists. Thus, once again, but with still another twist, philosophical development moved within a fundamentally Kantian context. Kant had distinguished between phenomena (the spatiotemporal manifold) and noumena (things-in-themselves), and he had held that, although our knowledge is limited to the former, we can nevertheless be confident that things-in-themselves exist. None of the philosophers of science believed in a noumenal realm beyond the spatiotemporal manifold; in this sense they were all phenomenalists. But some of them identified the spatiotemporal manifold with ultimate reality (which Kant, of course, had never done), and they went on to identify current scientific theories with ultimate truth (despite all the growing evidence that science itself has a history). This point of view may be called scientism. Though certainly rather naïve, it was widely accepted, and among its adherents were both materialists and vitalists.

MATERIALISM

Representative of the materialist thesis was the view of Ernst Haeckel.[20] Haeckel believed that science had indubitably proved that "the universe, or the cosmos, is eternal, infinite, and illimitable, [and that] its substance, with its two attributes (matter and energy), fills infinite space, and is in eternal motion. . . . This motion runs on through infinite time as an unbroken development" in the course of which "countless organic forms" gradually emerge. "Our mother-earth is a mere speck in the sunbeam in the illimitable universe, [and] man himself is but a tiny grain of protoplasm in the perishable framework of organic nature."[j]

There is no problem, Haeckel held, about the "origins of life" or about the nature of "sensation and rational thought." Everything can be explained in terms of the evolutionary development (in accordance with the "laws of the conservation of matter and the conservation of energy") of material substance. Haeckel called his philosophy "monism" to emphasize his denial of the various nonmaterial substances—minds, souls, and so on—of traditional philosophy.

> Monistic cosmology proved . . . that there is no personal God; comparative and genetic psychology showed that there cannot be an immortal soul; and monistic physiology proved the futility of the assumption of "free will." Finally, the science of evolution made it clear that the same eternal iron laws that rule in the inorganic world are valid too in the organic and moral world.[k]

20 Ernst Haeckel (1834–1919) was a biologist who taught at the University of Jena. He was one of the earliest German adherents of Darwinism.

This conclusion is very sweeping—and it is as dogmatic as any religion. But the crucial question for any materialistic monism is whether life can in fact be explained in mechanistic terms, by means of the "law of the evolution of substance," as Haeckel held. Long before Haeckel, Hobbes had held that it can be; Descartes had excluded only man—and not man's body but merely man's soul—from his otherwise universal mechanism. For such early modern philosophers, however, the question had been entirely theoretical; no one had regarded himself as being in a position to offer such an explanation in detail. But toward the end of the nineteenth century advances in biology made it seem likely that a complete explanation was actually possible. Many scientists came to believe that "ultimately life can be unequivocally explained in physico-chemical terms."[1]

In Jacques Loeb's[21] work on animal tropisms this point of view was explicitly asserted:

> That in the case of our inner life a physico-chemical explanation is not beyond the realm of possibility is proved by the fact that it is already possible for us to explain cases of simple manifestations of animal instinct and will on a physico-chemical basis; namely, the phenomena . . . of animal tropisms. As the most simple example we may mention [that] the tendency of certain animals to fly or creep to the light . . . might be explained by the . . . law of Bunsen and Roscoe, which explains the photochemical effects in inanimate nature. This law states that within wide limits the photochemical effect equals the product of the intensity of light into the duration of illumination. . . .
>
> The positively heliotropic animals—i.e., the animals which go instinctively to a source of light—have in their eyes (and occasionally also in their skin) photosensitive substances which undergo chemical alterations by light. The products formed in this process influence the contraction of the muscles. . . . If the animal is illuminated on one side only, the mass of photochemical reaction products formed on that side in the unit of time is greater than on the opposite side. Consequently the development of energy in the symmetrical muscles on both sides of the body becomes unequal. . . . [Therefore] the animal is automatically forced to turn toward one side [until] the symmetrical spots of its surface are struck by the light at the same angle. . . . Consequently the velocity of reaction of the photochemical processes on both sides of the animal become equal. There is no more reason for the animal to deviate from the motion in a straight line and the positively heliotropic animal will move in this line to the source of light. . . . Heliotropic animals are therefore in reality photometric machines.[m]

And what earlier philosophers had believed to be man's "free will"—his capacity for planning, and for appreciating values and choosing the best among them—has a similar source: "We eat, drink, and reproduce not because mankind has reached an agreement that this is desirable, but because, machine-like, we are compelled to do so."[n]

---

21 Jacques Loeb (1859–1924) was born in Germany. He studied medicine, worked at the zoological institute in Naples, and taught physiology before coming to the United States in 1891. He subsequently taught at the universities of Chicago and California.

VITALISM

Such mechanistic solutions to life's "riddles" were attacked by another school of metaphysician-scientists called vitalists. These thinkers held life to be *sui generis* and inexplicable in terms of physical or chemical laws. Characteristically, they did not use metaphysical and theological arguments to attack mechanism. For the vitalists, mechanism was poor philosophy because it was poor biology.

Representative of this version of scientism was the view of Hans Driesch.[22] According to Driesch, "the processes of life" have an "unanalysable autonomy"; they are not "the result of a special constellation of factors known already" in physics and chemistry. An organism differs from a machine because it operates as a whole, as an individual; hence it cannot be explained mechanistically. "Analytical experimental embryology" shows, for instance, that

> . . . there are many kinds of embryonic organs or even animals which, if by an operation deprived of part of their cells, behave in the following way: of whatever material you deprive these organs or animals, the remainder, unless it is very small, will always develop in the normal manner, though, so to speak, in miniature. That is to say: there will develop out of the part of the embryonic organ or animal left by the operation, as might be expected, not a part of the organization *but the whole,* only on a smaller scale. I have proposed the name of *harmonious-equipotential systems* for organs or animals of this type. . . .[o]

Driesch may well be correct in maintaining that "mechanical causality is *not* sufficient for an explanation of what happens" in this sort of situation. But the notion of "individualising causality," or "entelechy," that he puts forward as an alternative is also far from sufficient: "Entelechy . . . is itself neither 'an energy' nor 'a material substance' of any special kind: such an assumption would lead to absurdities. Entelechy is an agent *sui generis,* non-material and non-spatial, but acting 'into' space, so to speak; an agent, however, that belongs to nature."[p]

Thus, if (as Driesch points out) Loeb fell prey to the "materialistic dogmatism of his time" by stating "a very important *problem* in the form of a fact,"[q] Driesch himself was committed to an exactly opposite dogmatism. Indeed, the metaphysical tendency of both these thinkers, as well as of Haeckel, is obvious. Not only did they generalize too hastily from insufficient data—Loeb from his tropisms, Driesch from his harmonious-equipotential systems, Haeckel from his "two great laws." They were also philosophically naïve in assuming that what science reveals is the truth about ultimate reality. There is a question, as the second group of scientific philosophers were to show, about the status of scientific truth. If the dispute over mechanism and vitalism as rival explanations of behavior is now

22 Hans Driesch (1867–1941) began his career as a biologist and worked for a time at the zoological institute in Naples. In 1909 he went to Heidelberg to teach philosophy.

largely a dead issue, it is because more careful study of the methodology of science shows that neither "mechanism" nor "vitalism" has a very clear meaning and that "explanation" is itself subject to varying explanations.

POSITIVISM

Under the rubric of "positivism" may be grouped a number of thinkers who, in contrast to the disguised metaphysicians just considered, accepted the self-denying clause by which Kant had limited knowledge to phenomena. But they differed from Kant in rejecting the possibility of synthetical a priori knowledge and in being uninterested in making a place for faith, a task that Kant, of course, had regarded as the whole purpose of limiting knowledge to phenomena. Indeed, these thinkers combined Hume's mitigated scepticism with Kant's phenomenalism.

Comte can be considered a founder of this new point of view insofar as he insisted that the function of science is not to show why things happen but to generalize about how they happen—to provide, that is, an instrument of control rather than a knowledge of ultimate reality. Later positivist thinkers, of whom Ernst Mach[23] and Karl Pearson[24] are examples, carried forward and applied more systematically the empiricism and pragmatism that were implicit in Comte's point of view.

Mach's main contention was that metaphysics is no more justified in science than it is in philosophy. Why reject God, soul, and free will on the grounds that they are unobservable and then introduce equally unknowable elements—entelechies or, for that matter, atoms—as new ultimates? The ultimate reals of both the materialists and the vitalists are only "mental artifices." Reality, that is, consists neither in "minds" nor in "atoms." It consists in experiences—in colors, sounds, tastes, and other data of sensation. But are these data mental or physical? In themselves they are neither, according to Mach. In themselves experiences are "neutral." But no experience is isolated; each stands in relation to other experiences, and it is the context of an experience that determines whether we are to regard it as "mental" or "physical." Thus, in itself, a particular experience of red is neutral. If the context in which we are experiencing red includes, say, "light," we regard it as physical. If, on the other hand, the context includes "optic nerve," we regard it as mental. That is all. The various sciences deal with the same experiences in different contexts: In the former context, for instance, red is a part of the subject matter of physics; in the latter, it is a part of the subject matter of physiology.

What, then, is a science? It is merely an instrument that men use for summarizing and communicating about the various relations among their experiences.

23 Ernst Mach (1838–1916) was an Austrian. He taught mathematics and physics at the universities of Prague and Vienna.
24 Karl Pearson (1857–1936) studied mathematics at Cambridge. Later he became interested in law and eugenics. He taught mathematics and eugenics at the University of London.

My fundamental conception [is] the nature of science as Economy of Thought. . . .

It is the object of science to replace, or *save*, experiences, by the reproduction and anticipation of facts in thought. . . .

In the reproduction of facts in thought, we never reproduce the facts in full, but only that side of them which is important to us, moved to this directly or indirectly by a practical interest. Our reproductions are invariably abstractions. Here again is an economical tendency.

Nature is composed of sensations as its elements. Primitive man, however, first picks out certain compounds of these elements—those namely that are relatively permanent and of greater importance to him. The first and oldest words are names of "things." . . . No inalterable thing exists. The thing is an abstraction, the name a symbol, for a compound of elements from whose changes we abstract. The reason we assign a single word to a whole compound is that we need to suggest all the constituent sensations at once. . . . Sensations are not signs of things; but, on the contrary, a thing is a thought-symbol for a compound sensation of relative fixedness. Properly speaking the world is not composed of "things" as its elements, but of colors, tones, pressures, spaces, times, in short what we ordinarily call individual sensations.[s]

Everywhere we look for regularities among our sensations. We do so for the following reasons. First, the practical needs of everyday living—the "struggle to satisfy our wants"—require us to be able to anticipate the behavior of nature. Second, we want to communicate with our fellow men, and we cannot do so unless we discover regularities: "That only can be . . . conceptually represented which is uniform and conformable to law; for description presupposes the employment of names by which to designate its elements; and names can acquire meanings only when applied to elements that constantly reappear."[t] Third, experience of regularity is the basis of all explanation. The "uncommon" is always "perplexing and astonishing." When, however, as a result of repetition things become familiar, "we are no longer surprised, there is nothing new or strange to us in the phenomena, we feel at home with them . . . , they are *explained*."

It behooves us, therefore, to search out, in "the infinite variety of nature," those "simple elements" that "are the same, and that amid all multiplicity are ever present." In this undertaking there is no fundamental difference in kind between prescientific and scientific thinking. Scientific thinking is merely more "economical" in satisfying the basic requirements just enumerated. Thus, "water" is a prescientific word that fixes an enduring element amid change; "H_2O" is a more exact, and hence more economical, symbol. That is, the "sensations" designated by "H_2O" are more "comprehensive, compact, and consistent" than those designated by "water."

It follows that neither "water" nor "H_2O" names a real entity (as do, for instance, "cold" and "wet"); both are only "mental artifices." Further, scientific concepts evolve as much as does the world they describe. Science does not reveal "eternal iron laws," as Haeckel supposed. It gives us flexible instrumentalities for organizing and controlling our experience.

It follows, finally, that scientific concepts can be understood only in their historical setting.

> The history of the development of mechanics is quite indispensable to a full comprehension of the science in its present condition. . . .
>
> An *instinctive*, irreflective knowledge of the processes of nature will doubtless always precede the scientific, conscious apprehension, or *investigation*, of phenomena. The former is the outcome of the relation in which the processes of nature stand to the satisfaction of our wants. The acquisition of the most elementary truth does not devolve upon the individual alone: it is pre-effected in the development of the race. . . . [But] the experiments that man heedlessly and instinctively makes in his struggle to satisfy his wants, are just as thoughtlessly and unconsciously applied . . . , and as a rule will never supply an impetus to further thought. . . .
>
> [While] there is, therefore, no result of science which in point of principle could not have been arrived at wholly without methods, . . . as a matter of fact, within the short span of a human life and with man's limited powers of memory, any stock of knowledge worthy of the name is unattainable except by the *greatest* mental economy. Science itself, therefore, may be regarded as a minimal problem, consisting of the completest possible presentment of facts with the *least possible expenditure of thought.*[u]

These ideas were further developed by Pearson in *The Grammar of Science.* Scientific concepts, he held, are merely "conceptual shorthand by aid of which [we] can briefly describe and resume phenomena."

> Atom and molecule are intellectual conceptions by aid of which physicists classify phenomena and formulate the relationships between their sequences. From a certain standpoint, therefore, these conceptions of the physicist are *supersensuous*, that is, they do not . . . represent direct sense-impressions; but the reader must be careful not to confuse this kind of supersensuousness with that of the metaphysician. . . . [The physicist's supersensuousness is a] construct of his own imagination, just so far useful as it describes his experience, and certain to be replaced by a wider concept as his insight expands. . . . On the other hand, the metaphysician asserts an existence for the supersensuous which is unconditioned . . . and has a real existence apart from the imagination of men.[v]

From this "phenomenalistic," or positivistic, point of view, the whole dispute between the materialists and the vitalists became largely verbal:

> Mechanics does not differ, as so often has been asserted, from biology or any other branch of science in its essential principles. The laws of motion no more account than the laws of cell-development for the routine of perception; both solely attempt to describe as completely and simply as possible the repeated sequences of our sense perceptions. . . . The difference between the two branches of science is rather quantitative than qualitative; that is, the descriptions of mechanics are simpler and more general than those of

biology. . . . It is not a question of reducing the universe to a "dead mechanism," but of measuring the amount of probability that one description of change of a highly generalised and simple kind will ultimately be recognised as capable of replacing another description of a more specialised and complex character. . . . Regarded from this standpoint the laws of mechanics are seen to be essentially an intellectual product, and it appears absolutely unreasonable to contrast the mechanical with the intellectual when once these words are defined in an accurate manner.[w]

Thus the problem of the "origin of life," which Driesch and Loeb had believed themselves to be solving, turns out according to a positivistic analysis to be only a pseudo-problem. The metaphysician who asks about the "source" of life, and who seeks as an answer anything more than relations among sequences of sensations, "may call it *Matter*, or *God*, or *Will*, or *Mind-stuff*, but to do so serves no useful purpose. . . . I can as little accept or deny his assertion as he forsooth can demonstrate anything about his shadowy thing-in-itself."[x]

The only "intelligible definition which can be given of the word *knowledge*" limits it to experience, to the "careful and accurate classification of facts and observation of their correlation and sequence." In a word, "there is no sphere of inquiry which lies outside the legitimate field of science." "The metaphysician is a poet, often a very great one, but unfortunately he is not known to be a poet, because he strives to clothe his poetry in the language of reason, and hence it follows that he is liable to be a dangerous member of the community."[y]

But if metaphysics, which has been regarded traditionally as the core of philosophy, is ruled out, what is the business of philosophy? The philosopher can no longer build systems or criticize the concepts of science in the Hegelian manner. He can only accept the results of modern physics; "it is the language in which these results are stated that he believes needs reconsideration." Though much reduced, philosophy still has an important function. Its business is the kind of task to which *The Grammar of Science* was devoted: the analysis and definition of the various concepts employed by the scientists in their special fields—concepts like matter, force, cause, and external world.

In some respects—in their hostility to objective idealism,[25] in their tough-mindedness, and in their disrespect for the whole philosophical establishment—the positivists remind us of the pragmatists.[26] But, unlike the pragmatists, they were cognitivists; their goal was truth, not successful practice. But since—unlike Kierkegaard and Nietzsche,[27] it did not occur to them that truth might be problematical, they had no sympathy for what we have described as the countermovement in nineteenth-century culture. On the other hand, they anticipated many of the major preoccupations of philosophy in the twentieth century, and they were, indeed, the direct ancestors of logical positivism.[28]

---

25 See Ch. 9.   27 See Ch. 6.
26 See Ch. 8.   28 See Vol. V, Ch. 7.

Summary

Some twentieth-century writers look back on the nineteenth century, whether with scorn or with nostalgia, as a period of superb self-confidence, immutable belief, and rocklike stability. Actually, it was a century of tension and change, and of upheavals so great that even today we are struggling to adjust to them. The Industrial Revolution brought a massive shift of population to the towns, and although it created the long-range possibility of a vast improvement in man's lot, it actually produced distress, poverty, and disease—problems that we have not yet eradicated. Another and more gradual result of the Industrial Revolution was the economic unification of the world. In the course of the century Western industrial culture spread over large parts of the world, and everywhere the activities of formerly separate communities became closely meshed and inter-dependent. But, as society became economically more unified, other forces were working in a contrary direction. Among these was the sentiment of nationalism, the emergence of which was undoubtedly facilitated by another great nineteenth-century development—the awakening of the masses. For, although the old upper classes had been essentially cosmopolitan in outlook, with a common cultural heritage and a common ideal, the masses were rooted in the soil and in local traditions and found it natural to connect their claims to economic and political independence with a claim to national sovereignty. The new articulate-ness of the masses everywhere brought a broadening of the franchise, but, despite the optimism of some political theorists, it cannot be said that this development automatically solved the old problems of political control with which Plato and Aristotle had wrestled. Indeed, the new conditions of life in the nineteenth century and the development of techniques for the manipulation of public opinion made these problems even more acute.

Philosophical thinking naturally reflected all these complex currents and crosscurrents. However much they may have disagreed in other respects, all the philosophers whose views have been examined in this chapter were persuaded that reality is dynamic. But though they abandoned the Enlightenment's belief in immutable truths and inalienable rights, they held that there are "iron laws" of development that can be ascertained by applying scientific method to the study of man. Thus metaphysics was in effect replaced by philosophy of history. Comte's law of three stages, Marx's dialectical materialism, and Darwin's theory of "survival of the fittest" are examples of this development. Toward the end of the century, however, men began to suspect that all such formulas were as dogmatic in their own way as the much-scorned rationalism had been in its. Accordingly, a tendency was discernible for philosophers to conceive of their subject pragmatically and instrumentally, either as a critique of method and a means of clarifying linguistic confusion or—and here the influence of one of the major motifs of the century can be seen—as an instrument for the solution of pressing social and political problems.

CHAPTER 6

Kierkegaard and Nietzsche

However much Mill and Marx and the other philosophers discussed in the preceding chapter may have differed among themselves, they nevertheless shared certain basic assumptions. They all believed that an objective knowledge of man is attainable by applying the methods of empirical science to the study of social and psychological processes. They were all rationalists—in the broad sense that they attributed most of men's mistakes to ignorance, which is remediable, and not to sin, which Christian teaching considers "original." And they were optimists and meliorists in that they looked forward to a steady improvement in man's estate.

Though for many years this ethos remained dominant in Europe and America, a countermovement, hardly noticed at first, was also under way. The representatives of this countermovement, reflected in Dostoevsky's attack on "2 + 2" (science) and on the "Crystal Palace" (technology), rejected all the assumptions of the dominant ethos. They were as hostile to science as a cognitive enterprise as they were suspicious of the application of scientific method to the solution of economic and political problems; they were, indeed, indifferent to social welfare. All of this they wrote off contemptuously as mere "objectivity." The focus of their attention was on what they called "subjectivity." In this one respect they were a part of the mainstream of Western thought, for interest in the self had been a characteristic of philosophy since Descartes. And not only of philosophy: Since the time of the Renaissance, the culture in all its aspects had been marked by an increasing attention to the subjective flow of experience. But whereas most philosophers—Kant and Hegel, for instance—had thought of the self chiefly as a knower, the philosophers of the countermovement thought of the self as a decider and chooser; they held that we become truly a self not in the neutral contemplation of a truth but in the passionate commitment to a deed.

Kierkegaard and Nietzsche are representative of this countermovement. Both were born out of their time, when social and cultural conditions evoked neither sympathy nor understanding for their opinions. For many decades Kierkegaard was hardly known outside his native Denmark, and Nietzsche was easily written off as insane. But World War I—and, to a greater extent, World War II—drew men's attention forcefully to facts about human nature that earlier generations had ignored. The revelation of Nazi efforts to exterminate the Jews, the American atom-bomb attacks on Japanese cities, the insanities of the Cold War, the callous injustice done to Negroes, the repeated failure to resolve conflicts by peaceful means—all these suggested that man is indeed as "spiteful" as Dostoevsky had declared him to be.

In these circumstances the dominant philosophy of reasonableness and progress began to appear naïve. Almost two millenia earlier Augustine had gazed into the mirror of self-knowledge and had found himself to be ulcerous, sinful, and corrupt. During the centuries of the Enlightenment this view had been regarded not as a profound insight into human nature but as a distorted perception of a neurotic mind. But when, in the early twentieth century, men again experienced alienation and estrangement from their fellows and from the natural world, they began to regard Augustine as an unusually honest and perceptive psychologist. Even those men who were not by any means Christians came to share his—and Paul's—conviction that the human will is deeply divided and at odds with itself.

Thus, in the aftermath of World War II, the times seemed increasingly out of joint and men felt increasingly incapable of setting things right. At this point they began to take seriously thinkers like Kierkegaard and Nietzsche, philosophers who had condemned the culture that produced such alienation and estrangement, and who emphasized inwardness, rejected optimism, and taught that becoming a complete self is more important than improving one's relation with one's environment.

Kierkegaard

The bare facts of Kierkegaard's life are easily summarized. He was born in 1813. His mother had been a servant, and his father had grown up as a poverty-stricken peasant in Jutland before he settled in Copenhagen and made his fortune. Kierkegaard was a rather frail but clever boy; as a youth he lived a frivolous social life of which his father disapproved. As a result they became estranged, but just before his father's death in 1838 they were reconciled. In 1840 Kierkegaard became engaged to Regine Olsen, but the next year he broke off the engagement. Thereafter he wrote voluminously on a variety of subjects, and under a variety of complicated pseudonyms. In 1848, after experiencing a momentous conversion, he launched an attack on the Danish State Church, which seemed to him to be in a deplorable condition. While engaged in this controversy he died suddenly in 1855.

So much for externals. The facts about Kierkegaard's inner life are more interesting, and also more difficult to fathom. But it is important to ascertain them, for they stand in the closest possible relation to the development of his philosophy. That this should be the case is itself revelatory of the leading characteristic of that philosophy—its "existentialism" in fact.

Kierkegaard's Starting Point: What Am I To Do?

What I really lack is to be clear in my mind *what I am to do*, not what I am to know, except in so far as a certain understanding must precede every action. The thing is to understand myself, to see what God really wishes *me* to do; the thing is to find a truth which is true *for me*, to find *the idea for which I can live and die.* What would be the use of discovering so-called objective truth, of working through all the systems of philosophy and of being able if required, to review them all and show up the inconsistencies within each system;—what good would it do me to be able to develop a theory of the state and combine all the details into a single whole, and so construct a world in which I did not live, but only held up to the view of others;—what good would it do me to be able to explain the meaning of Christianity if it had *no* deeper significance *for me and for my life;*—what good would it do me if truth stood before me, cold and naked, not caring whether I recognised her or not, and producing in me a shudder of fear rather than a trusting devotion? I certainly do not deny that I still recognise an *imperative of understanding* and that through it one can work upon men, *but it must be taken up into my life,* and *that is* what I now recognise as the most important thing. That is what my soul longs after, as the African desert thirsts for water. That is what I lack, and that is why I am left standing like a man who has rented a house and gathered all the furniture and household things together, but has not yet found the beloved with whom to share the joys and sorrows of his life.[a]

Aristotle had believed that philosophy starts with wonder—with a kind of dispassionate curiosity about nature and about man; and most philosophers of the Western world have seemingly agreed with him. This is certainly true of Thomas, and even of Augustine, for though the latter was passionately concerned with getting into a right relation with God, he was also deeply interested in understanding what the fact of sin and the possibility of redemption tell us about the nature of God and man. Kierkegaard, however, was not a philosopher in the Aristotelian sense. For him, the philosophical enterprise was exhausted in a single, all-important question: What was he to do in order to find "peace and significance"? Or, to rephrase the question in the more psychological language Kierkegaard sometimes used: How was he to find a way of integrating his life, of giving it a "focus and a center," so that it would no longer be "a chance assemblage" of meaningless details? Kierkegaard's philosophy, then, was an intensely personal one that grew directly out of his deeply felt life-experiences. He left a detailed, if ambiguous and characteristically "indirect," record of some of these experiences—in particular, his relationship with his father and his relationship with Regine Olsen.

KIERKEGAARD AND HIS FATHER

Kierkegaard's father was an old man when Kierkegaard was born; he was a successful businessman who had risen from peasantry by a combination of good luck and hard work. He was deeply religious in a stern Protestant way, and he brought up his children to fear and venerate the Lord. The son also feared, loved, and deeply respected his father. As a child, even as a young man, Kierkegaard believed that his father led an exemplary Christian life. It was a terrible shock, then, to discover that this pious, God-fearing old man had lived in sin with his children's mother (who had been a servant in his house) before he married her. And even more shocking, to find out that his father had once cursed God in despair. "How terrible about the man who once as a little boy, while herding sheep on the heaths of Jutland, suffering greatly, in hunger and in want, stood upon a hill and cursed God—and the man was unable to forget it even when he was eighty-two years old."[b]

Kierkegaard's reaction to these discoveries is reflected at several points in his *Journals:*

> I still remember the impression it made upon me when some years ago [this entry was made in 1837, when Kierkegaard was twenty-four] . . . father said very solemnly: "there are offenses which one can only fight against with God's continual help." I hurried down to my room and looked at myself in the glass . . . —or when father said, as he often did, that it would be a good

thing to have "a venerable confessor to whom one could open one's heart." [c]

Then it was [1835] that the great earthquake occurred, the terrible revolution which suddenly forced upon me a new and infallible law of interpretation of all the facts. Then I suspected that my father's great age was not a divine blessing but rather a curse; that the outstanding intellectual gifts of our family were only given to us in order that we should rend each other to pieces. . . . There must be a guilt upon the whole family, the punishment of God must be on it. . . . [d]

I could perhaps reproduce the tragedy of my childhood . . . in a novel called "the mysterious family." It would begin on a completely idyllic, patriarchal note so that no one suspected anything until suddenly the word sounded which translated everything into terror. [e]

Thus the contrast between surface appearance and inner reality was dramatically called to the young man's attention. Furthermore, he experienced this contrast in his own life. He lived a gay and social life and was regarded by those who knew him as clever but rather superficial. Within was deep despair:

I have just returned from a party of which I was the life and soul; wit poured from my lips, everyone laughed and admired me—but I went away —and the dash should be as long as the earth's orbit _____

_____ and wanted to shoot myself. [f]

The *Journals* are full of references to "melancholy," which Kierkegaard was determined to hide from the world:

I feel so dull and so completely without joy, my soul is so empty and void that I cannot even conceive what could satisfy it—oh, not even the blessedness of heaven. [g]

It is terrible when I think, even for a single moment, over the dark background which, from the very earliest time, was part of my life. The dread[1] with which my father filled my soul, his own frightful melancholy, and all the things in this connection which I do not even note down. I felt a dread of Christianity and yet felt myself so strongly drawn towards it. [h]

An old man, himself prodigiously melancholy (wherefore I shall not write down) had a son in his old age upon whom the whole of that melancholy descended in inheritance—but at the same time he had such an elasticity of mind that he was able to conceal it. [i]

From a child I was under the sway of a prodigious melancholy, the depth of which finds its only adequate measure in the equally prodigious dexterity I possessed of hiding it under an apparent gaity and *joie de vivre*. [j]

---

1 [In another entry in the *Journals* (pp. 79–80) Kierkegaard defines dread as precisely this kind of ambivalence: "Dread is a desire for what one fears, a sympathetic antipathy; dread is an alien power which takes hold of the individual, and yet one cannot extricate oneself from it, does not wish to, because one is afraid, but what one fears attracts one. Dread renders the individual powerless." It is, he thought, the principal element in original sin—AUTHOR.]

But Kierkegaard had not only to hide his melancholy from the world; like his father, he had committed a secret sin:

> In his early youth a man once let himself be carried away while in a state of intoxication, and visited a prostitute. The whole thing is forgotten. Now he wants to marry. Then comes dread. The possibility of his being a father, that somewhere in the world there might be living a creature owing its existence to him, tortures him day and night. He cannot confide in anyone, he has not even any absolute assurance of the fact. —It must therefore have occurred with a prostitute, in the wild recklessness of youth; had it been a little love affair or a real seduction one could not imagine his being ignorant, but it is precisely his ignorance which is the disturbing element in his torture. On the other hand his doubt could only really appear when he falls in love, precisely because of the thoughtlessness of the whole affair.[2] [k]

KIERKEGAARD AND REGINE OLSEN

This brings us to the second life-experience that profoundly affected the development of Kierkegaard's philosophy. In 1837 he met Regine Olsen, who had just turned fourteen. For him it was love at first sight. They became engaged in 1840, but about a year later, despite Regine's protests, he broke off the engagement. When he had first proposed to her he had "warned her against myself, against my melancholy."[1] Yet he had not told her *all*, and since he could not bring himself to do so, he felt that their relationship was false (in a terminology that later became fashionable, he felt himself to be in "bad faith").

> If I had not been a penitent, . . . had not been melancholy, my union with her would have made me happier than I had ever dreamed of being. But in so far as I was what, alas, I was, I had to say that I could be happier in my unhappiness without her than with her. . . .
>
> There was a divine protest, that is how I understood it. The wedding. I had to hide such a tremendous amount from her, had to base the whole thing upon something untrue.[m]
>
> Had I not honoured her above myself, as my future wife, had I not been prouder of her honour than of mine, then I should have remained silent and have fulfilled her desire and mine, and have been married to her—there are so many marriages that conceal their little tale. That I did not want; in that way she would have become my concubine; I would rather have murdered her. —But if I had had to explain myself then I would have had to initiate her into terrible things, my relation to my father, his melancholy, the eternal darkness that broods deep within, my going astray, pleasures and excesses which in the eyes of God are not perhaps so terrible, for it was dread that drove me to excess, and where was I to look for something to hold on to when I knew, or suspected that the one man I revered for his power and strength had wavered.[n]

2 [Like so many of Kierkegaard's self-revelations, this was recorded as if it were the sketch of a plot for a novel. But there is little doubt that it had a real-life basis—AUTHOR.]

After he had sacrificed Regine, he apparently hoped that God would give her back to him—as Yahweh had returned Isaac to Abraham after Abraham had prepared himself to sacrifice Isaac for Yahweh.[3] He was greatly chagrined when Regine promptly married the suitor whom Kierkegaard had replaced, but later he concluded that this was for the best: Love for Regine was incompatible with love for God; he had to choose between them.

> She has not, after all, the first place in my life. No, no, humanly speaking certainly—and how willing would I not prove it, she has and shall have the first place in my life—but God has the first place. My engagement to her and the break are really my relation to God, they are, if I may say so, divinely speaking, my engagement with God.°

The inner struggle over what he should do, the terribly difficult decision, and the bitterly disappointing and humiliating aftermath produced a crisis:

> I was so deeply shaken that I understood perfectly well that I could not possibly succeed in striking the comforting and secure *via media* in which most people pass their lives: I had either to cast myself into perdition and sensuality, or to choose the religious absolutely as the only thing—either the world in a measure that would be dreadful, or the cloister. That it was the second I would and must choose was at bottom already determined . . . ; I had become thoroughly aware how impossible it would be for me to be religious only up to a certain point.ᴾ

By "cloister" Kierkegaard of course did not mean literally a monastic life. He meant a life that, though perhaps outwardly indistinguishable from that of other men, was wholly dedicated to God, a life in which he was to devote himself to the task of becoming a Christian and, at the same time, of bringing to the attention of others what is involved in becoming a Christian. It is in the light of this double task that his huge literary and philosophical production should be read.

Existence and Reality

Perhaps the most philosophical item in this production is the *Concluding Unscientific Postscript*. Its highly personal and "expressive" style reveals Kierkegaard's conception of the nature and function of philosophy. The purpose of philosophy is not to instruct, but to "edify," that is, to improve us by changing us. The point of view is passionate, not neutral; practical, not speculative; subjective, not objective; inner, not outer; existential, not systematic. And the

---

3 See pp. 225–26.

point of departure is the self—not the self in general but the particular, existing self of Søren Kierkegaard.

> It is impossible to exist without passion, unless we understand the word "exist" in the loose sense of a so-called existence. Every Greek thinker was therefore essentially a passionate thinker. I have often reflected how one might bring a man into a state of passion. I have thought in this connection that if I could get him seated on a horse and the horse made to take fright and gallop wildly, or better still, for the sake of bringing the passion out, if I could take a man who wanted to arrive at a certain place as quickly as possible, and hence already had some passion, and could set him astride a horse that can scarcely walk—and yet this is what existence is like if one is to become consciously aware of it. Or if a driver were otherwise not especially inclined toward passion, if someone hitched a team of horses to a wagon for him, one of them a Pegasus and the other a worn-out jade, and told him to drive—I think one might succeed. And it is just this that it means to exist, if one is to become conscious of it. Eternity is the winged horse, infinitely fast, and time is a worn-out jade; the existing individual is the driver. That is to say, he is such a driver when his mode of existence is not an existence loosely so called; for then he is no driver, but a drunken peasant who lies asleep in the wagon and lets the horses take care of themselves. To be sure, he also drives and is a driver; and so there are perhaps many who—also exist.q

Two important points are brought out in this passage. First, existence is a qualitative matter: It is true that there is something that people *call* existence—living the life of daily routine, conforming to social norms that others have established for them. But real existence differs qualitatively from what T. S. Eliot called "a little life of dried tubers." Truly to exist is to struggle, to strain, to encounter opposition, to experience passion; it is to make decisions, not to drift with the tide. Second, existence and selfhood are identical; to exist in what has just been called the "real" sense is to *become*, not merely to be, a self. Hence, though Kierkegaard did not draw this conclusion explicitly, things that are not selves do not have an independent status; they "are" only insofar as they are "for" selves.

Ironically, despite all the contempt he had for Hegel's philosophy, Kierkegaard's views are in many ways similar to Hegel's.[4] For instance, according to Kierkegaard the self is not a preexisting, fully formed thing that can be discovered by looking in the right direction, as the continent of North America was once discovered by sailing in the right direction; it is not something "shut in a box with a spring-lock."r To put this insight in Hegelian terms, the self is not substance but subject. But whereas Hegel's subject-self was primarily a self-conscious knower, Kierkegaard's was primarily a doer; and whereas Hegel

4 See pp. 110–13.

had held that things exist "for" minds, as objects of knowledge, Kierkegaard believed that things exist "for" agents, as objects encountered and mastered.

Furthermore, Hegel had certainly included passion in his theory. Nothing great, he said, is accomplished without passion: It is passion that moves those world-historical individuals (for instance, Julius Caesar and Napoleon) who destroy an outmoded society and create a new social order.[5] In some respects—in their energy and their passion—Hegel's world-historical figures are very close to Kierkegaard's "true" selves; but though Kierkegaard held that creativity involves the destruction of old social norms, he by no means identified creativity with the fashioning of new ones. And there are other differences of emphasis that made it easy for Kierkegaard—who was a passionate advocate, not a neutral judge—to regard Hegel as the very model of the abstract thinker. Above all, whatever Hegel might *say* about passion and subjectivity, he was certainly neither passionate nor subjective in his attitude toward them. In calling attention to the difference between saying and doing (or, rather, between saying and being), Kierkegaard scored effectively—and by no means merely against Hegel.

> The difficulty that inheres in existence, with which the existing individual is confronted, is one that never really comes to expression in the language of abstract thought, much less receives an explanation. . . . Abstract thought . . . ignores the concrete and the temporal, the existential process, the predicament of the existing individual arising from his being a synthesis of the temporal and the eternal situated in existence. . . .
>
> One must therefore be very careful in dealing with a philosopher of the Hegelian school, and, above all, to make certain of the identity of the being with whom one has the honor to discourse. Is he a human being, an existing human being? Is he himself *sub specie aeterni*, even when he sleeps, eats, blows his nose, or whatever else a human being does? Is he himself the pure "I am I"? . . . Does he in fact exist? And if he does, is he then not in process of becoming? And if he is in process of becoming, does he not face the future? And does he ever face the future by way of action? And if he never does, will he not forgive an ethical individuality for saying in passion and with dramatic truth, that he is an ass? But if he ever acts *sensu eminenti*, does he not in that case face the future with infinite passion? Is there not then for him an either-or? Is it not the case that eternity is for an existing individual not eternity, but the future, and that eternity is eternity only for the Eternal, who is not in process of becoming? . . .
>
> All logical thinking employs the language of abstraction, and is *sub specie aeterni*. To think existence logically is thus to ignore the difficulty, the difficulty, that is, of thinking the eternal as in process or becoming. But this difficulty is unavoidable, since the thinker himself is in process of becoming. It is easier to indulge in abstract thought than it is to exist, unless we understand by this latter term what is loosely called existing, in analogy with what is loosely called being a subject. Here we have again an example of the fact that the simplest tasks are the most difficult. Existing is ordinarily

5 See p. 188.

regarded as no very complex matter, much less an art, since we all exist; but abstract thinking takes rank as an accomplishment. But really to exist, so as to interpenetrate one's existence with consciousness, at one and the same time eternal and as if far removed from existence, and yet also present in existence and in the process of becoming: that is truly difficult. . . .[8]

THE AGONY OF DECISION

Here, then, are two contrasting notions of what it is to exist. One of these notions equates existing with thinking: Descartes' "I think, therefore I am" is typical of the point of view of abstract philosophy. The other view equates existing with the "predicament" of decision, with the suffering of a man who wants desperately to do right but who lacks the information he feels he needs for making a choice. These two notions of existence may be contrasted in the following way. One is characteristic of an observer who contemplates the agony of decision from the neutral vantage point of a thinker, who dispassionately "takes note of" the blood, sweat, and tears from outside. The other notion is characteristic of a participant, who shares in and directly experiences the agony of decision—he bleeds, sweats, and weeps with the decider.

Kierkegaard regarded the external and detached point of view as easy (anyone can be a "subject," if this means only to think) and also superficial. It wholly misses the inner reality of what it is to be human. Of course, when Kierkegaard equated existence with the agony of being in a predicament, he was really describing his own life-experience, which was characterized by conflict and division. He both loved and feared his father, both admired and condemned him. He both hoped to marry Regine and wished to reject her. Thus, Kierkegaard's approach to philosophy was in a sense empirical. Indeed, he can be said to have been more rigorously empirical than so-called empiricists like Locke or Hume: His conception of the self was rooted in the deepest, most direct life-experience; their conception was actually derived from metaphysical and logical considerations. Further, whereas most empiricists were interested in formulating generalizations (for instance, the "laws" of association) about the nature of the self, Kierkegaard was an empiricist only in order to shed light on the predicament of every man who is honest with himself and who takes decision seriously.

And, of course, Kierkegaard did not merely want men to take decision seriously. He wanted, first, to relate the predicament of decision to his religious beliefs and, second, to persuade others of what he himself had become persuaded—that the only "cure" for the agony was to become a Christian. Kierkegaard solved the first problem, and laid the basis for solving the second, by interweaving a number of closely related themes—the contrasts between infinity and finitude, eternity and time, movement and stasis, possibility and actuality.

Existence . . . is a difficult category to deal with; for if I think it, I abrogate it, and then I do not think it. It might therefore seem to be the proper thing to say that there is something which cannot be thought, namely, existence.

But the difficulty persists, in that existence itself combines thinking with existing, in so far as the thinker exists. . . .

It is on this point about existence, and the demand which the ethical makes upon each existing individual, that one must insist when an abstract philosophy and a pure thought assume to explain everything by explaining away what is decisive. It is necessary only to have the courage to be human, and to refuse to be terrified or tricked into becoming a phantom merely to save embarrassment. . . .

In so far as existence consists in movement there must be something which can give continuity to the movement and hold it together, for otherwise there is no movement. Just as the assertion that everything is true means that nothing is true, so the assertion that everything is in motion means that there is no motion as its measure and its end. . . . Now while pure thought either abrogates motion altogether, or meaninglessly imports it into logic, the difficulty facing an existing individual is now to give his existence the continuity without which everything simply vanishes. An abstract continuity is no continuity, and the very existence of the existing individual is sufficient to prevent his continuity from having essential stability; while passion gives him a momentary continuity, a continuity which at one and the same time is a restraining influence and a moving impulse. The goal of movement for an existing individual is to arrive at a decision, and to renew it.

Existence constitutes the highest interest of the existing individual, and his interest in his existence constitutes his reality. What reality is, cannot be expressed in the language of abstraction . . . Abstract thought can get hold of reality only by nullifying it. . . .

All knowledge about reality is possibility. The only reality to which an existing individual may have a relation that is more than cognitive, is his own reality, the fact that he exists; this reality constitutes his absolute interest. Abstract thought requires him to become disinterested in order to acquire knowledge; the ethical demand is that he become infinitely interested in existing.

The only reality that exists for an existing individual is his own ethical reality. To every other reality he stands in a cognitive relation; but true knowledge consists in translating the real into the possible.

The real subject is not the cognitive subject, since in knowing he moves in the sphere of the possible; the real subject is the ethically existing subject. . . .[t]

These, then, are the reasons why the self is divided and in conflict. To begin with, though we men live in time, we have an idea of eternity. Time—change through time, getting older, not having time for everything—is an omnipresent and painful feature of life-experience. Life would be easy indeed if we were merely animals. We would, of course, actually live out our lives in time—present, past, and future; but we would not be conscious of ourselves as temporal beings. However, since we are men and not animals, we know that we are going to die, that at some point time will stop for us. To live in time is to be limited with respect to what one can do. To be conscious is to be aware of this limitation;

it is to know that there are many options and that, when we choose one, all the others are excluded. Though we presumably gain something by choosing this option, we certainly lose something as well—we lose all the others. The trouble is that we can never be sure, it would seem, that what we have gained exceeds what we have lost. Hence the agony of decision.

THE CURE FOR THE AGONY

If these are the causes of agony, what is the cure? According to Kierkegaard, it is to become passionately committed to one of the options. It is a psychological fact that, to the extent that we commit ourselves utterly and passionately to one option (from the psychological point of view, it does not matter which one), we no longer care about the others. At this moment the agony of decision obviously disappears. Passion alone may be satisfactory psychologically, but it is hardly satisfactory ethically. It is possible, for instance, in a moment of passionate anger to strike out impulsively and kill a man. This is why Kierkegaard emphasized commitment as well as passion. His point was that the act to which one becomes passionately committed must be deliberately chosen. Or, as stated in the passage above, "Really to exist is to interpenetrate one's existence with consciousness. . . . Existence itself combines thinking with existence." Unfortunately, most men probably alternate between being conscious and being passionate. Like Hamlet, they find that consciousness makes them cowards—it makes them cautious, careful, and hesitant. And caution, care, and hesitation are incompatible with passion.

Yet, although the state in which an "interpenetration" of consciousness and passion occurs is perhaps rare, it is not a psychological impossibility. Would it then be the cure for which Kierkegaard was looking? No; there is one additional, and all-important, requirement. To understand what this is, contrast Kierkegaard's position with that of a psychiatrist who wishes to help a patient agonizing over decision. If the psychiatrist adopted Kierkegaard's psychological theory, he would aim at getting his patient to interpenetrate consciousness with passion. If the patient's agony were thereby alleviated, he would be satisfied; his job would be done. For Kierkegaard, this was not enough; he was not a psychiatrist but a Christian advocate. He was interested not in mental health but in salvation. Hence he could not be satisfied with any passionate commitment that happened to alleviate suffering; it had to be a passionate commitment to the Christian God. His contention was that only this commitment would alleviate the agony, and his reasoning seems to have been that a complete cure requires a complete commitment, that is, an "infinite" commitment. But only a commitment to an infinite person can be infinite. Hence only a religious—and, specifically, a Christian—commitment is really a solution to man's existential problem.

This move from a psychological to a religious resolution of despair was fundamental for Kierkegaard, who was, above all else, a Christian thinker. If it is doubtful that his discussion would convince anyone not already convinced on other grounds, it is also true that, unlike most other philosophers, Kierkegaard held that no discussion ever convinces on logical grounds. It may, however, edify; that is, it may move men to change their ways. If it does, that is enough; it is, indeed, everything. It is necessary to bear this point of view in mind as the discussion develops.

The Nature of Choice

Since Kierkegaard's starting point was the existential fact that men are faced with an either-or, we must understand the nature of choice. There is a fundamental difference—which everyone can experience within himself—between choosing and merely wishing or wanting. This distinction must not be confused with the difference between bringing about some external change and failing to bring it about. Choosing is inner; it is not at all dependent on successfully producing a change in the state of affairs. It is distinguished from mere wishing or wanting in that it is an act of will; that is, it involves a commitment, a movement, of the personality.

> The real action is not the external act, but an internal decision in which the individual puts an end to the mere possibility and identifies himself with the content of his thought in order to exist in it. . . .
>
> When I think of something good that I intend to do, is this identical with having done it? By no means. But neither is it the external that constitutes the criterion of action; for the human being who does not own a penny can be as charitable as one who gives away a kingdom. When the Levite journeyed along the road traversed by the unfortunate man who, between Jericho and Jerusalem, had fallen among thieves, it may well have occurred to him while he was still some distance away, how beautiful a deed it is to help a sufferer in his distress. He may perhaps even have thought, by way of anticipation, that a good deed of this sort has its reward in itself; and perhaps he rode more slowly because of his absorption in this thought. But as he came nearer the place where the victim was, the difficulties began to heap themselves up before his mind—and he rode past. Now he doubtless began to make haste, in order to get away quickly from the thought of the insecurity of the road, from the thought of the possible presence of the robbers near by, from the thought of how readily the victim might be led to confuse him with the robbers who had left him there to die. He failed to act. But now suppose that he was seized by remorse, that he turned quickly about, fearing neither the robbers nor other difficulties, but fearing only lest he arrive too late. Let us suppose that he did arrive too late, the good Samaritan having already managed to get the sufferer into the shelter of the inn. Had he not then acted? Certainly he had acted, and that in spite of the fact that he had no opportunity to act in the external sense. . . .[u]

In his emphasis on inner motivation rather than on overt action Kierkegaard was close to Kant; and both philosophers, of course, were echoing the Christian thesis that "it is what comes out of a man that pollutes him. For it is from inside, from men's hearts, that designs of evil come." [v] But Kierkegaard's interpretation of inwardness differs from Kant's in a way that reflects the great movement that culminated, before the end of the nineteenth century, in abandonment of the Enlightenment's emphasis on rationality and autonomy. Kant had distinguished between what he called heteronomy and freedom of the will. Man is free when he acts autonomously, that is, when he acts from respect for a law he has imposed on himself.[6] From Kierkegaard's point of view a self-imposed law is no law, for the essence of law is compulsion. To act from self-respect is not (as Kant had thought) to achieve the highest morality; it is to fall into the sin of pride.

> Kant held that man was his own law (autonomy), *i.e.* bound himself under the law which he gave himself. In a deeper sense that means to say: lawlessness or experimentation. It is no harder than the thwacks which Sancho Panza applied to his own bottom. . . . There [must be] some third and compelling factor, which is not the individual himself. . . .
>
> Not only is the law which I give myself . . . not a law; but there is a law which is given to me by one higher than I. And not only that; but that lawgiver takes the liberty of joining in at the same time in the character of educator and applies the compulsion.
>
> Now if during the whole of his life a man never acts in so decisive a way that the educator can get a hold on him: well, then the man is certainly allowed to live on complacently in a state of illusion, imagination, experimentation—but that also connotes: the greatest lack of grace.[w]

THE ETHICAL LIFE CONTRASTED WITH THE ESTHETIC

Whereas Kant had distinguished two kinds of choice, heteronomy and autonomy, Kierkegaard distinguished three. He called these three ways of choosing, or attitudes toward choice, the esthetic, the ethical, and the religious. In the esthetic life choice is not taken seriously. At this level a man may take the view that "it doesn't matter what I choose; it will all turn out equally well"—or, alternatively, "equally badly." Thus, the esthetic life is either happy-go-lucky or cynical. The ethical life, in contrast, is serious. At this level men live, not by whim or impulse, but by an ethical code. Choice becomes problematic and serious since ethical men must decide how their code applies to the various concrete situations in which they find themselves. From this point of view, the particular code that they live by is less important than the fact that they have chosen to live by a code—if, indeed, they have *chosen* their code instead of merely drifting into it as a part of their inheritance from the culture in which they grew up.

6 See pp. 81–82.

It is not so much a question of choosing the right as of the energy, the earnestness, the pathos with which one chooses. Thereby the personality announces its inner infinity, and thereby, in turn, the personality is consolidated. . . .

My either/or does not in the first instance denote the choice between good and evil; it denotes the choice whereby one chooses good *and* evil/or excludes them. Here the question is under what determinants one would contemplate the whole of existence and would himself live. That the man who chooses good and evil chooses good is indeed true, but this becomes evident only afterwards; for the aesthetical is not the evil but neutrality. . . . It is, therefore, not so much a question of choosing between willing the good *or* the evil, as of choosing to will, but by this in turn the good and the evil are posited. . . . Here you see again how important it is that a choice be made, and that the crucial thing is not deliberation but the baptism of the will which lifts up the choice into the ethical.[x]

If this passage sounds like Kant, it is because Kierkegaard has not yet reached the religious level in his discussion, and because Kant, in Kierkegaard's view, never remotely reached it. Thus, though both philosophers emphasized the primacy of motive (and moral seriousness, as distinct from a merely esthetic life), they differed profoundly about what this motive is. Kant believed that the morally good motive consisted in treating men as ends in themselves, not merely as means.[7] In this respect his view exemplified the Enlightenment's belief in self-respect and its high regard for human nature. But Kierkegaard held that this view turned everything upside down. Man is finite, God is infinite; man is a sinner, God is merciful. It is essential for each man to recognize these relations and to act on them—to give himself to God utterly and completely. Further, whereas Kant believed that it is possible to work out rationally how we ought to act (the categorical imperative is universal and demonstrable, since its denial involves a contradiction), Kierkegaard believed that nothing can be proved and that a leap of faith is necessary. And this leap is necessary not merely in the sense that it is something we have to put up with in our state of ignorance, in the way I might say that it is necessary to walk because I do not have the money for a taxi. Rather, the leap of faith is necessary in the sense that it makes religion "religion." Indeed, it is just that passionate commitment that has already been described at the psychological level.[8]

THE RELIGIOUS LIFE CONTRASTED WITH THE ETHICAL

Socrates' decision to believe in immortality when there was, and could be, no proof of immortality is an example of such a commitment and is thus religious in nature.

7 See pp. 79–80.
8 See pp. 214–15.

When one man investigates objectively the problem of immortality, and another embraces an uncertainty with the passion of the infinite: where is there most truth, and who has the greater certainty? The one has entered upon a never-ending approximation, for the certainty of immortality lies precisely in the subjectivity of the individual; the other is immortal, and fights for his immortality by struggling with the uncertainty. Let us consider Socrates. Nowadays everyone dabbles in a few proofs; some have several such proofs, others fewer. But Socrates! He puts the question objectively in a problematic manner: *if* there is an immortality. He must therefore be accounted a doubter in comparison with one of our modern thinkers with the three proofs?[9] By no means. On this "if" he risks his entire life, he has the courage to meet death, and he has with the passion of the infinite so determined the pattern of his life that it must be found acceptable—*if* there is an immortality. Is any better proof capable of being given for the immortality of the soul? But those who have the three proofs do not at all determine their lives in conformity therewith; if there is an immortality it must feel disgust over their manner of life: can any better refutation be given of these three proofs? The bit of uncertainty that Socrates had, helped him because he himself contributed the passion of the infinite; the three proofs that the others have do not profit them at all, because they are dead to spirit and enthusiasm. . . . The Socratic ignorance, which Socrates held fast with the entire passion of his inwardness, was thus an expression for the principle that the eternal truth is related to an existing individual, and that this truth must therefore be a paradox for him as long as he exists. . . .[y]

Though Socrates' passionate commitment to an immortality that he knew could not be proved shows him to have been religious "in the highest sense in which this was possible within paganism,"[z] there is an enormous difference between his religion and Christianity. For though there is no objective evidence for personal immortality, belief in immortality is not absurd. In contrast, the Christian belief in a God who became man and suffered on the cross for sinners is literally absurd. The Christian's commitment is, then, far more difficult than was Socrates'. Nevertheless, "carefully used," Socrates' story can be "adapted to the problem of becoming a Christian."[a] For the Socratic affirmation of immortality "is an analogue to faith; only that the inwardness of faith, corresponding as it does, not to the repulsion of the Socratic ignorance, but to the repulsion exerted by the absurd, is infinitely more profound."[b]

Thus the difference between the ethical stage and the religious stage is not the difference between two kinds of acts, for the same act may be done from a merely ethical motive (or indeed from an esthetic motive) as from a religious motive. Nor is it merely the difference between calculation and commitment, for a man may be passionately serious at the ethical stage. The difference, rather, is that between commitment to, say, a cause or code and commitment to God.

9 [Kierkegaard is referring to the three "classic" proofs of the existence of God, which Kant had criticized. See pp. 55–58—AUTHOR.]

Only when we make the latter commitment does our life acquire the focus and center for which we have been longing; this is because, as has been said, an infinite commitment is necessary, and it can be made only to an infinite person.

As long as a person lives by what Kant called the principle of autonomy he is in despair. He can be, as Kant himself was, passionately serious about duty. Indeed, in a sense, the more serious a person is, the more he is in despair, because he realizes that as long as he relies on his own judgment, he can never be sure what he is doing is right. It is not enough for someone to say to himself that he has done the best he can; the only exit from self-destructive doubt is for him to see that, if he relies on himself, he is *never* right. Then he is ready, in despair, to throw himself on God.

> No earnest doubt, no really deep concern, is put to rest by the saying that one does what one can. If a man is sometimes in the right, sometimes in the wrong, to a certain degree in the right, to a certain degree in the wrong, who, then, is to decide this except man; but in deciding it may he not be to a certain degree in the right, to a certain degree in the wrong? . . . Must doubt then prevail, constantly discovering new difficulties . . . ? We have, then, only the choice of being nothing before God, or the eternal torture of beginning over again every instant, but without being able to begin. For if we are to be able to determine definitely whether at the present instant we are in the right, this question must be definitely determined with a view to the preceding instant and then further and further back. . . .
>
> How might a man be able to depict his relationship to God by a more or a less, or by an approximate definition? . . . Only by an infinite relationship to God [can] doubt be calmed, only by an infinitely free relationship to God [can] anxiety be transformed into joy. [A man] is in an infinite relationship to God when he recognizes that God is always in the right, in an infinitely free relationship to God when he recognizes that he himself is always in the wrong. In this way, therefore, doubt is checked, for the movement of doubt consists precisely in the fact that at one instant he might be in the right, at another in the wrong, to a certain degree in the right, to a certain degree in the wrong. . . . So whenever doubt would . . . teach him that he suffers too much, that he is tried beyond his powers, he thereupon forgets the finite in the infinite thought that he is always in the wrong. Whenever the affliction of doubt would make him sad, he thereupon raises himself above the finite into the infinite; for the thought that he is always in the wrong is the wing whereby he soars above finitude, it is the longing wherewith he seeks God, it is the love wherein he finds God.[c]

In contrast to the despair of doubt is the assurance of faith. This assurance is compatible with uncertainty; indeed, what distinguishes faith from other states of mind is the tension between assurance and objective uncertainty. This brings us back to Kierkegaard's earlier distinction between the thinker and the existing individual. Truth for the thinker is an objective state of affairs that is capable of being formulated more and more precisely by an approximation process. Truth for the existing individual is that to which he is passionately committed. Thus for the existing individual, as distinct from the abstract thinker, truth and faith are the same. Both truth and faith involve

> . . . the tension of the subjective inwardness. Here is such a definition of truth: *An objective uncertainty held fast in an appropriation-process of the most passionate inwardness is the truth*, the highest truth attainable for an *existing* individual. . . . Thus the subject merely has, objectively, the uncertainty; but it is this which precisely increases the tension of that infinite passion which constitutes his inwardness. The truth is precisely the venture which chooses an objective uncertainty with the passion of the infinite. I contemplate the order of nature in the hope of finding God, and I see omnipotence and wisdom; but I also see much else that disturbs my mind and excites anxiety. The sum of all this is an objective uncertainty. But it is for this very reason that the inwardness becomes as intense as it is, for it embraces this objective uncertainty with the entire passion of the infinite. In the case of a mathematic proposition the objectivity is given, but for this reason the truth of such a proposition is an indifferent truth [that is, the sort of truth that is contemplated by a thinker].
>
> But the above definition of truth is an equivalent expression for faith. Without risk there is no faith. Faith is precisely the contradiction between the infinite passion of the individual's inwardness and the objective uncertainty. If I am capable of grasping God objectively, I do not believe, but precisely because I cannot do this I must believe. If I wish to preserve myself in faith I must constantly be intent upon holding fast to the objective uncertainty, so as to remain out upon the deep, over seventy thousand fathoms of water, still preserving my faith.[d]

Thus, as we have seen, the cure for doubt, the cure for the agonizing suspicion that despite all our efforts we *may* have chosen wrongly, is to realize that if we rely on our own efforts we *always* choose wrongly. We should, then, give up trying and put ourselves completely and unreservedly in God's hand. We must have faith that what we are doing has been chosen for us by God. A person who acts in this spirit is released from distress; he is "saved."

But, someone may ask, cannot such a person be mistaken? Of course, as long as he is persuaded that God has chosen for him, he will be spared all anxiety. But is he really saved, or does he only *think* he is saved? One answer to this question—and perhaps in the end the only answer—is that by raising this doubt one has adopted an abstract point of view. The questioner has become a "thinker". He is no longer an existing individual; he has taken himself out of the religious sphere. To reenter it he must once again enclose his doubt within the passionate commitment of faith.

This answer is admittedly a paradox. It is best to postpone further consideration of it until one of Kierkegaard's most characteristic notions—the teleological suspension of the ethical—has been examined, for this concept provides still another account of the all-important contrast between the ethical and the religious stages.

The Teleological Suspension of the Ethical

According to Kierkegaard, just as Socrates may be considered the paradigm of pagan religion, so Abraham can be taken as an exemplar of Christian attitudes. For both Socrates and Abraham truth was subjective; it involved a total commitment of their lives to something they knew could not be proved. But whereas Socrates' passion was directed toward an idea, Abraham's was directed toward a person, a God who commands absolute obedience and who will educate men[10] if they only act in a sufficiently decisive way.

This point about Abraham can best be understood by contrasting him with a tragic hero like Brutus. Both men disobeyed the universal moral requirement that fathers should succour, support, and defend the lives of their children. Brutus ordered his son killed when he was found to be conspiring against the Roman republic. This was a tragic decision, but it remained within the sphere of the ethical, for his decision was in accordance with a universal moral requirement—the duty of a political leader to preserve the state. In fact, this duty is an even higher expression of the ethical than is the universal moral requirement that parents love their children more than they love themselves.

> With Abraham the situation was different. By his act he overstepped the ethical entirely and possessed a higher *telos* outside of it, in relation to which he suspended the former. For I should very much like to know how one would bring Abraham's act into relation with the universal, and whether it is possible to discover any connection whatever between what Abraham did and the universal . . . except the fact that he transgressed it. It was not for the sake of saving a people, not to maintain the idea of the state, that Abraham did this. . . . Abraham's whole action stands in no relation to the universal, is a purely private undertaking. . . .
>
> Here is evident the necessity of a new category if one would understand Abraham. Such a relationship to the deity paganism did not know. The tragic hero does not enter into any private relationship with the deity, but for him the ethical is the divine, hence the paradox implied in his situation can be mediated in the universal.
>
> Therefore, though Abraham arouses my admiration, he at the same time appalls me. . . . The tragic hero gives up the certain for the still more certain, and the eye of the beholder rests upon him confidently. But he who gives up the universal in order to grasp something still higher which is not the universal—what is he doing? Is it possible that this can be anything else but a temptation (*Anfechtung*)? And if . . . the individual was mistaken—what can save him? He suffers all the pain of the tragic hero, he brings to naught his joy in the world, he renounces everything . . . and perhaps at the same instant debars himself from the sublime joy which to him was so precious that he would purchase it at any price. Him the beholder cannot understand nor let his eye rest confidently upon him. Perhaps it is not possible to do what the believer proposes, since it is indeed unthinkable. Or if it could be

10 See p. 220.

done, but if the individual had misunderstood the deity—what can save him? . . .

But now when the ethical is thus teleologically suspended, how does the individual exist in whom it is suspended? . . . How then did Abraham exist? He believed. This is the paradox which keeps him upon the sheer edge and which he cannot make clear to any other man, for the paradox is that he as the individual puts himself in an absolute relation to the absolute . . . .[e]

When Kierkegaard wrote this account of Abraham, he was thinking of his own situation. Just as Abraham had had to choose between God and Isaac, so, it seemed to Kierkegaard, he had had to choose between God and Regine. Now, it may be that on occasion religion demands this kind of choice; certainly individuals who have violated an existing moral code have sometimes justified their actions in this way. But the very drama of a decision like Abraham's, suggesting as it does that religion appertains only to exceptional circumstances, distorts the point Kierkegaard wanted to make: Actually, he wanted to bring together "the absoluteness of the religious and the particularities of life."[f] That is, he thought it important to show that it is possible for the ordinary man to be religious in even the most ordinary of circumstances.

The example Kierkegaard chose to illustrate this thesis was deliberately as trivial as possible. It was the question of how to choose to go on an outing to the Deer Park, a favorite expedition for the citizens of Copenhagen in Kierkegaard's day. He set out to show that it is not necessary to choose between God and the outing: One can become "so religious that he is able before God to resolve to take an outing in the Deer Park,"[g] just as Abraham was able before God to resolve to slay Isaac. Once again, the critical issue for religion is not what one does but the spirit in which one acts (the intense inwardness of one's commitment to that act).

What is necessary—whether a person is trying to decide to kill his son or whether he is only trying to decide to go to the Deer Park—is to recognize that he cannot reach certainty by an approximation process. Equally as many doubts can arise about whether he should make the excursion, and if so, when he should set out and at what hour he should return, as can arise about whether it is really God who is telling him to kill his son. Doubtless from the point of view of a utilitarian calculation of results in *this* world, the latter decision is much more difficult because so much more depends on it. But, in Kierkegaard's view, utilitarian results are trivial as compared with the need for getting in a right relation with God. Getting in a right relation with God consists in bringing one's will into loving obedience. This is no more difficult in the case of the Deer Park decision than in the case of Abraham's decision, for—and this is the whole point—the individual can *never* achieve this for himself. In every case, therefore, he must have faith that God has brought his will into obedience, for this is no more problematic in one case than in any other.

The religious individual is unable to bring the God-idea together with such accidental finitude as . . . taking a pleasure outing in the Deer Park. He feels the pain of this. . . . The difficulty is first and foremost to attain to a comprehension of his inability, and so to annul the illusion, since he should always bear in mind that he can do nothing of himself—this difficulty [the religious man] has conquered, and now there remains the second difficulty: with God to be able to do it.[h]

Abraham, or any man in his position, could never be certain he is obeying God; indeed, the more he knows (as a thinker, as a result of an approximation process), the more uncertain he must become. Since he cannot exclude the possibility that he is moved by unconscious jealousy, by a reverse Oedipal complex, he experiences agony as he presses the knife to his son's throat. The uncertainty holds also for the citizen of Copenhagen who is trying to decide whether to take an outing in the Deer Park. And the same is true for Kierkegaard himself: The more he thought about it, the less certain he was that he had really abandoned Regine for God's sake and not for his own sake—because he was ashamed to confess his earlier delinquencies, or because he was afraid of a sexual relationship, or simply because he was bored by the girl. In all three cases—in all cases whatever—the religious requirement is the same. One must be fully aware of the objective uncertainty and one must embrace this uncertainty with "the entire passion of the infinite." Thus religion does not consist simply in obeying God (an objective state of affairs), for one can never *know* that one is obeying God, and if one could know, one's faith would disappear. Rather, religion consists in having faith that one is obeying God.

Was Kierkegaard a Christian?

Holding such views as these, was Kierkegaard a Christian? He certainly wanted to be; he certainly thought he was. Indeed, in emphasizing inwardness he believed himself to be returning to the "true" Christianity. But, given his subjective view of truth, in what sense can any conception of Christianity be objectively truer than any other?

It is easy, of course, to understand why Kierkegaard emphasized inwardness. He saw that it had been relatively easy to be a Christian when Christianity consisted of but a small persecuted sect. In those days one knew whether or not one was a Christian, for it took a conscious decision, an act of will, a real commitment, to be a Christian. In nineteenth-century Europe, however, where "everyone" was a Christian, in a sense no one was. Someone who is born into a Christian family and is brought up as Christian finds himself going to Church on Sundays and performing the rites as a matter of routine, or possibly because he feels the service is "beautiful." This person calls himself a Christian without deciding to be one, or even thinking about what being a Christian means. It was natural, then, for Kierkegaard to insist on passion and commitment as the heart of inwardness.

But it may be that he went too far in the direction of subjectivity—farther than he himself intended to go. "If only the mode of this relationship is in the truth, the individual is in the truth even if he should happen to be thus related to what is not true." [i] When truth is defined as passionate inwardness, it seems to follow that the belief of a Hindu that Vishnu is God, the belief of a Mohammedan that Allah is God, the belief of a Nuer that *kwoth* is God—even the belief of an atheist that there is no God—are all true, providing only that in each of these beliefs an objective uncertainty is embraced with passionate intensity. "The objective accent falls on *what* is said, the subjective accent on *how* it is said." [j] This seems unequivocal: Though the beliefs differ with respect to content, the objective aspect is unimportant from the religious point of view; what is important from that point of view is the attitude adopted toward the content, and the same attitude can be adopted toward beliefs of very different contents. It would appear that religion has collapsed into feeling and that "God" is simply the name that Kierkegaard gave to the mental state in which he had come to feel a passionate commitment.

An analogous problem arises as soon as one tries to distinguish between true and false suspensions of the ethical. Kierkegaard wanted to hold that Abraham was truly a paradigm of Christian faith; he also wanted to hold that Magister Adler was deluded.[11] But if truth is subjective, Adler could have been false only if he were a deliberate liar. If Adler really experienced a passionate inwardness, his affirmation was as truly religious, in Kierkegaard's own account of religion, as was Abraham's. Indeed, it is possible that Adler was the only paradigm, for conceivably Abraham was lying.

Of course, Kierkegaard might have replied that he did not care about the lack of evidence on the basis of which it would be possible to infer that Abraham was true and Adler false: He did not want evidence; he had made a leap of faith for Abraham and against Adler. But then Adler could equally well have said (and believed) that *he* had made a leap of faith for himself and against Kierkegaard. It would seem, then, that Kierkegaard became involved in a kind of Protagoreanism in which every man is the measure of his own religiosity. Though Kierkegaard insisted that the believer's leap of faith "puts him in an absolute relation to the absolute," the only available criterion for judging whether he has in fact achieved this relation is his own private feeling. Thus Kierkegaard's absolutism turns out, on scrutiny, to be a radical relativism.

Kierkegaard attempted to extricate himself from this extreme position by defining God objectively as the being who has such-and-such properties—for instance, He commands, He educates. But can this account be brought into harmony with the other account in which God is defined subjectively as the being who (regardless of what objective properties he may have or lack) evokes such-and-such attitudes on the part of the believer? This would be possible if there

---

11   A. P. Adler (1812–69) was a Danish clergyman who, midway in a quiet and conventional career, suddenly announced that he had had a special revelation and proceeded to publish what God had told him.

were only one thing to which men can commit themselves absolutely, and if this thing were the being who possesses the properties of commanding, educating, and so on. But to take this line of defense is to rest one's case on an empirical, and therefore at best only probable, fact about human psychology.[12]

It is possible, of course, to avoid facing up to this consequence by shifting so swiftly between the subjective and the objective points of view that one does not see what is going on. This escape route is often taken by modern theologians who have been influenced by existentialism but who have also wanted to remain "orthodox." Though Kierkegaard himself sometimes used these tactics, he was not, as has already been pointed out, sufficiently interested in evidence, logic, or argument to feel the need of an escape route. Even if he could have been convinced that logic was against him and that the infinite person he called "God" might just possibly be Allah—or that Adler, not Abraham, might be the paradigmatic Christian—Kierkegaard would have replied that this is just one more objective uncertainty (which he had not thought of himself) that his leap of faith must embrace.

Subjective, Not Objective, Truth

Kierkegaard's distinction between subjective and objective truth deserves more detailed examination, for it plays an important role in defining his own view of religion and is highly interesting as a sign of the direction in which Western culture was moving. As we have seen, this distinction was important to Kierkegaard because he held faith to be the essence of religion. But since he also held faith to be incompatible with objective evidence, it was necessary for him to show that all the so-called proofs of Christianity are incompetent. Here again Kierkegaard may resemble Kant, who had undertaken to demonstrate that the three traditional proofs of the existence of God are invalid. But whereas Kant had criticized the proofs on logical grounds, Kierkegaard sought only to show that the mental state, or attitude, in which one is seeking to prove something is irreconcilable with religion.

---

12 In a parallel way, when Kierkegaard was attacking Adler, he cited a number of objective characteristics that supposedly distinguish true revelations from spurious ones. It appears that "a real *extraordinarius*" is silent; Adler talked and wrote a lot. Furthermore, Adler burned the theological treatise that he had been writing when he had his great experience; had he been an *extraordinarius* he would have kept it by him at least for a while. And so on. Poor Kierkegaard! it must have been evident to him that all these considerations were wholly irrelevant. Inferences from behavior to mental states are at best only probable. But even passing over the hazards of diagnosing delusional fantasy, insofar as Kierkegaard succeeded in making a case against Adler's claims, he did so only by converting questions about religious inwardness into questions about mental states. This "reduction" of religion to empirical psychology was a cost that Kierkegaard was certainly unwilling to pay. Kierkegaard's criticism of Adler is contained in *On Authority and Revelation*, translated by W. Lowrie with an introduction by F. Sontag (Harper & Row, New York, 1966). See, for instance, pp. 52 ff.

It was as a preliminary step in this undertaking that Kierkegaard distinguished between objective and subjective truth. The point of view of the seeker of objective truth is reflected in Kant's favorite image of the disinterested judge, who, because he is not a party to the case, listens to plaintiff and defendant and weighs their evidence impartially and dispassionately. For the most part, philosophers have accepted this ideal of impartiality and have merely disagreed about whether it is actually attainable or whether men can only approximate to it. Most philosophers, therefore, have regarded words like "impartial," "disinterested," and "dispassionate" as highly honorific. For Kierkegaard, however, they were pejorative. In his view, objective truth, like "system," is an impossible ideal. There is no such thing as an impartial observer, for all truth is in varying degrees interested. "Impartiality" is itself an interest, and, as it happens, an unfortunate one. In the first place, pursuit of impartiality, which is doomed to failure anyway, is a distraction insofar as it draws our energies away from what ought to be our sole concern—finding our center, becoming a Christian. In the second place, pursuit of impartiality is a form of escapism. Constructing systems, weighing evidence, attempting to reach an objective truth, are all subtle ways in which men seek to avoid the anguish of decision.

If Kierkegaard had been concerned with theory of knowledge, his notion of a truth that is always interested would have brought him into sympathetic relation with one important aspect of Marxism[13] and might even have made him anticipate pragmatism.[14] However, because his interests were so exclusively moral and religious, and because his bias in favor of inwardness was so strong, he failed to develop this idea. Instead, he was content to show that neither method of seeking objective truth—neither historical scholarship nor philosophical speculation—is a possible way to Christianity.

THE HISTORICAL POINT OF VIEW

Given Kierkegaard's demand for certainty, it was easy for him to show the inadequacy of historical research. Central to the Christians' claims are a number of historical assertions—that Jesus lived, that he was crucified, and so on. If we examine these claims objectively, that is, in the same way we would investigate the claim that Caesar was bald or that Cicero was the editor of Lucretius' poem, we see that, like all assertions about the past, they can be no more than merely probable.

> When one raises the historical question of the truth of Christianity, or of what is and is not Christian truth, the Scriptures at once present themselves as documents of decisive significance. The historical inquiry therefore first concentrates upon the Bible. . . . [But] even with the most stupendous learning and persistence in research, and even if all the brains of all the critics were

13 See pp. 190–91.
14 See Vol. V, pp. 55–56.

concentrated in one, it would still be impossible to obtain anything more than an approximation; and an approximation is essentially incommensurable with an infinite personal interest in an eternal happiness.

[But let us] assume that the critics have succeeded in proving about the Bible everything that any learned theologian in his happiest moment has ever wished to prove about the Bible. These books and no others belong to the canon; they are authentic; they are integral; their authors are trustworthy—one may well say, that it is as if every letter were inspired. . . .

Well, then, everything being assumed in order with respect to the Scriptures—what follows? Has anyone who previously did not have faith been brought a single step nearer to its acquisition? No, not a single step. Faith does not result simply from a scientific inquiry; it does not come directly at all. On the contrary, in this objectivity one tends to lose that infinite personal interestedness in passion which is the condition of faith.

. . . .

When the question is treated in an objective manner it becomes impossible for the subject to face the decision with passion, least of all with an infinitely interested passion. It is a self-contradiction and therefore comical, to be infinitely interested in that which in its maximum still always remains an approximation. If in spite of this, passion is nevertheless imported, we get fanaticism. . . . The fault is not in the infinitely interested passion, but in the fact that its object has become an approximation-object. . . .[k]

THE SPECULATIVE POINT OF VIEW

Having thus demolished the historical, or scientific, version of objectivity, Kierkegaard next directed his attack against the speculative version. By speculation Kierkegaard meant any interpretation of religion based on a very general set of metaphysical concepts, which thereby render it "intelligible." Kierkegaard was thinking primarily of Hegel's attempt to bring Christianity within the structure of his triadic system; but any philosophical theology—for instance, Aristotle's definition of God in terms of the basic metaphysical distinctions between form and matter, actuality and potentiality—represents the sort of procedure Kierkegaard found offensive. To try to make religious feeling "understandable" is to distort it by destroying its passionate inwardness. For any such undertaking Kierkegaard had even more contempt, if that be possible, than for historical scholarship. History at least restricts itself to the concrete and particular; philosophical theology is not only "objective" but abstract as well.

The speculative philosopher . . . proposes to contemplate Christianity from the philosophical standpoint . . . for the sake of interpenetrating it with his speculative thought; aye, with his genuinely speculative thought. But suppose this whole proceeding were a chimera, a sheer impossibility; suppose that Christianity is subjectivity, an inner transformation, an actualization of inwardness, and that only two kinds of people can know anything about it: those who with an infinite passionate interest in an eternal happiness base their happiness upon their believing relationship to Christianity, and those who with an opposite passion, but in passion, reject it—the happy and the unhappy lovers. Suppose that an objective indifference can therefore learn nothing at all. Only the like is understood by the like. . . .

Now if Christianity is essentially something objective, it is necessary for the observer to be objective. But if Christianity is essentially subjectivity, it is a mistake for the observer to be objective. In every case where the object of knowledge is the very inwardness of the subjectivity of the individual, it is necessary for the knower to be in a corresponding condition.[1]

Kierkegaard's attack on the abstraction of "speculative philosophy"—his reminder that it is individual men who speculate and that their speculations are inevitably affected by their beliefs, by their "passions"—is very salutary. In general, he is effective as long as he is criticizing one extreme position, but many people will think that he himself adopted the opposite, and equally mistaken, extreme. They will say that pure subjectivity is no more adequate than pure objectivity.

This criticism of Kierkegaard's position can be put in Kantian and in Hegelian terms. Kant drew a distinction between what he called percepts and concepts—between a direct, experiential element in cognition and an abstract, structural, and relational element.[15] Hegel developed this relatively simple distinction into the more subtle notion of there being a movement of thought from "immediacy" through "mediation" to "self-mediation"—from the immediacy and directness of feeling, through externalization and criticism, to a renewal of immediacy on a higher level of sophisticated understanding.[16] With respect to the quality of experience, Kierkegaard's subjectivity and Hegel's immediacy are about equivalent; but Kierkegaard would have lumped together Hegel's mediation and self-mediation. From Kierkegaard's point of view, the latter is as defective as the former because it too involves objectivity. In short, he would have held that thought can never become self-transcendent (its object always remains an other for it). As evidence of this, Kierkegaard would undoubtedly have cited the fact that Hegel himself, despite all the claims he made, never got beyond the level of *raisonnement*.

There is force to this criticism. Hegel certainly tended, in his own thought about thinking, to slip rather easily from the notion of degrees of adequacy (degrees of self-mediation) to the notion of complete adequacy (a self-mediation that is absolute). He sometimes wrote as if this ideal could actually be achieved; indeed, at times he wrote as if he thought that he had achieved it, and that his version of the system was the System itself. Kierkegaard's reminder that thought's object remains an other is a useful corrective to Hegel's tendency to suppose that *his* thought had somehow managed to incorporate the other in complete transcendence. Nevertheless, much can be said for Hegel's underlying

15 See pp. 33–34.
16 See pp. 119–20.

thesis that cognition involves not only an element of immediacy but also an element of conscious reflection and evaluation. To put this in Kantian terms, since percepts without concepts are blind and concepts without percepts are empty, all adequate thought involves a blend, or mix, of both elements.

Kant and Hegel would have agreed with Kierkegaard that consciousness involves externality, a kind of detachment from direct experience. And they would also have allowed that in this process of externalization something is lost—immediacy. But they would have argued that something is gained, which is even more valuable than what is lost—comparison, evaluation, interpretation, understanding, the setting of the moment of immediacy in a comparative context of earlier than, different from, similar to, and better than.

Kierkegaard would not have been responsive to this line of reasoning, for as a "line of reasoning" it had all the characteristics of objectivity that he hated. He also hated balance and compromise—attitudes that are associated with objectivity. Thus, if asked to weigh evidence that he had exaggerated the role of the direct, experiential element in cognition, he would have declined to do so, replying that he had direct experience of the preferred status of direct experience as compared with the weighing-of-evidence approach. If asked to consider whether he had not overemphasized the passionate element in cognition, he would have replied passionately that it is impossible to put too much emphasis on the passionate element. And he might well have added that to ask him to adopt a balanced, objective stance toward his thesis that imbalance and subjectivity are desirable was to invite him to fall into contradiction. Kierkegaard might have granted that the stance he adopted closed the issue in advance in his favor, but he could have added that Kant and Hegel, for their part, had done no better. They had closed the issue in their favor by the stance *they* had adopted—for they had adopted a judicious, balanced position toward a balanced blend of direct experience and abstract, conceptual knowledge.

Here, then, we are confronted with a major parting of the ways, one that reflects very deep temperamental differences. Despite the slippages just referred to, Hegel was essentially a gradualist: In his view, self-mediation was not an all-or-none affair but a matter of degree. On the whole, therefore, he was fairly reconciled to the notion of an "adequate" that was always becoming "more adequate," but that never actually became "completely" adequate. Kierkegaard was temperamentally impatient: Not to have all was as bad as to have none. He demanded certainty, finality, completeness; approximation was wholly inacceptable to him.

Kierkegaard had similar views regarding alienation. Alienation, considered in its social sense, is a concept closely related to mediation, considered as an element in cognition. Marx was greatly concerned about the existence of alienation in nineteenth-century culture, but he believed that this alienation could be, and would be, overcome in the course of time by the overthrow of capitalism. Moreover, he thought he could help this process along. His attitude was therefore not at all dissimilar to that of Hegel, who contemplated the history of thought in much the same way as Marx contemplated the history of class struggle. Basically, both were optimists. Kierkegaard was far more profoundly alienated, both in the intellectual sense and in the social sense, than was either Hegel or Marx. The division he experienced within himself was so intolerable that a philosophical theory offering no more than gradual improvement seemed utterly irrelevant. He was persuaded—again by direct personal experience—that no rational, scientific, or economic procedure could heal the break within the self and between the self and its world; only a leap of faith could accomplish that. And God—this was his faith—had helped him, Søren Kierkegaard, to make the leap that had brought his life into "focus" and given it a "center."

Kierkegaard and "The Age"

Kierkegaard expressed his experience of division and conflict in the religious language of sin and guilt. To many people today this language is foreign; they have not made, nor can they make, his leap of faith. Nonetheless, Kierkegaard speaks meaningfully to these "atheistic" (or perhaps "agnostic") existentialists because they too experience division, alienation, and loneliness and because they share his conviction that men are far less rational and far less capable of ordering and directing their affairs than they like to believe. Since these attitudes and beliefs increasingly characterize our own times, what Kierkegaard said about his own age seems even truer of the second half of the twentieth century:

> Our age reminds one vividly of the dissolution of the Greek city-state: everything goes on as usual, and yet there is no longer anyone who believes in it.
>
> Passion is the real thing. . . . And the age in which we live is wretched, because it is without passion.
>
> People must have lived ever so much more simply in the days when they believed that God made his will known in dreams. . . . Think of life in big cities and the manner of life: no wonder people attribute their dreams to devils and demons. —Moreover the poor opinion in which dreams are held nowadays is also connected with the intellectualism which really only values the conscious, while in simpler ages people piously believed that the unconscious life in man was the more important as well as the profounder.
>
> Have you seen a boat aground in the mud, it is almost impossible to float it again because it is impossible to punt, no punt-pole can touch bottom so that one can push against it. And so the whole generation is stuck in the mud banks of reason. . . .
>
> Mankind *en masse* gives itself up to evil, . . . nowadays it happens *en masse*. That is why people flock together, in order that natural and animal hysteria should get hold of them, in order to feel themselves stimulated, inflamed and *ausser sich*.

> Just as desert travellers combine into great caravans from fear of robbers
> and wild beasts, so the individuals of the contemporary generation are fearful
> of existence, because it is God-forsaken; only in great masses do they dare
> to live, and they cluster together *en masse* in order to feel that they amount
> to something.[m]

Wherever and whenever men evaluate their age and their culture in this
way, Kierkegaard will be read—despite his exaggeration, his one-sidedness, and
his radical subjectivity. Indeed, he will be read *because* of these qualities; they
are central to this view of man.

Nietzsche

Friedrich Nietzsche was born in 1844 in Prussian Saxony. His family background
was Lutheran, clerical, and royalist; his father and both his grandfathers were
pastors, and he was named for the reigning king of Prussia. Nietzsche's father
died when he was a child, and he was brought up in a house filled with
women—his mother, grandmother, two maiden aunts, and a sister. He was
educated at the universities of Bonn and Leipzig; at twenty-five (an unprece-
dentedly early age), even before he had taken his degree, he was appointed
to a professorship of classical philology at the University of Basel. Although
he had become a Swiss citizen, when the Franco-Prussian War broke out in
1870 Nietzsche volunteered and served briefly as a medical orderly in the Prussian
Army. Ill health caused him to withdraw from active duty and, in 1879, to
retire from teaching. However, despite terrible migraine headaches, severe
stomach upsets, insomnia, and very bad eyesight, he continued to write and
publish. He lived a solitary life in near poverty and spent his winters in boarding
houses in Italy and his summers in Switzerland. Early in 1889 he became
hopelessly insane, probably as a result of a syphilitic infection (which must have
been contracted very early, for he lived a very ascetic life). He died in 1900.

Nietzsche's life spanned almost exactly the second half of the nineteenth
century. When he was born, Hegel had been dead only thirteen years; Mill
was thirty-eight years old; and Kierkegaard was thirty-one. Nietzsche himself
was four when the *Manifesto of the Communist Party* was published and fifteen
when *The Origin of Species* appeared. In the year he died both Bergson and
Dewey were already forty-one and Russell was twenty-eight. During this period
the optimistic mood of the Enlightenment was ending and the democratization,
industrialization, and urbanization of Europe, which had initially been greeted
with enthusiasm, were seen to be having unpredicted consequences—the commer-
cialization, vulgarization, and impersonalization of life.

In many respects, Nietzsche's attitudes were similar to Kierkegaard's. He
too was deeply alienated from the contemporary culture and internally divided.

Hence, though he was more interested than Kierkegaard in the traditional problems of philosophy—for instance, theory of knowledge and esthetics—most of his writings bore directly or indirectly on the existential problem of a man who finds himself alone in a world that is irrational, purposeless, and ultimately meaningless. What stance should he adopt toward such a world? How can he find "a center and a focus" for his life? Nietzsche was as passionately concerned with this problem as Kierkegaard had been, but temperamentally he was more robust. He had nothing but contempt for Kierkegaard's leap of faith. In contrast, he found fulfillment precisely in the hardness and courage with which he faced up to the terrible truths he had discovered.

Which of these highly personal solutions appeals to the reader—if, indeed, either does—depends less on the evidence presented by the two philosophers than on the reader's own temperament and outlook. As a matter of fact, neither Kierkegaard nor Nietzsche offered any evidence in the strict sense; they agreed that a way of life is not subject to proof, and their writings were designed to draw the reader's attention to painful "truths" that he would prefer to ignore. Furthermore, since both believed that most readers have developed ingenious techniques for avoiding unpleasant facts, neither expected to make many converts. Neither addressed himself to the "masses," who they believed had been dehumanized by the conditions of life; but both these lonely men reached out with longing for the exceptional individual here and there who might understand the nature of selfhood and join in the quest for it.

Cognition an Interpretive Process

Although Nietzsche was almost as hostile to the idea of "system" as was Kierkegaard, it is nonetheless possible to find the elements of an epistemological theory scattered in his writings. A convenient starting point for discussing this theory is Nietzsche's own experience as a classical philologist—an experience dominated by the distinction between an original text and its various interpretations.

The printed version of a play by Sophocles or of a dialogue by Plato that is available to readers today is a reconstruction; it is the product of collating several surviving manuscript "sources." But these manuscripts themselves are only versions—and late ones at that, probably medieval copies of copies of copies, and so on—of the long-lost original, which (presumably) Sophocles or Plato had dictated to his own copyist. Beginning with the first copy, errors and mistakes have crept in; pages have been lost; paragraphs have been transposed. Each successive copyist, faced with something in the version before him that did not make sense, had to interpret it as best he could, and his interpretation was transmitted to later copyists. Although nineteenth- and twentieth-century philologists have more versions to work with and employ more scholarly techniques, basically their procedures do not differ from those of earlier copyists—they provide us only with more interpretations. And none of these can possibly be "final" or "definitive," for each reflects the "subjectivity" of the scholar making it—his temperament and outlook, his philological skills (and also his limitations), and his knowledge of classical history (and also his ignorance).

In a word, Nietzsche was impressed by the distinction between an inaccessible "original" and a plurality of "versions," or interpretations, of it. He then applied this model to the knowledge situation generally. In perception and thought, he held, we do not contemplate objects "out there," objects that are complete in themselves and independent of us. We are *active,* not passively receptive. Perceiving and thinking are acts of interpretation, in which our desires, memories, and passions affect in greater or less degree the outcome—the object that we perceive or think about.

> "Disinterested contemplation" . . . is a rank absurdity. . . . Let us, from now on, be on our guard against the hallowed philosophers' myth of a "pure, will-less, painless, timeless knower"; let us beware of the tentacles of such contradictory notions as "pure reason," "absolute knowledge," "absolute intelligence." All these concepts presuppose an eye such as no living creature can imagine, an eye required to have no direction, to abrogate its active and interpretative powers—precisely those powers that alone make of seeing, seeing *something.* All seeing is essentially perspective, and so is all knowing.
>
> Whoever has pursued the history of any single science finds in its development a clue for the understanding of the most ancient and common processes of all "knowing and cognizing." There as here, the premature hypotheses, the fictitious creations, the good stupid will to "believe," the lack of suspiciousness and patience, are developed first. Our senses learn late, and never wholly, to be subtle, faithful and cautious organs of cognition. It feels more comfortable to our eyes to reproduce upon a given stimulus an image already produced than to retain what is different and new in a given impression; the latter process requires more energy, more "morality." To hear something new is painful and difficult for the ear; we hear new music poorly. When we hear a foreign language we try unconsciously to reform the sounds into words that sound more familiar and home-like. Thus, for example, the Germans fixed up for themselves the word *Armbrust* (arm-breast) when they heard *arcubalista* (cross-bow). Everything new finds even our senses hostile and unwilling, and more than unwilling. The passions like fear, love, and hatred (including the passive passions like laziness) *rule* the "simplest" processes of our sense activity. As little as a modern reader reads the individual words (not to mention syllables) on a page, but out of every twenty words takes perhaps five at random and "guesses" the presumable sense that goes with these five, so little do we see a tree exactly and completely as to its leaves, branches, colors, and forms. It is so much easier to imagine an approximation of a tree. . . . We invent the largest part of the thing experienced and can hardly be compelled *not* to observe some process with

the eyes of an "inventor." All of this wants to say that we are basically and from time immemorial *accustomed to lying.* Or, to say it more virtuously and slyly, hence pleasantly: we are much greater artists than we know. —In the course of an animated conversation I often see the face of my partner, depending on the thought he has uttered or that I think I have evoked, so significantly and subtly defined that the degree of significance surpasses by far my visual capabilities. The subtlety of the play of muscles and the expression of the eyes that I "saw" *must* have been fictitiously created by me.[n]

Nietzsche's starting point, like the starting point of so many nineteenth-century philosophers, was Kantian. Kant had maintained that the objects we encounter in experience are actually constructs, products of a "transcendental synthesis." Kant, it is true, had limited the contribution of mind to a minimum. He held that it consisted in twelve "categories" that are universal and necessary features of all human minds. Hegel, as has been seen, greatly expanded the role of mind in experience and argued that this role has a history in that it varies with the level of mental and cultural development. That Nietzsche put even more emphasis on construction and interpretation than did Hegel is not only in accordance with his experience as a philologist; it also reflects a focus of attention on the individual person and his individual needs and problems that has already been encountered in Kierkegaard and that was becoming increasingly prominent in nineteenth-century thought.

It is indeed possible to hold that Nietzsche's insight into the nature of the cognitive process is itself an instance of his general thesis about cognition: It was his interest in subjectivity that caused him to interpret cognition as an interpretive process. Thus Nietzche attended to features of perceptual experience that Kant and Hegel did not notice but that they might have observed had these features interested them, such as the phenomenon of overlooking a typographical error in a sentence because the reader knows so well what the word "really" is—as, for instance, the erroneous spelling of the second word in this sentence. Another example is the phenomenon of hearing one's own name when it is mentioned across the room at a noisy party, even though one is not listening for it and can discriminate nothing else in the din. Here one's interest in oneself brings this part of the perceptual field into focus without conscious intent.

The Role of Language

That men's interests and expectations—what is sometimes called their perceptual set—influence their perceptions is now a commonplace. But Nietzsche was one of the first philosophers to observe this phenomenon and to see its relevance to theory of knowledge. He viewed it as derivative in part from what he called "laziness"—the tendency, once we have achieved a concept or hypothesis, to persist in using it to interpret our experiences, even though it may no longer apply when circumstances change. This kind of inertia, Nietzsche saw, increases as soon as the concept is formulated linguistically. To cast an interpretation into language is to rigidify it; it then becomes a Procrustean bed that our experience of the world is forced to fit. According to Nietzsche, many of the concepts that have seemed to be of fundamental importance in philosophy are nothing but linguistic traps of this kind—for instance, the concept of substance, conceived of either as an enduring encapsulated object that "has" properties or as an enduring encapsulated self that "has" various faculties and powers.

As regards the notion of object,

> ... there is no set of maxims more important for an historian than this: that the actual causes of a thing's origin and its eventual uses, the manner of its incorporation into a system of purposes, are worlds apart; that everything that exists, no matter what its origin, is periodically reinterpreted by those in power in terms of fresh intentions; that all processes in the organic world are processes of outstripping and overcoming, and that, in turn, all outstripping and overcoming means reinterpretation, rearrangment, in the course of which the earlier meaning and purpose are necessarily either obscured or lost. No matter how well we understand the utility of a certain physiological organ (or of a legal institution, a custom, a political convention, an artistic genre, a cultic trait) we do not thereby understand anything of its origin. I realize that this truth must distress the traditionalist. . . . But . . . the whole history of a thing, an organ, a custom, [is] a continuous *chain* of reinterpretations and rearrangements, which need not be causally connected among themselves, which may simply follow one another. The "evolution" of a thing, a custom, an organ is not its *progressus* towards a goal, let alone the most logical and shortest *progressus,* requiring the least energy and expenditure. Rather it is a sequence of more or less profound, more or less independent processes of appropriation, including the resistances used in each instance, the attempted transformations for purposes of defense or reaction, as well as the results of successful counterattacks. While forms are fluid, their "meaning" is even more so.°

In terms of the analogy of a long-lost classical text and its interpretations, Nietzsche's thesis is that since the original text is inaccessible, since it cannot enter into our calculations and reflections when we try to ascertain the meaning of Sophocles' play or of Plato's dialogue, and since all we ever do is compare one interpretation with others, we might as well abandon the "myth" that there was once an original. Similarly, the supposedly independently existing object with enduring properties of its own is also a myth. An uninterpreted original is never available; there are only the varied "meanings" that the object has had at different times for different people.

Or, to substitute "perspective"—another favorite term of Nietzsche's—for "interpretation," the history of mankind is the history of a succession of perspectives from which different social groups have viewed the universe. Each perspective shapes the social institutions, art, religion, and literature of that group. Questions about what is good, what is beautiful, and what is true are meaningless in the abstract; they are answerable only when a time has been specified, and the answers are to be ascertained by empirical inquiries, by investigations undertaken by anthropologists and psychologists into the basic drives that animate the dominant members of the group at that particular time. Further, changes in the culture—for instance, a shift from one "truth" or from one "good" to another—are explicable in terms of "appropriations and resistances" that occur at the level of values, and values in their turn are but reflections of the basic drives of the group.

Nietzsche's discussion of interpretation can be set in an interpretive context of its own. Considered from an historical point of view, which is the way Nietzsche recommended looking at things, it is easy to see that his view of history and culture is a typical nineteenth-century phenomenon. It stems from the Kantian distinction between things-in-themselves and appearances. And it is clear, further, that Nietzsche in effect duplicated Hegel's rejection of the unknown and unknowable things-in-themselves (that is, the inaccessible "original" play or dialogue). The result is that what Kant called "appearance" becomes reality and that this reality is viewed as a product—the phenomenology of spirit.

In this respect, Nietzsche was a Hegelian. But, according to Hegel, spirit expresses itself in an essentially rational manner: Successive stages in the development of spirit follow one another in a systematic way as "contradictions" emerge. Accordingly, in Hegel's view, the idea of progress or of teleology is applicable to the history of culture. In Nietzsche's view, however, there may not even be causal relations among the stages; indeed, the so-called stages are stages in name only, and the idea of purpose or teleology is only an idea—just another interpretation that reflects the underlying values of Hegel and other scholars and philosophers.

Spirit was perceived by Nietzsche chiefly in terms of will and volition, rather than in terms of thought. The life of the spirit was a struggle between the desire to appropriate and the desire to resist appropriation—note his use of such terms as "counterattack," "outstrip," and "overcome." In this respect—in de-emphasizing the logicality of the course of historical change—Nietzsche was closer to Marx and to Darwin than he was to Hegel, for both Marx and Darwin saw the world process as a struggle. According to the one it was for class supremacy; according to the other, for material survival. Nevertheless, like Hegel, they regarded successive stages of this struggle as constituting a development; if it did not have a *telos*, it had a pattern. Hence in their view the outcome of the struggle was sufficiently predictable for a science of culture to be possible. This Nietzsche denied.

Nietzsche's discussion of the way language encapsulates objects can be applied to the self. Just as, if we are not careful, we slip into thinking of an object as having a nature of its own that exists independently of us and our interpretations, so we easily slip into the fallacy of thinking of the self (our own self, for instance) as existing "completely, laid out as if in an illuminated glass case."[p] In both cases language is to blame:

> A quantum of strength is equivalent to a quantum of urge, will, activity, and it is only the snare of language (of the arch-fallacies of reason petrified in language), presenting all activity as conditioned by an agent—the "subject"—that blinds us to this fact. For, just as popular superstition divorces the lightning from its brilliance, viewing the latter as an activity whose subject is the lightning, so does popular morality divorce strength from its manifestations, as though there were behind the strong a neutral agent, free to manifest its strength or contain it. But no such agent exists; there is no "being" behind the doing, acting, becoming; the "doer" has simply been added to the deed by the imagination—the doing is everything. The common man actually doubles the doing by making the lightning flash; he states the same event once as cause and then again as effect. The natural scientists are no better when they say that "energy *moves*," "energy *causes*." For all its detachment and freedom from emotion, our science is still the dupe of linguistic habits; it has never yet got rid of those changelings called "subjects." The atom is one such changeling, another is the Kantian "thing-in-itself." [q]

Nietzsche's point here is that everything that anyone might ever say about the self can be expressed by verbs (doing, acting, becoming); we introduce the complexity of a subject that acts and becomes only because it happens that a declarative sentence takes a noun as its grammatical subject.

> A thought comes when "it" will and not when "I" will. It is thus a *falsification* of the evidence to say that the subject "I" conditions the predicate "think." *It* is thought, to be sure, but that this "it" should be that old famous "I" is, to put it mildly, only a supposition, an assertion. Above all it is not an "immediate certainty." In the end even "it is thought" says too much. Even this "it" contains an *interpretation* of the process and does not belong to the process itself. Our conclusion is here formulated out of our grammatical custom: "Thinking is an activity; every activity presumes something which is active, hence. . . ."[r]

The Psychological Bases of Thought

In some respects these comments can be viewed as but another attack in the long series of criticisms—begun by the British Empiricists and continued by Kant, Hegel, and Kierkegaard—of the Cartesian concept of substance. Nietzsche's attack, however, was far more drastic than any of the others. Whereas Kant and Hegel had held the philosophical enterprise as a whole to be the most significant of human activities (though they had, of course, criticized specific philosophical practices), and whereas Kierkegaard had merely declared it to be idle and distracting, Nietzsche regarded it as thoroughly phony. Philosophers think that they aim at Truth (with a capital "T"), but their theories are only elaborate attempts to justify the beliefs that they hold on instinctive (and hence unthinking) grounds. Philosophers are in fact like lawyers, who are hired to "make a case" for their clients. They differ from lawyers only in being too simpleminded to recognize what they are doing; they are lawyers who are taken in by their own statements to the jury:

> After keeping an eye on and reading between the lines of the philosophers for a long time, I find that I must tell myself the following: the largest part of conscious thinking must be considered an instinctual activity, even in the case of philosophical thinking. . . . Most of the conscious thinking of a philosopher is secretly guided by his instincts and forced along certain lines. Even behind logic and its apparent sovereignty of development stand value judgments, or, to speak more plainly, physiological demands for preserving a certain type of life. Such as for example, that the definite is worth more than the indefinite, that appearance is less valuable than "the truth." . . .
>
> What tempts us to look at all philosophers half suspiciously and half mockingly is not so much that we recognize again and again how innocent they are, how often and how easily they make mistakes and lose their way, in short their childishness and childlike-ness—but rather that they are not sufficiently candid, though they make a great virtuous noisy to-do as soon as the problem of truthfulness is even remotely touched upon. Every one of them pretends that he has discovered and reached his opinions through the self-development of cold, pure, divinely untroubled dialectic (in distinction to the mystics of every rank who, more honest and fatuous, talk about "inspiration"), whereas, at bottom, a pre-conceived dogma, a notion, an "institution," or mostly a heart's desire, made abstract and refined, is defended by them with arguments sought after the fact. They are all of them lawyers (though wanting to be called anything but that). . . .
>
> Gradually I have come to realize what every great philosophy up to now has been: the personal confession of its originator, a type of involuntary and unaware memoirs. . . .[s]

And what is true of philosophy is also true of science. "Physics, too, is only an interpretation of the universe, an arrangement of it (to suit us, if I may be so bold!), rather than a clarification."[t] As examples Nietzsche chose "causality" and "natural law," which all the sciences uncritically assume to be fundamental concepts:

> One should make use of "cause" and "effect" only as pure *concepts,* i.e., as conventional fictions for the purpose of designation and mutual understanding, *not* for explanation. In "being-as-such" there are no "causal connections" or "necessities" or "psychological lack of freedom"; effect there does *not* follow upon a cause; there *is* no "law" which rules phenomena. It is *we,* we alone, who have dreamed up the causes, the one-thing-after-

anothers, the one-thing-reciprocating-anothers, the relativity, the constraint, the numbers, the laws, the freedom, the "reason why," the purpose. And when we mix up this world of symbols with the world of things as though the symbols existed "in themselves," then we are merely doing once more what we have always done: we are creating myths. . . .

One will forgive, I hope, an old philologist who cannot desist from the malice of pointing his finger at poor interpretation. But really, that "conformity of nature unto law" of which you physicists talk so proudly as if . . . , that lawfulness is the result only of your *explication de texte*, of your bad philology! It is not a fact, not a "text" at all, but only a naive, humanitarian arrangement and misinterpretation that you use for truckling to the democratic instincts of the modern soul. "Everywhere equality before the law—and nature is no better off than we are"—surely a fine *arrière-pensée*. . . . This is explication, not text, and someone might come along who, with opposite intention and interpretive skill, might read out of the same nature and the same phenomena quite another thing: a tyrannical, inconsiderate, relentless enforcement of claims to power. . . . Let us admit that this, too, would be only an interpretation—and you will be eager enough to make this objection! Well, all the better! [u]

Consciousness a Disease

Indeed, *all* thinking, not merely the thinking of professional philosophers and scientists, must be regarded as an aberration. Thought is a product of consciousness, and consciousness is an evolutionary blind alley.

In some remote corner of the universe, poured out and glittering in innumerable solar systems, there once was a star on which clever animals invented knowledge. That was the haughtiest and most mendacious minute of "world history"—yet only a minute. After nature had drawn a few breaths the star grew cold, and the clever animals had to die.

One might invent such a fable and still not have illustrated sufficiently how wretched, how shadowy and flighty, how aimless and arbitrary, the human intellect appears in nature. There have been eternities when it did not exist; and when it is done for again, nothing will have happened. For this intellect has no further mission that would lead beyond human life. . . .

The intellect, as a means for the preservation of the individual, unfolds its chief powers in simulation; for this is the means by which the weaker, less robust individuals preserve themselves, since they are denied the chance of waging the struggle for existence with horns or the fangs of beast of prey. In man this art of simulation reaches its peak: here deception, flattery, lying and cheating, talking behind the back, posing, living in borrowed splendor, being masked . . . [are] so much the rule and the law that almost nothing is more incomprehensible than how an honest and pure urge for truth could make its appearance among men. They are deeply immersed in illusions and dream images; their eye glides only over the surface of things and sees "forms"; their feeling nowhere leads into truth, but contents itself with the reception of stimuli, playing, as it were, a game of blindman's buff on the backs of things. . . .

Let us give special consideration to the formation of concepts. Every word immediately becomes a concept, inasmuch as it is not intended to serve as a reminder of the unique and wholly individualized original experience to which it owes its birth, but must at the same time fit innumerable, more or less similar cases—which means, strictly speaking, never equal—in other words, a lot of unequal cases. Every concept originates through our equating what is unequal. No leaf ever wholly equals another, and the concept "leaf" is formed through an arbitrary abstraction from these individual differences, through forgetting the distinctions; and now it gives rise to the idea that in nature there might be something besides the leaves which would be "leaf"—some kind of original form after which all leaves have been woven, marked, copied, colored, curled, and painted, but by unskilled hands, so that no copy turned out to be a correct, reliable, and faithful image of the original form. We call a person "honest." Why did he act so honestly today? we ask. Our answer usually sounds like this: because of his honesty. Honesty! That is to say again: the leaf is the cause of the leaves. After all, we know nothing of an essence-like quality named "honesty"; we know only numerous individualized, and thus unequal actions, which we equate by omitting the unequal and by then calling them honest actions. In the end, we distill from them a *qualitas occulta* with the name of "honesty." . . .

What, then, is truth? A mobile army of metaphors, metonyms, and anthropomorphisms— . . . truths are illusions about which one has forgotten that this is what they are; metaphors which are worn out and without sensuous power; coins which have lost their pictures and now matter only as metal, no longer as coins. . . .[v]

This attack on Truth is far more radical than the criticism that has already been considered. According to the latter, cognition is a series of interpretations of a world that is inaccessible save through interpretations; nevertheless, the various interpretations can be compared among themselves with respect to their adequacy—just as one philologist's reconstruction of the *Bacchae* can be adjudged better than another's, even though the original text has disappeared. But from the point of view presented in the passage above all interpretations are equally inadequate just because they are interpretations. Better by far is the relationship in which the plants and the lower animals stand to the world, a relationship that is simple and direct because it does not involve interpretation at all.

Nietzsche was not troubled by the conflict between this romantic primitivism (as it may be called) and his perspectival theory. Instead, he pointed out that consciousness not only brings "knowledge"—that is, interpretations—in its train; it also brings conscience. Lacking the capacity to reflect, animals are happily without the notion of an abstract good, just as they are without the concept of an abstract Truth to which, supposedly, their beliefs fail to correspond, and an abstract Reality from which, supposedly, the actual spaciotemporal world deviates. Accordingly, since they do not have the illusory notion of an "ideal" from which their behavior deviates, animals do not experience a sense of duty, sin, guilt, or bad conscience. Animal behavior is simply the spontaneous response of instinct to the external world; it is not mediated by consciousness and hence is without the complications that thought and deliberation inevitably introduce.

Why did consciousness and conscience evolve? Nietzsche's answer is that man became socialized, that socialization necessitated the repression of many of his most powerful instincts, and that repressed instincts then turned within. The result was that for the first time an interior psychic life developed—a mental world of thoughts, motives, hypotheses, dreams, illusions, and simulations.

> I take bad conscience to be a deep-seated malady to which man succumbed under the pressure of the most profound transformation he ever underwent— the one that made him once and for all a sociable and pacific creature. Just as happened in the case of those sea creatures who were forced to become land animals in order to survive, these semi-animals, happily adapted to the wilderness, to war, free roaming, and adventure, were forced to change their nature. Of a sudden they found all their instincts devalued, unhinged. They must walk on legs and carry themselves, where before the water had carried them: a terrible heaviness weighed upon them. They felt inapt for the simplest manipulations, for in this new, unknown world they could no longer count on the guidance of their unconscious drives. They were forced to think, deduce, calculate, weigh cause and effect—unhappy people, reduced to their weakest, most fallible organ, their consciousness! I doubt that there has ever been on earth such a feeling of misery, such a leaden discomfort. It was not that those old instincts had abruptly ceased making their demands; but now their satisfaction was rare and difficult. . . . All instincts that are not allowed free play turn inward. This is what I call man's interiorization; it alone provides the soil for the growth of what is later called man's *soul*. Man's interior world, originally meager and tenuous, was expanding in every dimension, in proportion as the outward discharge of his feelings was curtailed. The formidable bulwarks by means of which the polity protected itself against the ancient instincts of freedom (punishment was one of the strongest of these bulwarks) caused those wild, extravagant instincts to turn in upon man. Hostility, cruelty, the delight in persecution, raids, excitement, destruction all turned against their begetter. Lacking external enemies and resistances, and confined within an oppressive narrowness and regularity, man began rending, persecuting, terrifying himself, like a wild beast hurling itself against the bars of its cage. . . . Also the generator of the greatest and most disastrous of maladies, of which humanity has not to this day been cured: his sickness of himself, brought on by the violent severance from his animal past, by his sudden leap and fall into new layers and conditions of existence, by his declaration of war against the old instincts that had hitherto been the foundation of his power, his joy, and his awesomeness.

> Man, with his need for self-torture, his sublimated cruelty resulting from the cooping up of his animal nature within a polity, invented bad conscience in order to hurt himself, after the blocking of the more natural outlet of his cruelty.ᵂ

NIETZSCHE AND THE WAVE OF THE FUTURE

It is astounding to see the prodigality with which Nietzsche tossed off seminal ideas. Such notions as repression, sublimation, and the mythical element in science were enunciated in these scattered paragraphs and aphorisms (without being developed in detail, it is true) long before they were formulated by Freud, Jung, and the other psychoanalysts. Indeed, in the last paragraphs quoted, Nietzsche anticipated the main arguments of Freud's *Civilization and Its Discontents* by almost half a century.

Even more impressive perhaps than such specific insights are the two themes that dominate Nietzsche's whole discussion. The first of these is the derogation of consciousness as a mode of life and experience. Men came to feel that consciousness entailed externality and objectivity (or, in Hegel's terminology, "mediation") and hence the repression of freedom, spontaneity, and inwardness. This hostility to consciousness, which had been expressed very early in Dostoevsky's account of underground man, became increasingly prominent in the next century: Surrealism, Dadaism, sensitivity training, encounter groups, happenings in the theater, "mind-expanding" drugs, Zen, the antinovel, the new wave in the cinema, are all manifestations of the emphasis on immediacy and so of the Nietzschian attitude toward consciousness.[17]

The second main theme is the "expressiveness" of cultural phenomena. That all cultural phenomena are expressive of deep, often unconscious, elements in the psyche has become one of the most widely held articles of faith in contemporary society, influencing not only the art and literature but also the science and philosophy of our time. It has influenced, for example, the writing of this chapter on Kierkegaard and Nietzsche, and, quite specifically, the last sentence of the paragraph above, which asserts that surrealism, Zen, and other twentieth-century phenomena are "manifestations" of a particular attitude toward consciousness. In these respects, and in so many others, Nietzsche was a pioneer, truly one of those "creative" individuals whom he so much admired.

One paragraph quoted above—the discussion of the formation of concepts—requires more detailed examination. Nietzsche's insistence that concepts are inevitably distorting because they treat as "equal" things that are unequal echoes Schopenhauer and the Romantic poets (for instance, Wordsworth's castigation of reason as "that false secondary power by which we multiply distinctions"). But Nietzsche's line of attack was far more destructive than Schopenhauer's. Schopenhauer's argument would be convincing only to an extreme nominalist who held that every individual object is unique. Nietzsche agreed with Schopen-

---

17 About consciousness, as about many things, Nietzsche was of two minds. See pp. 249 and 259.

hauer that abstract universals falsify the facts of empirical diversity, but he then proceeded to undermine the case for conceptualism as much as for realism by uncovering the psychological source of our love of universals, concepts, and Platonic "forms." They are all products of "laziness." And not only of laziness. Platonism, like the Egyptian pyramids, is evidence of a hatred of becoming. Belief in abstract universals and eternal forms is a way of escaping from the real world of growth, decay, and death into the security of a changeless realm.

NIETZSCHE'S RELATIVISM

This psychologizing strategy is almost too powerful an instrument of destruction. The theory that all theories are expressions of underlying elements in the psyche is presumably an expression of underlying elements in the personality of Nietzsche. What Nietzsche says about consciousness as an evolutionary mistake is, on his own account, only an interpretation, not a text. Furthermore, this interpretation is a reflection of Nietzsche's values and attitudes—his alienation, his isolation, and his own tormented consciousness. It is clear, for instance, that Nietzsche greatly prized smoothness, rapidity, and sureness of response—perhaps because he himself was hesitant, shy, and introspective. "Happiness," he wrote in 1874, "lies in the swiftness of feeling and thinking: all the rest of the world is slow, gradual, and stupid. Whoever could feel the course of a light ray would be very happy, for it is very swift." [x] There is no reason, of course, why Nietzsche should not have found happiness in the swiftness of feeling, and no reason why he should not have derogated consciousness insofar as it impedes the swift flow of feeling. But why should another man, who prizes deliberation, reflection, and calculation and who is therefore led to make a different evaluation of consciousness, accept Nietzsche's conclusion that consciousness is an "ineluctable disaster"? [y] If all criteria are subjective, every man is the measure of his own conclusion regarding the value of consciousness.

Nietzsche might have attempted to extricate himself from such a radical conclusion by introducing an "objective" criterion. Indeed, on occasion he did exactly this. At one point, for instance, he suggested that interpretations can be assessed objectively as life-preserving or life-defeating. This suggestion, had he developed it, would have taken him in the direction that Bergson and Dewey were to go. But whatever one thinks of *their* use of this argument, Nietzsche's version of it was inadequate. First, using empirical evidence, one would conclude that consciousness is more life-preserving than instinct—the opposite conclusion from the one Nietzsche wanted to draw. Second, his psychological stance makes the very notion of empirical evidence suspect. The conclusion that consciousness is in fact destructive—if this indeed is the conclusion the evidence seems to call for—is itself an interpretation, not a text. One's assessment of the empirical evidence is in part a reflection of one's bias against (or in favor of) consciousness and hence adds no independent support to one's initial assessment of the value of consciousness.

Nietzsche was, of course, much too acute not to see that this objection could be raised against him. A sentence in which he referred to this possibility has already been quoted: "Let us admit that this, too, would be only an interpretation—and you will be eager to make this objection! Well, all the better." [18] This cavalier attitude will disturb philosophers who take truth seriously. But, for his part, Nietzsche did not take such philosophers seriously. He regarded them as old maids: respectable, dull, uninspiring, and full of petty jealousies. Nietzsche could afford to be cavalier because, like Kierkegaard, he distinguished two kinds of truth—objective and subjective. Objective truth is a fiction of the philosophers, a product of their insecurity and laziness. Subjective truth is any new interpretation launched by a creative individual. Every such truth, precisely because it is novel, must do battle for survival against old, entrenched interpretations that claim to be objectively true. In this struggle, the new interpretation may win or may lose; but even if it wins, victory is only temporary: Sooner or later it will be replaced by newer, more creative interpretations. Nietzsche would have been inconsistent had he claimed objective truth for his view, but he was content to claim only subjective truth for it. Because it was only an interpretation that he had placed in competition, it was "all the better" to have objections raised against him. To raise objections was to launch an attack; and only by meeting and surviving an attack could his view become true in the way in which he wanted it to be true.

The Will to Power

So much for comment on what may be called the ontological status of Nietzsche's interpretation. The central feature of that interpretation was Nietzsche's discovery of the will to power. This insight was, he felt, creative in the way in which subjective truth always is creative: It offered men a new perspective from which to view themselves and nature.

But what, exactly, is the will to power? To begin with, it is a cosmological principle. Let us, Nietzsche in effect said, replace the old billiard-ball model of the physical universe with one derived from our experience of life. The trouble with the billiard-ball model (apart from the fact that it involves the "lazy" fiction of encapsulated, enduring things) is that it commits us to dualism, for this model is inapplicable in biology, psychology, and sociology. It is worth experimenting, therefore, to see whether the notion of drive, which is common to these fields, may not also serve in physics; if it does, we will have a single, unified world view.

> Let us assume that nothing is "given" as real except our world of desires and passions, that we cannot step down or step up to any kind of "reality"

18 See p. 243.

except the reality of our drives. . . . Would we not be allowed to experiment with the question whether these "givens" are not *sufficient* for understanding the so-called mechanistic (or material) world? . . . To understand the material world as a *pre-form* of life? In the end this experimental question is not merely allowed; it is demanded by the conscience of *methodology*. Not to assume several types of causality until the experiment of getting along with a single one has been followed to its utmost conclusion: . . . this is the morality of methodology. . . . In the end, the question is whether we really acknowledge the will as *effective;* whether we believe in the causality of the will. If we do (and basically our faith in the causality of the will amounts to our belief in causality itself), we *must* experiment with taking will-causality as our only hypothesis. Will, of course, can only act on will, not on matter (on "nerves," for example). Enough said: we must risk the hypothesis that everywhere we recognize "effects" there is an effect of will upon will; that all mechanical happenings, insofar as they are activated by some energy, are will-power, will-effects. —Assuming, finally, that we succeeded in explaining our entire instinctual life as the development and ramification of one basic form of will (of the will to power, as I hold); assuming that one could trace back all the organic functions to this will to power, including the solution of the problem of generation and nutrition (they are one problem)—if this were done, we should be justified in defining *all* effective energy unequivocally as *will to power*.[z]

Characteristically, Nietzsche never worked out this insight in detail. But that it was not merely an idle fantasy is shown by Whitehead's "process" philosophy. His notion of prehension and Nietzsche's concept of power drive are similar, and the basic strategies of the two philosophers—their attempts to achieve a unified world view by replacing the billiard-ball model with a more organic one—are identical.[19]

Although the will to power remained for Nietzsche a mere undeveloped suggestion at the level of cosmology, he worked it out in considerable detail at the level of psychology. His aim here was to show that all the multiform drives that seemingly motivate men's acts are but variants of this one basic drive, the will to power. At the preconscious level the will to power expresses itself directly and immediately in the attempt of every organism to use, and thus to overcome, those that are less powerful than itself. "Life itself is essential assimilation, injury, violation of the foreign and the weaker, suppression, hardness, the forcing of one's own forms upon something else, ingestion and—at least in its mildest form—exploitation."[a]

At the human level, consciousness naturally adds complications, but these complications do not alter the basic nature of the drive. Consciousness introduces inhibitions ("bad conscience") in the instinctive exercise of power on the part of those who possess power and provides justifications, excuses, and alternative routes to power for those who lack power. In this way a variety of goods emerge,

19 See Vol. V, pp. 71–78.

but the only thing good in itself is power. All other goods, all values, and all virtues are expressions of, and hence relative to, the power positions of various individuals and groups. Thus there is one set of goods and virtues for the strong and another for the weak. The latter, which Nietzsche called "slave morality" or "herd morality," is essentially the morality that was taught by the Greek philosophers and the Christian theologians. It emphasizes justice, prudence, equality, consideration for others, respect for the law, and moderation—all of which are virtues of the weak and based, ultimately, on the resentment and rancor that the weak feel against the strong.

THE GENESIS OF SLAVE MORALITY

The slave revolt in morals begins by rancor turning creative and giving birth to values—the rancor of beings who, deprived of the direct outlet of action, compensate by an imaginary vengeance. All truly noble morality grows out of triumphant self-affirmation. Slave ethics, on the other hand, begins by saying no to an "outside," an "other," a non-self, and that no is its creative act. This reversal of direction of the evaluating look, this invariable looking outward instead of inward, is a fundamental feature of rancor. Slave ethics requires for its inception a sphere different from and hostile to its own. Physiologically speaking, it requires an outside stimulus in order to act at all; all its action is reaction. The opposite is true of aristocratic valuations: such values grow and act spontaneously, seeking out their contraries only in order to affirm themselves even more gratefully and delightedly. . . . The Greek aristocracy, for example . . . , did not have to construct their happiness factitiously by looking at their enemies, as all rancorous men are wont to do, and being fully active, energetic people they were incapable of divorcing happiness from action. . . .

All this stands in utter contrast to what is called happiness among the impotent and oppressed, who are full of bottled-up aggressions. Their happiness is purely passive and takes the form of drugged tranquility, . . . peace, . . . emotional slackness. Whereas the noble lives before his own conscience with confidence and frankness . . . , the rancorous person is neither truthful nor ingenuous nor honest and forthright with himself. His soul squints; his mind loves hide-outs, secret paths, and back doors. . . ; he is expert in silence, in long memory, in waiting, in provisional self-depreciation, and in self-humiliation.[b]

This resentful slave is in fact Dostoevsky's underground man. And the function of all religions and transcendent moralities (for example, Platonism) is to make life tolerable for such men by appeasing and reducing their feelings of resentment—"the black melancholy of the physiologically incapacitated." "To put it quite generally, the main object of all great religions has been to counteract a certain epidemic malaise due to unreleased tension"—the tension that is built up as a result of the interiorization of instinctual drives.[c] Nietzsche proceeded to outline the "main forms" in which the weak have waged their "battle against anxiety."

Since melancholy and depression are the products of the repression of natural drives, the first way to relieve depression is to try to "reduce the vital energy [of these drives] to its lowest point." This is why religion advocates asceticism:

> No love; no hate; equanimity; no retaliation; no acquisition of riches; no work; mendicancy; preferably no woman, or as little woman as possible; in intellectual matters, Pascal's maxim, "We must stultify ourselves." . . . The result . . . in physiological terms is hypnosis—the attempt to achieve for man something approximating the hibernation of certain animal species. . . .[d]

This technique has had considerable success. It is true that it has also had a number of unfortunate by-products, including "all kind of mental disorders." But since these by-products are explained by the sufferers themselves in quite different terms—"as a return to the ground of being, a deliverance from all illusion"—the technique is not impaired for those who use it. "Though it goes without saying that the subjects' own explanations of these phenomena have always been extravagantly false, we cannot fail to notice the sincere gratitude that makes them *want* to give explanations of this kind."[e]

A second "regimen for combatting depression" is mechanical activity:

> There is no doubt that such activity can appreciably alleviate man's suffering. Nowadays it is spoken of rather dishonestly as "the blessing of labor." It brings relief by turning the attention of the sufferer away from his suffering. Since he is constantly preoccupied with doing, there is little room left in his mind for suffering—the chamber of man's consciousness is pretty narrow, after all.[f]

A third prescription for relieving melancholy is "emotional debauch." Naturally, it is described by its priestly advocates "under the most sacred names," but "any strong emotion will do—rage, fear, lust, vengeance, hope, triumph, despair, cruelty—provided it has sudden release."[g]

To sum up, religion and transcendental ethics are instruments for preserving the unfit and for suborning the strong by duping them into accepting the small virtues of small people.

> [Religions] side with the defectives; . . . they confirm the rights of all those who suffer from life as though it were a disease; they would like to render invalid and impossible any other sentiment besides theirs. . . . They [have] preserved too much of what *should have perished*. . . . To turn upside down all valuations—*that* is what they had to do! To shatter the strong, to infect great hopes, to cast suspicion on the enjoyment of beauty, to break down everything autonomous, manly, victorious, dominating, all the instincts natural to the highest and best turned-out type of mankind, and bend it over

into uncertainty, distress of conscience, and self-destruction—to reverse every bit of love for the earth and things earthly and control of the earth into hatred of things earthly and of the earth: this was the self-assumed task of the church.[h]

The Decadence of Contemporary Culture

In every age the great majority of people are weak; slave morality therefore always tends to predominate. But Nietzsche believed that the nineteenth century was even more mediocre, flat, conventional, and cautious than earlier periods. So-called progress was producing the "factory-slave," who was no longer a person but a gear, and who was so debased that he thought his shame was a virtue. Nietzsche concentrated his attack on the new German *Reich*, which Bismarck had brought into being after Prussia's victory over France and which (it seemed to Nietzsche) represented in advanced form every vice of the times. His discussion of German universities, for instance, has an extraordinarily modern sound:

> For seventeen years I have never tired of calling attention to the *despiritualizing* influence of our current science-industry. The hard helotism[20] to which the tremendous range of the sciences condemns every scholar today is a main reason why those with a fuller, richer, *profounder* disposition no longer find a congenial education and congenial *educators*. There is nothing of which our culture suffers more than of the super-abundance of pretentious jobbers and fragments of humanity; our universities are, *against* their will, the real hothouses for this kind of withering of the instincts of the spirit. And the whole of Europe already has some idea of this—power politics deceives nobody. Germany is considered more and more as Europe's *flatland*.[i]

And, in a passage prophetic of the rise of totalitarian dictatorships in the twentieth century, Nietzsche points out that the circumstances that have turned most men into factory slaves also tend to produce a few strong types:

> The same new conditions which will, on the average, bring about an equalization and mediocritization of man, a useful, hardworking, adaptable herd-animal of many uses, are also disposed in the highest degree to the creation of exceptional men of most dangerous and fascinating quality. For while . . . the total impression that these future Europeans will make will probably be one of manifold, gossipy, willpower-poor and extremely employable workers who *need* a boss, a master who gives them commands, as they need their daily bread; while, in other words, the democratization of Europe will amount to the creation of a type prepared in the subtlest sense for

---

20 [Helots were the slaves of ancient Sparta—AUTHOR.]

slavery—the individual, meanwhile, the exceptional case, the *strong* man, will turn out to be stronger and richer than he has probably ever been, thanks to the lack of prejudice in his schooling, thanks to the enormous varied practice he can get in skills and disguises. . . . The democratization of Europe is at the same time an involuntary arrangement for the training of tyrants. . . .[j]

The Existential Problem

Some of the sociological, economic, and political causes of herd mentality have been mentioned above, but Nietzsche believed that the most fundamental cause is our horror at the "abyss" in man and nature. There have always been a few perceptive individuals who have known that man is "merciless, greedy, insatiable, murderous," that he hangs "upon the back of a tiger."[k] But for centuries most men have managed to repress this knowledge by the fiction that man is a unique species specially created by a beneficent God and that the universe in which He placed him is a neat and tidy teleological system. According to Nietzsche, science has finally exploded these rationalizations; the knowledge that they are myths is beginning to enter our consciousness, despite our desire not to hear. Our conventionality, our blandness, and our discretion are actually protective devices, designed to prevent us from recognizing the true nature of the world. We are determined to stay at the surface, to think safe thoughts and to live by safe values, because we are terrified to look beyond them and find that the world is purposeless and meaningless—simply brute fact.

These insights were expressed by Nietzsche in two phrases that have become famous as a summary of his view—"God is dead" and "Everything eternally recurs." To say that God is dead is to say that men no longer believe there is a cosmic order. What looks like an objective order is merely a projection into chaos of man's desperate human need to believe there is reason and purpose in the universe. From this point of view a universe in which there is a malevolent god who could be held responsible for our misfortunes would be better than a universe in which God is dead and everything that happens might just as well not have happened. This is the feeling expressed in Hardy's poem *Hap*:

> If but some vengeful god would call to me
> From up the sky, and laugh: "Thou suffering thing,
> Know that thy sorrow is my ecstasy,
> That thy love's loss is my hate's profiting!"
>
> Then would I bear it, clench myself, and die,
> Steeled by the sense of ire unmerited;
> Half-eased in that a Powerfuller than I
> Had willed and meted me the tears I shed.

> But not so. How arrives it joy lies slain,
> And why unblooms the best hope ever sown?
> —Cross Causality obstructs the sun and rain,
> And dicing Time for gladness casts a moan. . . .
> These purblind Doomsters had as readily strown
> Blisses about my pilgrimage as pain.[1]

To say that everything eternally recurs is to say that everything that has ever happened happens again and again an infinite number of times. At first, there may seem to be a conflict between this statement and the assertion that God is dead (that there is no order). The assurance that everything happens again and again implies a kind of order after all. But these poetical expressions of Nietzsche's must not be taken too literally. Underlying both of them is the denial that there is anything in the universe that could provide a rationale for human struggles. Men make great sacrifices for causes in which they believe and to whose eventual triumph they are committed. But if God is dead, progress is an illusion. All our efforts, all our seeming achievements, become infinitely inconsequential as they eternally recur. This, according to Nietzsche, is the terrible truth that every man must sooner or later face. How he himself faced it is described in "The Vision of the Loneliest."

"THE VISION OF THE LONELIEST"

Not long ago I walked gloomily through the deadly pallor of dusk—gloomy and hard, with lips pressed together. Not only one sun had set for me. A path that ascended defiantly through stones, malicious, lonely, not cheered by herb or shrub—a mountain path crunched under the defiance of my foot. . . . Upward—defying the spirit that drew it downward toward the abyss, the spirit of gravity, my devil and archenemy. Upward—although he sat on me, half dwarf, half mole, lame, making lame, dripping lead into my ear, leaden thoughts into my brain. . . .

But there is something in me that I call courage; that has so far slain my every discouragement. This courage finally bade me stand still and speak: "Dwarf! It is you or I!"

For courage is the best slayer, courage which attacks. . . .

Courage also slays dizziness at the edge of abysses: and where does man not stand at the edge of abysses? Is not seeing always—seeing abysses?

Courage is the best slayer: courage slays even pity. But pity is the deepest abyss: as deeply as man sees into life, he also sees into suffering.

Courage, however, is the best slayer—courage which attacks: which slays even death itself, for it says, "Was *that* life? Well then! Once more!" . . .

Then something happened that made me lighter, for the dwarf jumped from my shoulder, being curious, and he crouched on a stone before me. But there was a gateway just where he had stopped.

"Behold this gateway, dwarf!" I continued. "It has two faces. Two paths meet here; no one has yet followed either to its end. This long lane stretches back for an eternity. And the long lane out there, that is another eternity. They contradict each other, these paths; they offend each other face to face; and it is here at this gateway that they come together. The name of the gateway is inscribed above: 'Moment.' . . .

"Behold," I continued, "this moment! From this gateway, Moment, a long eternal lane leads *backward:* behind us lies an eternity. Must not whatever *can* walk have walked on this lane before? Must not whatever *can* happen have happened, have been done, have passed by before? And if everything has been there before—what do you think, dwarf, of this moment? Must not this gateway too have been there before? And are not all things knotted together so firmly that this moment draws after it *all* that is to come? Therefore—itself too? For whatever *can* walk—in this long lane out *there,* too, it *must* walk once more.

"And this slow spider, which crawls in the moonlight, and this moonlight itself, and I and you in the gateway, whispering together, whispering of eternal things—must not all of us have been there before? And return and walk in that other lane, out there, before us, in this long dreadful lane,—must we not eternally return?"

Thus I spoke, more and more softly; for I was afraid of my own thoughts and the thoughts behind my thoughts. . . .

Where was the dwarf gone now? And the gateway? And the spider? And all the whispering? Was I dreaming, then? Was I waking up?

Among wild cliffs, I stood suddenly alone, bleak, in the bleakest moonlight. But *there lay a man.* . . . A young shepherd I saw, writhing, gagging, in spasms, his face distorted, and a heavy black snake hung out of his mouth. Had I ever seen so much nausea and pale dread on one face? He seemed to have been asleep when the snake crawled into his throat, and there bit itself fast. My hand tore at the snake and tore in vain; it did not tear the snake out of his throat. Then it cried out of me: "Bite! Bite its head off! Bite!" Thus it cried out of me—my dread, my hatred, my nausea, my pity, all that is good and wicked in me cried out of me with a single cry.

The shepherd . . . bit as my cry counseled him; he bit with a good bite. Far away he spewed the head of the snake—and he jumped up. No longer shepherd, no longer human—one changed, radiant, *laughing!* Never yet on earth has a human being laughed as he laughed! O my brothers, I heard a laughter that was no human laughter; and now a thirst gnaws at me, a longing that never grows still. My longing for this laughter gnaws at me; oh, how do I bear to go on living! And how could I bear to die now! [m]

It is instructive to compare this vision of the loneliest with Plato's myth of the cave. In the *Republic* Plato pictured men as chained deep in a cave, contemplating flickering shadows that they mistakenly hold to be real objects. Nietzsche—and Kierkegaard, too, of course—would have agreed with this view of man; indeed, they would have said that nineteenth-century Europeans were chained in an even deeper and darker cave than Plato's Greeks. Furthermore, according to Plato's myth, here and there an exceptional man manages to free himself from his chains and begins the long and difficult climb out of the cave.

Again, Kierkegaard and Nietzsche would have agreed that there is an ascent, and that this ascent is difficult and rare. Finally, according to Plato, the climbers eventually reach the mouth of the cave and find themselves in a world that is beautiful and good and that is illumined by the splendid light of the sun. Here Kierkegaard and Nietzsche part company with Plato. Of course, Kierkegaard held that there is a world outside the cave, and that this world is beautiful and good. But he wholly rejected Plato's view that men can find their way to this world by their own, unaided "natural" powers. Escape is possible, he held, only by a leap of faith—by the climber's passionate commitment to the sun outside that he has never seen and for whose existence he has, as yet, no evidence.

According to Nietzsche, Plato and Kierkegaard were deluding themselves: There is no world outside the cave. Both Plato's conviction that the existence of such a world can be established by rational means and Kierkegaard's admitted leap of faith are refuges of "slaves" who, having become fainthearted, weary, and dizzy from looking into the abyss, have given up the climb. Where does the climb lead? Nowhere. There is only the climber and his knowledge that, however far and long he climbs, he is doomed to repeat the same ascent endlessly. Why climb at all then? Because it is our nature to do so. The only question is how well we climb and how we cope with our knowledge that the climb is meaningless. A man who is strong enough to accept this "truth" and to laugh—a man who can bite the snake and spew it forth—is strong indeed. He is, in fact, no mere man but a master, a superman, an overman.

Overman

Nietzsche's overman, it is clear, is not a future evolutionary product that will someday emerge and "lord it over" man, as man now lords it over the species from which he has evolved. Overmen in fact are just those rare individuals (those "windfalls") who become masters by mastering themselves and their passions, their powers, and their weaknesses. They feel nausea as they contemplate the nature of existence, for they are human; but they are not "all too human," because they are strong enough to overcome their nausea. They are those exceptional individuals who pass through pessimism to affirmation. An overman, wherever and whenever he appears, is simply

> . . . the truly exuberant, alive and world-affirming man who does not merely resign himself to and learn to get along with all that was and is, but who wants everything *as it was and is* back again, back forever and ever, insatiably calling *da capo*, not only to himself but to the whole spectacle and performance, and not only to the performance but basically to that which necessitates and needs the performance because it forever and ever necessitates and needs itself![n]

Among the overmen whom Nietzsche specifically mentioned are Alcibiades, Alexander the Great, Julius Caesar, Cesare Borgia, and Napoleon. Their chief characteristics, apart from will power, were hardness, courage, and creativity. To be creative, if one is a politician, is to take existing institutions and shape them to new uses: For instance, Alexander destroyed the Greek city-state and Caesar destroyed the Roman republic in order to create great empires. To be creative is necessarily to be "hard," "beyond good and evil," indifferent to existing traditions, institutions, and values, and courageous enough to operate without norms because one is creating new ones. Thus the overman "suspends the ethical" (in Kierkegaard's terminology), but he does so out of the strength of his self-affirmation, not out of a weakness disguised as affirmation of a transcendent being.

Most of the overmen whom Nietzsche mentioned by name were politicians and generals whose creativity often expressed itself in the conquest of alien peoples or the subjugation of their fellow citizens. It would appear, however, that the creativity Nietzsche most admired was that of the artist; and everything that he says about the hardness, ruthlessness, and destructiveness of his overmen applies to Leonardo and Michelangelo as well as to Alexander and Caesar.

ARTISTIC CREATIVITY

The nature of artistic creativity was a theme that recurred in Nietzsche's writing from the start. His first book, *The Birth of Tragedy*, was a pioneering work on the psychology of the artist and on the Greek psyche. According to Nietzsche, the Greeks were not, as men of the Enlightenment had thought, a people of balance and moderation. On the contrary, they were unusually passionate and violent. Anyone who looks closely at Homeric and pre-Homeric man will see the "abyss of a terrifying savagery of hatred and the lust to annihilate." The Greek dramatists—Aeschylus and Sophocles, for instance—were fully aware of the abyss, but they were strong enough to look into it and still create works of art. The calm of mind achieved in their dramas should not deceive us:

> The luminous images of the Sophoclean heroes—those Apollonian masks— are the necessary productions of a deep look into the horror of nature; luminous spots, as it were, designed to cure an eye hurt by the ghastly night. Only in this way can we form an adequate notion of the seriousness of Greek "serenity"; whereas we find that serenity generally misinterpreted nowadays as a condition of undisturbed complacence.°

The balance of a great work of art is not static but dynamic. Like the balancing act of a tightrope walker, it reflects a continuous tension, an over-coming of opposing forces. The Greeks realized that artistic achievement is *won:* It is the outcome of a struggle against intractable materials and a competition for supremacy against other artists. This is why the *agon*, or contest, was so important in Greek life. The institution of ostracism, the educational practices of the Sophists, the musical theories of Pindar and Simonides, the dialogue form in which Plato wrote—all of these were expressions of the Greek preference for competition. "The Greek knows the artist *only as engaged in a personal fight*,"[p] and it is the omnipresence of competition in Greek society that brought about the superiority of Greek culture.

Nietzsche held that artistic creativity, like all creativity, is an expression of power; it is the overcoming of passion. Without passion, without frenzy, there would be no creativity.

> If there is to be art, if there is to be any aesthetic doing and seeing, one physiological condition is indispensable: frenzy. Frenzy must first have enhanced the excitability of the whole machine; else there is no art. All kinds of frenzy, however diversely conditioned, have the strength to accomplish this: above all, the frenzy of sexual excitement, this most ancient and original form of frenzy. Also the frenzy that follows all great cravings, all strong affects; the frenzy of feasts, contests, feats of daring, victory, all extreme movement; the frenzy of cruelty; the frenzy in destruction; the frenzy under certain meteorological influences, as for example the frenzy of spring; or under the influence of narcotics; and finally the frenzy of will, the frenzy of an overcharged and swollen will. What is essential in such frenzy is the feeling of increased strength and fullness. Out of this feeling one lends to things, one *forces* them to accept from us, one violates them. . . . A man in this state transforms things until they mirror his power—until they are reflections of his perfection. This *having to* transform into perfection is—art.[q]

Or, as Zarathustra put it more succinctly, "One must still have chaos in oneself to be able to give birth to a dancing star."[r] Thus frenzy is the precondition of creativity, but it is only the precondition. There must be the achievement, the projection, of order and pattern. That which is given order and pattern is the work of art, whether this be a painting, a symphony, a new state, or a dancing star.

Nietzsche's view of creativity can be rephrased in terms of the concept of sublimation—one of those seminal ideas in which Nietzsche anticipated Freud.[21] The will to power can, and on occasion does, express itself simply in hitting out in all directions, in a wild, unrestrained thrashing about. But this is animal; there is nothing human about it. What makes man human is the ability to contain and direct his will to power. Such self-discipline is not a sign of weakness, as is knuckling under to someone else's ideas and orders. Indeed, to be able to exercise self-restraint for the sake of an ideal of order that a person has himself chosen is the highest possible expression of the will to power. What the noblest of all overmen overcome is themselves, not others.

From the fact that Nietzsche made "self-overcoming" the fundamental aspect of artistic creativity it follows that in his view the greatest work of art a

21 See p. 246.

man can create is himself. Goethe is an example of this latter, and best, type of overman, for of all the works of art Goethe created, the finest was Goethe himself.

> Goethe—not a German event, but a European one; a magnificent attempt to overcome the eighteenth century by a return to nature, by an *ascent* to the naturalness of the Renaissance—a kind of self-overcoming on the part of that century. He bore its strongest instincts within himself: the sensibility, the idolatry of nature, the anti-historic, the idealistic, the unreal and revolutionary (the latter being merely a form of the unreal). He sought help from history, natural science, antiquity, and also Spinoza, but, above all, from practical activity; he surrounded himself with limited horizons; he did not retire from life but put himself into the midst of it; he was not fainthearted but took as much as possible upon himself, over himself, into himself. What he wanted was *totality;* he fought the mutual extraneousness of reason, sense, feeling, and will (preached with the most abhorrent scholasticism by *Kant,* the antipode of Goethe); he disciplined himself to wholeness, he *created* himself.ˢ

Nietzsche the admirer of overman evaluated consciousness very differently from Nietzsche the romantic primitivist. When the latter strain was dominant in Nietzsche's thought, consciousness seemed to him to have been an evolutionary mistake.[22] As an admirer of overman, however, he believed that it is precisely consciousness that makes it possible for the strong man to be strong. If, for instance, a man was, like the animals and plants, unconscious (even if he was only partially conscious, as ordinary men are), he would not know that God is dead. He would never experience cosmic loneliness, and there would be nothing to overcome. Nor, obviously, would it be possible for him to be a creator—to conceive of an ideal of order and to impose discipline on himself—without the fullest kind of consciousness and self-awareness. From the one point of view Nietzsche dreaded the snake of consciousness. This is the point of view that he shared with Dostoevsky and that is echoed in much of twentieth-century culture. From the other point of view Nietzsche welcomed the snake, for its bite is the peculiar mark and badge of overman.

It may seem that the aspect of Nietzsche's thought that emphasizes the superiority of the intellect and the nobility of the ideal of self-realization does no more than express, with the fervor of personal discovery, ideas that have been familiar at least since Aristotle. That there are similarities with Aristotle's philosophy is obvious, but there are also differences. It is easy to maintain one's balance when one walks on the ground; it is an achievement to do so on a tightrope. Aristotle's ethics focused on the beauty of balance achieved; Nietzsche's focused on the overcoming of difficulties. Nietzsche may well have been right in maintaining that the Greeks themselves did not achieve balance easily, but it is also probably true (as Nietzsche himself would certainly have maintained) that balance was much harder to achieve in the nineteenth century. In his

22 See pp. 249–50.

interpretation of the ideal of self-realization he thus reflected the age in which he lived. In a world in which every man is alone, confronted with an alien and hostile environment, and aware of the ultimate meaninglessness and futility of his life, the achievement of balance is rare indeed and must be continuously renewed.

It is suggestive, too, of the differences between Greek and modern culture that whereas for Aristotle the citizen was the model for self-realization, for Nietzsche the artist was the paradigm. In former times men believed that God created the universal cosmos out of chaos. In a world in which the myth of the creator god has been exploded, the artist is the most godlike of beings, for in the work of art he creates a miniature cosmos from the chaos within him. Perhaps it is a thought such as this, first enunciated by Nietzsche, that explains the preoccupation of modern writers (Joyce, Mann, Hesse, and Eliot, to name a few) with the artist and his creativity.

Interpretations of Nietzsche's Interpretation

Nietzsche held that men can never get back to the "original text"; they are confined to interpretations that reflect their biases and preconceptions. This at least is the interpretation of Nietzsche presented in this chapter. But few philosophers have been the subject of more varied interpretations. For instance, though most of his writing was strongly anti-anti-Semitic, Nietzsche sometimes sounded like those he criticized.[23] It is not surprising, therefore, that he has been regarded as an anti-Semite. He has also been called a precursor of the Nazis; he was certainly claimed by them as one of their own. It is not difficult to see why: He too praised war and warriors, hardness and cruelty; he too loathed such bourgeois virtues as respect for the "sanctity" of promises and contracts. If he praised Leonardo and Goethe, he also praised Alcibiades and Cesare Borgia, who were overmen only in the magnitude of their self-affirmation and destructiveness.

What would Nietzsche have thought of Hitler? It is impossible to say—except that, like most people, he would probably have made different assessments at different times, depending on his own mood and also, of course, on the stage in Hitler's career. And like many people, but unlike most philosophers, Nietzsche would have written down and published all these assessments just as they occurred to him, without making an effort to reach an overall, balanced appraisal. This approach characterized Nietzsche's writing generally. Far from being systematic, he was, like Kierkegaard, positively antisystematic: For Nietzsche, to aim at consistency was a sign of weakness. Thus in discussing creativity, if he sometimes

23 For instance, "It was the Jew who . . . dared to invert the aristocratic value equations good/ noble/powerful/beautiful/happy/favored-of-the-gods and . . . who started the slave revolt in morals . . ."—*Genealogy of Morals*, pp. 167–68.

emphasized the "dancing star" that is finally achieved, he also on occasion emphasized the initial chaos, frenzy, and destruction. Similarly, though much of his enthusiastic talk about war and warriors was undoubtedly metaphorical, some of it appears to have been literal praise of war and the destruction it entails.

But Nietzsche was not inconsistent merely as a result of carelessness and indifference. He was quite deliberately ambiguous. To be misunderstood by the many was the risk he ran in order to be understood by the few. "Every deep thinker fears being understood more than he fears being misunderstood." [t] Nietzsche meant that he did not want to pass along nuggets of meaning unchanged to his readers; he wanted, rather, to induce them to be creative by finding new meanings for themselves in his writings. This is why he so often wrote in aphorisms. They were designed to shock, to challenge convictions and prejudices. "An aphorism that has been honestly struck cannot be deciphered simply by reading it off; this is only the beginning of the work of interpretation. . . ." [u]

But Nietzsche also desperately wanted to be understood in the ordinary sense of "being understood"—that is, he wanted to establish a real communion with his readers. At one and the same time, then, he wanted his writings to be both a text and also only a starting point for other men's interpretations. This paradox reflects the basic division in Nietzsche's personality and in his view of man: On the one hand, man is a creature capable of transcending himself and becoming an overman. On the other hand, he is a mere evolutionary quirk, an oddity. From this point of view, the whole conception of the overman is only a rationalization— a rationalization that, try as we may, we men never quite manage to believe in. Hence, if men cannot learn to laugh at themselves, their only alternative is to weep. This is Nietzsche's central "message." It is significant of the great change that has occurred in contemporary culture that what was once regarded as a madman's ravings is now more and more widely regarded as a realistic assessment of the human condition.

CHAPTER 7

C. S. Peirce

Peirce[1] and James were contemporaries and friends, and in many respects their views were similar. Both rejected the prevailing orthodoxies, transcendental idealism and positivism; both were empirically oriented. Yet the end results of their philosophical development could hardly be more dissimilar. It is tempting to explain this dissimilarity by reference to James's notion of temperamental difference. Peirce's view stemmed from a basic need of his nature—the passion

---

1 Charles Sanders Peirce (1839–1914) was the son of Benjamin Peirce, a distinguished mathematician. He graduated from Harvard, where his father taught, in 1859, and was employed as a scientist by the United States Coast and Geodetic Survey from 1861 to 1891. For despite his brilliance and originality—indeed, perhaps because of his brilliance and originality, and his refusal to "popularize" his writings—he was unable to obtain a regular teaching post in any American university. His last years were spent in poverty and ill health. During his whole life he wrote voluminously, but much of what he wrote remained unpublished until long after his death.

to get his ideas clear. For ideas to be clear there has to *be* something for them to be clear *about*, and Peirce's approach to philosophy was to follow the clue that the objective character of the world must be such that men, with the mental equipment they possess, can come to understand clearly what this objective character is. That is, his main interest in the empirical world was metaphysical. James, as we shall see, was anything but a metaphysician. He was the advocate of a particular way of life, and far from clarity being necessary for a man of his temperament, it was actually undesirable. A little muddle and vagueness helped wonderfully! Characteristically, James, with all his enthusiasm, openness, and friendliness, never quite understood the great differences between his views and Peirce's, while Peirce, again characteristically, was completely clear about what divided him from James.

Pragmatism, Pragmaticism, and the Pursuit of Clarity

In 1878, in an article on "How to Make Our Ideas Clear," Peirce formulated a view that he called "pragmatism." Like almost everything else Peirce wrote, this essay was ignored by the philosophical public, and it was not until James gave a series of lectures on the subject,[2] almost thirty years later, that pragmatism began to attract attention. Unfortunately for Peirce, though James thought he was only demonstrating "the importance of Peirce's principle [by] applying it to concrete cases," [a] he badly misconstrued Peirce—so badly, indeed, that Peirce proceeded to hand the term "pragmatism" over to James and adopt a new term, "pragmaticism," for his own view. The

> . . . word "pragmatism" has gained general recognition in a generalized sense that seems to argue power of growth and vitality. The famed psychologist, James, first took it up. . . . So then, the writer, finding his bantling "pragmatism" so promoted, feels that it is time to kiss his child good-by and relinquish it to its higher destiny; while to serve the precise purpose of expressing the original definition, he begs to announce the birth of the word "pragmaticism," which is ugly enough to be safe from kidnappers.[b]

It was not pique that caused Peirce to abandon "pragmatism" to the "kidnappers." His drive for clarity led him to have very strong feelings about nomenclature. Every distinct idea should be denominated by a special term, and the relations, if any, between ideas should be reflected in corresponding relations between the terms. Peirce's aim, in fact, was to achieve an isomorphism between a vocabulary and the objects named by this vocabulary. Since common-sense

2 See p. 324.

language lacks such an isomorphism, a new technical language is needed, and until a discipline achieves such a language it can make no claim to being a science.

> Concerning the matter of philosophical nomenclature, there are a few plain considerations, which the writer has for many years longed to submit to the deliberate judgment of those few fellow-students of philosophy, who deplore the present state of that study, and who are intent upon rescuing it therefrom and bringing it to a condition like that of the natural sciences, where . . . every observation is repeated, and isolated observations go for little; where every hypothesis that merits attention is subjected to severe but fair examination, and only after the predictions to which it leads have been remarkably borne out by experience is trusted at all, and even then only provisionally; where a radically false step is rarely taken. . . . No study can become scientific in the sense described, until it provides itself with a suitable technical nomenclature, whose every term has a single definite meaning universally accepted among students of the subject, and whose vocables have no such sweetness or charms as might tempt loose writers to abuse them—which is a virtue of scientific nomenclature too little appreciated. . . . The one only way in which the requisite unanimity and requisite ruptures with individual habits and preferences can be brought about is so to shape the canons of terminology that . . . he who introduces a new conception into philosophy is under an obligation to invent acceptable terms to express it, and that when he has done so, the duty of his fellow-students is to accept those terms.[c]

This passage, short as it is and devoted to a seemingly minor topic, goes to the very heart of Peirce's conception of philosophy. In the first place, everything, including "sweetness or charms,"[3] is to be sacrificed to the achievement of clarity, and the possibility of achieving clarity presupposes that the universe includes a set—doubtless a very large set—of determinate entities, each with a nature of its own. In the second place, the best way—indeed the only way—of achieving clarity and reaching a knowledge of these entities is the method already worked out and put into effect in the sciences. The superiority of this method will become obvious, Peirce thought, if we compare it with the available alternatives.

The Fixation of Belief

What, in the most general terms, is the purpose of inquiry? It is to move from doubt to belief—from an unsettled, restless, uneasy state to a settled one, for belief is nothing other than a mental state in which there is no doubt. Of course, a settled mental state may, at some future time, become unsettled. Hence, though any belief is per se good, more settled and stable beliefs are better than less stable

---

3 One unfortunate by-product of sacrificing "sweetness or charms" was the loss of readers.

beliefs. Again, any method of resolving doubt and of reaching belief is per se good, but some methods are better than others, namely those that tend, on the whole, to lead us to more stable beliefs. Let us, then, in the light of these definitions and criteria, examine the various methods of attaining belief. These are tenacity, authority, a priori rationalism, and empirical science.

If the settlement of opinion is the sole object of inquiry, and if belief is of the nature of a habit, why should we not attain the desired end, by taking as answer to a question any we may fancy, and constantly reiterating it to ourselves, dwelling on all which may conduce to that belief, and learning to turn with contempt and hatred from anything that might disturb it? . . . A man may go through life, systematically keeping out of view all that might cause a change in his opinions, and if he only succeeds . . . I do not see what can be said against his doing so. . . .

But this method of fixing belief, which may be called the method of tenacity, will be unable to hold its ground in practice. The social impulse is against it. The man who adopts it will find that other men think differently from him, and it will be apt to occur to him, in some saner moment, that their opinions are quite as good as his own, and this will shake his confidence in his belief. . . . Unless we make ourselves hermits, we shall necessarily influence each other's opinions; so that the problem becomes how to fix belief, not in the individual merely, but in the community.

Let the will of the state act, then, instead of that of the individual. Let an institution be created which shall have for its object to keep correct doctrines before the attention of the people, to reiterate them perpetually, and to teach them to the young; having at the same time power to prevent contrary doctrines from being taught, advocated, or expressed. Let all . . . who reject the established belief be terrified into silence. . . .

In judging this method of fixing belief, which may be called the method of authority, we must, in the first place, allow its immeasurable mental and moral superiority to the method of tenacity. Its success is proportionately greater; and, in fact, it has over and over again worked the most majestic results. . . .

But [even] . . . in the most priest-ridden states some individuals will . . . see that men in other countries and in other ages have held to very different doctrines from those which they themselves have been brought up to believe; and they cannot help seeing that it is the mere accident of their having been taught as they have, and of their having been surrounded with the manners and associations they have, that has caused them to believe as they do and not far differently. . . .

A different new method of settling opinions must be adopted, that shall not only produce an impulse to believe, but shall also decide what proposition it is which is to be believed. Let the action of natural preferences be unimpeded, then, and under their influence let men, conversing together and regarding matters in different lights, gradually develop beliefs in harmony with natural causes. . . . The most perfect example of it is to be found in the history of metaphysical philosophy. Systems of this sort have not usually rested upon any observed facts, at least not in any great degree. They have been chiefly adopted because their fundamental propositions seemed "agreeable to reason." This is an apt expression; it does not mean that which agrees with experience, but that which we find ourselves inclined to believe. . . .

This method is far more intellectual and respectable from the point of view of reason than either of the others which we have noticed. . . . But its failure has been the most manifest. It makes of inquiry something similar to the development of taste.[d]

Though these methods all have the short-run advantage of fixing belief relatively easily, they have no way of preventing these beliefs from becoming unfixed over the long run. Further, none of them is self-corrective. The scientific method, on the contrary, is self-corrective, and, though it unsettles our beliefs over the short run by exposing them to criticism, over the long run it brings us closer and closer to beliefs that are permanently settled because they correspond more and more closely with "some external permanency."

To satisfy our doubts, therefore, it is necessary that a method should be found by which our beliefs may be determined by nothing human, but by some external permanency—by something upon which our thinking has no effect. . . . The method must be such that the ultimate conclusion of every man shall be the same. Such is the method of science. Its fundamental hypothesis, restated in more familiar language, is this: There are Real things, whose characters are entirely independent of our opinions about them; those Reals affect our senses according to regular laws, and, though our sensations are as different as are our relations to the objects, yet, by taking advantage of the laws of perception, we can ascertain by reasoning how things really and truly are; and any man, if he have sufficient experience and he reason enough about it, will be led to the one True conclusion. The new conception here involved is that of Reality.[e]

Belief in the existence of external reality thus underlies and warrants our confidence that the method of science is one of gradual approximation toward settled beliefs. But what in turn warrants this belief in an external reality? Well, like all other beliefs it is corrigible—Peirce did not claim that it is an a priori truth; he did not appeal to authority. It is, on the contrary, an hypothesis, but it is an hypothesis for which empirical support exists.

It may be asked how I know that there are any Reals. If this hypothesis is the sole support of my method of inquiry, my method of inquiry must not be used to support my hypothesis. The reply is this: 1. If investigation cannot be regarded as proving that there are Real things, it at least does not lead to a contrary conclusion; but the method and the conception on which it is based remain ever in harmony. No doubts of the method, therefore, necessarily arise from its practice, as is the case with all the others. 2. The feeling which gives rise to any method of fixing belief is a dissatisfaction at two repugnant propositions. But here already is a vague concession that there is some *one* thing which a proposition should represent. Nobody, therefore, can really doubt that there are Reals, for, if he did, doubt would not be a source of dissatisfaction. The hypothesis, therefore, is one which every mind admits. So that the social impulse does not cause men to doubt it. 3. Everybody uses the scientific method about a great many things, and only ceases to use it when he does not know how to apply it. 4. Experience of the method has not led us to doubt it, but, on the contrary, scientific investigation has had the most wonderful triumphs in the way of settling opinion.[f]

So much, then, for the superiority of the scientific method over other methods of fixing belief and for the hypothesis on which this method rests. But why is this method superior in fixing belief? The reason is that it confines belief to what is empirically, experimentally verifiable. Consideration of the actual practice of scientists led Peirce to formulate a general theory of meaning:

> The writer of this article has been led by much experience to believe that every physicist, and every chemist, and, in short, every master in any department of experimental science, has had his mind moulded by his life in the laboratory to a degree that is little suspected. . . . You will find that whatever assertion you may make to [the typical scientist], he will either understand as meaning that if a given prescription for an experiment ever can be and ever is carried out in act, an experience of a given description will result, or else he will see no sense at all in what you say. . . .
>
> Endeavouring . . . to formulate what he so approved, [the writer] framed the theory that a *conception*, that is, the rational purport of a word or other expression, lies exclusively in its conceivable bearing upon the conduct of life; so that, since obviously nothing that might not result from experiment can have any direct bearing upon conduct, if one can define accurately all the conceivable experimental phenomena which the affirmation or denial of a concept could imply, one will have therein a complete definition of the concept, and *there is absolutely nothing more in it.* . . .
>
> Let us illustrate this rule by some examples; and, to begin with the simplest one possible, let us ask what we mean by calling a thing *hard*. Evidently that it will not be scratched by many other substances. The whole conception of this quality, as of every other, lies in its conceived effects. There is absolutely no difference between a hard thing and a soft thing so long as they are not brought to the test. . . .
>
> Let us next seek a clear idea of Weight. This is another very easy case. To say that a body is heavy means simply that, in the absence of opposing force, it will fall. This (neglecting certain specifications of how it will fall, etc., which exist in the mind of the physicist who uses the word) is evidently the whole conception of weight.[g]

This has a close affinity with what later came to be called by some the Verifiability Principle, and by others the Operational Definition of Truth. Peirce himself, partly as a result of the difficulties in which James was soon entangled, came to see that his initial formulation of the principle was ambiguous, and it is instructive to watch him getting his own ideas about clarity clearer.

> My original essay, having been written for a popular monthly, assumes, for no better reason than that real inquiry cannot begin until a state of real doubt arises and ends as soon as Belief is attained, that "a settlement of Belief," or, in other words, a state of *satisfaction*, is all that Truth, or the aim of inquiry, consists in. . . . [But] if Truth consists in satisfaction, it cannot be any *actual* satisfaction, but must be the satisfaction which *would* ultimately be found if the inquiry were pushed to its ultimate and indefeasible issue.[h]

If one defines "truth" as "satisfaction," one must not define it as "what satisfies," for then anything and everything that satisfies would be true. There must, Peirce saw, be a way of distinguishing between warranted and unwarranted satisfactions. One way would be to define truth in terms of what would, in the long run, satisfy. But Peirce concluded that a feeling of satisfaction—even what *would*, in distinction from what *does*, satisfy—is still too subjective.

Accordingly, phrases in the earliest version (such as, "have a practical bearing" and "have no other function than to affect our action"), which had not unnaturally suggested to James that he and Peirce were in agreement on the pragmatic criterion, have disappeared; action now comes in only as behavior by which predictions are verified. James's vague "working" has been narrowly and precisely defined as empirical verification of scientific hypotheses.

> When an experimentalist speaks of a *phenomenon*, such as "Hall's phenomenon," "Zeemann's phenomenon" and its modification, "Michelson's phenomenon," or "the chessboard phenomenon," he does not mean any particular event that did happen to somebody in the dead past, but what *surely will* happen to everybody in the living future who shall fulfill certain conditions. The phenomenon consists in the fact that when an experimentalist shall come to *act* according to a certain scheme that he has in mind, then will something else happen. . . .
>
> The rational meaning of every proposition lies in the future. How so? The meaning of a proposition is . . . simply the general description of all the experimental phenomena which the assertion of the proposition virtually predicts. . . . Whenever a man acts purposively, he acts under a belief in some experimental phenomenon. Consequently, the sum of the experimental phenomena that a proposition implies makes up its entire bearing upon human conduct.[i]

Thus Peirce placed himself squarely in the camp of the cognitivists. In this emphasis on the pursuit of truth, in contrast to James's feeling of "rest and ease," Peirce differed not at all from the traditional philosophers. Far from being destructive of all metaphysics, as James intended his pragmatism to be, Peirce's pragmaticism eliminates only "ontological metaphysics" and does so in order to clear the ground to make possible the development of a true metaphysics, whose outlines we shall have to examine later.[4] But first we must examine Peirce's

4 See pp. 275–83.

attack on an antimetaphysical theory that seemed far more formidable than James's version of pragmatism. This is the positivism of Comte, Pearson, and Mach.[5]

Peirce and Positivism

Unlike James, who wobbled between holding that the contents of pure experience are sensations, and holding that they are the shoes, ships, and sealing wax of the common-sense world,[6] the positivists distinguished sharply between the data of sensation, which we "directly experience," and the concepts, theories, and other "mental artifices" by means of which we organize these data into the objects of experience. Peirce subjected this distinction to a merciless criticism.

> Auguste Comte . . . condemn[ed] every theory that was not "verifiable." Like the majority of Comte's ideas, this is a bad interpretation of a *truth*. An explanatory hypothesis . . . ought . . . to be *verifiable;* that is to say, it ought to be little more than a ligament of numberless possible predictions concerning future experience, so that if they fail, it fails. Thus, when Schliemann entertained the hypothesis that there really had been a city of Troy and a Trojan War, this meant to his mind among other things that when he should come to make excavations at Hissarlik he would probably find remains of a city with evidences of a civilization more or less answering to the descriptions of the *Iliad*, and which would correspond with other probable finds at Mycenae, Ithaca, and elsewhere. So understood, Comte's maxim is sound. Nothing but that *is* an explanatory hypothesis. But Comte's own notion of a *verifiable* hypothesis was that it must not suppose anything that you are not able directly to observe. From such a rule it would be fair to infer that he would permit Mr. Schliemann to suppose he was going to find arms and utensils at Hissarlik, but would forbid him to suppose that they were either made or used by any human being, since no such beings could ever be detected by direct percept. He ought on the same principle to forbid us to suppose that a fossil skeleton had ever belonged to a living ichthyosaurus. . . . You must not believe that you hear me speaking to you, but only that you hear certain sounds while you see before you a spot of black, white, and flesh color; and those sounds somehow seem to suggest certain ideas which you must not connect at all with the black and white spot. A man would have to devote years to training his mind to such habits of thought, and even then it is doubtful whether it would be possible. And what would be gained? . . . Comte . . . and Karl Pearson take what they consider to be the first impressions of sense, but which are really nothing of the sort, but are percepts that are products of psychical operations, and they separate these from all

5 See pp. 202–04.
6 See pp. 300–02.

the intellectual part of our knowledge, and arbitrarily call the first *real* and the second *fictions*. These two words *real* and *fictive* bear no significations whatever except as marks of *good* and *bad*. But the truth is that what they call *bad* or *fictitious*, or *subjective*, the intellectual part of our knowledge, comprises all that is valuable on its own account, while what they mark *good*, or *real*, or *objective*, is nothing but the pretty vessel that carries the precious thought.[j]

The first part of this argument simply points out that the positivists were far from clear about what is directly observable and, so, about what is the terminus of the verification process. The second part attacks the whole notion of the direct observation. Since this notion—that there are things with which we are directly acquainted—has been a central feature of the theories of many philosophers, it is worth examining Peirce's criticisms in some detail.

There are many things about, say, my desk with which I am not directly acquainted, but which I know by hearsay or by inference (such as that it once belonged to my uncle and that it is too large to go through the door of my study). But many people would say that when I am looking at it under normal light, I am directly acquainted with its continuous, spread-out, mahogany-colored surface. Peirce pointed out that the findings of physiology show that this cannot be the case. When I look at something—say, my desk—there is a very large number of separate inputs to my brain, each of them originating in one of the many "needlelike" nerve endings in my retinas. There must, then, be some sort of synthesizing activity that "constructs" the continuous surface. And there must be similar activity as regards the blind spot, which physiology tells us exists in the retina. Since what is actually occurring (pinpoints of light with gap) is quite different from what seems to be occurring (direct presentation of continuous surface with no gap), it follows that "we have no intuitive faculty of distinguishing direct from mediate cognitions."

The next argument does not rest on physiological theory. Suppose I have made an appointment to meet a friend at a certain place and time. When he turns up I recognize him at once. It seems to me that, once he comes into view, he is directly present to me in my perception of him. But when we consider what is involved in my being able to recognize the approaching man as my friend, we find that, though "we think that something is presented to us as a picture, . . . it is really constructed from slight data by the understanding."[k] For instance, I certainly would not recognize the man who is approaching unless I had had numerous earlier encounters with him and unless I had brought my memories of these encounters to the present meeting. Again, if I did not expect my friend to arrive, or if I happened to be preoccupied with something else, I might fail to recognize him as he approached. On the other hand, the fact that I am eagerly awaiting him might cause me to mistake a complete stranger for him; if it were not for this expectation, I would see a stranger, not mistakenly recognize a friend. Thus, it is memories of the past and expectations of the future that make it possible for the understanding to construct the ordinary objects of ordinary experience "from slight data." Even the simplest perception of objects involves a "process of reasoning," or of "interpretation," a process that Peirce called "abduction," in order to distinguish it from induction and deduction, the only two "processes of reasoning" that the traditional philosophy had recognized.

> All our knowledge may be said to rest upon *observed facts*. It is true that there are psychological states which antecede our observing facts as such. Thus, it is a fact that I see an inkstand before me; but before I can say that I am obliged to have impressions of sense into which no idea of an inkstand, or of any separate object, or of an "I," or of seeing, enter at all; and it is true that my judging that I see an inkstand before me is the product of mental operations upon these impressions of sense. . . .
>
> I call all such inference by the peculiar name, *abduction*, because its legitimacy depends upon altogether different principles from those of other kinds of inference.[1]
>
> Abductive inference shades into perceptual judgment without any sharp line of demarcation between them. . . . On its side, the perceptive judgment is the result of a process, although of a process not sufficiently conscious to be controlled, or, to state it more truly, not controllable and therefore not fully conscious. If we were to subject this subconscious process to logical analysis, we should find that it terminated in what that analysis would represent as an abductive inference, resting on the result of a similar process which a similar logical analysis would represent to be terminated by a similar abductive inference, and so on *ad infinitum*. This analysis would be precisely analogous to that which the sophism of Achilles and the Tortoise applies to the chase of the Tortoise by Achilles, and it would fail to represent the real process for the same reason. Namely, just as Achilles does not have to make the series of distinct endeavours which he is represented as making, so this process of forming the perceptual judgment, because it is subconscious and so not amenable to logical criticism, does not have to make separate acts of inference, but performs its act in one continuous process.[m]

This analysis not only undermines the positivism with which Peirce was familiar; it also undermines twentieth-century Logical Positivism and, equally, the "common-sense" realism of Moore and the "logical" realism of Russell.[7] If Peirce is correct, neither sense data nor ordinary objects are directly present in perception. *Nothing* is directly present in perception. The seemingly obvious fundamental distinction between direct percepts and mediate cognitions has been replaced by the notion of a process of interpretation which is unconscious and continuous, but which can be represented, for the purpose of analysis, as a series of inferences. The end product of this process at any particular time is a perceptible object; the starting point of this process at any particular time is an abductive inference. Every end product is subject to further interpretation at some

7 See Vol. V, Chs. 3, 4, and 5.

subsequent time; every starting point is subject to analysis into more elementary abductive inferences. What is the ultimate end product? It is a real object that we are approaching asymptotically. What is the original starting point? It is the limit, the "extreme case," of abductive inference. Thus there is an infinite series of abductive inferences, stretching in both directions. Before we make any inductive abductive inference there is an earlier one we must have made, just as, before Achilles took his first step, there was an earlier step he must have taken. But this is true only from the point of view of "logical analysis": Achilles *did* take his first step; he *did* overtake the tortoise. So, too, perceptions occur and are "completed"; our experience is the experience of a world of objects.

In these pages Peirce has been giving an analysis of the contents of what James called "pure experience," and it is instructive to compare his approach with James's relatively superficial discussion.[8] James's "sensations and feelings" have become the *termini a quo* of an interpretative process, and his ordinary objects have become the *termini ad quem* of this process.

To talk, as Peirce does, about an unconscious process of reasoning, and about the mind's constructive activity, may suggest that his view is a sophisticated, as James's was a muddled, version of Kantianism. But Peirce insisted that he was a realist. It is true that a constructive activity is going on, but this activity is directed toward, and is approximating to, an objective world that is wholly independent of us. Hence he avoided the subjectivism that "infected" so much of nineteenth-century philosophy and from which twentieth-century philosophy, as we shall see,[9] sought to escape. It is unfortunate that Peirce's writings remained unknown for so long. Otherwise, philosophy in this century could have developed in a very different way.

Peirce's Realism

We have already seen Peirce arguing that there are "external permanencies" to which our thought can more and more closely approximate. We must now examine this thesis in more detail.

First, as regards universals, there are just two possibilities. Either they are fictions, which is the view of the nominalists (or "Occamists," as Peirce called them), or they are reals, which is the view of Duns Scotus and the scholastic realists.[10]

> Are universals real? We have only to stop and consider a moment what was meant by the word *real*, when the whole issue soon becomes apparent. Objects are divided into figments, dreams, etc., on the one hand, and realities

8 See pp. 299–302.
9 See Vol. V, Ch. 1.
10 See Vol. II, Ch. 8.

on the other. The former are those which exist only inasmuch as you or I or some man imagines them; the latter are those which have an existence independent of your mind or mine or that of any number of persons. The real is that which is not whatever we happen to think it, but is unaffected by what we may think of it. The question, therefore, is whether *man, horse,* and other names of natural classes, correspond with anything which all men, or all horses, really have in common, independent of our thought, or whether these classes are constituted simply by a likeness in the way in which our minds are affected by individual objects which have in themselves no resemblance or relationship whatsoever.[n]

Although the realist answer to this question is "less familiar" than the nominalist answer, it is "more natural and obvious."

> All human thought and opinion . . . universally [tend] in the long run to a definite form, which is the truth. . . . There is, then, to every question a true answer, a final conclusion, to which the opinion of every man is constantly gravitating. He may for a time recede from it, but give him more experience and time for consideration, and he will finally approach it. The individual may not live to reach the truth; there is a residuum of error in every individual's opinions. No matter; it remains that there is a definite opinion to which the mind of man is, on the whole and in the long run, tending. . . . This final opinion, then, is independent, not indeed of thought in general, but of all that is arbitrary and individual in thought; is quite independent of how you, or I, or any number of men think.
>
> Everything, therefore, which will be thought to exist in the final opinion is real, and nothing else. . . . It is plain that this view of reality is inevitably realistic, because general conceptions enter into all judgments, and therefore into true opinions. Consequently a thing in the general is as real as in the concrete.[o]

Similarly as regards the so-called laws of nature. Here again there are but two possibilities. One is that the so-called laws of nature are devices we introduce to facilitate our traffic with nature. The other is that there are genuine laws and that the regularities we observe may very well be instances of such laws.

It is an easy matter, Peirce thought, to prove that the second alternative is correct. Indeed, everybody, except a few doctrinaire Occamists, is a realist regarding the laws of nature.

> Suppose we attack the question experimentally. Here is a stone. Now I place that stone where there will be no obstacle between it and the floor, and I will predict with confidence that as soon as I let go my hold upon the stone it will fall to the floor. . . .
>
> But *how can* I know what is going to happen? You certainly do not think that it is by clairvoyance. . . . Still, it remains true that I *do know* that that stone will drop, as a *fact,* as soon as I let go my hold. If I *truly know* anything, that which I know must be *real.* . . .

It is the same with [all] the operations of nature. With overwhelming uniformity, in our past experience, direct and indirect, stones left free to fall have fallen. Thereupon two hypotheses only are open to us. Either—

1. the uniformity with which those stones have fallen has been due to mere chance and affords no ground whatever, not the slightest, for any expectation that the next stone that shall be let go will fall; or

2. the uniformity with which stones have fallen has been due to some *active general principle,* in which case it would be a strange coincidence that it should cease to act at the moment my prediction was based upon it. . . .

Of course, every sane man will adopt the latter hypothesis . . . that *general principles are really operative in nature.* That is the doctrine of scholastic realism.[p]

How are we to assess this argument? It seems to consist in a definition and two empirical generalizations. Reality is defined as that on which the opinions of individual minds would finally converge, if in fact opinions do converge. The first generalization is that the history of science shows that opinions are in fact converging, and the second is that the converging opinions involve, or are about, universals and laws. From these theses it follows that universals and laws are not fictions but real. "If you believe that modern science has made any general discovery at all, you believe that general so discovered to be real, and so you *are* a *scholastic realist* whether you are aware of it or not."[q]

Though the claim that opinions are converging and that they will continue to converge is an essential step in the argument, Peirce hardly subjected this historical generalization to his usual critical scrutiny. It is true, as he pointed out, that

. . . all the followers of science are animated by a cheerful hope that the processes of investigation, if only pushed far enough, will give one certain solution to each question to which they apply it. One man may investigate the velocity of light by studying the transits of Venus and the aberration of the stars; another by the oppositions of Mars and the eclipses of Jupiter's satellites; a third by the method of Fizeau; a fourth by that of Foucault; a fifth by the motions of the curves of Lissajoux; a sixth, a seventh, an eighth, and a ninth, may follow the different methods of comparing the measures of statical and dynamical electricity. They may at first obtain different results, but, as each perfects his method and his processes, the results are found to move steadily together toward a destined centre. So with all scientific research. Different minds may set out with the most antagonistic views, but the progress of investigation carries them by a force outside of themselves to one and the same conclusion. . . . The opinion which is fated to be ultimately agreed to by all who investigate, is what we mean by the truth, and the object represented in this opinion is the real. That is the way I would explain reality.[r]

Doubtless, many scientists have been animated by just the belief Peirce describes. If Kepler,[11] for instance, had not been convinced that the orbits of the planets are external permanencies, he would hardly have persisted for years in his research. But the psychology of scientists is one thing and what is the case about the world is another, as Peirce himself would be the first to insist. Again, historians of science by no means agree that science has in fact progressed in a more or less continuous linear fashion, as Peirce supposed. But his assertion of continuing convergence is really not an empirical generalization based on the history of science; it is, rather, a declaration of faith, as the phrase "cheerful hope" suggests. Peirce was a metaphysical realist because the pursuit of truth was for him a central passion and because it seemed to him that this pursuit is meaningful and rational only if there is some objectively existing state of affairs toward which opinion is moving.

Metaphysics as Scientia Generalis

"The business of metaphysics," according to Peirce, "is to study the most general features of reality and real objects."[8] In defining metaphysics as *scientia generalis*—as the most general of the sciences—Peirce was explicitly turning his back on the currently fashionable positions in philosophy and reverting to the Aristotelian tradition. From Aristotle down to Kant, philosophers had assumed, almost without exception, that metaphysics is the most general of the sciences. Whereas physics is confined to the study of one sort of being (inanimate nature) and biology is confined to the study of another sort of being (living things), metaphysics, it was held, is the science of being as such, of being in general. It was Kant, of course, who first undermined this whole conception by distinguishing between things as they appear and things as they are in themselves and by arguing that the human mind is forever limited to knowledge of the former. But the positivists and the pragmatists added new considerations: Metaphysical assertions are not verifiable and are therefore meaningless, and the pursuit of metaphysical truth is only a clumsy, if unconscious, attempt to escape into a realm of certainty.

As a scholastic realist Peirce naturally rejected this whole school of thought: If there is an objective reality it ought to be knowable. And his first task in rehabilitating metaphysics was to explain why, if indeed it is a possible science, it has remained in such a "puny, rickety and scrofulous" condition.

> The common opinion has been that Metaphysics is backward because it is intrinsically beyond the reach of human cognition. But that, I think I can clearly discern, is a complete mistake. Why should metaphysics be so difficult?

11 See Vol. III, pp. 95–98.

Because it is abstract? But the abstracter a science is, the easier it is, both as a general rule of experience and as a corollary from logical principles. . . . [Again,] it will be said that metaphysics is inscrutable because its objects are not open to observation. This is doubtless true of some systems of metaphysics, though not to the extent that it is supposed to be true. The things that any science discovers are beyond the reach of direct observation. We cannot see energy, nor the attraction of gravitation, nor the flying molecules of gases, nor the luminiferous ether, nor the forests of the carbonaceous era, nor the explosions in nerve-cells. It is only the premises of science, not its conclusions, which are directly observed. . . . The data of metaphysics are not less open to observation, but immeasurably more so, than the data, say, of the very highly developed science of astronomy. . . . No, I think we must abandon the idea that metaphysics is backward owing to any intrinsic difficulty of it.

In my opinion the chief cause of its backward condition is that its leading professors have been theologians. . . . Theology, I am persuaded, derives its initial impulse from a religious wavering. . . . As far as I can penetrate into the motive of theology, it begins in an effort of men who have joined the Christian army and sworn fidelity to it to silence the suggestions of their hearts that they renounce their allegiance. . . . Nothing can be more unscientific than the attitude of minds who are trying to confirm themselves in early beliefs. . . . To sum up, the case is this:

We should expect to find metaphysics, judging from its position in the scheme of the sciences, to be somewhat more difficult than logic, but still on the whole one of the simplest of sciences, . . . and it is [therefore] worth trying [to discover] whether by proceeding modestly, recognizing in metaphysics an observational science, and applying to it the universal methods of such science, without caring one straw what kind of conclusions we reach or what their tendencies may be, but just honestly applying induction and hypothesis, we cannot gain some ground for hoping that the disputes and obscurities of the subject may at last disappear.[t]

Accordingly, Peirce proposed to proceed systematically and to begin by making "a complete survey of human knowledge," taking "note of all the valuable ideas in each branch of science."[u] Among the most promising of these, Peirce thought, are the ideas of force and of law (derived from dynamics), the idea of evolution (derived from biology), the ideas of feeling, reaction, and habit (derived from psychology), and the idea of continuity (derived from mathematics).

Such are the materials out of which chiefly a philosophical theory ought to be built, in order to represent the state of knowledge to which the nineteenth century has brought us. Without going into other important questions of philosophical architectonic, we can readily foresee what sort of a metaphysics would appropriately be constructed from those conceptions. . . . It would suppose that in the beginning—infinitely remote—there was a chaos of unpersonalized feeling, which being without connection or regularity would properly be without existence. This feeling, sporting here and there in pure arbitrariness, would have started the germ of a generalizing tendency. Its other sportings would be evanescent, but this would have a growing virtue. Thus, the tendency to habit would be started; and from this, with the other principles of evolution, all the regularities of the universe would be evolved. At any time, however, an element of pure chance survives and will remain until the world becomes an absolutely perfect, rational, and symmetrical system, in which mind is at last crystallized in the infinitely distant future.

That idea . . . accounts for the main features of the universe as we know it—the characters of time, space, matter, force, gravitation, electricity, etc. It predicts many more things which new observations can alone bring to the test.[v]

But the chief task of the metaphysician is to describe the leading characteristics of this universe that has evolved and is still evolving from a "chaos of feeling," rather than to trace the path of its evolutionary development. The features to which Peirce directed most attention are chance and continuity, or—to use the terms that, in accordance with his own advocacy of linguistic precision, he preferred—"tychism" and "synechism."

TYCHISM

Tychism, or the doctrine of chance, is adumbrated in what Peirce has already said about feeling originally "sporting in pure arbitrariness" and in his emphasis on habit. He did not, of course, think of denying the lawfulness of nature. That the behavior of nature is on the whole regular, is an empirical fact. What he was chiefly concerned to deny was the notion—widely held by scientists in his own day—that the laws of nature are "iron necessities." They are, rather, in his view, statistical regularities. Hence the importance of the notion of habit, for a habit is precisely a regularity that obtains only on the whole and that is compatible with the idea of growth and of novelty. In more than one prophetic passage Peirce suggested what has become a commonplace of quantum physics, that "there is room for serious doubt whether the fundamental laws of mechanics hold good for single atoms,"[w] and that "the peculiar function of the molecular hypothesis in physics is to open an entry for the calculus of probabilities."[x] But his main concern was less to establish tychism than to show that the concept of determinism is riddled with inconsistencies.

I propose here to examine the common belief that every single fact in the universe is precisely determined by law. . . .

The proposition in question is that the state of things existing at any time, together with certain immutable laws, completely determine the state of things at every other time (for a limitation to *future* time is indefensible). Thus, given the state of the universe in the original nebula, and given the laws of mechanics, a sufficiently powerful mind could deduce from these data the precise form of every curlicue of every letter I am now writing.[y]

Having defined the doctrine of necessity, Peirce proceeded to demolish in turn each argument by which the doctrine has been defended. The first argument Peirce considered claims that the doctrine of necessity is a postulate.

> When I have asked thinking men what reason they had to believe that every fact in the universe is precisely determined by law, the first answer has usually been that the proposition is a "presupposition" or postulate of scientific reasoning. Well, if that is the best that can be said for it, the belief is doomed. Suppose it be "postulated": that does not make it true, nor so much as afford the slightest rational motive for yielding it any credence. It is as if a man should come to borrow money and, when asked for his security, should reply he "postulated" the loan. To "postulate" a proposition is no more than to hope it is true.[z]

A second argument that has been used to support the doctrine of necessity is that it is "proved to be true, or at least rendered highly probable, by the observation of nature."[a] But

> . . . to one who is behind the scenes, and knows that the most refined comparisons of masses, lengths, and angles, far surpassing in precision all other measurements, yet fall behind the accuracy of bank accounts, and that the ordinary determinations of physical constants, such as appear from month to month in the journals, are about on a par with an upholsterer's measurements of carpets and curtains, the idea of mathematical exactitude being demonstrated in the laboratory will appear simply ridiculous. . . .
>
> Those observations which are generally adduced in favour of mechanical causation simply prove that there is an element of regularity in nature, and have no bearing whatever upon the question of whether such regularity is exact and universal or not. Nay, in regard to this *exactitude*, all observation is directly *opposed* to it; and the most that can be said is that a good deal of this observation can be explained away.[b]

A third argument has it that chance is "unintelligible, that is to say . . . it does not disclose to the eye of reason the how or why of things."[c] But the necessitarian does not get rid of arbitrariness and unintelligibility. He merely introduces it all

> . . . in one dose, in the beginning, if there was a beginning, and [holds] that the variety and complication of nature has always been just as much as it is now, [whereas] I, for my part, think that the diversification, the specification, has been continually taking place. Should you condescend to ask me why I so think, I should give my reasons as follows:
>
> 1. Question any science which deals with the course of time. . . . Glance at the history of states, of institutions, of language, of ideas. Examine the successions of forms shown by paleontology, the history of the globe as set forth in geology, of what the astronomer is able to make out concerning the

changes of stellar systems. Everywhere the main fact is growth and increasing complexity. . . . From these broad and ubiquitous facts we may fairly infer, by the most unexceptionable logic, that there is probably in nature some agency by which the complexity and diversity of things can be increased; and that consequently the rule of mechanical necessity meets in some way with interference.

2. . . . When I ask the necessitarian how he would explain the diversity and irregularity of the universe, he replies to me out of the treasury of his wisdom that irregularity is something which from the nature of things we must not seek to explain. Abashed at this, I seek to cover my confusion by asking how he would explain the uniformity and regularity of the universe, whereupon he tells me that the laws of nature are immutable and ultimate facts, and no account is to be given of them. But my hypothesis of spontaneity does explain irregularity, in a certain sense; that is, it explains the general fact of irregularity, though not, of course, what each lawless event is to be. At the same time, by thus loosening the bond of necessity, it gives room for the influence of another kind of causation, such as seems to be operative in the mind in the formation of associations, and enables us to understand how the uniformity of nature could have been brought about. . . .

I believe I have thus subjected to fair examination all the important reasons for adhering to the theory of universal necessity, and have shown their nullity.[d]

But, though Peirce held he had demolished necessitarianism, he did not hold that he had established the truth of tychism. In accordance with his own doctrine of fallibilism[12] he pointed out that

. . . a serious student of philosophy will be in no haste to accept or reject this doctrine; but he will see in it one of the chief attitudes which speculative thought may take, feeling that it is not for an individual, nor for an age, to pronounce upon a fundamental question of philosophy. That is a task for a whole era to work out.[e]

Thus the doctrine of convergence toward, rather than achievement of, truth applies in the field of metaphysics just as it does in the other sciences. And it was just Peirce's insistence on the possibility of continuous progress toward truth that underlay his hostility to necessitarianism, which argues that, given the state of the material universe at any time and the laws of motion, the state of the universe at any other time is, in principle, predictable. But it takes the laws of motion as givens; they are themselves inexplicable. Hence necessitarianism sooner or later reaches a dead end. Tychism, in contrast, by taking the universe as an evolutionary development in which habits successively emerge, eliminates the threat of dead ends. *Everything*, from this point of view, becomes a stage

12 See p. 293.

in an ongoing process and is therefore capable, at least theoretically, of being explained as the outgrowth of a still earlier stage, in accordance with the laws of evolutionary development. But these laws are themselves only habits. That is, unlike the laws of nature, as conceived by the materialists and the necessitarians, the laws of evolutionary development undergo development and therefore themselves are capable, at least theoretically, of explication, even though chance plays a part in their development.

SYNECHISM

Peirce's second basic metaphysical category is synechism—the belief that continuity, as much as chance, is a pervasive feature of the world. Though Peirce found the clue to this category in the field of mathematics, some of the best (in the sense of the most readily understood) examples of continuity are to be found in psychology. Indeed, continuity is the basic law of the mind.

> Logical analysis applied to mental phenomena shows that there is but one law of mind, namely, that ideas tend to spread continuously and to affect certain others which stand to them in a peculiar relation of affectibility. In this spreading they lose intensity, and especially the power of affecting others, but gain generality and become welded with other ideas.
>
> I set down this formula at the beginning, for convenience, and now proceed to comment upon it.
>
> We are accustomed to speak of ideas as reproduced, as passed from mind to mind, as similar or dissimilar to one another, and, in short, as if they were substantial things; nor can any reasonable objections be raised to such expressions. But taking the word "idea" in the sense of an event in an individual consciousness, it is clear that an idea once past is gone forever, and any supposed recurrence of it is another idea. . . .
>
> Some minds will here jump to the conclusion that a past idea cannot in any sense be present. But that is hasty and illogical. How extravagant, too, to pronounce our whole knowledge of the past to be mere delusion! . . .
>
> How can a past idea be present? Not vicariously. Then, only by direct perception. In other words, to be present, it must be *ipso facto* present. That is, it cannot be wholly past; it can only be going, infinitesimally past, less past than any assignable past date. We are thus brought to the conclusion that the present is connected with the past by a series of real infinitesimal steps.[f]

What Peirce is discussing here is what James called "the stream of consciousness."[13] But note how different Peirce's approach is. Where James's is descriptive, Peirce's is analytical. Characteristically, he starts from a problem in the theory of knowledge: If our experience consists in a number of particular, encapsulated ideas, we could never have access to (or indeed any notion of) the past. For

13 See pp. 299–300.

each such particular encapsulated idea, once past, would be irrecoverable. But we do have access to the past. Hence our mental life is a continuum, not a series of encapsulated events.

> We find that when we regard ideas from a nominalistic, individualistic, sensualistic way, the simplest facts of mind become utterly meaningless. That one idea should resemble another or influence another, or that one state of mind should so much as be thought of in another is, from that standpoint sheer nonsense. . . . By this and other means we are driven to perceive, what is quite evident of itself, that instantaneous feelings flow together into a continuum of feeling.[g]

So far, we have seen the principle of continuity applied to a psychological problem. But, because it is a basic metaphysical category, it is equally applicable in all the sciences. For instance,

> . . . when a naturalist wishes to study a species, he collects a considerable number of specimens more or less similar. In contemplating them, he observes certain ones which are more or less alike in some particular respect. They all have, for instance, a certain S-shaped marking. He observes that they are not *precisely* alike, in this respect; the S has not precisely the same shape, but the differences are such as to lead him to believe that forms could be found intermediate between any two of those he possesses. He, now, finds other forms apparently quite dissimilar—say a marking in the form of a C—and the question is, whether he can find intermediate ones which will connect these latter with the others. . . . In this way, he builds up from the study of Nature a new general conception of the character in question. . . . I surely need not say much to show what a logical engine is here. It is the essence of the method of the naturalist.[h]

COMMUNITY

From the idea of continuity it was easy for Peirce to pass (by continuous degrees, as it were) to the idea of community. Characteristically, Peirce set out a formal argument for community, and this argument began, interestingly enough, with a consideration of what is implied by the notion of rational choice in a world of chance.

Peirce first points out that "the idea of probability essentially belongs to a kind of inference which is repeated indefinitely."[i] We can be confident that a penny will turn up heads as often as tails only if the penny is tossed an indefinitely large number of times. Peirce next points out that sooner or later we all will die. We will die before an indefinitely large number of throws of the penny can be made, for an indefinitely large number of throws requires an indefinitely long time. Nonetheless, it is rational to bet, on any particular occasion, that the odds are 1 to 2 that the penny will turn up heads, and to go on betting in this way on every toss. But how can it be rational to use what happens only during an indefinitely large number of cases as a warrant for deciding what to do in a smaller number of cases, however large? The answer can only be that we are interested not merely in what happens in this smaller number of cases but in what happens *in the long run*—that is, in what happens in the indefinitely large number of cases that extend beyond our own finite lives.

> I can see but one solution. . . . It seems to me that we are driven to this, that logicality inexorably requires that our interests shall *not* be limited. They must not stop at our own fate, but must embrace the whole community. This community, again, must not be limited, but must extend to all races of beings with whom we can come into immediate or mediate intellectual relation. It must reach, however vaguely, beyond this geological epoch, beyond all bounds. He who would not sacrifice his own soul to save the whole world, is, as it seems to me, illogical in all his inferences, collectively. Logic is rooted in the social principle.
>
> To be logical men should not be selfish.[j]

Accordingly, Peirce concluded that "no man can be logical whose supreme desire is the well-being of himself or of any other existing person or collection of persons." To be rational "requires a conceived identification of one's interests with those of an unlimited community."[k]

A less technical argument leading to the same conclusion, that "individualism and falsity are one and the same," can be developed from Peirce's discussion of the relative merits of the various methods of fixing beliefs. As we have already seen, he rejected the method of tenacity because, as he said, "the social impulse is against it." It follows that even the most efficient police state cannot prevent people from comparing notes and so discovering that the official version is not universally accepted. But this is merely a sociological fact. We now see that the social impulse is inextricably bound up with the notion—so central in Peirce's view—of the truth as the opinion toward which belief is gradually converging. Thus the notion of truth involves the notion of community. The pursuit of truth is, and can only be, a community effort—not the effort of some finite community over some limited period of time, but of the indefinitely large community that we call mankind, over an indefinitely long period of time.

> The great bulk of mankind . . . never have leisure to labor for anything but the necessities of life for themselves and their families. But, without directly striving for it, far less comprehending it, they perform' all that civilization requires, and bring forth another generation to advance history another step. Their fruit is, therefore, collective; it is the achievement of the whole people. What is it, then, that the whole people is about, what is this civilization that is the outcome of history, but is never completed? We cannot expect to attain a complete conception of it; but we can see that it is a gradual process . . . whereby man, with all his miserable littleness, becomes gradually more and more imbued with the Spirit of God, in which Nature and History are rife. . . . The great principle of logic is self-surrender.

Individual action is a means and not our end. Individual pleasure is not our end; we are all putting our shoulders to the wheel for an end that none of us can catch more than a glimpse at—that which the generations are working out.[1]

Thus the doctrines of realism (in contrast to nominalism), chance (in contrast to determinism), and community (in contrast to individualism) came together as central features of Peirce's philosophical theory because all three of these doctrines seemed to him to be required if the continuous pursuit of truth, not its actual achievement, is to be possible.

Phaneroscopy

In the past few pages we have been outlining some of the main features of Peirce's metaphysics, yet Peirce's metaphysics itself remained only an outline; illness, poverty, and isolation prevented him from developing these ideas systematically. But meanwhile, his thoughts had begun to focus on a different aspect of the philosophical enterprise, an attempt to describe the contents of experience—not the contents of this or that individual's experience but the structural features of all experience. Of course, from Peirce's point of view, these two inquiries —metaphysics as *scientia generalis* and the description of the general structure of experience—ought to converge in the same results. This follows from Peirce's realist thesis that what is real and what is before the mind when it entertains a true opinion are one and the same.

In accordance with his preference for terminological precision rather than "sweetness or charms," Peirce called his descriptive approach "phaneroscopy." Since this approach was intended to be presuppositionless (we are to frame no hypotheses; we are to make no predictions; we are merely to describe the structures we discover), phaneroscopy amounts to what came to be called "phenomenology"—a term Peirce also used, though less frequently. Here again, along with James, Peirce anticipated a major theme of twentieth-century philosophy.[14]

> PHANEROSCOPY is the description of the *phaneron;* and by the *phaneron* I mean the collective total of all that is in any way or in any sense present to the mind, quite regardless of whether it corresponds to any real thing or not. . . .
> English philosophers have quite commonly used the word *idea* in a sense approaching to that which I give to *phaneron*. But in various ways they have . . . given a psychological connotation to their word which I am careful to exclude. . . . What I term *phaneroscopy* is that study which, supported by

14 See p. 299 and Vol. V, Ch. 6.

the direct observation of phanerons and generalizing its observations, signalizes several very broad classes of phanerons; describes the features of each; shows that although they are so inextricably mixed together that no one can be isolated, yet it is manifest that their characters are quite disparate; then proves, beyond question, that a certain very short list comprises all of these broadest categories of phanerons there are; and finally proceeds to the laborious and difficult task of enumerating the principal subdivisions of those categories.

It will be plain from what has been said that phaneroscopy has nothing at all to do with the question of how far the phanerons it studies correspond to any realities. It religiously abstains from all speculation as to any relations between its categories and physiological facts, cerebral or other. . . . It simply scrutinizes the direct appearances, and endeavours to combine minute accuracy with the broadest possible generalization. The student's great effort is not to be influenced by any tradition, any authority, any reasons for supposing that such and such ought to be the facts, or any fancies of any kind, and to confine himself to honest, single-minded observation of the appearances.[m]

The "short list of categories" is very short. There are, Peirce believed, only three such categories, and to them he gave the names "Firstness," "Secondness," and "Thirdness."

FIRSTNESS

Firstness is just the felt characteristic of being whatever something is felt to be—the redness of red, the middle-C-ness of middle C, the saltiness of salt. If we want to get a pure example of Firstness, we must progressively eliminate every other aspect of experience until, say, the redness of red fully occupies the mind, because, in actual expression, the three categories are "inextricably mixed" together. Suppose, for instance, one were aloft in a balloon at night alone and "enjoying absolute calm and stillness." If one were *totally* absorbed in the calm and stillness—not experiencing any contrasting somatic data or thinking about the earth below or the heavens above—that would be pure Firstness. Pure Firstness, then, is exactly that state of affairs from which, according to the hypotheses of metaphysics, the evolution of the universe started.[15]

> Among phanerons there are certain qualities of feeling, such as the colour of magenta, the odour of attar, the sound of a railway whistle, the taste of quinine, the quality of the emotion upon contemplating a fine mathematical demonstration, the quality of feeling of love, etc. . . .
>
> By a feeling, I mean an instance of that kind of consciousness which involves no analysis, comparison or any process whatsoever, nor consists in whole or in part of any act by which one stretch of consciousness is distinguished from another, which has its own positive quality which consists in nothing else,

15 See pp. 276–77.

and which is of itself all that it is, however it may have been brought about; so that if this feeling is present during a lapse of time, it is wholly and equally present at every moment of that time.[n]

Though it would be only in very unusual circumstances that we would ever approach a mental state that was an experience of pure Firstness, Firstness is an inherent aspect of all experience, for "whatever is in the mind in any mode of consciousness there is necessarily an immediate consciousness and consequently a feeling."[o]

SECONDNESS

Secondness is most strikingly displayed in the phenomena of resistance and reaction. Suppose again that one were in a balloon enjoying absolute calm and stillness. The feeling of calm and stillness is Firstness. Now suppose that suddenly the stillness is broken by a piercing steam whistle. The sound, simply as the feeling of piercingness, is also Firstness. But the breaking of the stillness by the whistle is Secondness, for this interruption is something that happens to someone and so involves one's drawing a distinction—which one does not draw at the level of pure feeling—between ego and nonego. Thus, Secondness is the characteristic of actuality, factuality, constraint, causation, and force—and these are as much categorial features of experience as is feeling.

> The idea of second is predominant in the ideas of causation and of statical force. For cause and effect are two; and statical forces always occur between pairs. Constraint is a Secondness. . . . In the idea of reality, Secondness is predominant; for the real is that which insists upon forcing its way to recognition as something *other* than the mind's creation.[p]

THIRDNESS

If Firstness is called Firstness because feeling is the mode of being that involves nothing else (no contrast), and Secondness is so called because it does involve a second, then Thirdness is so called because it is the mode of being in which a second is brought into relation with a third. Thirdness is the aspect of lawfulness, as distinct from factuality. Law takes us beyond fact and the resistance (or constraint, or actuality) of facts to our will. "No collection of facts can constitute a law, for the law goes beyond any accomplished facts and determines how facts that *may be,* but *all* of which never can have happened, shall be characterized."[q]

To bring out the way in which law involves not merely a dyad but a triad, Peirce calls our attention to what is involved in the notion of giving something to somebody. Suppose A gives B to C. There is a relation between A and B (A rids himself of B) and there is a relation between B and C (B is acquired by C). But giving does not consist in either of the dyadic relations taken separately or in both taken together. That is, giving does not consist merely in A ridding himself of B, nor in C acquiring B, nor yet in A ridding himself of B and C acquiring B. For A to give B to C, C must come into possession of B according to law. "There must be some kind of law before there can be any kind of giving—be it but the law of the strongest."ʳ

But important as law is, the preeminent aspect of Thirdness is meaning, or what Peirce preferred to call "significance." For instance, a sign, as Peirce pointed out, is clearly a third:

> Suppose, for example, an officer of a squad or company of infantry gives the word of command, "Ground arms!" This order is, of course, a sign. That thing which causes a sign as such is called the *object* (according to the usage of speech, the "real," but more accurately, the *existent* object) represented by the sign: the sign is determined to some species of correspondence with that object. In the present case, the object the command represents is the will of the officer that the butts of the muskets be brought down to the ground. Nevertheless, the action of his will upon the sign is not simply dyadic; for if he thought the soldiers were deaf mutes, or did not know a word of English, or were raw recruits utterly undrilled, or were indisposed to obedience, his will probably would not produce the word of command. . . . For the proper significate outcome of a sign, I propose the name, the *interpretant* of the sign. The example of the imperative command shows that it need not be of a mental mode of being.ˢ

So much for definitions of the three elements involved in the action of a sign. The analysis continues:

> Now the problem of what the "meaning" of an intellectual concept is can only be solved by the study of the interpretants, or proper significate effects, of signs. These we find to be of three general classes with some important subdivisions. The first proper significate effect of a sign is a feeling produced by it. . . . This "emotional interpretant," as I call it, may amount to much more than that feeling of recognition; and in some cases, it is the only proper significate effect that the sign produces. Thus, the performance of a piece of concerted music is a sign. It conveys, and is intended to convey, the composer's musical ideas; but these usually consist merely in a series of feelings. If a sign produces any further proper significate effect, it will do so through the mediation of the emotional interpretant, and such further effect will always involve an effort. I call it the energetic interpretant. The effort may be a muscular one, as it is in the case of the command to ground arms; but it is much more usually an exertion upon the Inner World, a mental effort. It never can be the meaning of an intellectual concept, since it is a single act, [while] such a concept is of a general nature. But what further kind of effect can there be?
>
> In advance of ascertaining the nature of this effect, it will be convenient to adopt a designation for it, and I will call it the *logical interpretant,* without as yet determining whether this term shall extend to anything beside the

meaning of a general concept, though certainly closely related to that, or not. . . .

Although the definition does not require the logical interpretant (or, for that matter, either of the other two interpretants) to be a modification of consciousness, yet our lack of experience of any semiosis in which this is not the case, leaves us no alternative to beginning our inquiry into its general nature with a provisional assumption that the interpretant is, at least, in all cases, a sufficiently close analogue of a modification of consciousness to keep our conclusion pretty near to the general truth. We can only hope that, once that conclusion is reached, it may be susceptible of such a generalization as will eliminate any possible error due to the falsity of that assumption. . . .

Making that provisional assumption, then, I ask myself, since . . . the logical interpretant is general in its possibilities of reference (*i.e.*, refers or is related to whatever there may be of a certain description), what categories of mental facts there be that are of general reference. I can find only these four: conceptions, desires (including hopes, fears, etc.), expectations, and habits. I trust I have made no important omission. Now it is no explanation of the nature of the logical interpretant (which, we already know, is a concept) to say that it is a concept. This objection applies also to desire and expectation, as explanations of the same interpretant; since neither of these is general otherwise than through connection with a concept. . . . Therefore, there remains only habit, as the essence of the logical interpretant. Let us see, then, just how, . . . this habit is produced; and what sort of a habit it is. . . .

Every concept . . . first came to us as a conjecture. These ideas are the *first logical interpretants* of the phenomena that suggest them, and which, as suggesting them, are signs. . . . Thus, the primitive man must have been sometimes asked by his son whether the sun that rose in the morning was the same as the one that set the previous evening; and he may have replied, "I do not know, my boy; but I think that if I could put my brand on the evening sun, I should be able to see it on the morning sun again; and I once knew an old man who could look at the sun though he could hardly see anything else; and he told me that he had once seen a peculiarly shaped spot on the sun; and that it was to be recognized quite unmistakably for several days." [Readiness] to act in a certain way under given circumstances and when actuated by a given motive is a habit; and a deliberate, or self-controlled, habit is precisely a belief.

In the next step of thought, those first logical interpretants stimulate us to various voluntary performances in the inner world. We imagine ourselves in various situations and animated by various motives; and we proceed to trace out the alternative lines of conduct which the conjectures would leave open to us. We are, moreover, led, by the same inward activity, to remark different ways in which our conjectures could be slightly modified. The logical interpretant must, therefore, be in a relatively future tense. . . .

The real and living logical conclusion [is always a] habit; the verbal formulation merely expresses it. I do not deny that a concept, proposition, or argument may be a logical interpretant. I only insist that it cannot be the final logical interpretant, for the reason that it is itself a sign of that very kind that has itself a logical interpretant. . . . If we now revert to the psychological assumption originally made, we shall see that it is already largely eliminated by the consideration that habit is by no means exclusively a mental fact. Empirically, we find that some plants take habits. The stream of water that wears a bed for itself is forming a habit. Every ditcher so thinks of it.[t]

This discussion is difficult, but only because, like all of Peirce's writing, it is dense; the main ideas are both clear and important.

1. That a sign is a third will become clear if we consider the circumstances in which nobody would say that "Ground arms!" is a sign. Suppose that the officer lets drop the words "Ground arms!" by accident, not intending to give an order and suppose by coincidence just at that moment the soldiers lower their rifle butts to the ground because they suddenly have been overcome by fatigue. In these circumstances we would not say that an order had been issued nor that an order had been obeyed. We would say that in these circumstances "Ground arms!" was not a sign, even though the movement had occurred which, in other circumstances, is the logical interpretant of "Ground arms!" The analysis of the sign situation exactly parallels the analysis of what is involved in giving a gift. These two dyadic relations (that between the officer and "Ground arms!" and that between "Ground arms!" and the lowering of the rifle butts) no more amount to a sign than, as we have seen, the two dyadic relations whereby A puts down B and C picks up B amount to A giving B to C. In a word, the notion of law is as much involved in something being a sign as it is involved in something being a gift.

2. As regards the three types of interpretant: (a) The emotional interpretant is simply the feeling that the sign is indeed a sign—for instance, a recognition on the part of the soldiers that the words "Ground arms!" are not just random noises issuing from the officer's mouth but are intended by him to be an order to ground arms. Note that the emotional interpretant *may* be the only proper significant effect of a sign, as when we know that the speaker is saying something meaningful but do not understand what he is saying—for example, we hear someone speaking a language we do not ourselves speak. (b) What Peirce says about the energetic interpretant is clear enough. An example would be trying to figure out what is being said to us in a foreign language which we understand only poorly. (c) The assimilation of the logical interpretant to a habit was of fundamental importance to Peirce. That it is sometimes a habit is obvious. In Peirce's own example, for instance, the sign "Ground arms!" means (signifies) the lowering of the rifle butts to the ground, and since this is its regular meaning whenever the sign is uttered, it is fair to say that "Ground arms!" means the *habit* of lowering rifle butts to the ground. It is easy to see that this can be generalized to cover all signs that eventuate in action on somebody's part (for instance, the sign of a red traffic light means the habit of slowing down and coming to a stop).

But what about signs that assert facts, or truths, and that convey information instead of suggesting or ordering action? Surely here the interpretant is a concept, that is, the concept of the fact or truth asserted. Peirce's reply is that concepts may very well be involved, but the *final* logical interpretant is always a habit. Consider the word "hard" in the sentence "Diamonds are hard." We know what this means without having had to analyze either "diamond" or "hard" because we are familiar in a general way with both concepts from prior experience. In many—perhaps most—circumstances, interpretants that are much more elementary than the logical interpretant suffice, for in most circumstances the sign has only a "rude function."[u] But if for any reason we *do* want to analyze the significance of "hard," we eventually arrive at a habit—the behavior on our part that the concept "hard" produces, which is quite different from the behavior that the concept "soft" produces. This "habit of acting" is the ultimate logical interpretant of "hard." It is, speaking loosely, what "hard" means. Peirce has now reformulated his pragmaticism in terms of his doctrine of signs.[16]

3. Earlier we saw that a habit is all that a law can ever be in a tychistic universe. We have just seen that the notion of sign involves the notion of habit as a sign's logical interpretant. This brings us back once more to the notion of law. We watch A put B down and C pick it up. How do we know that this is an instance of giving, not just a coincidence? This amounts to asking, How do we know that a triadic relation is involved, not merely two dyadic relations? The answer must be that we have heard or seen A make a sign to C that C has recognized. A may have said formally, "I, A, give thee, C, this B." Or, less formally, A may have said, "Happy Birthday, C," and offered him B. Or again, A may have said nothing and C may have heard nothing, but A may have wrapped B in tissue paper, tied it with ribbon and left it under C's Christmas tree. Unless *some* sign has been made and recognized, this transaction in which C acquires the B that A once possessed is not an instance of giving. And so, generally speaking, we can say that, from the social point of view, the function of signs is to create expectations and so to introduce order and regularity into men's interactions. "The essential function of a sign is to render inefficient relations efficient—not to set them into action, but to establish a habit or general rule whereby they will act on occasion."[v]

4. It follows that *anything* can be a sign, providing only that it serves as a third, and so introduces a habit, or regularity, or lawfulness into behavior.

5. It follows also that Thirdness is not by any means limited to human experience. Animals certainly take some of their experiences as signs (for a dog, his master's whistle is a sign that dinner is ready or that he is to be taken for a walk), and perhaps to some limited extent all of an animal's experience is faintly tinged by Thirdness: It is not *mere* feeling and nothing else. But as we go up

16 See p. 267.

the evolutionary scale, Thirdness becomes more and more prominent. "With the exception of knowledge, in the present instant, of the contents of consciousness in that instant (the existence of which knowledge is open to doubt) all our thought & knowledge is by signs."[w] Suppose we begin to daydream or grow sleepy: we may fixate on some object—for example, a candle flame. As we do so, the object's significance fades away. We no longer recognize it as our candle, or even as a candle, but only as a sort of brightness. That is the limiting case, beyond which there is only feeling—feeling experienced but not recognized, even, as "brightness." Except in such a limiting case, human experience is always saturated with Thirdness.

6. That experience seemed to Peirce to be saturated with Thirdness is no accident. Though, like all phenomenologists, he claimed to give a presuppositionless (neutral) description of experience, his description, like those of other phenomenologists, was greatly influenced by what seemed to him especially important. Thus, the fact that Thirdness is so prominent in Peirce's phenomenology is connected with the primacy, in his personal hierarchy of values, of the pursuit of truth. Since Peirce was a cognitivist—since he held philosophy to be an inquiry into the general characteristics of the universe—he held it essential to distinguish between a psychological description of "thought processes" and logic as a normative science, and he condemned most of the logicians among his contemporaries precisely because they slipped into "psychologizing."

> Almost all the stronger logicians of today, present company excepted, make the fundamental mistake of confounding the logical question with the psychological question. The psychological question is what processes the mind goes through. But the logical question is whether the conclusion that will be reached, by applying this or that maxim, will or will not accord with the *fact*.[x]

By calling attention to the quality, or category, of Thirdness in experience, phenomenology—or phaneroscopy, as Peirce also termed it—escaped this trap and made the transition from psychology to logic. It is not too much to say that Peirce's whole phenomenological investigation was directed toward developing a doctrine of signs and that the whole doctrine of signs, in turn, was directed toward establishing logic as an independent and normative science, instead of merely a description of "how the mind works."

Logic as Semiotic

As usual, Peirce introduced technical terms to fix the various concepts he had distinguished. Thus the action by which some triadic relation is established (for instance, A's action of saying "Happy Birthday" to C on the occasion of offering

B to C, which brings about an instance of giving) is called by Peirce *"semiosis."*
"By 'semiosis' I mean . . . an action, or influence, which is, or involves, a cooperation of *three* subjects, such as a sign, its object, and its interpretant, this tri-relative
influence not being in any way resolvable into actions between pairs."[y]

Accordingly, Peirce's technical term for the doctrine of signs is "semiotic."
As he said, it is "the doctrine of the essential nature and fundamental varieties
of possible semiosis." And this is the study with which Peirce held logic to be
equivalent.

> Logic, in its general sense, is . . . only another name for *semiotic*, the
> quasi-necessary, or formal, doctrine of signs. By describing the doctrine as
> "quasi-necessary," or formal, I mean that we observe the characters of such
> signs as we know, and from such an observation, by a process which I will
> not object to naming Abstraction, we are led to statements, eminently fallible,
> and therefore in one sense by no means necessary, as to what *must be* the
> characters of all signs used by a "scientific" intelligence, that is to say, by
> an intelligence capable of learning by experience. . . . By such a process,
> which is at bottom very much like mathematical reasoning, we can reach
> conclusions as to what *would be* true of signs in all cases, so long as the
> intelligence using them was scientific. The modes of thought of a God, who
> should possess an intuitive omniscience superseding reason, are put out of
> the question.[z]

That is, logic is the study of what must "quasi-necessarily" be the case about
signs "in order that they may hold good of any *object*, that is, may be true."[a]

THE CLASSES OF SIGNS

Before it is possible to study logic, before it is possible to study those properties of signs by virtue of which they are true, the different kinds of signs must
be distinguished from one another. Though, as we have seen, a sign always stands
in "some species of correspondence" to its object, there are many different species
of correspondence, and these different species furnish the basis for Peirce's
classification of signs. For instance, names and photographs are both signs, but
a name stands in a different kind of correspondence to its object from the kind
of correspondence in which a photograph stands to its object. The former is an
instance of what Peirce called a "Legisign"; the latter, of what he called an
"Index." In the end Peirce decided that there are ten trichotomies and sixty-six
classes of signs, but the following passage from an earlier and simpler classification, in which there are but three trichotomies, will serve our purpose, which
is not to produce an exhaustive list of signs but to give some indication of the
subtlety of Peirce's analysis and of the skill with which he displayed the complex
interrelationships among the signs that he distinguished.

Signs are divisible into three trichotomies: first,

. . . according as the sign in itself is a mere quality, is an actual existent, or is a general law; secondly, according as the relation of the sign to its object consists in the sign's having some character in itself, or in some existential relation to that object, or in its relation to an interpretant; thirdly, according as its Interpretant represents it as a sign of possibility or as a sign of fact or a sign of reason.

According to the first division, a Sign may be termed a *Qualisign*, a *Sinsign*, or a *Legisign*.

A *Qualisign* is a quality which is a sign. It cannot actually act as a sign until it is embodied; but the embodiment has nothing to do with its character as a sign.

A *Sinsign* (where the syllable *sin* is taken as meaning "being only once," as in *single, simple,* Latin *semel*, etc.) is an actual existent thing or event which is a sign. It can only be so through its qualities; so that it involves a qualisign, or rather, several qualisigns. . . .

A *Legisign* is a law that is a Sign. This law is usually established by men. Every conventional sign is a legisign [but not conversely]. It is not a single object, but a general type which, it has been agreed, shall be significant. Every legisign signifies through an instance of its application, which may be termed a *Replica* of it. Thus, the word "the" will usually occur from fifteen to twenty-five times on a page. It is in all these occurrences one and the same word, the same legisign. Each single instance of it is a Replica. . . .

According to the second trichotomy, a Sign may be termed an *Icon*, an *Index*, or a *Symbol*.

An *Icon* is a sign which refers to the Object that it denotes merely by virtue of characters of its own, and which it possesses, just the same, whether any such Object actually exists or not. . . . Anything whatever, be it quality, existent individual, or law, is an Icon of anything, in so far as it is like that thing and used as a sign of it.

An *Index* is a sign which refers to the Object that it denotes by virtue of being really affected by that Object. . . .

A *Symbol* is a sign which refers to the Object that it denotes by virtue of a law, usually an association of general ideas, which operates to cause the Symbol to be interpreted as referring to that Object. It is thus itself a general type or law, that is, is a Legisign. As such it acts through a Replica. . . .

According to the third trichotomy, a Sign may be termed a *Rheme*, a *Dicisign* or *Dicent Sign* (that is, a proposition or quasi-proposition), or an *Argument*.

A *Rheme* is a Sign which, for its Interpretant, is a Sign of qualitative Possibility, that is, is understood as representing such and such a kind of possible Object. . . .

A *Dicent Sign* is a Sign, which, for its Interpretant, is a Sign of actual existence. It cannot, therefore, be an Icon, which affords no ground for an interpretation of it as referring to actual existence. A Dicisign necessarily involves, as a part of it, a Rheme, to describe the fact which it is interpreted as indicating. . . .

An *Argument* is a Sign which, for its Interpretant, is a Sign of law. Or we may say that a Rheme is a sign which is understood to represent its object in its characters merely; that a Dicisign is a sign which is understood to represent its object in respect to actual existence; and that an Argument is a Sign which is understood to represent its Object in its character as Sign.[b]

In treating logic as semiotic, as a study of the properties of signs, Peirce was once again a pioneer, and it is his logical studies, rather than the metaphysical inquiries for which in Peirce's view the logical studies were only preliminary, that chiefly caught and held the attention of philosophers when, many years after his death, Peirce's writings came to be read and discussed.

Here we will discuss two of Peirce's many theses, both of which are of great importance.

LOGIC AND FALLIBILISM

We have seen that, according to Peirce's definition, logic is concerned with what *must* be the characters of signs if these signs are true. But the statements logic makes about what these characters must be are "eminently fallible."[17] Here again Peirce differed from most logicians, who have insisted that the principles of logic are absolutely certain—even though, as he pointed out, the most elementary acquaintance with the history of logic shows that logicians are anything but infallible. "This historical proof is, of course not infallible"—naturally!—"but it is very strong."[c]

In a word, what Peirce held about the other sciences—that the best we can hope to do is to approach the truth asymptotically—applies equally, in his view, to the science of logic. The only exceptions to fallibility are "the mind's own creations," and for Peirce the truths about truth conditions are emphatically *not* the mind's creations. Just as there must be a reality independent of ourselves if progress in knowledge is possible, so there must be, independently of ourselves, ways of distinguishing what is knowledge from what is not knowledge. We can never know these ways completely, but we can make progress toward a knowledge of them asymptotically. This progressive inquiry is what the science of logic is.

LOGIC AND SELF-CONTROL

In a letter to Lady Welby in 1909, Peirce wrote: "I regard Logic as the Ethics of the Intellect—that is, in the sense in which Ethics is the science of the methods of bringing Self-Control to bear to gain our Satisfactions."[d]

Let us start our explication of this sentence from the fact of habit and the

17 See p. 291.

fact that habits are constantly being modified. Some of these modifications occur as a result of environmental changes that cause a habit to be inoperable or no longer effective. Still "every man exercises more or less control over himself by means of modifying his own habits."[e] But self-control is not something that we possess in an "arbitrarily assignable" amount: like almost everything else it is learned, that is, acquired, by doing. We can measure the amount of self-control we have acquired by reflecting on "the absence (or slightness) of the feeling of self-reproach, which subsequent reflection will induce." Further, the self-reproach we experience after doing some particular act is likely to modify our behavior on the next occasion that this act is appropriate. As a result of this feedback, "there is a tendency, as action is repeated again and again, for the action to approximate indefinitely toward the perfection of that fixed character, which would be marked by entire absence of self-reproach."[f]

Ethics is the study of the methods of increasing self-control. Alternatively put, it is the science of learning to do what we really want to do—that is, what we will not regret having done. Ethics is not an absolutely certain science; like all inquiry, it is fallible. But "control may itself be controlled, criticism itself subjected to criticism; and ideally there is no obvious limit to the sequence."[g] What is possible, and what is desirable, is continuous progress toward fixed rules and self-mastery.

Now—this is the point—everything that Peirce says about ethical self-control, that is, the progressive control of conduct, applies equally to logical self-control, or the progressive control of thought. "Logical self-control is a perfect mirror of ethical self-control—unless it be rather a species under that genus."[h] That Peirce can so easily think of logical self-control as a species of ethical self-control results, of course, from his conception of thought as, in essence, experimental, and so a mode of action.

Finally, in the continuous development of self-control, both logical and ethical, we pass beyond the individual to society as a whole. The twin goals for which I seek to increase my self-control are not *my personal satisfactions,* whether with respect to belief or behavior, but "truth" and "justice"—those "great facts [which] . . . notwithstanding the iniquity of the world, [are] the mightiest of the forces that move it."[i]

Peirce and the Spirit of the Age

Thus we are brought back to the configuration of beliefs that formed the central core of Peirce's philosophy. His devotion to truth committed him to affirming the existence of an independently real world that consists not merely of particulars but of "generals"; his devotion to justice committed him to denying the self-sufficiency of the individual and to asserting the superior value of "society," conceived as "a sort of loosely compacted person, in some respects of higher rank than the person of an individual organism."[j] Coupled with these was a belief in progress—progress toward truth, progress toward justice. And as a scholastic realist he could take comfort in the fact that these ideals are not mere ideals but objectively real features of the universe.

These convictions mark Peirce off decisively from most nineteenth-century philosophers. Though he shared the positivist admiration for science, he rejected the claim to certainty which was for the positivists the chief appeal of science. If he did not, like James, relish uncertainty, he nevertheless had a high tolerance for it, and this sufficiently distinguished him from Kierkegaard and Nietzsche, both of whom (though in radically different ways) held that uncertainty had to be "overcome." Though he was a formidable critic of individualism, he did not share the Utilitarians' interest in society. The progress that was important for him was increase in knowledge, not improvement of social conditions. Yet Peirce was very much a man of the nineteenth, not of the twentieth, century. Though he criticized contemporary society as strongly as Kierkegaard and Nietzsche, he was not dispirited. He believed that the failures of science and of technology could be, and would be, gradually corrected by the application of intelligence—that is, by improved science and improved technology. Peirce died the year the First World War began. Those who have lived through the destructiveness of this century may feel that Peirce's optimism was a bit naïve—for optimistic he was. Despite all the "iniquities of the world," a good many of which he had personally experienced, Peirce believed that love—love in exactly the sense in which the New Testament asserts that "God is love"—is the animating force in the evolution of the cosmos.[k]

But even here we have not reached the most central of Peirce's beliefs. This surely was his commitment to what he called the first rule of reason. Since he thought this rule deserved to be inscribed on every wall of the city of philosophy, it is appropriate to let Peirce's description of it stand as the conclusion of this chapter.

> Upon this first, and in one sense this sole, rule of reason, that in order to learn you must desire to learn, and in so desiring not to be satisfied with what you already incline to think, there follows one corollary which itself deserves to be inscribed upon every wall of the city of philosophy:
>
> Do not block the way of inquiry.
>
> Although it is better to be methodical in our investigations, and to consider the economics of research, yet there is no positive sin against logic in *trying* any theory which may come into our heads, so long as it is adopted in such a sense as to permit the investigation to go on unimpeded and undiscouraged. On the other hand, to set up a philosophy which barricades the road of further advance toward the truth is the one unpardonable offence in reasoning.[l]

CHAPTER 8

William James

Philosophy and Temperament

James[1] was primarily a psychologist—a truly original one—and an advocate and preacher—an immensely persuasive one. He was also a philosopher. But his background in psychology and his self-chosen role in life as advocate and preacher

---

1 William James (1842–1910) was born into a well-to-do and cultivated New York family. His father was a prolific writer on ethical and religious subjects; his brother Henry was the distinguished novelist. James was educated privately, mostly abroad, and at Harvard, where he studied medicine. In 1872 he became a member of the Harvard faculty, at first teaching physiology, then shifting to psychology, and finally to philosophy. His *Principles of Psychology* (1890) was a pioneering work that greatly influenced the development of the science; his popular lectures made him the best-known philosopher of his time; his personal charm, gaiety, and kindliness won him the friendship of even his most severe critics.

greatly influenced his philosophy—not only the specific theories he developed but also, at a second level, his conception of what a philosophical theory ought to be. Most philosophers have regarded philosophy as a primarily cognitive enterprise. James disagreed. Its task, he thought, is not to inform us about the world but to help us make a successful adjustment to that world, and a successful adjustment depends less on holding beliefs that are true than on holding beliefs that suit our temperament.

If we take the whole history of philosophy, the systems reduce themselves to a few main types which, under all the technical verbiage in which the ingenious intellect of man envelops them, are just so many visions, modes of feeling the whole push, and seeing the whole drift of life, forced on one by one's total character and experience, and on the whole *preferred*—there is no other truthful word—as one's best working attitude. . . .[a]

Of course I am talking here of very positively marked men, men of radical idiosyncrasy, who have set their stamp and likeness on philosophy and figure in its history. Plato, Locke, Hegel, Spencer, are such temperamental thinkers. Most of us have, of course, no very definite intellectual temperament, we are a mixture of opposite ingredients, each one present very moderately. We hardly know our own preferences in abstract matters; some of us are easily talked out of them, and end by following the fashion or taking up with the beliefs of the most impressive philosopher in our neighborhood, whoever he may be.

Now the particular difference of temperament that I have in mind in making these remarks is one that has counted in literature, art, government, and manners as well as in philosophy. In manners we find formalists and free-and-easy persons. In government, authoritarians and anarchists. In literature, purists or academicals, and realists. In art, classics and romantics. You recognize these contrasts as familiar; well, in philosophy we have a very similar contrast.

I will write these traits down in two columns. I think you will practically recognize the two types of mental make-up that I mean if I head the columns by the titles "tender-minded" and "tough-minded" respectively.

THE TENDER-MINDED	THE TOUGH-MINDED
Rationalistic (going by "principles"),	Empiricist (going by "facts"),
Intellectualistic,	Sensationalistic,
Idealistic,	Materialistic,
Optimistic,	Pessimistic,
Religious,	Irreligious,
Free-willist,	Fatalistic,
Monistic,	Pluralistic,
Dogmatical.	Sceptical.

Each of you probably knows some well-marked example of each type, and you know what each example thinks of the example on the other side of the line. They have a low opinion of each other. Their antagonism, whenever as individuals their temperaments have been intense, has formed in all ages a part of the philosophic atmosphere of the time. It forms a part of the philosophic atmosphere to-day. The tough think of the tender as senti-mentalists and soft-heads. The tender feel the tough to be unrefined, callous, or brutal. Their mutual reaction is very much like that that takes place when Bostonian tourists mingle with a population like that of Cripple Creek. . . . [But] few of us are tender-foot Bostonians pure and simple, and few are typical Rocky Mountain toughs, in philosophy. Most of us have a hankering for the good things on both sides of the line.[b]

It follows that philosophy, as orthodox philosophers conceive and practice it, is doubly a failure. In the first place, far from providing an understanding of the deep nature of things that it claims to do, it merely reflects the temperament of its practitioners. In the second place, it does not help us make the adjustment that is its real business to provide. Since the orthodox philosophers have all been men whose temperament is "very positively marked," their theories have all been skewed in one direction or the other. Such polar visions can never satisfy the average man, whose temperament is "a mixture of opposite ingredients, each one present only moderately." Yet, unfortunately, these men of the mixed type of temperament (that is, the vast majority) are easily swayed and therefore end up "by following fashion or by taking up the belief of the most impressive philosopher" in their neighborhood. The result is unhappiness—they come to accept a philosophy that is out of harmony with their own "dumb sense" of the world.

Never were as many men of a decidedly empiricist proclivity in existence as there are at the present day. Our children, one may say, are almost born scientific. But our esteem for facts has not neutralized in us all religiousness. It is itself almost religious. Our scientific temper is devout. Now take a man of this type, and let him be also a philosophic amateur, unwilling to mix a hodge-podge system after the fashion of a common layman, and what does he find his situation to be, in this blessed year of our Lord 1906? He wants facts; he wants science; but he also wants a religion. And being an amateur and not an independent originator in philosophy he naturally looks for guidance to the experts and professionals whom he finds already in the field. A very large number of you here present, possibly a majority of you, are amateurs of just this sort.

Now what kinds of philosophy do you find actually offered to meet your need? You find an empirical philosophy that is not religious enough, and a religious philosophy that is not empirical enough for your purpose.[c]

What is needed, and what James proposed to supply, is a philosophy that will show "scientifically oriented circles" that they are entitled to satisfy the religious and moral side of their natures, show them, for instance, that belief in immortality, which is "one of the greatest spiritual needs of man," is not incompatible with acceptance of the findings of physiological psychology; show them that belief in freedom of the will, on which the moral life depends, is not incompatible with acceptance of scientific claims to predict human behavior; show them that belief in the existence of God is not incompatible with the findings of science.

"Pure" Experience

All philosophical theory must start from human experience; that is agreed. But both the rationalist-idealists and the traditional empiricists, being alike men of polar temperaments, have given us descriptions badly biased by the need for security, for absolutes, for "truth," and for certainty that most of them felt. Let us then start from a pure—that is, an unbiased—description of experience. On this basis it will be possible to develop a theory of the self, of knowledge, and of God that will satisfy men of moderate temperament. This is the program laid out in *Essays in Radical Empiricism,* and it shows James to have been one of the first philosophers to adopt what subsequently came to be called the "phenomenological" approach, that is, an approach that seeks to start from, and confine itself to, a presuppositionless description of experience as it comes.

> I give the name of "radical empiricism" to my Weltanschauung. . . . To be radical, an empiricism must neither admit into its constructions any element that is not directly experienced, nor exclude from them any element that is directly experienced. For such a philosophy, *the relations that connect experiences must themselves be experienced relations, and any kind of relation experienced must be accounted as "real" as anything else in the system.* . . .
>
> Now, ordinary empiricism, in spite of the fact that conjunctive and disjunctive relations present themselves as being fully coordinate parts of experience, has always shown a tendency to do away with the connections of things, and to insist most on the disjunctions. Berkeley's nominalism, Hume's statement that whatever things we distinguish are as "loose and separate" as if they had "no manner of connection" . . . and the general pulverization of all Experience by association and the mind-dust theory, are examples of what I mean.
>
> The natural result of such a world picture has been the efforts of rationalism to correct its incoherencies by the addition of transexperiential agents of unification, substances, intellectual categories and powers, or Selves; whereas, if empiricism had only been radical and taken everything that comes without disfavor, conjunction as well as separation, each at its face value, the results would have called for no such artificial correction. *Radical empiricism,* as I understand it, *does full justice to conjunctive relations,* without, however, treating them as rationalism always tends to treat them, as being true in some supernal way, as if the unity of things and their variety belonged to different orders of truth and vitality altogether. . . .

Personal histories are processes of change in time, and *the change itself is one of the things immediately experienced.* "Change" in this case means continuous as opposed to discontinuous transition. But continuous transition is one sort of a conjunctive relation; and to be a radical empiricist means to hold fast to this conjunctive relation of all others, for this is the strategic point, the position through which, if a hole be made, all the corruptions of dialectics and all the metaphysical fictions pour into our philosophy. The holding fast to this relation means taking it at its face value, neither less nor more; and to take it at its face value means first of all to take it just as we feel it, and not to confuse ourselves with abstract talk *about* it, involving words that drive us to invent secondary conceptions in order to neutralize their suggestions and to make our actual experience again seem rationally possible.

What I do feel simply when a later moment of my experience succeeds an earlier one is that though they are two moments, the transition from the one to the other is *continuous.* Continuity here is a definite sort of experience; just as definite as is the *discontinuity-experience*, which I find it impossible to avoid when I seek to make the transition from an experience of my own to one of yours. . . .

There is no other *nature*, no other whatness than this absence of break and this sense of continuity in that most intimate of all conjunctive relations, the passing of one experience into another when they belong to the same self. And this whatness is real empirical "content," just as the whatness of separation and discontinuity is real content in the contrasted case. Practically to experience one's personal continuum in this living way is to know the originals of the ideas of continuity and of sameness, to know what the words stand for concretely, to know all that they can ever mean. But all experiences have their conditions; and oversubtle intellects, thinking about the facts here, and asking how they are possible, have ended by substituting a lot of static objects of conception for the direct perceptual experiences.[d]

THE CONTENTS OF EXPERIENCE

So far, so good. Experience does indeed seem more like a continuous stream than like a series of billiard balls. But this is only the starting point, and the real test of James's phenomenological approach is what sort of philosophy he constructed on this base. However, before turning to his theory of knowledge, his view of freedom, and his philosophy of religion, it is necessary to point out some ambiguities in his account of pure experience. First, what are the contents of pure experience? Sometimes, perhaps usually, James's answer is that the contents of the stream are the "objects" of the ordinary, everyday, common-sense world. His essays and lectures are full of examples: the pen with which he was writing, the chair across the room, the sheet of paper from which he was reading, Memorial Hall in Cambridge, Massachusetts. But part of the time he saw that this reply would not do. Common sense, as he said, is only one "stage in the mind's development."[e] It is very ancient and venerable; its categories (for example, "thing," "mind," "body," "the real," "the fancied") obviously have considerable utility. This, indeed, is why they have survived to this day. But

> . . . in spite of their being so venerable, of their being so universally used and built into the very structure of language, [these] categories may after all be only a collection of extraordinarily successful hypotheses (historically discovered or invented by single men, but gradually communicated, and used by everybody) by which our forefathers have from time immemorial unified and straightened the discontinuity of their immediate experiences, and put themselves into an equilibrium with the surface of nature so satisfactory for ordinary practical purposes that it certainly would have lasted forever, but for the excessive intellectual vivacity of Democritus, Archimedes, Galileo, Berkeley, and of other eccentric geniuses whom the example of such men inflamed. Retain, I pray you, this suspicion about common sense.[f]

This answer was reenforced by what we may call James's genetic bias. Hence he tended to look for examples of pure experience in the earliest experience of the infant.

> "Pure experience" is the name which I gave to the immediate flux of life which furnishes the material to our later reflection with its conceptual categories. Only newborn babes, or men in semicoma from sleep, drugs, illnesses, or blows, may be assumed to have an experience pure in the literal sense of a *that* which is not yet any definite *what*, although ready to be all sorts of whats; full both of oneness and of manyness, but in respects that don't appear; changing throughout, yet so confusedly that its phases interpenetrate and no points, either of distinction or of identity, can be caught. Pure experience in this state is but another name for feeling or sensation. But the flux of it no sooner comes than it tends to fill itself with emphases, and these salient parts become identified and fixed and abstracted; so that experience now flows as if shot through with adjectives and nouns and prepositions and conjunctions. Its purity is only a relative term, meaning the proportional amount of unverbalized sensation which it still embodies.[g]

From this point of view, the "purity" of pure experience does not consist in its freedom from the presuppositions of orthodox philosophers; it consists in its freedom from any learning whatever. Concepts are now constructs—"labor-saving devices," "instrumentalities," "explanatory devices" are some of the terms he uses to characterize them. Accordingly, experience itself, "the flow of feeling or sensation," is "a quasi-chaos," and is to be contrasted with our stable, organized "verbal pictures" of it; the latter "never take us off the superficial plane."[h] It would seem to follow that feeling and sensation—the ultimate reality—can only be felt, not accurately described. To describe is to name, and to name is to distort.

> When we talk of reality "independent" of human thinking, then, it seems a thing very hard to find. . . . We may glimpse it, but we never grasp it;

what we grasp is always some substitute for it which previous human thinking has peptonized and cooked for our consumption. If so vulgar an expression were allowed us, we might say that wherever we find it, it has been already *faked*.[i]

Clearly, James has moved a long way from the simple, common-sensical view of the contents of experience from which he started. Far from the pen with which he is writing or the sheet of paper from which he is reading being real, "pen" and "paper" are merely convenient "constructs," "verbal images"—in fact, "fakes." His position is now hardly distinguishable from Schopenhauer's. But Schopenhauer's (and later, Bergson's) attack on conceptual knowledge was a preliminary move in a plan to exalt intuition as the mode of access to a truer and deeper reality. James's temperament was such that he had even less use for intuition than for concepts, since concepts were, and intuitions were not, effective instruments for dealing with the practical problems that interested him.

Hence, if James occasionally slipped into a nominalism as extreme as that of the intuitionists, he also slipped—perhaps in overreaction—into a curious kind of realism. Starting from the proposition that "anything is real of which we find ourselves obliged to take account in any way," he found it easy to conclude that "concepts are thus as real as percepts, for we cannot live a moment without taking account of them."[j] Moreover, concepts, it now occurred to him, are as much elements in the stream of experience as are feeling and sensation. Concepts form "a co-ordinate realm of reality,"[k] along with percepts. But "a concept means always the same thing. Change means always change, white always white, a circle always a circle."[l] Hence (at least James's reasoning runs) there must be an "'eternal' kind of being" involved in, contained within, the flow of pure experience. "What I am affirming here is the platonic doctrine that concepts are singulars, that concept-stuff is inalterable, and that physical realities are constituted by the various concept-stuffs of which they 'partake.'"[m]

JAMES AND KANT

All the shifts that we have been describing were oscillations, as it were, around a central tendency, and this central tendency (as James himself on occasion saw) falls within the Kantian framework: "Superficially this sounds like Kant's view; but between categories fulminated before nature began, and categories gradually forming themselves in nature's presence, the whole chasm between rationalism and empiricism yawns."[n]

What James meant was that he had retained Kant's basic notion of experience as the construction of a stable world out of a sensuous manifold. But he abandoned the notions of the synthetical a priori and the transcendental unity of apperception, and Kant might well have exclaimed that, these deletions made, not much was left of Kantianism. This comment brings into focus the profound difference in temperament between Kant and James. Experience, in James's view, does not have and does not need, a universal or necessary structure. It is a natural growth through time. Whatever structure it has at any particular time is just the structure that it happens to have at that time, the result of a process in which the relatively more viable concepts and theories have survived and the less viable ones have dropped out. And a "viable" theory or concept is not one that has special ontological properties; it is simply one that allows us to cope with the future as it streams toward us in the flow of experience; it is one that tends, "in a general way at least, to banish uncertainty from the future."

The operative words here are "in a general way at least." Since Kant had wanted to banish uncertainty—at least in principle, if not in detail—it had seemed to him essential to demonstrate that an a priori science of nature is possible. Hence the centrality in his theory of the transcendental deduction of the categories. James could eliminate the deduction, and with it the synthetical a priori, because, unlike Kant, he was willing—nay, really eager—to live in an uncertain world. For the same reason he did not feel the need for a transcendental unity of apperception. The unity actually found in experience was enough for him—the unity, that is, that experience has because it is a stream, not a series of discrete elements.

As for Kant's doctrine of the phenomenal object, this did not even so much as enter into James's consideration, since, as we have seen, he never really settled on whether pure experience consists in the common-sense world of pens and sheets of paper or only in the flow of "sensation and feeling."

In reply to the challenge that this was something he *ought* to have settled on, James would probably have retorted that these are merely "fine distinctions" elaborated by "oversubtle intellects."

Since the purpose of his description of pure experience was to provide the basis for a philosophy that would satisfy the "spiritual needs" of men of "moderate" temperament—needs that were thwarted both by transcendental idealism and by Humian-positivist empiricism—the confusions that philosophers detected in his description were of little consequence to James. He was interested in the traditional problems of metaphysics and epistemology only so far as the answers philosophers have given to these problems affect our moral and religious beliefs.

Does Consciousness Exist?

One theoretical problem that, as James held, does affect men's moral and religious beliefs is the mind-body problem, an inheritance from Descartes. Descartes assumed that there are two fundamentally different kinds of substance: mind and matter. Matter is extended and its behavior is fully predictable. Mind is unextended and free. This corresponds to the common-sensical distinction between the things I experience and the I who experiences them. But in the body of every man these two substances seem to interact. When my body has a fever, my mind is sluggish; I may hallucinate. When I will to raise my arm, my arm rises. How can this be? How can two such different kinds of substance act causally on one another? How can what is unextended (my mind) cause changes in what is extended (my body)? How can what is extended cause changes in what is unextended?

Descartes himself was unable to answer these questions to anyone's satisfaction save his own, and subsequent generations of philosophers tackled them in vain. The whole history of philosophy from Descartes down to James's day had been, in effect, a series of efforts to overcome the dualism with which Cartesianism had infected philosophy. If James, starting from his doctrine of pure experience, could solve the mind-body problem, he would make a major contribution to philosophical theory, quite apart from the possible effect this solution might have on men's spiritual needs.

The key to solving the problem, James thought, is consciousness. Dualism seems plausible—indeed, inevitable—only if minds are conscious and bodies are not; it seems to follow that minds and bodies are fundamentally different kinds of things.

> We are supposed by almost every one to have an immediate consciousness of consciousness itself. When the world of outer fact ceases to be materially present, and we merely recall it in memory, or fancy it, the consciousness is believed to stand out and to be felt as a kind of impalpable inner flowing, which, once known in this sort of experience, may equally be detected in presentations of the outer world.°

But is consciousness the distinct, if impalpable, sort of thing that common sense and the traditional philosophy alike have taken it to be? James held that if we look at experience in its purity, that is, without the distortions introduced by metaphysical presuppositions, we do not find any such distinct entity at all. Once the myth of a distinct entity is exposed, dualism and the seemingly irreconcilable opposition between mind and matter disappear.

> To deny plumply that "consciousness" exists seems so absurd on the face of it—for undeniably "thoughts" do exist—that I fear some readers will follow me no farther. Let me then immediately explain that I mean only to deny that the word stands for an entity, but to insist most emphatically that it does stand for a function. There is, I mean, no aboriginal stuff or quality of being, contrasted with that of which material objects are made, out of which our thoughts of them are made; but there is a function in experience which thoughts perform, and for the performance of which this quality of being is invoked. That function is *knowing*. "Consciousness" is supposed necessary to explain the fact that things not only are, but get reported, are known. Whoever blots out the notion of consciousness from his list of first principles must still provide in some way for that function's being carried on.
>
> My thesis is that if we start with the supposition that there is only one

primal stuff or material in the world, a stuff of which everything is composed, and if we call that stuff "pure experience," then knowing can easily be explained as a particular sort of relation toward one another into which portions of pure experience may enter. The relation itself is a part of pure experience. . . .

If the reader will take his own experiences, he will see what I mean. Let him begin with a perceptual experience, the "presentation," so called, of a physical object, his actual field of vision, the room he sits in, with the book he is reading as its center; and let him for the present treat this complex object in the commonsense way as being "really" what it seems to be, namely, a collection of physical things cut out from an environing world of other physical things with which these physical things have actual or potential relations. Now at the same time it is just *those selfsame things* which his mind, as we say, perceives; and the whole philosophy of perception from Democritus' time downward has been just one long wrangle over the paradox that what is evidently one reality should be in two places at once, both in outer space and in a person's mind. . . .

The puzzle of how the one identical room can be in two places is at bottom just the puzzle of how one identical point can be on two lines. It can, if it be situated at their intersection; and similarly, if the "pure experience" of the room were a place of intersection of two processes, which connected it with different groups of associates respectively, it could be counted twice over, as belonging to either group, and spoken of loosely as existing in two places, although it would remain all the time a numerically single thing.

Well, the experience is a member of diverse processes that can be followed away from it along entirely different lines. The one self-identical thing has so many relations to the rest of experience that you can take it in disparate systems of association, and treat is as belonging with opposite contexts. In one of these contexts it is your "field of consciousness"; in another it is "the room in which you sit," and it enters both contexts in its wholeness, giving no pretext for being said to attach itself to consciousness by one of its parts or aspects, and to outer reality by another. What are the two processes, now, into which the room-experience simultaneously enters in this way?

One of them is the reader's personal biography, the other is the history of the house of which the room is part.

The room thought-of, namely, has many thought-of couplings with many thought-of things. Some of these couplings are inconstant, others are stable. In the reader's personal history the room occupies a single date—he saw it only once perhaps, a year ago. Of the house's history, on the other hand, it forms a permanent ingredient. . . . Grouped with the rest of its house, with the name of its town, of its owner, builder, value, decorative plan, the room maintains a definite foothold, to which, if we try to loosen it, it tends to return, and to reassert itself with force. With these associates, in a word, it coheres, while to other houses, other towns, other owners, etc., it shows no tendency to cohere at all. The two collections, first of its cohesive, and, second, of its loose associates, inevitably come to be contrasted. We call the first collection the system of external realities, in the midst of which the room, as "real," exists; the other we call the stream of our internal thinking, in which, as a "mental image," it for a moment floats. The room thus again gets counted twice over. It plays two different roles. . . .

As "subjective" we say that the experience represents; as "objective" it is represented. What represents and what is represented is here numerically the same; but we must remember that no dualism of being represented and representing resides in the experience per se. In its pure state, or when isolated, there is no self-splitting of it into consciousness and what the consciousness is "of." Its subjectivity and objectivity are functional attributes solely, realized only when the experience is "taken," i.e., talked-of, twice, considered along with its two differing contexts respectively, by a new retrospective experience, of which that whole past complication now forms the fresh content.[p]

One more step was necessary to round out James's case. Since, as he knew, many philosophers were persuaded that in introspection they could fix their attention on an impalpable but quite distinct element to which they gave the name "consciousness," James saw that he must show, not that they are conscious of nothing at all when they think they are conscious of consciousness—that would never convince them—but that they are experiencing something else, which they have misnamed "consciousness." Very well, what is it that they have carelessly mistaken to be a consciousness of consciousness? James's answer is that, if they look carefully, they will see that they have been obscurely aware of breathing.

The stream of thinking (which I recognize emphatically as a phenomenon) is only a careless name for what, when scrutinized, reveals itself to consist chiefly of the stream of my breathing. The "I think" which Kant said must be able to accompany all my objects, is the "I breathe" which actually does accompany them. There are other internal facts besides breathing (intra-cephalic muscular adjustments, etc. . . .), and these increase the assets of "consciousness," so far as the latter is subject to immediate perception; but breath, which was ever the original of "spirit," breath moving outward, between the glottis and the nostrils, is, I am persuaded, the essence out of which philosophers have constructed the entity known to them as consciousness.[q]

The Nature of Knowledge

As James said, most philosophers took consciousness for granted not only because they thought they were aware of it but because they regarded consciousness as necessary to account for knowledge, and in eliminating consciousness, James of course did not want also to eliminate knowledge. Although he optimistically thought that "knowing can easily be explained as a particular sort of relation toward one another into which portions of pure experience may enter,"[r] it is doubtful whether, given the frame of reference in which he was operating, he could give a plausible account of the nature of knowledge.[2]

Let us spell this out in detail. We have seen how the stream of pure experience gets differentiated functionally into two different contexts, a self context and an object context. Further, as James pointed out, some (not all) of those "pieces of experience" that have entered into the self context "know" other pieces of experience that are not part of this self but parts of what has become differentiated into the object context. Here I sit (to use one of James's own examples) and think about Memorial Hall at Harvard University. Memorial Hall is not directly present in my experience now, for I am not looking at Memorial Hall and I am not even in Cambridge. Let us say that what is in my experience now is perhaps some visual memory of what Memorial Hall looks like, or perhaps the words (written or spoken) "Memorial Hall," and that this "piece of experience" *represents* Memorial Hall for me. Alternatively it is a token of Memorial Hall, or a sign of Memorial Hall; alternatively, again, it refers to Memorial Hall, it means Memorial Hall.

James's first problem was to give an account of meaning (alternatively, an account of referring, representing, or being a sign). And, since continuity and succession are the only relations that, according to his description, characterize pure experience, he must account for meaning in terms of these two relations.

> The key to this difficulty lies in the distinction between knowing as verified and completed, and the same knowing as in transit and on its way. To recur to the Memorial Hall example lately used, it is only when our idea of the Hall has actually terminated in the percept that we know "for certain" that from the beginning it was truly cognitive of *that*. Until established by the end of the process, its quality of knowing that, or indeed of knowing anything, could still be doubted; and yet the knowing really was there, as the result now shows. We were *virtual* knowers of the Hall long before we were certified to have been its actual knowers, by the percept's retroactive validating power. . . .
>
> Now the immensely greater part of all our knowing never gets beyond this virtual stage. It never is completed or nailed down. . . . We live, as it were, upon the front edge of an advancing wave crest, and our sense of a determinate direction in falling forward is all we cover of the future of our path. It is as if a differential quotient should be conscious and treat itself as an adequate substitute for a traced-out curve. Our experience, *inter alia*, is of variations of rate and of direction, and lives in these transitions more than in the journey's end. The experiences of tendency are sufficient to act upon—what more could we have *done* at those moments even if the later verification comes complete?[s]

But it is not a question of the difference between "knowledge in transit" and "knowledge completed." It is a question of what is involved in there being

2 See pp. 302–03.

knowledge at all, whether incomplete or completed. Let us grant for the sake of argument that one "piece of experience" (for example, the image of Memorial Hall) comes to be taken as the sign of another piece of experience only if the one leads frequently, smoothly, and continuously into the other. But there are many pieces of experiences that lead frequently, smoothly, and continuously into others that are nevertheless not taken as signs of those others. For instance, since stepping through the door of Memorial Hall usually leads to seeing the interior, we come to expect (as Hume had pointed out) that when we step through the door, we shall see the interior, and expectations are certainly parts of the flow of experience. But expectations and meanings are not identical. For instance, though we expect the interior when we step through the door, stepping through the door does not mean the interior. Stepping through the door may, on occasion, mean something, but normally it does not mean *that*.

It is true that, in one of the possible sorts of sign relations (for example, when we say that black clouds are a sign of rain), the occurrence of the sign leads us to expect the signification. But this is not always the case: The occurrence of the sign "Memorial Hall" on this page does not lead a normal reader to expect Memorial Hall to appear before him. In a word, since some sign relations do not involve expectations and since some expectations do not involve the sign relationship, the notion of meaning cannot be reduced to a feeling of expectation.

There are two ways in which James could have tackled this problem. The first would have been to undertake a new description of the experience of meaning—one in which expectation is no longer the central feature. This would have been a natural course for James, with his psychological orientation, if only he had realized that, as we have just pointed out, meaning and expectation are not identical. He would then have been led to look for some other feature in virtue of which any experience, including the experience of expectation, is a sign. Could he have found it? Well, there was a group of psychologists-turned-philosophers who, as it happened, were contemporaries of James and who believed that they had discovered this feature. They called it "intentionality" or "directionality." To be conscious, they maintained, is to be conscious *of*. From the point of view of this group, James was correct in holding that consciousness is not a datum but mistaken in concluding that because it is not a datum consciousness does not exist. They saw James's failure as one of observation. Because he was looking for a datum, and not for a direction, he missed the whole essence of consciousness, and having missed it, he could not possibly give an adequate account of meaning.

The second course James might have adopted would have been to shift from psychological description to epistemological analysis. It is one thing to describe the difference between how it feels to be in a meaningful situation (for example, how it feels to be taking "Memorial Hall" to refer to Memorial Hall) and how it feels to be expecting to see Memorial Hall when one turns the next corner; it is another thing to analyze what the sign-signification relation entails. We should not criticize James for limiting himself to description if that was all that he claimed to be doing. But he also set out to "explain knowing," and he thought he had succeeded in doing so. Yet this proposed explanation turns out to be only more description. Thus he wrote, "To be 'conscious' is not simply to be, but to be reported, known, to have awareness of one's being added to that being, . . ." which calls attention to the sign relationship. But then the sentence continues, "and this is just what happens when the appropriative experience intervenes." This phrase, "the appropriative experience," is just another way of describing how it feels to mean something. It throws no light at all on what is involved in something being a sign of something else.

It is not that James was too muddled to see the distinction between being "a particular sort of relation into which portions of pure experience may enter" and being a sign. Rather, the distinction was too remote from what chiefly interested him for him to attend to it. Apparently he satisfied his own "spiritual needs" without entangling himself in the kinds of problem and difficulty we have just been raising, and he thought (probably rightly) that he could satisfy the spiritual needs of his popular audiences without entangling them. This being the case, we shall now leave these epistemological questions unresolved and turn to the great practical issues with which James was personally concerned and with which he believed his audiences were concerned.

The Moral Life

The first of the great practical issues is "How do we lead the good life?" Life consists of innumerable points at which we must make a choice, and, James held, we are free to choose what we shall do. James was concerned that at each of these points we really do choose, that is, we decide what to do. This means, on the one hand, not acting merely capriciously or casually, and on the other, not evading the problem of choice by putting our trust in any so-called moral law handed down by some allegedly superior authority. Ethics, for James, was a serious and personal matter, and he thought that others should take the problem of choice as seriously and as personally as he did. Ethics was to James, not so much a theory of the good or a theory of obligation, as an appeal to people to become concerned about choice and about the whole moral tone of their lives.

THE GOOD

To lead the good life we must know what the good is. In James's view this was not a metaphysical question but an empirical and psychological question, involving what people actually aim at. Happily, the answer is obvious: The good is, generally speaking, whatever satisfies a demand.

Various essences of good have thus been . . . proposed as bases of the ethical system. Thus, to be a mean between two extremes; to be recognized by a special intuitive faculty; to make the agent happy for the moment; to make others as well as him happy in the long run; to add to his perfection or dignity; to harm no one; to follow from reason or flow from universal law; to be in accordance with the will of God; to promote the survival of the human species on this planet,—are so many tests, each of which has been maintained by somebody to constitute the essence of all good things or actions so far as they are good.

No one of the measures that have been actually proposed has, however, given general satisfaction. Some are obviously not universally present in all cases,—e.g., the character of harming no one, or that of following a universal law; for the best course is often cruel; and many acts are reckoned good on the sole condition that they be exceptions, and serve not as examples of a universal law. Other characters, such as following the will of God, are unascertainable and vague. Others again, like survival, are quite indeterminate in their consequences, and leave us in the lurch where we most need their help: a philosopher of the Sioux Nation, for example, will be certain to use the survival-criterion in a very different way from ourselves. The best, on the whole, of these marks and measures of goodness seems to be the capacity to bring happiness. But in order not to break down fatally, this test must be taken to cover innumerable acts and impulses that never *aim* at happiness; so that, after all, in seeking for a universal principle we inevitably are carried onward to the *most* universal principle,—that *the essence of good is simply to satisfy demand.* The demand may be for anything under the sun. There is really no more ground for supposing that all our demands can be accounted for by one universal underlying kind of motive than there is ground for supposing that all physical phenomena are cases of a single law.[t]

Every satisfied demand is so far good, but the world being what it is, the satisfaction of one demand usually involves the frustration of others.

There is hardly a good which we can imagine except as competing for the possession of the same bit of space and time with some other imagined good. Every end of desire that presents itself appears exclusive of some other end of desire. Shall a man drink and smoke, *or* keep his nerves in condition?—he cannot do both. Shall he follow his fancy for Amelia, *or* for Henrietta?—both cannot be the choice of his heart. Shall he have the dear old Republican party, *or* a spirit of unsophistication in public affairs?—he cannot have both, etc. So that the ethical philosopher's demand for the right scale of subordination in ideals is the fruit of an altogether practical need. Some part of the ideal must be butchered, and he needs to know which part. It is a tragic situation, and no mere speculative conundrum, with which he has to deal.[u]

This leads to the notion of "obligation." In this sort of situation one ought to act so as to maximize satisfactions and minimize dissatisfactions. The maximization problem would be sufficiently complicated if there were but one person on earth—he would have to weigh against each other the "imperativeness" of the many demands he from time to time experienced. But since there are millions upon millions of men with as many demands as my own, my obligation is not merely to maximize my own private satisfaction but, to the best of my abilities, to act so as to maximize the total amount of satisfaction in the world.

There are no moral *laws*. There are only moral guidelines and all of these are provisional, corrigible, and subject to revision in the light of experience. The experimental method is as applicable in ethics as it is in natural science. Just as our research methods in physics or biology or medicine are constantly being refined by reflection on the effectiveness of whatever methodological procedures we are using at any given time, so in morals, reflection on the outcome of the decisions we make results in a gradual improvement of our decision-making techniques.

It follows that the worst possible belief a man can have is a belief in moral absolutes, for such a belief encourages unthinking inflexibility rather than the flexibility that is essential, given the fact that real life is complex and always changing. "No philosophy of ethics is possible in the old-fashioned absolute sense of the term. . . . There can be no final truth in ethics any more than in physics until the last man has had his experience and said his say."[v]

Nevertheless, James thought that it is possible to make a few generalizations about the moral life. First, we never start with a clean slate. We are born into an ongoing society where certain procedures for distributing satisfactions and dissatisfactions already exist as a result of an enormous number of decisions made in the past. It would be foolish not to accept this framework and work within it for its improvements. "The presumption in cases of conflict must always be in favor of the conventionally recognized good. The philosopher must be a conservative, and in the construction of his casuistic scale must put the things most in accordance with the customs of the community on top."[w]

Nevertheless we cannot rule out on a priori grounds (James, of course, held that nothing can ever be ruled out on a priori grounds) the possibility that some revolutionary genius may, if he is willing to run the risks, achieve a better distribution of satisfactions and dissatisfactions.

> Although a man always risks much when he breaks away from established rules and strives to realize a larger ideal whole than they permit, yet the philosopher must allow that it is at all times open to any one to make the experiment, provided he fear not to stake his life and character upon the throw. . . . See the abuses which the institution of private property covers, so that even to-day it is shamelessly asserted among us that one of the prime functions of the national government is to help the adroiter citizens to grow rich. See the unnamed and unnamable sorrows which the tyranny, on the whole so beneficent, of the marriage-institution brings to so many, both of the married and the unwed. . . .
>
> The anarchists, nihilists, and free-lovers; the free-silverites, socialists, and

single-tax men; the free-traders and civil-service reformers; the prohibitionists and anti-vivisectionists; the radical darwinians with their idea of the suppression of the weak,—these and all the conservative sentiments of society arrayed against them, are simply deciding through actual experiment by what sort of conduct the maximum amount of good can be gained and kept in this world.[x]

Second, despite persisting abuses, there has been immense progress in the distribution of satisfactions and dissatisfactions.

The course of history is nothing but the story of men's struggles from generation to generation to find the more and more inclusive order. . . . Polyandry and polygamy and slavery, private warfare and liberty to kill, judicial torture and arbitrary royal power have slowly succumbed to actually aroused complaints; and though some one's ideals are unquestionably the worse off for each improvement, yet a vastly greater total number of them find shelter in our civilized society than in the older savage ways.[y]

Third, given the world as it is, a plurality of decision-makers, each aiming at the maximization of satisfactions for all, is preferable to a single decision-maker aiming at a similar maximization.

All one's slumbering revolutionary instincts waken at the thought of any single moralist wielding such powers of life and death. Better chaos forever than an order based on any closet-philosopher's rule, even though he were the most enlightened possible member of his tribe.[z]

These passages reveal James's own temperament: his optimism, his openness to differences of opinion, his devotion to democracy. They also show that his ethical theory (if indeed we want to call his reflections a "theory") is a version of altruistic utilitarianism. Like Mill, he held (1) that the only ground for claiming that anything is desirable is the fact that it is desired, and (2) that it is desirable to maximize the common good.[3]

The only possible reason there can be why any phenomenon ought to exist is that such a phenomenon actually is desired. Any desire is imperative to the extent of its amount; it *makes* itself valid by the fact that it exists at all. Some desires, truly enough, are small desires; they are put forward by insignificant persons, and we customarily make light of the obligations which they bring.[a]

Now consider a dispute between James and some egoistic Utilitarian. As against the latter, James maintains that "there is but one unconditional commandment, which is that we should seek incessantly, with fear and trembling, so to vote and to act as to bring about the very largest total universe of good

3 See pp. 166–73.

which we can see."[b] Not at all, the egoist replies; since I desire only my own good, it follows, on your own grounds, that it is my duty to maximize my own happiness, not the general good. James could only retort that the egoist is an "insignificant person" with "small" desires, which seems less an argument than a bit of name-calling. So much for James's proof that altruistic utilitarianism is the "one unconditional commandment."

Again, James deeply believed that the "strenuous mood," in which one struggles to maximize satisfactions (whether one's own or everybody's is irrelevant here) is better than the "easy-going mood," in which one sits back and lets things take their course. But how could he prove that the strenuous mood is morally better than the quietism of the Stoics and the Epicureans, who chose to reduce their demands rather than to struggle to maximize their satisfactions? Were they not, in their way and from their point of view, maximizing their one "urgent and tyrannical demand," the demand to be easy rather than to be strenuous?

But when James declared that the "strenuous mood" is natural, that "the strenuous type of character will on the battle-field of human history always outwear the easy-going type,"[c] he was not so much adducing arguments to support a particular moral theory as he was advocating a particular kind of life, the strenuous one. His use of the language of theory was a part of the rhetoric of his appeal: telling us that the strenuous life will win out is a way of winning us over to a strenuous life. And this—again from James's point of view—is eminently fair. Since there are no moral certainties, no moral absolutes, each of us is entitled both to believe what he wants to believe and to try to induce others to accept our beliefs, especially since we are convinced that these beliefs will be best for others in the long run.

INDETERMINACY

James did not have much use for the term "free will." He rightly thought that it had been contaminated by arguments about grace and predestination—theological considerations that did not interest him. What did interest him was possibility, chance, change, and serendipity. To him "change is an essential ingredient" in the world. "There is history. There are novelties, struggles, losses, gains." What he meant by freedom, then, was simply that "some things at least are decided here and now, that the passing moment may contain some novelty, be an original starting-point of events, and not merely a push from elsewhere."[d]

Underlying everything James had to say on this subject was his conviction that most people—of moderate temperament, that is—have a deeply rooted "spiritual need" to believe that what they do makes, or may make, a difference. But this need is blocked by the "dogma" of determinism, according to which "whatever is is necessary and . . . aught else is impossible," and which they tend to accept because of the prestige of science. Accordingly, James's case for indeterminacy can be divided into two stages: the first consists in arguing that since neither determinacy nor indeterminacy can be conclusively proved, we are "entitled" to believe in either; the second consists of an appeal to choose to believe in indeterminacy on the grounds that this belief satisfies a deeply felt human need.

> I disclaim openly on the threshold all pretension to prove to you that freedom of the will is true. The most I hope is to induce some of you to follow my own example in assuming it true, and acting as if it were true. . . .
> All the magnificent achievements of mathematical and physical science— our doctrines of evolution, of uniformity to law, and the rest—proceed from our indomitable desire to cast the world into a more rational shape in our minds than the shape into which it is thrown there by the crude order of our experience. . . . I, for one, feel as free to try conceptions of moral as of mechanical or of logical rationality. If a certain formula for expressing the nature of the world violates my moral demand, I shall feel as free to throw it overboard, or at least to doubt it, as if it disappointed my demand for uniformity of sequence, for example; the one demand being, so far as I can see, quite as subjective and emotional as the other is. The principle of causality, for example—what is it but a postulate, an empty name covering simply a demand that the sequence of events shall some day manifest a deeper kind of belonging of one thing with another than the mere arbitrary juxtaposition which now phenomenally appears? It is as much an altar to an unknown god as the one that Saint Paul found at Athens. All our scientific and philosophic ideals are altars to unknown gods. Uniformity is as much so as is free will.[e]

Since "evidence of an external kind to decide between determinism and indeterminism is impossible to find," we must decide between them on practical, or moral, grounds. As soon as we see what each professes, it will be clear that indeterminacy is preferable (and so, "more rational").

> What does determinism profess? It professes that those parts of the universe already laid down absolutely appoint and decree what the other parts shall be. . . . Indeterminism, on the contrary, says that the parts have a certain amount of loose play on one another, so that the laying down of one of them does not necessarily determine what the others shall be. It admits that possibilities may be in excess of actualities, and that things not yet revealed to our knowledge may really in themselves be ambiguous.[f]

This is why indeterminism is the preferable philosophy.

> What interest, zest, or excitement can there be in achieving the right way, unless we are enabled to feel that the wrong way is also a possible and a natural way,—nay, more, a menacing and an imminent way? And what sense can there be in condemning ourselves for taking the wrong way, unless we need have done nothing of the sort, unless the right way was open to us as well? . . .

The indeterminism I defend, the free-will theory of popular sense based on the judgment of regret, represents the world as vulnerable and liable to be injured by certain of its parts if they act wrong. And it represents their acting wrong as a matter of possibility or accident, neither inevitable nor yet to be infallibly warded off. . . .

The great point is that . . . the issue is decided nowhere else than *here* and *now*. *That* is what gives the palpitating reality to our moral life and makes it tingle . . . with so strange and elaborate an excitement. This reality, this excitement, are what determinism . . . suppress[es] by [its] denial that *anything* is decided here and now, and [its] dogma that all things were foredoomed and settled long ago.[g]

It will be seen that here again James did not try to present evidence or marshal formal arguments, as a traditional philosopher would. Since he was convinced that indeterminacy would be "forever inacceptable" to "a mind possessed of the love of unity at any cost,"[h] his case was addressed exclusively to men of the more moderate type,[4] and his strategy was simply to call their attention to aspects of their own experience (the flow of their feeling and sensation) that they might otherwise overlook but that, when attended to, might shift their beliefs from a configuration in which they experienced unease and perplexity, because some of their deepest needs were frustrated, to a configuration in which they experienced "ease, peace, and rest," because these needs were satisfied. We shall see this strategy used again in connection with religious beliefs.

Religion

In the preface to *The Varieties of Religious Experience* James remarked that his original intention had been to write two books of about equal length: "a descriptive one on 'Man's Religious Appetites,' and the second a metaphysical one on 'Their Satisfaction through Philosophy.'"[i] As it turned out, nineteen of the twenty chapters that he actually wrote were devoted to description and only one to metaphysics—a distribution that represents very fairly James's own interests. Throughout the book James constantly brought up, and as constantly postponed, the question of "the philosophical significance" of man's "religious propensities." The truth is that his primary aim was to describe religion and its "fruits" in such a way as to win a favorable judgment on these fruits from his readers. At the end, therefore, he found little to say by way of philosophical assessment—the case that he wanted to make and that he thought was persuasive had already been made in the course of his presentation of the testimony.

What, then, is James's case? Since he was a psychologist, not a sociologist or anthropologist, he concentrated on "the subjective phenomena." *The Varieties*

4 See p. 298.

is in fact a series of case studies, based on the writings of a relatively few religious geniuses, not a sampling of mass opinions and attitudes as reported in questionnaires. James believed that the essence of religion stands out more prominently in the cases of these exceptional men, precisely because they were exceptional, than in the masses of ordinary men. The first question to be dealt with is the argument that since religious geniuses have often been neurotics, their testimony is worthless.

> In the natural sciences and industrial arts it never occurs to anyone to try to refute opinions by showing up their author's neurotic constitution. Opinions here are invariably tested by logic and by experiment, no matter what may be their author's neurological type. It should be no otherwise with religious opinions. Their value can only be ascertained by spiritual judgments directly passed upon them, judgments based on our own immediate feeling primarily; and secondarily on what we can ascertain of their experiential relations to our moral needs and to the rest of what we hold as true.[j]

Accordingly, "we must judge the religious life by its results exclusively,"[k] that is, by its fruits in the life of the religious genius himself and in the lives of those touched by his work. But before assessing these fruits, James distinguished two basic types of personality: "the healthy minded, who need to be born only once, and the sick souls, who must be born twice—born in order to be happy. The result is two different conceptions of the universe of our experience," and since both of these types exist in large numbers, they deserve "to be studied with respect."[l]

THE HEALTHY-MINDED

The healthy-minded are those who "look on all things and see that they are good." Although "there are shallower and profounder levels" of healthy-mindedness, ranging all the way from "happiness like that of the mere animal" to the "more regenerate sorts of happiness,"[m] all of the healthy-minded are characterized by overwhelming joy and enthusiasm.

> In these states, the ordinary contrast of good and ill seems to be swallowed up in a higher denomination, an omnipotent excitement which engulfs the evil, and which the human being welcomes as the crowning experience of his life. This, he says, is truly to live, and I exult in the heroic opportunity and adventure. . . .
>
> The advance of liberalism, so-called, in Christianity, during the past fifty years, may fairly be called a victory of healthy-mindedness within the church over the morbidness with which the old hell-fire theology was more harmoniously related.[n]

THE SICK SOULS

If we think of the healthy-minded as "deliberately minimizing evil," there is an exactly opposite view "based on the persuasion that the evil aspects of our life are of its very essence, and that the world's meaning most comes home to us when we lay them most to heart."° As with the healthy mind

> . . . there [are] different levels of the morbid mind, and the one is much more formidable than the other. There are people for whom evil means only a mal-adjustment with *things*, a wrong correspondence of one's life with the environment. Such evil as this is curable, in principle at least, upon the natural plane, for merely by modifying either the self or the things, or both at once, the two terms may be made to fit, and all go merry as a marriage bell again. But there are others for whom evil is no mere relation of the subject to particular outer things, but something more radical and general, a wrongness or vice in his essential nature, which no alteration of the environment, or any superficial rearrangement of the inner self, can cure, and which requires a supernatural remedy.ᴾ

THE TWO TYPES COMPARED

> In our own attitude, not yet abandoned, of impartial onlookers, what are we to say of [these two different conceptions]? It seems to me that we are bound to say that morbid-mindedness ranges over the wider scale of experience. . . . The method of averting one's attention from evil, and living simply in the light of good is splendid as long as it will work. It will work with many persons; it will work far more generally than most of us are ready to suppose; and within the sphere of its successful operation there is nothing to be said against it as a religious solution. But it breaks down impotently as soon as melancholy comes. . . .
>
> The normal process of life contains moments as bad as any of those which insane melancholy is filled with, moments in which radical evil gets its innings and takes its solid turn. The lunatic's visions of horror are all drawn from the material of daily fact. Our civilization is founded on the shambles, and every individual existence goes out in a lonely spasm of helpless agony. If you protest, my friend, wait till you arrive there yourself! To believe in the carnivorous reptiles of geologic times is hard for our imagination—they seem too much like mere museum specimens. Yet there is no tooth in any one of those museum-skulls that did not daily through long years of the foretime hold fast to the body struggling in despair of some fated living victim. Forms of horror just as dreadful to the victims, if on a smaller spatial scale, fill the world about us to-day. Here on our very hearths and in our gardens the infernal cat plays with the panting mouse, or holds the hot bird fluttering in her jaws. Crocodiles and rattlesnakes and pythons are at this moment vessels of life as real as we are; their loathsome existence fills every minute

of every day that drags its length along; and whenever they or other wild beasts clutch their living prey, the deadly horror which an agitated melancholiac feels is the literally right reaction on the situation. . . . The completest religions would therefore seem to be those in which the pessimistic elements are best developed.[q]

Thus sick souls have a more realistic view of the world than the healthy-minded; more important, only out of the despair of sick souls does the most profound religious phenomenon—conversion—emerge.

CONVERSION

Conversion, James concluded from the large number of cases he examined, occurs in every religion, though the members of the various sects naturally describe their experience in the vocabulary of their particular theology. And, though some conversions are so gradual as to be almost imperceptible, others are "instantaneous." It is these latter that seem to some people conclusive of divine intervention. Accordingly, the fundamental question about conversion is whether "instantaneous conversion [is] a miracle in which God is present"[r] or whether a naturalistic explanation can be given. James's answer was that a naturalistic explanation of the origins of conversion is possible, but that this does not in any way affect the importance of its fruits.

First, as regards the naturalistic explanation of conversion:

> The expression "field of consciousness" has but recently come into vogue in the psychology books. Until quite lately the unit of mental life which figured most was the single "idea," supposed to be a definitely outlined thing. But at present psychologists are tending, first, to admit that the actual unit is more probably the total mental state, the entire wave of consciousness or field of objects present to the thought at any time; and, second, to see that it is impossible to outline this wave, this field, with any definiteness. . . .
>
> The important fact which this "field" formula commemorates is the indetermination of the margin. . . . Our whole past store of memories floats beyond this margin, ready at a touch to come in; and the entire mass of residual powers, impulses, and knowledges that constitute our empirical self stretches continuously beyond it. So vaguely drawn are the outlines between what is actual and what is only potential at any moment of our conscious life, that it is always hard to say of certain mental elements whether we are conscious of them or not. . . .
>
> And having reached this point, I must now ask you to recall what I said in my last lecture about the subconscious life. . . . I cannot but think that the most important step forward that has occurred in psychology since I have been a student of that science is the discovery, first made in 1886, that, in certain subjects at least, there is not only the consciousness of the ordinary field, with its usual centre and margin, but an addition thereto in the shape of a set of memories, thoughts, and feelings which are extra-marginal and

outside of the primary consciousness altogether, but yet must be classed as conscious facts of some sort, able to reveal their presence by unmistakable signs. . . .

The most important consequence of having a strongly developed ultra-marginal life of this sort is that one's ordinary fields of consciousness are liable to incursions from it of which the subject does not guess the source, and which, therefore, take for him the form of unaccountable impulses to act, or inhibitions of action, of obsessive ideas, or even of hallucinations of sight or hearing. The impulses may take the direction of automatic speech or writing, the meaning of which the subject himself may not understand even while he utters it. . . .

In the wonderful explorations by Binet, Janet, Breuer, Freud, Mason, Prince, and others, of the subliminal consciousness of patients with hysteria, we have revealed to us whole systems of underground life, in the shape of memories of a painful sort which lead a parasitic existence, buried outside of the primary fields of consciousness, and making irruptions thereinto with hallucinations, pains, convulsions, paralyses of feeling and of motion, and the whole procession of symptoms of hysteric disease of body and of mind. . . .

And thus I return to our own specific subject of [religious] conversions. . . . If, abstracting altogether from the question of their value for the future spiritual life of the individual, we take them on their psychological side exclusively, so many peculiarities in them remind us of what we find outside of conversion that we are tempted to class them along with other automatisms, and to suspect that what makes the difference between a sudden and a gradual convert is not necessarily the presence of divine miracle in the case of one and of something less divine in that of the other, but rather a simple psychological peculiarity, the fact, namely, that in the recipient of the more instantaneous grace we have one of those subjects who are in possession of a large region in which mental work can go on subliminally, and from which invasive experiences, abruptly upsetting the equilibrium of the primary consciousness, may come.[s]

If this, then, is the naturalistic explanation of the process of conversion, what are its fruits? They are, first, saintliness, which is a matter of conduct, and, second, mysticism, which is a matter of "seeing the truth in a special manner."[t]

SAINTLINESS

Once again basing his findings on extensive case studies, James concluded that saintliness has the following "practical consequences": (1) asceticism, (2) strength of soul, (3) purity, and (4) charity. The next task is to ascertain how valuable these consequences are. This is an empirical question, and, as with all empirical questions, we must be content with answers that are only probable; "we can never hope for clear-cut and scholastic results."[u]

> What I propose to do is, briefly stated, to test saintliness by common sense, to use human standards to help us decide how far the religious life commends

> itself as an ideal kind of human activity. . . . The fruits of religion are like all human products, liable to corruption by excess. Common sense must judge them.[v]

Thus it is true that some saints are fanatics and that others are otherworldly and naïve. But our case studies show that "fanaticism is found only where the character is masterful and aggressive." And as for otherworldliness, far from being useless, it is "a genuinely creative social force."[w]

> If things are ever to move upward, some one must be ready to take the first step, and assume the risk of it. No one who is not willing to try charity, to try non-resistance as the saint is always willing, can tell whether these methods will or will not succeed. When they do succeed, they are far more powerfully successful than force or worldly prudence. Force destroys enemies; and the best that can be said of prudence is that it keeps what we already have in safety. But non-resistance, when successful, turns enemies into friends; and charity regenerates its objects. These saintly methods are, as I said, creative energies; and genuine saints find in the elevated excitement with which their faith endows them an authority and impressiveness which makes them irresistible in situations where men of shallower nature cannot get on at all without the use of worldly prudence. This practical proof that worldly widom may be safely transcended is the saint's magic gift to mankind.[x]

MYSTICISM

When James finally came to deal with mysticism, the limitations of his descriptive psychological approach became more noticeable. Saintliness is a matter of behavior; it is relatively easy to describe this behavior and to ask whether it is valuable—that is, tends, on the whole, to maximize satisfaction. But mysticism makes cognitive claims, and in addition to assessing its possible beneficial effects on conduct and on the subjective feelings of the mystic, we have to ask, it would seem, whether its cognitive claims are warranted. James fudged this issue badly.

Let us look at the "marks" of mysticism, of which there are four. First and "handiest," mystical states are ineffable: "No one can make clear to another who has never had a certain feeling, in what the quality or worth of it consists. One must have musical ears to know the value of a symphony. . . . The mystic finds that most of us accord to his experiences an equally incompetent treatment." Second, mystical states are transient: "Except in rare instances, half an hour, or at most an hour or two, seems to be the limit beyond which they fade into the light of common day." Third, mystical states are passive: "Although the oncoming of mystical states may be facilitated by preliminary voluntary operations, . . . yet when the characteristic sort of consciousness once has set in, the mystic feels as if his own will were in abeyance, and indeed sometimes as if he were grasped and held by a superior power." Finally, "mystical states seem to those who experience them to be . . . states of insight into depths of truth unplumbed by the discursive intellect."ʸ

The psychological basis for mystical experiences is to be explained, James thought, in terms of those sub-, un-, and co-conscious phenomena that account for conversion. In a mystical experience one is in touch with the ultramarginal aspects of one's field of experience. What is more, alcohol, anesthetics, and other drugs also open us to this otherwise closed region. For instance,

> . . . nitrous oxide and ether, especially nitrous oxide, when sufficiently diluted with air, stimulate the mystical consciousness in an extraordinary degree. . . .
>
> Some years ago I myself made some observations on this aspect of nitrous oxide intoxication, and reported them in print. One conclusion was forced upon my mind at that time, and my impression of its truth has ever since remained unshaken. It is that our normal waking consciousness, rational consciousness as we call it, is but one special type of consciousness, whilst all about it, parted from it by the filmiest of screens, there lie potential forms of consciousness entirely different. . . . No account of the universe in its totality can be final which leaves these other forms of consciousness quite disregarded. How to regard them is the question—for they are so discontinuous with ordinary consciousness. Yet they may determine attitudes though they cannot furnish formulas, and open a region though they fail to give a map. At any rate, they forbid a premature closing of our accounts with reality. Looking back on my own experiences, they all converge towards a kind of insight to which I cannot help ascribing some metaphysical significance. The keynote of it is invariably a reconciliation. It is as if the opposites of the world, whose contradictoriness and conflict make all our difficulties and troubles, were melted into unity. Not only do they, as contrasted species, belong to one and the same genus, but *one of the species,* the nobler and better one, *is itself the genus, and so soaks up and absorbs its opposite into itself.* This is a dark saying, I know, when thus expressed in terms of common logic, but I cannot wholly escape from its authority. I feel as if it must mean something, something like what the hegelian philosophy means, if one could only lay hold of it more clearly. Those who have ears to hear, let them hear; to me the living sense of its reality only comes in the artificial mystic state of mind.ᶻ

In attributing "metaphysical significance" to these states, James accepted the mystic's belief that one mark of mysticism is "insight into depths of truth." And since this is a cognitive claim, James was at long last face to face with the cognitive issue. But of course it had been hovering in the background all the time. The twice-born man is not content merely to *feel* converted; he wants his feeling to be warranted, and for it to be warranted certain of his beliefs about the world must be true. Similarly as regards the saint. Saintliness may, as James insisted, be justified, socially and morally, by its beneficial effect on mankind. But the saint himself is moved to perform his acts of tenderness and charity less by such considerations than because he holds certain beliefs about the nature of the universe. In the saint's opinion, if not in James's, these beliefs must be true if the saint's saintliness is warranted.

This is the problem that religion has always created for empiricism, or, rather, it is the problem that empiricism creates for any religiously disposed man, such as James himself certainly was. James's "radical" empiricism, with its emphasis on experience as a stream of sensation and feeling, is doubtless better psychology than the traditional empiricist's notion of encapsulated impressions and ideas. But does it provide a better basis for religious belief? Let us consider James's claim that it does.

He began by distinguishing between what he called "over-beliefs" and beliefs that are "literally and objectively true." An over-belief, it would appear, is a belief that is not justified by evidence but that is "essential" to some individual's religion. Thus over-beliefs are so called presumably because they go beyond, or over, the evidence. Examples are "Vedantism and transcendental idealism [which] bring in their monistic interpretations and tell us that the finite self rejoins the absolute self, . . . the soul of the world." Though the specific over-beliefs of different individuals tend to cancel each other out—"they neutralize one another and leave no fixed results"—there is nevertheless something that is "common and generic" to them all. This common core is the belief that "the conscious person is continuous with a wider sense through which saving experiences come."[a] And it is this core belief, in distinction from the varying specific over-beliefs of different sects and religions, that James maintained is compatible with the empirical point of view and with scientific thought.

> Let me then propose, as an hypothesis, that whatever it may be on its farther side, the "more" with which in religious experience we feel ourselves connected is on its hither side the subconscious continuation of our conscious life. Starting thus with a recognized psychological fact as our basis, we seem to preserve a contact with "science" which the ordinary theologian lacks. At the same time the theologian's contention that the religious man is moved by an external power is vindicated, for it is one of the peculiarities of invasions from the subconscious region to take on objective appearances, and to suggest to the Subject an external control. In the religious life the control is felt as "higher"; but since in our hypothesis it is primarily the higher faculties of our own hidden mind which are controlling, the sense of union with the power beyond us is a sense of something, not merely apparently, but literally true.[b]

Here we find James rejecting the distinction on which most philosophers would insist, that between the psychological factors that lead someone to hold such-and-such a belief and the (logical) reasons that would warrant anybody's holding this belief. Let us grant for the sake of argument that James's description of these experiences is correct: in them control is felt as issuing from a higher power. But is this feeling warranted? James seems simply to have assumed that the strength of a feeling is evidence of its reliability. But though the strength of our feeling can indeed explain why we become convinced that a higher power is controlling us, its strength is quite irrelevant to the question whether a higher power is actually controlling us.

Note, too, James's characteristically easy shift from talk about the "hither side" to talk about the "farther side"—that is, his shift from the empirical hypothesis that "our own hidden mind" (our unconscious) is operative in these experiences to the transcendental hypothesis that "a power beyond us" is operative in them. Let us once again grant, for the sake of argument, James's claim that there are "ultramarginal" aspects of experience that are "continuous" with conscious experience and that these irrupt into consciousness during periods of intoxication and trance and on other occasions as well. The question is: Are such irruptions from subconscious experience evidence of the existence of something we are justified in "calling by the name God"? To allow an inference from what is in experience (whether conscious or subconscious is irrelevant here) to something wholly beyond any experience is a far cry, surely, from radical empiricism.

Consider James's contention that there is at least as much evidence for the religious hypothesis as for the materialistic hypothesis. "The drift of all the evidence seems to me to sweep us toward the belief in some form of superhuman life with which we may, unknown to ourselves, be coconscious."[c] Now the "positive evidence" to which James referred was that adduced by the Society for Psychical Research, of which he had been president. Some of its reports, a neutral observer might say, are impressive evidence for the existence of modes of communication not yet understood and not understandable in terms of current physical and psychological theory. However, that is a long way, such a neutral observer might add, from being evidence for "superhuman life."

But, of course, from James's point of view, there are no neutral observers. "We all, scientists and non-scientists, live on some inclined plane of credulity. The plane tips one way in one man, another way in another; and may he whose plane tips in no way be the first to cast a stone."[d] Thus the very data that seemed to James persuasive evidence for the religious hypothesis will be adjudged by a tougher-minded empiricist to be of no relevance whatever.

In the end, then, James came to the inconclusive conclusion that, since nothing can be proved one way or the other, each of us is entitled to believe what he wants to believe. On the one hand, "mystical states, when well developed, usually are, and have the right to be, absolutely authoritative over the individuals to whom they come." On the other hand, "no authority emanates from them which should make it a duty for those who stand outside of them to accept their revelations uncritically."[e]

This, then, is the argument that underlies the proposal of the short, "philosophical" part of *The Varieties of Religious Experience*. How shall we assess it? Let us turn, finally, to James's defense of the pragmatic test of truth, the doctrine for which he is best known in the history of philosophy.

The Pragmatic Criterion
of Meaning and Truth

It was Peirce, as we have seen, who first formulated pragmatism.[5] It was James who later popularized it and, in popularizing it, bowdlerized it—at least from Peirce's point of view. It is easy to see how James came to misconstrue Peirce. After all, Peirce had written: "The whole function of thought is to produce habits of action; and whatever there is connected with a thought but irrelevant to its purpose, is an accretion to it, but no part of it." And: "Consider what effects that might conceivably have practical bearing, we conceive the object of our conception to have. Then, our conception of these effects is the whole of our conception of the object."

James naturally read "purpose" and "practical" in terms of his own voluntarism; Peirce's pragmatic maxim meant to him that we are entitled to believe whatever suits our purposes, whatever "works," whatever has "cash value" in terms of our temperamental needs. For him, then, pragmatism is not a way of fixing our beliefs cognitively; it is a way of eliminating metaphysical puzzles that, though trivial in themselves, stand in the way of our accepting those beliefs that would satisfy our spiritual needs.

> The pragmatic method is primarily a method of settling metaphysical disputes that otherwise might be interminable. Is the world one or many?—fated or free?—material or spiritual?—here are notions either of which may or may not hold good of the world; and disputes over such notions are unending. The pragmatic method in such cases is to try to interpret each notion by tracing its respective practical consequences. What difference would it practically make to any one if this notion rather than that notion were true? If no practical difference whatever can be traced, then the alternatives mean practically the same thing, and all dispute is idle. Whenever a dispute is serious, we ought to be able to show some practical difference that must follow from one side or the other's being right. . . .
>
> A pragmatist turns his back resolutely and once for all upon a lot of inveterate habits dear to professional philosophers. He turns away from abstraction and insufficiency, from verbal solutions, from bad *a priori* reasons, from fixed principles, closed systems, and pretended absolutes and origins. He turns towards concreteness and adequacy, towards facts, towards action and towards power.[f]

From Peirce's point of view (and from that of other cognitivists) there is a fatal flaw in this formulation. What does "practical" mean? Whereas they thought chiefly of experiences that verify or refute empirical hypotheses, James, with

5 See pp. 263–64.

his anti-intellectualist and voluntaristic bias, thought chiefly of what sustains or impedes our temperament, our "passional nature."

It is this conception of pragmatism that underlies the whole "philosophical" case for religious belief that we have just examined. When James was in this mood he drew a sharp distinction between the facts (pure experience) and "the ulterior judgments we may eventually come to make"[g] about these facts. All of our theories, all of our verbalizations, are "only a man-made language, a conceptual shorthand . . . in which we write our reports of nature; and languages, as is well known, tolerate much choice of expression and many dialects."[h] Our religious sentiments and emotions "are certainly not mere derivatives of theism. . . . They harmonize with paternal theism beautifully," but they harmonize equally well with Stoicism, Hinduism, and Buddhism, and presumably with primitivism, animism or, for that matter, descriptive psychology. Pure experience, which includes the feeling of "more than," of "beyond," "antedates theologies and is independent of philosophies. . . . It is capable of entering into closest marriage with every speculative creed." But by the same token it is capable of divorcing itself from any or all of them, and it remains intact and pure when it does so. All of its marriages with theory or speculations are marriages of convenience, temporary affairs. Hence you may "call it by any other name you please."[i]

From this point of view theories are only so many "over-beliefs"; all are equally valuable and equally worthless. All are worthless if what one is after is the feeling itself. To become acquainted with it, one must encounter it directly in pure experience, and if one does not experience it directly, no amount of theory or verbalization will help. On the other hand, all theories are equally valuable, since, given the direct experience, what a theory does is satisfy other needs. Different kinds of theory satisfy different needs, and what sort of theory one prefers reflects what interest animates one to employ it to verbalize one's feelings. Since we do not choose between theories on cognitive grounds (for only direct feeling, not theory, is cognitive), we choose between them on practical grounds. Thus objective idealism is true for those who assert it—true in the sense that it satisfies their need for unity, security, and peace.[j]

This magnanimous gesture to the objective idealists caused great mirth among professional philosophers. They pointed out that since on this view every theory that anybody has ever held or will ever hold is true, the word "true" as James used it has no meaning whatever. But James had characteristically overstated his case. He did not want to hold—or at least part of the time he did not want to hold—such an extreme anti-intellectualism. For he maintained that he was putting forward a theory, including a theory of truth, that is cognitively superior to alternative theories.

> Pragmatism . . . asks its usual question. "Grant an idea or belief to be true," it says, "what concrete difference will its being true make in any one's actual life? How will the truth be realized? What experiences will be different from

those which would obtain if the belief were false? What, in short, is the truth's cash-value in experiential terms?"

The moment pragmatism asks this question, it sees the answer: *True ideas are those that we can assimilate, validate, corroborate and verify. False ideas are those that we cannot.* That is the practical difference it makes to us to have true ideas; that, therefore, is the meaning of truth, for it is all that truth is known-as. . . .

Our ideas must agree with realities, be such realities concrete or abstract. . . . Primarily, no doubt, to agree means to copy. . . . To "agree" in the widest sense with a reality *can only mean to be guided either straight up to it or into its surroundings, or to be put into such working touch with it as to handle either it or something connected with it better than if we disagreed.* Better either intellectually or practically! . . .

Our account of truth is an account of truths in the plural, of processes of leading, realized *in rebus,* and having only this quality in common, that they *pay.* They pay by guiding us into or towards some part of a system that dips at numerous points into sense-percepts, which we may copy mentally or not, but with which at any rate we are now in the kind of commerce vaguely designated as verification. Truth for us is simply a collective name for verification-processes.[k]

Note what a variety of verification procedures is proposed in these paragraphs: There is talk about "agreement," which sounds like the correspondence theory; talk about "assimilation" and being "connected with," which sounds like the coherence theory; talk about "corroborate and verify," which sounds like scientific method generalized; and talk about "working" and "paying," which sounds like the sheerest anti-intellectualism. The phrase "better either intellectually or practically!" (including the exclamation point) is typically Jamesian. In his philosophy there is room for everybody and for all theories—the more the merrier; the more, indeed, the better and the "truer." In the end, then, "truth" becomes simply the "collective name" for a whole grab-bag collection of wholly different verification procedures.

The fact is that, so far as James was setting out a theory of knowledge and attempting to prove it, he was caught in a trap. On the one hand, he wanted to maintain that pragmatism (or, rather, his version of it) is true; on the other hand, this version of pragmatism undermines the concepts of theory and truth. The twistings and slidings we have been examining are evidence both of his struggle to escape and his failure to extricate himself.

But James was a theorist only part of the time; another part of the time, as we have seen all along, James was an advocate, and perhaps in the end he would have settled for the latter role. From this standpoint the arguments we have criticized look very different, for he has not been putting forward an argument—that is, a line of reasoning that is intended to be carefully scrutinized and considered on its merits—but something quite different: a diplomatic formula. Thus he wrote at one point, "This doorway into the subject [the proposal we are now considering] seems to me the best one for a science of religions, for it mediates between a number of different points of view."[1] In other words, the proposal was designed as a compromise that would be acceptable to scientists and theologians alike. Now a diplomatic formula is not intended to be carefully scrutinized and considered on its merits; indeed it works only as long as it is sufficiently ambiguous (though, of course, not obviously ambiguous) for each party to the dispute to believe he is getting most of what he wants and not giving up anything he regards as indispensable.

This interpretation of what James was up to—which exonerates him from charges of having argued in a muddled and confused way by claiming that he was not arguing at all but presenting a formula that he hoped would enable scientists and theologians alike to believe what they want to believe—fits in with his frequent assertion that even the sciences, whose business it is to present arguments and test empirical hypotheses, themselves rest on nothing more secure, or ultimate, than a vision of the universe—a vision different from the vision of the religious man but no less a matter of ardent faith. In this connection James liked to quote W. K. Clifford[6] on the creed of the scientist, or at least on the creed of the mid-nineteenth-century scientist with positivist leanings:

> "Belief is desecrated when given to unproved and unquestioned statements for the solace and private pleasure of the believer. . . . Whoso would deserve well of his fellows in this matter will guard the purity of his belief with a very fanaticism of jealous care, lest at any time it should rest on an unworthy object, and catch a stain which can never be wiped away. . . . If [a] belief has been accepted on insufficient evidence [even though the belief be true, as Clifford on the same page explains] the pleasure is a stolen one. . . . It is sinful because it is stolen in defiance of our duty to mankind. That duty is to guard ourselves from such beliefs as from a pestilence which may shortly master our own body and then spread to the rest of the town. . . . It is wrong always, everywhere, and for everyone, to believe anything upon insufficient evidence."[m]

James could point out with good effect that this itself is, precisely, a *creed*, that is, a belief that, far from being based on evidence, "is only an expression of our passional life."

> He who says, "Better go without belief forever than believe a lie!" merely shows his own preponderant private horror of becoming a dupe. He may be critical of many of his desires and fears, but this fear he slavishly obeys. He cannot imagine any one questioning its binding force. For my own part, I have also a horror of being duped; but I can believe that worse things than being duped may happen to a man in this world: so Clifford's exhortation has to my ears a thoroughly fantastic sound.[n]

---

6 W. K. Clifford (1845–79) was an English mathematician who also wrote on philosophical subjects.

Since belief in scientific method is itself a matter of faith, scientific method is not sacrosanct. It has to compete for men's allegiance with other visions, and ultimately that vision will win out which makes the strongest appeal to our nature. James had no doubt that this is the religious vision; even scientists are religious—about science. One thing, and one thing alone, prevents the triumph of the religious vision. This is the unwarranted belief in the infallibility of science. If that belief could be shaken, all faiths would compete on even terms. Note that belief in the infallibility of science is "unwarranted" only on the criterion that science itself puts forward, namely, evidential grounds. Belief in the infallibility of science is warranted on the criterion James himself put forward, that is, it is warranted for those whose deepest need is not to be duped. We are not entitled to commit ourselves to any passing whim or fancy. But we are all—and not merely scientists—entitled to commit ourselves to those beliefs that are expressions of the deepest elements in our "passional life."

From this point of view James's excursions into theory, including his exposition of the pragmatic theory of truth, are not momentary aberrations but parts of a single and consistent strategy of advocacy. In a word, we can think of the whole discussion, from start to finish, as being a diplomatic formula that he dressed in the rhetoric of argument because he thought this rhetoric would appeal to those whom he wished to win over to his vision of the universe. And in this vision the role of theory is simply to lend support to his advocacy of his vision. Theory, within this vision, is useful, but useful only as a kind of therapy with which to dissipate the bad effects of theory conceived as a search for eternal verities.

From this point of view again, James would have wished to be judged by the power of his vision not by the logical consistency of his theory. This is the vision of an open universe, growing, incomplete, unpredictable as to its outcome. To live in such a universe people need flexibility, resourcefulness, a sense of humor, and a readiness to gamble on their convictions. They need not only learn to live with insecurity but even to enjoy it. These are the qualities James prized, but what he prized above all was individuality. "Probably a crab," he wrote, "would be filled with a sense of personal outrage if it could hear us class it without ado or apology as a crustacean, and thus dispose of it. 'I am no such thing,' it would say; 'I am MYSELF, MYSELF alone.'"⁰ The root of his anti-intellectualism was his appreciation of individual differences, for he thought it was the nature of the intellect to classify and so to make crustaceans more real than crabs.

James's vision, then, is of a pluralistic universe—a "universe" only by courtesy, for there is no fit among its parts. What people do in this loose universe makes, or may make, a difference. Nothing is guaranteed, but because the future is open it would be folly—or, worse, cowardice—not to act as if it is in our hands. James's function in the historical development of philosophy was to state this vision with passionate conviction. It was the function of other, more intellectually inclined philosophers, to develop theories that gave formal expression to it. Thus James anticipated some of the major themes of twentieth-century philosophy—

existentialism's emphasis on the centrality of choice, phenomenology's emphasis on pure experience, Wittgenstein's emphasis on the extent to which language can hold us captive and on the role of philosophy in freeing us from these conceptual "frames." If James was not, like Moore or Frege, a philosopher's philosopher, he was a seminal thinker whose ideas, pouring forth with almost careless abandon, entered the stream of Western culture at many points, influencing the way in which people came to view their world. This surely is the role he would have wished to play.

CHAPTER 9

F. H. Bradley

In the last three chapters we have been examining the theories of philosophers who, however much they differed among themselves, were at one in their hostility to Hegel. But alongside of positivism, existentialism, and pragmatism, various versions of Hegelianism continued to flourish.

The continuing appeal of Hegelianism reflects the survival of that Romantic view of the world which, as we have seen, was a late eighteenth-century reaction to the atomism that had dominated thought in the preceding period. For the Enlightenment, society consisted in a number of autonomous individuals who contracted together to form a state; the minds of these individuals were composed of a number of separate "faculties"—reason, sense perception, volition; the physical world consisted in a vast number of particles interacting according to completely deterministic laws. Hegel, and those thinkers to whom Hegelianism appealed, agreed with the romantic poets in rejecting all of this as a "fragmentation" of reality. The universe is one, they insisted; its parts are not merely externally juxtaposed, but, as Wordsworth believed, deeply "interfused." And since they thought that the past is as organically involved in the present as the parts of the present are involved in one another, they took very seriously the notions of historical development.

The Hegelians were not alone, of course, in attacking atomism, mechanism, and an unhistorical point of view. Nevertheless, it was to them that the romantic vision appealed most strongly, and it was they who developed it systematically into a philosophical theory.

A second reason for the survival of Hegelianism was a hostility to science. Some of this antagonism merely reflected the attitude of humanistic scholars who knew no science and were proud of their ignorance—and who were also, doubtless, a bit defensive about it. But some of it had a more respectable source. To many men, science, or rather the fashionable antimetaphysical metaphysics based on science, left no place for God or for human choice. The world that science disclosed reminded Matthew Arnold of the beach at low tide: All that had made life worth living turned out, in the scientific view, to be illusion; what was left was merely meaningless flotsam and jetsam tossed about by the sea.

> The Sea of Faith
> Was once too at the full, and round earth's shore
> Lay like the folds of a bright girdle furl'd.
> But now I only hear
> Its melancholy, long withdrawing roar,
> Retreating to the breath
> Of the night-wind, down the vast edges drear
> And naked shingles of the world.[a]

Unlike the positivists, Arnold could not accept this view of things; on the other hand, unlike the orthodox theologians, he could not contemptuously reject it. Hence he found himself, as he said,

> Wandering between two worlds, one dead,
> The other powerless to be born,
> With nowhere yet to rest my head.[b]

Whereas James undertook to give the Arnolds of this world a place to rest their heads by persuading them that they had a right to believe whatever they wanted to believe, the Neo-Hegelians claimed to have proved that people have adequate grounds for believing what they want to believe. Or, to put the source of its attraction in different terms, Neo-Hegelianism claimed that men do not face the hard decision with which Nietzsche confronted them: They do not have to bite off and spit out the black snake lodged in their throat. On the contrary, they can tame the snake of science and keep it in its proper place—subordinating it to, and including it within, a wider view of things.

No wonder, then, that Neo-Hegelianism became the dominant philosophical school in the late nineteenth century. Because it was dominant, it naturally became the target of attack for all those who, for whatever reason, opposed the philosophical establishment. The leading philosophers of the early part of the twentieth century—Moore, Russell, the Logical Positivists—are virtually incomprehensible except in the context of the doctrine they opposed. Accordingly, it is fitting to end this volume with a chapter on Neo-Hegelianism, marking both the concluding phase of nineteenth-century philosophy and the departure point for the twentieth-century revolt. But rather than try to cover a number of representatives of this school, we shall concentrate on one—F. H. Bradley[1]—one of the most original and most interesting of the Neo-Hegelians.

Bradley and Hegel

Although we have just characterized Bradley as a Hegelian, and although he freely acknowledged his debt to Hegel, he did not want to be called a Hegelian: His differences from Hegel were, in his view, more important than their similarities. Let us begin, then, with what seemed to Bradley the essence of Hegel's position. According to Bradley, Hegel held that

> . . . the whole reality is so immanent and so active in every partial element, that you have only to make an object of anything short of the whole, in order to see this object pass beyond itself. The object visibly contradicts itself and goes on to include its complementary opposite in a wider unity. And this process repeats itself as long as and wherever the whole fails to express itself entirely in the object. Hence the two principles of coherence and comprehensiveness are one. And not only are they one but they include also the principle of non-contradiction. The order to express yourself in such a way as to avoid visible contradiction, may be said in the end to contain the whole criterion. . . .
>
> No one who has not seen this view at work, and seen it applied to a wide area of fact, can realize its practical efficiency. But, for myself, if this solution of our puzzle ever satisfied me entirely, there came a time when it ceased to satisfy. And when attempting to discuss first principles this was not the answer which I offered. However immanent in each element the whole is really, I cannot persuade myself that everywhere in the above way it is

---

1 Francis Herbert Bradley (1846–1924) was almost an exact contemporary of Peirce and James. Bradley, whose father was a clergyman, was educated at Oxford, where he studied classical languages and literature. In 1870 he was elected to a fellowship at Merton College, Oxford, which was tenable for life and required no teaching. These were fortunate circumstances, since he shortly developed a serious kidney infection that necessitated his wintering in a warmer climate than Oxford's. Despite ill health and increasing deafness, which made him something of a recluse, he published intensively and was a formidable antagonist.

immanent visibly. . . . The visible internal self-transcendence of every object is a thing which I cannot everywhere verify.[c]

So, to Bradley what was important in Hegelianism was the doctrine that "immediate experience is the beginning" but that, because "contradictions" develop within it, we are driven to seek an ever more inclusive and completely unified experience. But Bradley rejected Hegel's view that the process of resolving contradiction is dialectical in nature.[2] Even more important, though Bradley accepted coherence and system as cognitive ideals, he became sceptical (as we see in the passage just quoted) of Hegel's claim that the human intellect can achieve coherent and systematic knowledge. Hence, Bradley was as ambivalent as Hegel was sure about the nature and role of metaphysics.[3] On the one hand, Bradley shared Hegel's view that the goal of philosophy is a grand metaphysical system; on the other hand, he concluded that such a system cannot be worked out in detail. On the one hand, he held that the principle of contradiction is an infallible criterion of truth and reality; on the other hand, he held that this infallible criterion never yields and, as a matter of principle can never yield, any absolutely certain truth. On the one hand, Bradley struck the high, rationalist note that we found in Hegel: The real is rational and the rational is real:

> Is there an absolute criterion? . . . You can scarcely propose to be quite passive when presented with statements about reality. . . . If you think at all so as to discriminate between truth and falsehood, you will find that you cannot accept open self-contradiction. . . . Ultimate reality is such that it does not contradict itself; here is an absolute criterion. And it is proved absolute by the fact that, either in endeavouring to deny it, or even in attempting to doubt it, we tacitly assume its validity.[d]

Here, and in many similar passages, Bradley was as extreme a rationalist as Parmenides or Zeno.[4] As we shall see, he rejected such "obvious" sensory experiences as those of motion and change, on the grounds that when we examine these two concepts, we find that they are contradictory. What distinguishes philosophy from the sciences, and what renders it superior to them, is that we do not ask about some assertion, "Can it be verified in experience?" but simply, "Is it self-contradictory?"

On the other hand, thought contains a fatal flaw, as will become evident when we examine Bradley's view of the nature of thought. Though thought, according to this view, seeks the self-consistent and can never be content until

---

2 Bradley's criticism of Hegel's intellectualism and formalism (as when he referred contemptuously to Hegel's "ballet of bloodless categories") and of what he felt was Hegel's minimization of the role of feeling and emotion in life, sounds very much like James. But he and James differed too much in other ways to recognize their fellow-feeling in this respect.

3 Hegel would certainly not have subscribed to, or even understood, Bradley's aphorism: "Metaphysics is the finding of bad reasons for what we believe upon instinct, but to find these reasons is no less an instinct" (*Appearance and Reality*, p. xii).

4 See Vol. I, pp. 21 and 25.

it finds it, thought is doomed never to find the wholly self-consistent. Hence, "in the end" thought necessarily fails in its quest for truth and reality. For these reasons some critics have not unnaturally concluded (Bradley's protestations to the contrary) that he was a sceptic, not a rationalist, and others have argued that he was really a mystic.

The Nature of Thought

There is no such thing, Bradley held, as a passive contemplation of an idea or of some passing experience: "Without exception, to think must be, in some sense, to judge."[e] Accordingly, to understand the nature of thought and to grasp why it inevitably fails in its quest for truth and reality, we must ascertain the nature of judgment. We will start, by contrast, with feeling—that level of immediate experience which is prejudgmental.

> The recognition of the fact of immediate experience opens the one road, I submit, to the solution of ultimate problems. But, though opening the road, it does not of itself supply an answer to our questions. . . .
>
> The solution, if I may anticipate, is in general supplied by considering this fact, that immediate experience, however much transcended, both remains and is active. It is not a stage which shows itself at the beginning and then disappears, but it remains at the bottom throughout as fundamental. And further, remaining it contains within itself every development which in a sense transcends it. Nor does it merely contain all developments, but in its own way it acts to some extent as their judge. Its blind uneasiness, we may say, insists tacitly on visible satisfaction. We have on one hand a demand, explicit or otherwise, for an object which is complete. On the other hand the object which fails to include immediate experience in its content, is by the unrest of that experience condemned as defective. We are thus forced to the idea of an object containing the required element, and in this object we find at last theoretical satisfaction and rest. . . .
>
> I must however, before proceeding further, try to explain what I mean by immediate experience. . . . Immediate experience [is] that which is comprised wholly within a single state of undivided awareness or feeling. As against anything "unconscious," in the sense of falling outside, this is immediate as being my actual conscious experience. And further it is immediate as against those other special and immediate developments which throughout rest on it, and, while transcending, still remain within itself.[f]
>
> Questions at once arise on some of which we may first touch in passing. Was there and is there in the development of the race and the individual a stage at which experience is merely immediate? And, further, do we all perhaps at moments sink back to such a level? . . . I think it probable that such a stage of mind not only, with all of us, comes first in fact, but that at times it recurs even in the life of the developed individual. . . . What I

would here insist on is the point that feeling, so understood, need not be devoid of internal diversity. Its content need not in this sense be simple, and possibly never is simple. By feeling, in short, I understand, and, I believe, always have understood, an awareness which, though non-relational, may comprise simply in itself an indefinite amount of difference. There are no distinctions in the proper sense, and yet there is a many felt in one. . . . And, not only this, but such a whole admits in itself a conflict and struggle of elements, not of course experienced as struggle but as discomfort, unrest and uneasiness. . . .

Whether there is a stage where experience is *merely* immediate I have agreed to leave doubtful. Feeling is transcended always, if you please, in the sense that we have always contents which are more than merely felt. But on the other side at no moment can feeling ever be transcended, if this means that we are to have contents which are not felt. In a sense, therefore, we never can at any time pass beyond immediate experience. . . .

At any moment my actual experience, however relational its contents, is in the end non-relational. No analysis into relations and terms can ever exhaust its nature or fail in the end to belie its essence. What analysis leaves for ever outstanding is no mere residue, but is a vital condition of the analysis itself. Everything which is got out into the form of an object implies still the felt background against which the object comes, and further, the whole experience of both feeling and object is a non-relational immediate felt unity. The entire relational consciousness, in short, is experienced as falling within a direct awareness. This direct awareness is itself non-relational. It escapes from all attempts to exhibit it by analysis as one or more elements in a relational scheme, or as that scheme itself, or as a relation or relations, or as the sum or collection of any of these abstractions. And immediate experience not only escapes, but it serves as the basis on which the analysis is made. Itself is the vital element within which every analysis still moves, while, and so far as, and however much, that analysis transcends immediacy.

Everything therefore, no matter how objective and how relational, is experienced only in feeling, and, so far as it is experienced, still depends upon feeling.[g]

IMMEDIATE EXPERIENCE

It will be seen that though this description of immediate experience is concerned with what James called pure experience and Peirce called feeling, differences in emphasis are striking:

1. For Bradley what is important about immediate experience is its "non-relational unity." For good examples of such nonrelational unity we can go to the romantic poets. Here is Wordsworth on the experience of a baby:

> Blest the Babe,
> Nursed in his Mother's arms, who sinks to sleep
> Rocked on his Mother's breast; who with his soul

Drinks in the feelings of his Mother's eye!
For him, in one dear Presence, there exists
A virtue which irradiates and exalts
Objects through widest intercourse of sense. . . .
Is there a flower, to which he points with hand
Too weak to gather it, already love
Drawn from love's purest earthly fount for him
Hath beautified that flower.[h]

The baby—this was one of Wordsworth's, and Bradley's, main points—does not distinguish between the flower's beauty and his mother's love. Nor does the baby "conclude," on the basis of what his mother does and says, that she loves him. On the contrary, he "drinks in" her love.

2. The operative word in this passage is the first, "blest": the romantic poet typically longs to return to the unmediated experience of the baby. Bradley would have agreed that the human mind is fully satisfied by nothing less than nonrelational unity; but this, according to Bradley, is not the nonrelational unity of prejudgmental experience; it is the nonrelational unity of an experience that has passed beyond judgment. In this romantic appreciation of the "blessedness" of a nonrelational unity, Bradley differed markedly from James and Peirce. For James, a baby's experience is only a buzzing, booming confusion; he felt at home in the level of experience in which we encounter the objects of the common-sense world—flowers on the one hand and mothers on the other—as quite distinct objects. As for Peirce, pure feeling is the theoretical limit from which the universe has evolved, and since evolutionary progress is good, it follows that the nonrelational unity of feeling is inferior to the relational structures that develop out of it. Thirdness, not Firstness, is the important feature of human experience for Peirce.

3. What is essential for Bradley about immediate experience is the fact that "we can never pass beyond" it. That is, there is never an experienced content, however articulate and analytically grasped it may be, that is not imbedded in a larger "whole of which I am immediately aware." Here again we can go to Wordsworth for an example: When Wordsworth was strolling through the countryside around Tintern Abbey he took note, as any passerby might, of the "steep and lofty cliffs," the "plots of cottage-ground," the "pastoral farms," the "wreaths of smoke." But at the same time that he noted these distinct and separate objects, he felt

A presence that disturbs me with the joy
Of elevated thoughts; a sense sublime
Of something far more deeply interfused,
Whose dwelling is the light of setting suns
And the round ocean and the living air,

And the blue sky, and in the mind of man:
A motion and a spirit, that impels
All thinking things, all objects of all thought,
And rolls through all things.[i]

Wordsworth believed that awareness of presences surrounding and impregnating our everyday experience of objects is a special prerogative of poets, that even poets attain such awareness only occasionally. Bradley, in contrast, held that everybody's experience is continuously characterized by a "more than." And this is not merely a curious psychological fact about human experience. That experience always includes more than what is now present follows necessarily from the nature of awareness. If we did not from the start transcend the now, we would never transcend it: We would live in a succession of encapsulated nows, which, under these circumstances, could not even be experienced by us as a succession. We would never *know* anything at all, because there would be no relation between what we experience now and anything else. In short, logical considerations, as well as experiences such as those Wordsworth described led Bradley to invoke what we may call the doctrine of presence.

4. Further, Bradley agreed with Wordsworth about the cosmic dimensions of the presence that is so deeply interfused in ordinary things. But here again, whereas Wordsworth merely *felt* the cosmos, Bradley held that he could *prove* its presence. Since it is impossible in principle, according to Bradley, to draw any line between what is present and given and what is present and not given, it follows that the whole universe is present (but not given) at every moment. Each of us carries with him continuously the whole universe, or, rather, the universe carries with it innumerable "finite centers" that are in varying degrees conscious of that universe in which they are embedded. This is the high metaphysical thesis that Bradley extracted from what we would now call his phenomenology of immediate, or pure, experience; and this is a thesis that James and Peirce, despite the many similarities between their phenomenological descriptions and Bradley's, would have entirely rejected.

5. We have noted that, according to Bradley, if immediate experience did not, from the start, contain or involve a "more than," we would never know anything at all. Bradley's emphasis, like Peirce's, was thus on the need to give a description of experience on which an epistemological theory can be erected. He was just as dissatisfied as Peirce was with James's "psychologizing" tendency and far less restrained in expressing his dissatisfaction.

> What according to Prof. James is to become of the fact of knowledge and truth, a fact apparently not included in mere immediate experience [according, at least, to his account of it]? His answer, however unsatisfactory, will, I think, up to a certain point be found to be instructive and interesting.
> Since only particular events are real, Prof. James denies that an idea can

be more, and can be self-transcendent. The psychical fact must know, without itself referring beyond itself. And what is it to know? The answer obviously is "other events," for there is nothing else to know. And, in order for these events to be *real*, they (the logic is not mine) must be *future*. If now, following the same logic, we ask what knowledge is and where it falls, the answer is that knowledge is essentially a temporal process of facts. It falls in, and it *is*, the mere series of experienced events, beginning with the idea and ending with the object. . . .

Suppose that I know that somewhere near there is a spring of water. Does my present knowledge consist in my actually finding this water? Has it, in order to be knowledge now, got to wait for this future event? Such a contention seems obviously absurd, and it forthwith is covertly modified. . . . While the self-reference of the idea beyond itself is explicitly denied by Prof. James, he uses, and is forced to use, words which re-affirm it. The present idea of water, he says, *leads* to the finding. There is a continuous advance to the object, with an experience of developing progress, and therefore the object was *meant*. But is it not, I ask, obvious that such language implies at the start, and before the finding, a self-transcendent idea of the water?[j]

This criticism of James consists in pointing out (a) that reference—what Bradley himself called "transcendence," what Peirce called "significance"—is a fundamental feature of cognition; (b) that reference is not identical with, nor reducible to, temporal succession; (c) that temporal succession and similarity (for example, "association of ideas") are the only relations James's purely psychological approach permits; hence (d) that James cannot give an adequate account of cognition; and finally (e) that this otherwise obvious inadequacy is hidden from James only because he has illicitly allowed reference to slip unnoticed into his account.

JUDGMENT

We have already seen that, according to Bradley, to think is to judge. And we have now seen that thinking, or judging, arises naturally, inevitably, and by no abrupt transition, out of immediate experience.

If we take up anything considered real, no matter what it is, we find in it two aspects. There are always two things we can say about it; and, if we cannot say both, we have not got reality. There is a "what" and a "that," an existence and a content, and the two are inseparable. That anything should be, and should yet be nothing in particular, or that a quality should not qualify and give a character to anything, is obviously impossible. If we try to get the "that" by itself, we do not get it, for either we have it qualified, or else we fail utterly. If we try to get the "what" by itself, we find at once that it is not all. It points to something beyond, and cannot exist by itself and as a bare adjective. Neither of these aspects, if you isolate it, can be taken as real, or indeed in that case is itself any longer. They are distinguishable only and are not divisible.

And yet thought seems essentially to consist in their division. For thought is clearly, to some extent at least, ideal. Without an idea there is no thinking, and an idea implies the separation of content from existence. It is a "what" which, so far as it is a mere idea, clearly *is* not, and if it also *were*, could, so far, not be called ideal. For ideality lies in the disjoining of quality from being. . . .

We can understand this most clearly if we consider the nature of judgement, for there we find thought in its completed form. In judgement an idea is predicated of a reality. Now, in the first place, what is predicated is . . . a mere "what," a mere feature of content, which is used to qualify further the "that" of the subject. . . . The predicate is a content which has been made loose from its own immediate existence and is used in divorce from that first unity. . . . If this were not so, there would be no judgement; for neither distinction nor predication would have taken place. . . .

And in the second place, when we turn to the subject of the judgement, we clearly find the other aspect, in other words, the "that." Just as in "this horse is a mammal" the predicate was *not* a fact, so most assuredly the subject is an actual existence. And the same thing holds good with every judgement. No one ever means to assert about anything but reality, or to do anything but qualify a "that" by a "what." . . .

Judgement is essentially the re-union of two sides, "what" and "that," provisionally estranged. But it is the alienation of these aspects in which thought's ideality consists.[k]

SOME EXAMPLES

This passage may have an initial difficulty, but what Bradley is talking about is familiar enough. Let us begin with a simpler example than his "This horse is a mammal," that is, an example drawn from an earlier developmental stage. Consider, then, Wordsworth's blessed babe, for whom flower's scent and mother's loving glance are a felt, nonrelational whole. At some point in the baby's development, presumably long before he has distinguished between his mother and the flower, he has what we may call an experience of "This again." On some occasion, that is, when this felt unity presents itself, the baby recalls an earlier presentation of it. He experiences it as "the same," as occurring again. And the baby responds *differentially* to the second presentation of the felt unity, not merely because it has been presented before, but because he recognizes it as the same as that earlier one. The baby is no longer merely reacting to the presentation (by way of conditioning or association); it is responding to it. In Peirce's language, this recurrence of the felt unity has become a sign of that earlier occurrence of it. In Bradley's language, the baby has separated its "what" from its "that": The felt unity has been "loosened" from its context. Without this "looseness"—Bradley also calls it "ideality"—the baby could never judge (nonverbally, of course) "This again." It experiences this felt unity as being the same as that earlier one only because, and to the extent that, it is able to detach the felt unity from the rest of what is presented on those two occasions.

A further development occurs—but no radical novelty is introduced—when the baby comes to distinguish, within the felt unity, between mother and flower.

To distinguish at all, there has to be a more extensive "loosening." Let the distinguishing mark be as elementary as one likes—mother cuddles; flower does not. Still, in order to distinguish at all, the baby must be able mentally to isolate (detach) cuddle as one aspect of the whole felt unity; and having managed to do this, he must then be able to assign this quality to one region of the felt unity and to exclude it from other regions. Assigning ("Cuddle coming now" on the presentation of mother) is a nonverbal judgment; so is excluding ("No cuddle coming now" on the presentation of flower). And these judgments are merely more complex forms of the same process of differentiation and recombination that we have seen to be involved in "This again."

"This horse is a mammal," to come now to Bradley's own example, is simply a more complex form of the same double process. To be able, on looking at the horse, to recognize (judge) that it is a mammal, one must have in one's repertoire the concept (ideal content) "mammal." This is an aspect that we have been able to detach not only from our experience of *this* horse (as the baby is able to detach cuddle as an aspect of the felt unity), but from other horses, and from dogs and cats, lions and tigers, and so on, as well. And we have stored away this quality in its loosened ("ideal") form for future use, when we will recombine it with appropriate regions of experience.

WHY DO WE JUDGE?

We judge because "to remain within the presented is neither defensible nor possible. We are compelled alike by necessity and by logic to transcend it."[1] That is, we judge only because we experience some unrest, due to a discrepancy we encounter. In the most elementary case, the baby judges (nonverbally) because the felt unity has become sufficiently detached from its context for him to notice it. To notice is to experience a minor unrest; a small discrepancy has occurred that disturbs the even flow of the baby's life. Hence the baby asks, in effect, "What is it?" and answers himself, "It's this again." The baby's recognition of what has disturbed the even flow removes the discrepancy and allays his unrest.

Or, to take an example of explicit judgment, think of the circumstances in which someone might judge, "Whales are mammals." He has many times seen whales swimming in the sea, but now, by chance, for the first time he sees a whale suckling her young. He feels unrest because he "knows" that creatures that swim in the sea do not suckle their young. Here, then, is a major discrepancy, or, as Bradley termed it, "contradiction," which he naturally wants to remove. It occurs to him (he judges) that whales are mammals who live in the sea, and harmony is restored.

ALL JUDGMENT IS CONDITIONAL

It will be seen that Bradley's whole emphasis was on judging—on the act, not on the proposition that is the result of the act. For this reason, and because of all his talk about movement and development, it may seem that Bradley himself, despite all his criticism of James, lapsed into psychology. But Bradley would have maintained that the goal-directed movement from unrest to rest that he took judging to be is a logical development, not a psychological process. He was not describing how the human mind, as a matter of fact, happens to work; he was setting down the logically necessary requirements for reaching the truth—exactly what Peirce claimed to be doing in his studies of semiotic. The difference is that, in Bradley's view, no judgment is either true or false as it stands. To put this differently, all judgments, however categorical they may look in respect to form (for example, "Whales are mammals"), are conditional. Because they are conditional, we need to specify the conditions under which they are true; this, it will be seen, is a logical need, not a psychological one.

It may not be immediately evident why, in Bradley's view, all judgments are conditional. But it must be recalled that judging is a process of isolating and recombining elements and aspects within a larger whole—the "more than" that is present but not given. We know that the elements we have isolated and that we are recombining are somehow related to the "more than," but we cannot know how they are related to it nor what bearing the "more than" may have on them. The conditional character of the judgment (whatever its apparent form) is the mark of our ignorance—"Whales are mammals, if . . ." where the "if . . ." represents the unknown conditions which may indeed make it true that whales are mammals.

> Judgements are conditional in this sense, that what they affirm is incomplete. It cannot be attributed to Reality, as such, and before its necessary complement is added. And, in addition, this complement in the end remains unknown. But while it remains unknown, we obviously cannot tell how, if present, it would act upon and alter our predicate. For to suppose that its presence would make no difference is plainly absurd, while the precise nature of the difference falls outside our knowledge. But, if so, this unknown modification of our predicate may, in various degrees, destroy its special character. The content in fact might so be altered, be so redistributed and blended, as utterly to be transformed. And, in brief, the predicate may, taken as such, be more or less completely untrue. Thus we really always have asserted subject to, and at the mercy of, the unknown. And hence our judgement, always but to a varying extent, must in the end be called conditional.[m]

PREDICATION

The same conclusion can be reached by considering the nature of predication. Suppose we predicate some quality (say, sweetness) of some substance (say, sugar). But "Sugar is sweet" is either a flat-out contradiction or a tautology. (1) If "sweet" means sweet, then we contradict ourselves when we say, "Sugar is sweet," for sugar is *not* sweet. Sugar is sugar, and sweet is sweet. On the other hand (2), if "sweet" means sugar, then when we say that "Sugar is sweet," we have only said that sugar is sugar—a true but empty assertion. "If you predicate what is different, you ascribe to the subject what it is *not;* and if you predicate what is *not* different, you say nothing at all." The only exit from this "old dilemma," in Bradley's view, is to admit that whenever we predicate P of S, "there must be a whole embracing what is related, or there would be no differences and no relation."[n] In other words, whenever we make a judgment of the ostensible form, S is P, we are really making a judgment of the form, R-S is P, where R is the whole universe—always present but not given—and S is the part of R that is now in focus.

To maintain that the judgment "Sugar is sweet" is either a self-contradiction or a tautology may seem in its turn to be either a poor joke or a bad muddle, and this is exactly what many—indeed, most—logicians would hold. But Bradley cannot be disposed of quite so easily. Suppose we encounter a man who has red hair and is freckled, or, for that matter, we simply encounter two redheaded men. In both cases, according to Bradley, we are confronted with a contradiction that we must try to dissolve.

> Any such irrationality and externality cannot be the last truth about things. Somewhere there must be a reason why this [red hair] and that [freckles] appear together. And this reason and reality must reside in the whole from which [red hair and freckles] are abstractions, a whole in which their internal connexion must lie. . . . The merely external is, in short, our ignorance set up as a reality, and to find it anywhere, except as an inconsistent aspect of a fact . . . is impossible.[o]

Now certainly felt discrepancies (such as the coincidence of red hair and freckles) may evoke the question, "Why?" and so lead to the discovery of new truths, such as a genetic linkage between red hair and freckles. But perhaps no linkage is discovered; perhaps the coincidence remains a coincidence. We can add, if we like, that it is a "presupposition," or a "working hypothesis," of science that there are no coincidences (for if one did not assume that there are no coincidences, one would not persist in research), or, again, that it is the "faith" of the scientist. These are things that have satisfied some philosophers, but presuppositions, assumptions, and faith would not satisfy Bradley. He wanted to *prove*, and he thought he could prove, that there are, and can be, no coincidences.

> The correlation of the other circumstances of and characters in the two men with the quality of red-hairedness cannot in other words possibly be bare chance. And if you could have a perfect relational knowledge of the world, you could go from the nature of red-hairedness to these other characters which qualify it, and you could from the nature of red-hairedness reconstruct all the red-haired men. . . .
>
> For example, a red-haired man who knew himself utterly would and must, starting from within, go on to know every one else who has red hair, and he would not know himself until he knew them. But, as things are, he does not know how or why he himself has red hair, nor how or why a different

man is also the same in that point, and therefore, because he does not know the ground, the how and why, of his relation to the other man, it remains for him relatively external, contingent, and fortuitous. But there is really no mere externality except in his ignorance.[p]

We have now made a step forward. It turns out that the alleged logical truth that only the unconditioned is free from contradiction rests on the alleged truth that everything must be capable of explanation, that is, that there are no coincidences. Bradley's argument is that a coincidence would be a "bare" juxtaposition (for example, red hair *and* freckles—sheer "and," without any reason), and that to assert "and" is itself a contradiction. "Take a diversity (here is the point), a diversity used simply to qualify the same subject, and with that you have a contradiction, and that is what contradiction means. The 'And,' if you take it *simply as mere* 'And,' is itself contradiction."[q]

We get a clue to what underlies this argument if we note how much broader a meaning "contradiction" has for Bradley than for most logicians. For most logicians it is a contradiction to assert that S is both A and not-A at the same time, but it is no contradiction to assert that S is both A and not B. For Bradley, as we have seen, it is a contradiction even to assert that S is A. In his view *any* sort of felt discrepancy, any sort of felt unrest, is a contradiction—"contradiction" and "discrepancy" are coterminous.

This "broader" view of contradiction led Bradley to conclusions that are so paradoxical and of such consequences for his whole theory that we will briefly recapitulate the argument.

Bradley started, then, from the unrest that infects even the nonrelational unity of immediate experience—the unrest occasioned by the imperfect interfusion of past and future in the now. Judgment is the process by which we seek to achieve a perfect interfusion of our experience. But judgment cannot reach this state of completion, for two reasons.

The first reason is that, though we take in more and more of the "more than," there is always still more that eludes us—more that is present as a "presence" but that is not yet fully developed and articulated. Indeed, in a sense, the more we take in, the more there is still left to take in, for everything that we take in and manage to articulate, has extensive connections with what, as yet, lies outside, that is, is present but not given. To put this differently, the universe is, for us, inexhaustible; therefore, since the relation between what we have so far articulated and what we feel but have not yet articulated, is unknown, the universe is a source of "discomfort, unrest, and uneasiness."[r]

The second reason is that even if, *per impossible,* judgment could complete the articulated relational structure at which it is constantly at work, this structure would be only a complete description of the universe. The universe and the complete relational structure would be two, not one; they would be barely juxtaposed, related by a contradictory "and." Hence the so-called completed relational structure would not really be complete; it would not be unconditioned.

It may be helpful to state Bradley's point in Peirce's language. At the level of judgment, then, we always have a relation between a sign and what the sign signifies. If the sign were not different from its signification, the sign obviously would not signify—there would be no meaning, no reference, no signification. Or in Bradley's own language: At the level of judgment there is always a loosening of the "what" from the "that"; if the "what" were not loosened from the "that," there would be no judgment and, so, no truth.

So far, Bradley and Peirce agreed. But for Peirce the gap between sign and signification is not problematic; far from being problematic, it is essential. If the mind could close the gap (instead of merely approaching its object asymptotically), the object would not be independent, and truth would, at best, be only relative. Peirce, that is to say, was a Realist; his deepest passion was the quest for truth. Bradley's deepest passion, in contrast, was the quest for unity. Hence all separations—including the gap between the "that" and the loosened "what"—must be overcome, transcended, healed; the separated elements must be reunited. But now this quest for perfect unity creates a dilemma: On the one hand, the mind assuredly seeks to know its object. On the other hand, it is never content until it becomes that object. If that could happen, if the gap between sign and signification could be overcome, knowledge, and with it truth, would disappear. "The essential inconsistency of truth may, perhaps, be best stated thus. If there is any difference between *what it means* and *what it stands for,* then truth is clearly not realized. But, if there is no such difference, then truth has ceased to exist."[s]

Relations

We can reach the same radical conclusion by another route: by examining the nature of relations. Happily it is unnecessary to examine the argument in close detail; it not only ends at the same point as the discussion of judgment, but covers much the same ground. This is the case, of course, because thought, in contrast to feeling, is, in its essential nature, relational. The weaknesses of thought that we have just examined are due, in the last analysis, to the fact that all relations are contradictory.

> The arrangement of given facts into relations and qualities may be necessary in practice, but it is theoretically unintelligible. . . .
> The conclusion to which I am brought is that a relational way of thought—any one that moves by the machinery of terms and relations—must give appearance, and not truth. It is a makeshift, a device, a mere practical compromise, most necessary, but in the end most indefensible.[t]

Bradley's arguments may be summarized in the following way: First he considered the claim that there can be qualities without relations, and replied that there cannot be *a* quality unless there are at least two qualities; we would never get the notion of a unit unless we had another unit to contrast this one with. Very well, then, if there are two units there must be a relation between them, if only the relation of being different. Hence there are no qualities without relations.

Next he considered the claim that qualities with relations are intelligible, and argued that this too must be rejected. We have two units related by being different (one earlier than the other; one larger than the other . . .). Surely the first unit must be, in order to be related to the second. But, as we have seen in the first argument, it cannot be until, or unless, it is related to another. Philosophers may try to evade this conclusion by dividing the unit A into two parts; part *a*, which makes possible the relation with the other unit, B, and part α, which is made possible by the relation with B. But now our unit is a unit no longer; it is two units: *a* and α. The first argument now applies, and a vicious circle has been generated.

In short, terms, with or without relations, are unintelligible. The same conclusion follows if we consider the matter from the side of terms. Relations without terms are manifestly impossible—what would a relation be that related nothing? But relations with terms are equally impossible. Consider the relation *r* that relates A to B. Is *r* related to A? Obviously so. Then there must be a relation *r'* that relates *r* to A, a relation *r''* that relates *r'* to *r*, and so on. Clearly another infinite regress has broken out.

These arguments may sound sophistical. They are, however, only "ramifications and refinements"[u] of Bradley's critique of "and."[5] Some pair of juxtaposed elements, A and B, may be so familiar that their juxtaposition does not puzzle us. If so, that is a comment on us, not on them. Their juxtaposition *ought* to puzzle us, for, as a "mere" juxtaposition, it is a contradiction. To resolve the contradiction we need to understand why they are juxtaposed, and this means articulating the context in which the merely juxtaposed elements occur. But this context is itself a relational structure. That is, it consists in juxtaposed elements that, in their turn, must be explicated—made intelligible—in the same way. And clearly this process of explication can never end. The logical conclusion is that, rather than continue the process endlessly, we must pass beyond—transcend—the whole "relational way" of seeking intelligibility.

Leaving aside possible quibbles over the ramifications and refinements, is this critique of relations valid? No simple answer seems possible, for here we face again that major parting of the ways that reflects differing attitudes toward unity. Consider the blessed babe once more. To distinguish between mother and flower is to replace a felt unity by a relational structure. Doubtless something has been lost, but surely something has been gained. Has more been lost or has more been gained? And does one believe that by substituting for the initial crude structure, a complex and highly differentiated relational structure one can make up the losses and keep the gains? In particular, is "Mother + flower" (letting " + "

5 See p. 343.

represent the most complex and subtle set of interrelations that can be worked out and set down) ever adequate to the original felt unity, mother/flower?

Or, as another example, consider the judgments, "This horse is a mammal" and "That whale is a mammal." Does it seem reasonable to say that, since both judgments are true, the two animals have an identical property—mammality—in common? Or does one insist that the mammality of this horse is different from the mammality of every other horse, let alone the mammality of whales? Is one impressed by the mammality one experiences as one watches, say, one's mare nurse its foal? *That* mammality is a synthesis of all sorts of visual, olfactory, and tactile experiences, together with one's affection for the mare and one's hopes for the foal. Is it this directly experienced mammality that is important? Or is it the bare, abstract, universal "mammality" that, loosened from its context, can be asserted indifferently of gorillas, lions, and whales, as well as of one's own mare? We may suspect that people will answer these questions differently, and on these differences assessments of Bradley's critique will turn. Those who share his passion for unity will agree that the essential nature of reality escapes through the interstices of a relational net, however highly structured and articulated it may be, and they will conclude that Bradley's critique is profound. Others will regard it as nonsensical.

Degrees of Truth, Degrees of Reality, and Error

We have now seen that the truth "is corrected only by passing outside the intellect," and that "in this passage the proper nature of truth is, of course, transformed and perishes."[v] This conclusion may suggest that Bradley fell victim to the same fatal mistake he found in all relativism and scepticism. As he himself put it, "If a man asserts there is no truth, you can formally convict him out of his own mouth,"[w] and it has seemed to some philosophers that Bradley's insistence that the whole relational way of thought is self-defeating amounts to just such a self-convicting assertion.

But Bradley held otherwise. If truth and falsity were, as most logicians hold, contraries, so that if a judgment, J, is true, it is not false and if it is false it is not true, then he would indeed be involved in the contradiction just described. But Bradley's account of the nature of thought entails that no judgment is wholly true and none is wholly false. Every judgment is to some extent true, depending on how much experience is articulated in it; every judgment is to some extent false, depending on what is excluded, omitted, or ignored. In short, there are degrees of truth, depending on the comprehensiveness of what is articulated in the judgment; but there is no absolute truth, for there can be no judgment that includes everything, that is *identical* with reality. Similarly, there are degrees of error, depending on the incoherence and partiality of the judgment;

but there is no absolute error, for even the most elementary judgment, to be a judgment at all, makes some distinction, however fragmentary and partial, within the felt unity of immediate experience.

This doctrine of degrees of truth and error follows directly from the notion of the ideality of judgment, which we have already discussed.[6] It follows, that is, from the contention that judgment inevitably involves

> . . . the loosening of that which an idea itself is from that which it means and stands for. And in my opinion this breach is at once essential and fatal to truth. For truth is not perfect until this sundering of aspects is somehow made good, until that which in fact is, forms a consistent whole with that which it stands for and means. In other words, truth demands at once the essential difference and identity of ideas and reality. It demands (we may say) that the idea should in the end be reconstituted by the subject of the judgement and should in no sense whatever fall outside. But the possibility of such an implication involves, in my view, a passage beyond mere truth to actual reality, a passage in which truth would have completed itself beyond itself. Truth, in other words, content with nothing short of reality, has, in order to remain truth, to come short for ever of its own ideal and to remain imperfect. But on the other side there is no possible judgement the predicate of which can fail somehow to qualify the Real; and there is hence no mere error.
>
> The more the conditions of your assertion are included in your assertion, so much the truer and less erroneous does your judgement become. But can the conditions of the judgement ever be made complete and comprised within the judgement? In my opinion this is impossible. And hence with every truth there still remains some truth, however little, in its opposite. In other words, you never can pass wholly beyond degree. . . .[x] Error *is* truth, it is partial truth that is false only because it is partial and left incomplete.[y]

Appearance

Having studied Bradley's theory of knowledge, we are now ready to turn to his metaphysics. We have, in the first place, to distinguish mere appearance from reality.

What has just been said about degrees of truth and error is highly relevant to the discussion of appearance, for appearance is not illusion (as the term may suggest), nor is it something different from reality. To allow that would be to lapse into dualism. Appearance *is* reality, but it is reality only partially grasped and, so, only partially true.

> Certainly a man knows and experiences everywhere the ultimate Reality, and indeed is able to know and experience nothing else. But to know it or experience it, fully and as such, is a thing utterly impossible. . . .

6 See pp. 338–39.

No one aspect of experience, as such, is real. None is primary, or can serve to explain the others or the whole. They are all alike appearances, all one-sided, and passing away beyond themselves. But I may be asked why, admitting this, we should call them appearances. For such a term belongs solely of right to the perceptual side of things, and the perceptual side, we agreed, was but one aspect among others. . . . We must . . . admit that . . . a licence is involved in our use of the term. Our attitude, however, in metaphysics must be theoretical. It is our business here to measure and to judge the various aspects of things. And hence for us anything which comes short when compared with Reality, gets the name of appearance. . . . When the term is thus defined, its employment seems certainly harmless. . . .

Reality (we must repeat this) is not the sum of things. It is the unity in which all things, coming together, are transmuted, in which they are changed all alike, though not changed equally. . . .

Since the amount of change is different in each case, appearances differ widely in their degrees of truth and reality. There are predicates which, in comparison with others, are false and unreal. To survey the field of appearances, to measure each by the idea of perfect individuality, and to arrange them in an order and in a system of reality and merit—would be the task of metaphysics.[z]

Bradley did not attempt, in the fashion of Hegel, to carry the "task of metaphysics" through to completion, and it may be doubted whether, given his radical attack on truth, it would be possible for him to have done so. Instead, he examined several typical conceptual schemes that philosophers and others have used in attempting to understand the world and showed that each falls into contradiction. This conclusion hardly has to be worked out in detail for each conceptual scheme; it follows directly, of course, from Bradley's critique of relations, for a conceptual scheme is nothing but a relational structure by means of which we organize experience. Nevertheless it will be useful to examine a few of the more important of the arguments, especially since the criticisms do not always depend on a prior acceptance of Bradley's general thesis that the relational way of thought is inadequate.

SPACE, TIME, MOTION, AND CHANGE

Space: In summary Bradley's argument is that "space is a relation—which it cannot be; and it is a quality or substance—which again it cannot be. . . . It is a . . . special attempt to combine the irreconcilable."[a] Expanded and set out in the antithetical form Bradley liked, the argument runs as follows:

1. Space is not a mere relation. For any space must consist of extended parts, and these parts clearly are spaces. So that, even if we could take our space as a collection, it would be a collection of solids. The relation would join spaces which would not be mere relations. And hence the collection, if taken as a *mere* inter-relation, would not be space. We should be brought

to the proposition that space is nothing but a relation of spaces. And this proposition contradicts itself. . . .

2. But space is nothing but a relation. For, in the first place, any space must consist of parts; and, if the parts are not spaces, the whole is not space. Take then in a space any parts. These, it is assumed, must be solid, but they are obviously extended. If extended, however, they will themselves consist of parts, and these again of further parts, and so on without end. A space, or a part of space, that really means to be solid, is a self-contradiction. Anything extended is a collection, a relation of extendeds, which again are relations of extendeds, and so on indefinitely. The terms are essential to the relation, and the terms do not exist. Searching without end, we never find anything more than relations; and we see that we cannot. Space is essentially a relation of what vanishes into relations, which seek in vain for their terms. It is lengths of lengths of—nothing that we can find. . . .

[In short,] space vanishes internally into relations between units which never can exist. But, on the other side, when taken itself as a unit, it passes away into the search for an illusory whole. . . . For take space as large and as complete as you possibly can. Still, if it has not definite boundaries, it is not space; and to make it end in a cloud, or in nothing, is mere blindness and *our* mere failure to perceive. A space limited, and yet without space that is outside, is a self-contradiction. But the outside, unfortunately, is compelled likewise to pass beyond itself; and the end cannot be reached.[b]

Time:

It is usual to consider time under a spatial form, [and] time, apprehended in this way, is open to the objection we have just urged against space. It is a relation—and, on the other side, it is not a relation; and it is, again, incapable of being anything beyond a relation.[c]

Motion:

Motion has from an early time been criticized severely, and it has never been defended with much success. I will briefly point to the principle on which these criticisms are founded. Motion implies that what is moved is in two places in one time; and this seems not possible. That motion implies two places is obvious; that these places are successive is no less obvious. But, on the other hand, it is clear that the process must have unity. The thing moved must be one; and, again, the time must be one. If the time were only many times, out of relation, and not parts of a single temporal whole, then no motion would be found. But if the time is one, then, as we have seen, it cannot also be many.[d]

Change:

Something, A, changes, and therefore it cannot be permanent. On the other hand, if A is not permanent, what is it that changes? It will no longer be A, but something else. In other words, let A be free from change in time, and it does not change. But let it contain change, and at once it becomes A^1, A^2, A^3. Then what becomes of A, and of its change, for we are left with something else? Again, we may put the problem thus. The diverse states of A must exist within one time; and yet they cannot, because they are successive. . . .

Change, upon any hypotheses, is impossible. It can be no more than appearance.[e]

COMMENT ON THESE ARGUMENTS

These arguments sound very much like—and are almost certainly deliberately modeled on—Zeno's paradoxes. Like those paradoxes they all depend on an alleged puzzle about the continuum. But whatever Zeno may have thought, Bradley did not hold that space, time, motion, and change are illusions. When we see swift Achilles overtake the slow tortoise we are not, in Bradley's view, experiencing something like the mirage a thirsty traveler sees in the desert or the pink rats a dipsomaniac sees on his hearth rug. What then—if he is not claiming that perceptual experiences of space, time, motion, and change are illusory—is Bradley asserting when he claims that they are "mere" appearances? It is that a coherent analysis of these concepts is impossible for the reason that they all involve the notion of infinite divisibility, which is contradictory. We can use our perceptual experiences of space, time, motion, and change as a guide for action and as a basis for prediction. Further, most people are so familiar with such experiences that they are never puzzled about them. But if they ever do attempt to *understand* them they find that they cannot.

Bradley's worry about infinite divisibility seems to have been based on the feeling that sooner or later we must come to an end, but that we cannot come to an end because, no matter how many times we have divided our space (or our time), there is always more space (or time) left to divide. The contradiction he felt is between "we must" and "we cannot." A possible reply (as courteous as some of Bradley's replies to his own critics) might be that, however much a philosopher "wholly ignorant of mathematics" may feel "unrest and discomfort," the differential calculus has long provided an entirely satisfactory way of representing infinite divisibility.

But of course Bradley would not deny that, for the purpose of, say, getting to the moon and back, a curve drawn on a piece of graph paper or an equation written on a blackboard is a satisfactory representation of space and time. Such "devices . . . may work," he would say, in the sense that they help us get to the moon and back, but they are only "makeshifts." They leave wholly unsolved "the theoretical problem." They are "theoretically unintelligible."[f]

What do you mean by "theoretically unintelligible"? a critic might retort. What remains to be understood about the meaning of space and time when you have specified procedures for measuring time and space? All that is left is a metaphysician's vague feeling of unrest, and this can be safely disregarded: It is just a psychological quirk of this metaphysician. Bradley's situation is exactly the sort that Peirce's pragmaticism was designed to deal with. On the one hand, you have the obvious fact that Achilles does overtake the tortoise; on the other hand, you have a device that enables you to specify, as precisely as you like, the instant at which he overtakes him. What more do you want?

Well, one might reply, one wants an adequate representation of the felt passage of time experienced by the mathematician as he computes Achilles' acceleration. That felt passage of time—the time the mathematician lives through—is experienced by him as a continuous flow, and this is not well represented by the concept of an "instant" as a unit that can be made as small as the mathematician likes. And what about the claustrophobic feeling of being crowded into too small a space, or the agrophobic feeling of being lost in too large a space? What about the way time speeds up and slows down in different circumstances? It could be argued that a novel like Thomas Mann's *Magic Mountain* is a much more satisfactory representation of these felt features of space and time than is any mathematical representation.

This reply, which is in the spirit of much of what Bradley said, unfortunately does not establish all that he wanted. It leaves us with a plurality of different types of representations, each of which is adequate to an appropriate region of experience and inadequate to other regions of experience. Bradley wanted to hold that there is a hierarchy of representations, all of which are adequate in varying degrees, to the one all-inclusive Reality.

FACTS

Bradley started with the common-sense view of fact: A fact is "either an event, or else what is directly experienced."[g] Thus it is either a fact that I am now experiencing a pain and seeing a blue sense datum, or it is not. Either it is a fact that Caesar crossed the Rubicon or it is a fact that he did not. In short, for common sense, the chief characteristic of a fact is its ultimacy, its givenness or "brutality." There is nothing we can do about a fact but ignore it, or accept it and try to account for it as best we can. It is the business of a scientific theory to explain the facts, and scientific theories stand or fall depending on whether they fit the facts or conflict with them.

This common-sense view of facts Bradley of course wholly rejected, and with it the "pretensions" of science to truth, in distinction from utility. Facts "(a) cannot make the world intelligible, and again (b) they are not given, and (c) in themselves they are self-contradictory, and not truth but appearance."[h] We say that Bradley *of course* rejected the ultimacy (and the reality) of facts because a fact claims to be an encapsulated event that is what it is, regardless of its context (either Caesar crossed the Rubicon or he did not). And it follows both from Bradley's theory of judgment and from his critique of relations that context is always relevant. Whatever else a fact is, it is a finite being, and "we have found that the very essence of finite beings is self-contradictory, that their own nature includes relation to others, and that they *are* already each outside of its own existence."[i]

But the common-sense view of the sheer factuality of facts can be attacked in a way that is not dependent on Bradley's general metaphysical theory. Every fact, according to this line of argument, is the end product of an inference and therefore relative to the assumptions, beliefs, and theories on which this inference rests. In an early essay, "The Presuppositions of Critical History," Bradley effectively criticizes historians of the Ranke school of thought, who hold that the task of the historian is simply to ascertain what "really happened"—what the facts really are. This is naïve, Bradley points out. Even where we have reports of eyewitnesses to some past event, these reports always reflect the varying perspectives of those witnesses. The reports are not simply passive recordings of what occurred; they are "constructions," selective interpretations, colored, both in what they include and in what they exclude, by the biases and by the ignorance of the observers. And on top of these constructions, we have the successive contributions of historians, each adding his own construction, which reflects his biases and ignorance.

> The historical fact then (for us) is a conclusion; and a conclusion, however much it may appear so, is never the fiction of a random invention. We bring to its assertion the formed world of existing beliefs, and the new matter of a fresh instance. They are grounds for our position, and we know them as such, or at least we may know them. For everything that we say we think we have reasons, our realities are built up of explicit or hidden inferences; in a single word, our facts are inferential, and their actuality depends on the correctness of the reasoning which makes them what they are. . . .
>
> The correctness of the isolated event as recorded rests upon a theory, and the recorded train of circumstances which makes a narrative is a still wider theory, which must depart yet farther from the fact as imagined to consist in passive sensation, and must imply, together with its greater possibilities of truth and falsehood, the increased existence of active combination. We cannot recall accurately what we have not rightly observed, and rightly to observe is not to receive a series of chaotic impressions, but to grasp the course of events as a connected whole.[j]

Bradley's view of the relation between the given and the constructions by means of which we organize and interpret it was quite different from that of the positivists (and of James, so far as James ever settled on any one view).[7] According to them, the ultimate facts are sense data; the shoes and ships and sealing wax of ordinary experience are constructions to be evaluated in terms of their capacity to help us accomplish our practical ends. But for Bradley, though constructions do have practical value, they should, above all else, be self-consistent, and, ultimately, no construction can be. As for the given, it is simply the name for the region within experience (whatever it happens to be on this occasion) that is relatively clear and in focus, in contrast to the penumbra that

7 See pp. 202–03, 300–03.

is felt as present but is not now in focus. There is no given, in the positivists' sense of ultimate unanalyzable building blocks; everything is subject to interpretation. And sense data, far from being given, are extremely artificial abstractions.

> There is a view which takes, or attempts to take, sense-perception as the one known reality. . . . This conclusion is radically erroneous. No perception ever . . . has a character contained within itself. In order to be a fact at all, each presentation must exhibit ideality. . . . The union in all perception of thought with sense, the co-presence everywhere in all appearances of fact with ideality—this is the one foundation of truth.[k]

Bradley's criticism of positivism was thus very close to Peirce's.[8] He would have agreed with Peirce that what I happen to see when I meet a man in the street (an old friend or, alternatively, a complete stranger) is a function of my present interests and my past knowledge. But he drew a completely different conclusion from the inferential or "constructive" character of facts. Whereas Peirce held that the end product of construction (an end product that we never reach but only approach asymptotically) is this particular man as he really is (either old friend or complete stranger), Bradley held that the end product (which we can never reach but which we know must be) is the Absolute, in which this and every other particular is included but transcended.

THE SELF

That the self is mere appearance is a foregone conclusion, for it is certainly a finite being, and, as we have seen, "the very essence of finite beings is self-contradictory." It remains, therefore, only to consider any claims that might be made for exempting the self from this general condemnation. Since finite beings are self-contradictory because, in any finite being, it is impossible to reconcile unity and diversity, a claim might be put forward that in the feeling of self-identity—in my feeling that I am the same self I was a year ago—we have an instance of the way "in which diversity is harmonized." But

> . . . mere feeling is no answer to our riddle. . . . Either you do not descend low enough to get rid of relations with all their inconsistency, or else you have reached a level where subject and object are in no sense distinguished, and where, therefore, neither self nor its opposite exists.[1]

And if it is claimed that I have an intuition, not a mere feeling, of self-identity, the case is no better:

> Self-consciousness, we may be told, is a special way of intuition, or perception, or what you will. And this experience of both subject and object in one self, or of the identity of the Ego through and in the opposition of itself

8 See pp. 269–70.

to itself, or generally the self-apprehension of the self as one and many, is at last the full answer to our whole series of riddles. But to my mind such an answer brings no satisfaction. For it seems liable to the objections which proved fatal to mere feeling. Suppose, for argument's sake, that the intuition (as you describe it) actually exists; suppose that in this intuition, while you keep to it, you possess a diversity without discrepancy. This is one thing, but it is quite another thing to possess a principle which can serve for the understanding of reality. For how does this way of apprehension . . . satisfy the claims of understanding? This, to my mind, forms a wholly insuperable obstacle. For the contents of the intuition (this many in one), if you try to reconstruct them relationally, fall asunder forthwith. And the attempt to find in self-consciousness an apprehension at a level, not below, but above relations—a way of apprehension superior to discursive thought, and including its mere process in a higher harmony—appears to me not successful. I am, in short, compelled to this conclusion: even if your intuition is a fact, it is not an *understanding* of the self or of the world. It is a mere experience, and it furnishes no consistent view about itself or about reality in general.[m]

The self, then, is not a primordial feature of the universe but a construction that has developed in the course of dealing with, interpreting, and trying to make sense of experience as it comes. The self is as much a construction as is a field of force, a gravitational attraction, social mobility, or class struggle. These and all other constructions have an initial usefulness, they are constantly exposed to criticism, revised, and again applied to the interpretation of experience. The self is more viable than most such constructions; indeed, "it is the highest form of experience which we have."[n] But for all that, it is only a construction: It does not give us reality as it is in itself, but only as it appears to, or through, a particular relational structure.

GOODNESS

The good, in the most general sense, is simply "that which satisfies desire. It is that which we approve of, and in which we can rest with a feeling of contentment." Having thus fixed the meaning of goodness, "we may proceed to lay stress on its contradictory character."[o] In the first place, goodness

> . . . always [is] the adjective of something not itself. Beauty, truth, pleasure, and sensation are all things that are good. We desire them all, and all can serve as types or "norms" by which to guide our approbation. And hence, in a sense, they all will fall under and be included in goodness. But when we ask, on the other hand, if goodness exhausts all that lies in these regions, the answer must be different. For we see at once that each possesses a character of its own; and, in order to be good, the other aspects of the universe must also be themselves. The good then, as such, is obviously not so wide as the totality of things.[p]

Being less than the Whole, goodness is finite and therefore mere appearance. Alternatively, since goodness is a quality or characteristic predicated of other things, for example, "beauty, truth, strength, even luck," it stands in a relation to these things and is therefore exposed to the general critique of relations.

Also, goodness is in a special way characterized by "ideality." The "inmost being" of the good "implies a distinction of idea from existence": If the good is what we desire, then, when we attain it and so no longer desire it, it is no longer good.

> A satisfied desire is, in short, inconsistent with itself. For, so far as it is quite satisfied, it is not a desire; and, so far as it is a desire, it must remain at least partly unsatisfied. And where we are said to want nothing but what we have, . . . we have, first, an ideal continuance of character in conflict with change. But in any case, apart from this, there is implied the suggestion of an idea, distinct from the fact while identified with it. Each of these features is necessary, and each is inconsistent with the other. And the resolution of this difference between idea and existence is both demanded by the good, and yet remains unattainable. Its accomplishment, indeed, would destroy the proper essence of goodness, and the good is therefore in itself incomplete and self-transcendent.[q]

Finally, we desire no mere balance of satisfactions over dissatisfactions; we desire perfect satisfaction. But perfect satisfaction—like absolute truth—is unattainable, and the pursuit of it leads to an infinite regress.

> A mere balance of advantage, however satisfactory the means by which I come to possess it, is most assuredly *not* the fulfilment of my desire. For the desire of human beings (this is surely a commonplace) has no limit. Goodness, in other words, must imply an attempt to reach perfection, and it is the nature of the finite to seek for that which nothing finite can satisfy. . . . Goodness, or the attainment of such an impossible end, is still self-contradictory.[r]

For these reasons goodness is "a subordinate and, therefore, a self-contradictory aspect of the universe."

GOD

If God is less than the Whole, then God is finite and, so, like everything finite, mere appearance. But certainly the God of Christianity is less than the Whole, for He is held to have created a universe that is other than Himself, and He stands in a complex set of relations to this created universe. Unfortunately, since relations are self-contradictory, God's relation to man is unintelligible.

> Religion naturally implies a relation between Man and God. Now a relation always (we have seen throughout) is self-contradictory. It implies always two

terms which are finite and which claim independence. On the other hand a relation is unmeaning, unless both itself and the relateds are the adjectives of a whole. And to find a solution of this discrepancy would be to pass entirely beyond the relational point of view. This general conclusion may at once be verified in the sphere of religion.

Man is on the one hand a finite subject, who is over against God, and merely "standing in relation." And yet, upon the other hand, apart from God man is merely an abstraction. And religion perceives this truth, and it affirms that man is good and real only through grace, or that again, attempting to be independent, he perishes through wrath. He does not merely "stand in relation," but is moved inly by his opposite, and indeed, apart from that inward working, could not stand at all. God again is a finite object, standing above and apart from man, and is something independent of all relation to his will and intelligence. Hence God, if taken as a thinking and feeling being, has a private personality. But, sundered from those relations which qualify him, God is inconsistent emptiness; and, qualified by his relation to an Other, he is distracted finitude. . . .

Religion prefers to put forth statements which it feels are untenable, and to correct them at once by counter-statements which it finds are no better. It is then driven forwards and back between both, like a dog which seeks to follow two masters. A discrepancy worth our notice is the position of God in the universe. We may say that in religion God tends always to pass beyond himself. He is necessarily led to end in the Absolute, which for religion is not God. God, whether a "person" or not, is, on the one hand, a finite being and an object to man. On the other hand, the consummation, sought by the religious consciousness, is the perfect unity of these terms. . . . The unity implies a complete suppression of the relation, as such; but, with that suppression, religion and the good have altogether, as such, disappeared. If you identify the Absolute with God, that is not the God of religion. If again you separate them, God becomes a finite factor in the Whole. And the effort of religion is to put an end to, and break down, this relation—a relation which, none the less, it essentially presupposes. Hence, short of the Absolute, God cannot rest, and, having reached that goal, he is lost and religion with him. . . .

In short, God, as the highest expression of the realized good, shows the contradiction which we found to be inherent in that principle. The falling apart of idea and existence is at once essential to goodness and negated by Reality. And the process, which moves within Reality, is not Reality itself. We may say that God is not God, till he has become all in all, and that a God which is all in all is not the God of religion. God is but an aspect, and that must mean but an appearance, of the Absolute.[8]

Reality

So far we have been discussing appearance, that is, partially true but ultimately inadequate ways of characterizing Reality. What we know about Reality so far, in distinction from appearance, is only that its character, whatever it is, is such that it "excludes contradiction. . . . We may say that everything, which appears, is somehow real in such a way as to be self-consistent. The character of the real is to possess everything phenomenal in a harmonious form."[t]

What, then, can we—applying the absolute criterion of self-consistency—affirm about Reality? It is one; it is of the nature of experience; it is suprarelational; it is such that all sides of our nature and not merely our intellect find satisfaction in it. Let us examine these features of Reality in turn.

REALITY IS ONE

That Reality is one, not many, follows directly from the critique of relations. For suppose there were a plurality of reals: These reals would stand in *some* relation to each other, even if only the relation of being independent of each other. And being in relation, they would be self-contradictory and, so, by definition, not Reality.

> Reality is one. It must be single, because plurality, taken as real, contradicts itself. Plurality implies relations, and, through its relations, it unwillingly asserts always a superior unity. To suppose the universe plural is therefore to contradict oneself and, after all, to suppose that it is one. Add one world to another, and forthwith both worlds have become relative, each the finite appearance of a higher and single Reality.[u]

How, in detail, the plurality comes together in unity we do not, and cannot, know. *That* it does we are assured, for the unity of Reality is a necessity of logic.

REALITY IS SENTIENCE

As far as the content of this unity goes, Bradley argued that it must be of the nature of experience. The reason is simple but, to him, compelling: There is nothing else it could be.

> Can we . . . say anything about the concrete nature of [the Absolute]?
> Certainly, I think, this is possible. When we ask as to the matter which fills up the empty outline, we can reply in one word, that this matter is experience. And experience means something much the same as given and present fact. We perceive, on reflection, that to be real, or even barely to exist, must be to fall within sentience. Sentient experience, in short, is reality, and what is not this is not real. . . .
> Find any piece of existence, take up anything that any one could possibly call a fact, or could in any sense assert to have being, and then judge if it does not consist in sentient experience. Try to discover any sense in which you can still continue to speak of it, when all perception and feeling have been removed; or point out any fragment of its matter, any aspect of its being, which is not derived from and is not still relative to this source. When the

experiment is made strictly, I can myself conceive of nothing else than the experienced. Anything, in no sense felt or perceived, becomes to me quite unmeaning. And as I cannot try to think of it without realizing either that I am not thinking at all, or that I am thinking of it against my will as being experienced, I am driven to the conclusion that for me experience is the same as reality.[v]

The argument is Berkeley's *esse est percipi*, "to be is to be perceived."[9] And Bradley's challenge to an objector is the same as Berkeley's: Find something that is not *for* a percipient. Whatever you find, whatever you point to, is—just by the fact that you find it, that you point to it—*for* a percipient, namely you. This challenge, which seems so completely unanswerable to idealists like Berkeley and Bradley, leaves realists like Peirce wholly unmoved. That an object is "for a percipient" seems to the realist an accidental circumstance of the object; its nature is untouched by the fact that somebody happens to perceive it. Here we reach another major parting of the ways in philosophy, though it should be pointed out that Bradley had in his armory of weapons a reply not available to idealists of the Berkelian school. To hold, as the realist does, that the percipient and the perceived object are independent of each other is to fall into "vicious" abstraction; nothing is independent of anything else. But since this reply rests on the critique of relations, with it we reach still another parting of the ways.

REALITY IS SUPRARELATIONAL

To myself it seems that ultimate reality is supra-relational. We find it first below relations, and again relations are necessary to its development, and yet the relations cannot rightly be predicated of the original unity. They remain in a sense contained in it, but none the less again they transcend it. And the natural conclusion in my judgement is to a higher unity which is supra-relational. . . . The higher form of union, which satisfies at once our feeling, sense, and intelligence, is not found, in my opinion, within truth itself. It lies beyond and on the other side of judgement and intelligence.[w]

If relations are self-contradictory, it follows with logical necessity that Reality is nonrelational. But why not subrelational, instead of suprarelational? It would seem to be an argument in favor of this move that at least we have some experience of feeling, which is a subrelational state, whereas of suprarelational states we have none. Though it is obvious why Bradley wanted to avoid this conclusion, it is not easy to see how he managed to do so. He wanted to avoid it because (1) what the intellect seeks is understanding and to feel is not to understand, and (2) feeling, though nonrelational, is not without discrepancy; indeed, it is the felt discrepancy in immediate experience that generates the process that only ends in the Absolute. On the other hand, since understanding is relational ("to think is to judge"), how can we understand a suprarelational unity any better than we understand a subrelational unity?

9 See Vol. III, pp. 287–88.

REALITY MUST SATISFY ALL SIDES OF OUR NATURE

> I admit, or rather I would assert, that a result, if it fails to satisfy our whole nature, comes short of perfection. And I could not rest tranquilly in a truth if I were compelled to regard it as hateful. While unable, that is, to deny it, I should, rightly or wrongly, insist that the inquiry was not yet closed, and that the result was but partial. And if metaphysics is to stand, it must, I think, take account of all sides of our being. I do not mean that every one of our desires must be met by a promise of particular satisfaction; for that would be absurd and utterly impossible. But if the main tendencies of our nature do not reach consummation in the Absolute, we cannot believe that we have attained to perfection and truth. . . . We cannot argue directly that all sides of our nature must be satisfied, but indirectly we are led to the same result. For we are forced to assume theoretical satisfaction; and to suppose that existing one-sidedly, and together with practical discomfort, appears inadmissible. Such a state is a possibility which seems to contradict itself.[x]

Bradley's contention that Reality must satisfy every side of our nature thus depends on his identification of discrepancy with contradiction. If we knew Reality to be such that some deep human need could not be satisfied, this would certainly be experienced by us as a discrepancy. Since this amounts, in Bradley's view, to a contradiction, it follows that the universe is such that all deep human needs must be satisfied. But even if the identification of discrepancy and contradiction, which we have had occasion to question, were accepted, Bradley's conclusion would not necessarily follow. The existentialists, for instance, have argued in exactly the opposite direction: Since the universe is such that our deepest needs cannot be satisfied, it follows that the universe is absurd.

This difference in the direction in which the same argument can run reflects a profound difference between the mentality of the nineteenth and the twentieth centuries. From this point of view, argument and evidence are less important than tonality and overall outlook. Clearly, Bradley belonged to the great tradition that, stemming from Aristotle, sees philosophy distinguished from all other inquiry by being an attempt to give a complete, well-rounded, and balanced account of things—the attempt, in Arnold's words, to "see life steadily and see it whole."[y]

In Bradley's universe, as in Aristotle's, intellect has a special, and preeminent, place. For it is intellect that, after weighing the demands of the "other sides" of our nature, determines what the balance is.

> The other sides of our nature . . . must make their appeal not only to, but also through, the intelligence. In life it is otherwise, but there is a difference between philosophy and life. And in philosophy my need for beauty and for practical goodness may have a voice, but, for all that, they have not a vote. They cannot address the intellect and insist, "We are not satisfied, and therefore you also shall not be satisfied." They must be content to ask and to repeat, "Are you in fact satisfied with yourself as long as we remain unsatisfied? It is for you to decide, and we can only suggest."[z]

But in Aristotle's universe, intellect is equal to the task assigned it. In Bradley's universe, intellect is not equal to the task.

The Central Issue

We are brought once more to the paradox we have encountered so often in our account of Bradley and the one that set him off not only from Hegel and the Hegelians but from the whole intellectualist tradition in philosophy. Here was a rationalist who had such great confidence in thought that he relied solely on the criterion of self-consistency, assigning to perception and the other sides of our nature only voices, not votes. But at the same time he held that thought is self-contradictory, since, in thought, we are always divorced from the object we seek. (We seek, not to *think* it, but to *be* it.)

On the one hand, we are assured that "our conclusion"—that Reality is one, suprarelational, and so on—"is certain; . . . to doubt it logically is impossible. . . . It is impossible rationally even to entertain the question of another possibility."[a] And this is a *conclusion*, the terminus of a logical argument. It is reached, that is, by thinking. There speaks Bradley the rationalist. On the other hand, we are told that "Reality offers a problem not soluble by any relational thought."[b] There speaks Bradley the mystic.

The qualifier "relational" may suggest a possible escape from the dilemma. But is there any thought that is not relational? Bradley rejected intuition—it cannot "satisfy the claims of understanding." And feeling, of course, is subrelational. What other nonrelational thought might there be? Bradley, certainly, never suggested that there is any. A means of escape from the dilemma that he *did* attempt was to distinguish between the "general nature" of Reality, about which, he held, we can be assured, and the "details," which are admittedly forever hidden from us. But, apart from the fact that in Bradley's view all distinctions are mere appearance, it would seem that—so far as it is by thinking that we reach a conclusion, however general, about the nature of Reality—Bradley was attributing to thought a validity that he explicitly denied to it.

But need we hold that thought is intrinsically and in essence self-defeating? Why is a relational structure and a relational way of thought not good enough? Our answer to these questions depends, as we have already suggested, on our attitude toward unity. The central issue, perhaps, is whether one accepts or rejects Bradley's attack on "and" as an intolerable discrepancy. If one rejects it—and most philosophers today probably do reject it—Bradley's whole theory "collapses in ruin," to adopt a phrase he liked to apply to the views of his opponents. But there is something in the scale and boldness of the enterprise he undertook that surely ought to elicit our respect. He had a vision of the universe "in all its sensible glory, . . . in all its sensible splendor," as contrasted with the "poor fictions" and "paltry abstractions"—whether they be those of science or of religion—that attempt to sum up the universe in a formula. Granted that his attempt to give a truly synoptic account of the universe was a failure; still it was a noble failure.

Bradley was not quite the last speculative philosopher, but most philosophers in recent times have had a much more modest view of their subject. In the words of one of the most eminent practitioners of the newer fashion, the main business of philosophy "conststs in criticizing and clarifying notions which are apt to be regarded as fundamental and accepted uncritically."[c] In short, most twentieth-century philosophers have been content to concentrate on what Bradley called "appearance." It is noteworthy that Bradley's own writings themselves fore-shadow the coming change. He repeatedly insisted that *Appearance and Reality* was only a "sketch," not a systematic treatise on metaphysics, though we may suspect that it was a treatise that he had orginally hoped and expected to write. And even if he had actually accomplished all in the sketch that he believed himself to have accomplished, his contribution would still be more critical than constructive. This is why Bradley is such an interesting and pivotal writer: His work is paradigmatic of the century that was ending—paradigmatic not only of philosophy but of the culture as a whole: great expectations unfulfilled.

Notes

Chapter 1 / The Age of Reason

a   Antoine Nicholas de Caritat, Marquis de Condorcet, *Sketch for a Historical Picture of the Progress of the Human Mind,* translated by J. Barraclough (Weidenfeld and Nicolson, London, 1955), pp. 173–75, 179, 187–88, 199, and 200–01.
b   *Emile* (J. M. Dent, London, 1930), p. 239. The passage is from "The Creed of a Savoyard Priest," Bk. IV.
c   *Decline and Fall of the Roman Empire,* Ch. XV.
d   *Ibid.,* Ch. XX.
e   *The Spirit of the Laws,* translated by T. Nugent and revised by F. V. Prichard (Bohn, London, 1896–97), I, i.
f   *Ibid.,* XIV, i.
g   *Ibid.,* XIV, ii.
h   This condensation is made from the German text in *Immanuel Kants Werke,* edited by E. Cassirer (E. Cassirer, Berlin, 1922), Vol. IV, pp. 169–76.

i *Ibid.*, Vol. VI, pp. 452–53.
j *Notes from Underground*, in *The Best Short Stories of Dostoyevsky*, translated by D. Magarshack (Modern Library, New York, n.d.), pp. 107–08, 111–13, 117–18, 129–30, 133, and 136.
k *Ibid.*, pp. 239–40.
l *Ibid.*, p. 174.
m *Ibid.*, p. 108.
n *Ibid.*, p. 142.
o *Ibid.*, p. 138.
p *Ibid.*, p. 163.
q *Ibid.*, p. 144.
r *Ibid.*, p. 234.

Chapter 2 / Kant: Theory of Knowledge

a *Critique of Pure Reason*, translated by N. Kemp Smith (Macmillan, London, 1929), B xii–xviii. (A refers to text of first edition, B to text of second edition.)
b *Ibid.*, B 3–4.
c *Ibid.*, B 1–2.
d *Ibid.*, B 14–16.
e *Ibid.*, A 23–25 = B 38–40.
f *Ibid.*, B 40–41.
g *Ibid.*, A 26–28 = B 42–44.
h *Ibid.*, A 51 = B 75.
i *Ibid.*, A 70 = B 95.
j *Ibid.*, A 80 = B 106.
k *Ibid.*, A 79 = B 104–05.
l *Ibid.*, A 104–06.
m *Ibid.*, A 107–08 and 111 = B 164–65.
n *Ibid.*, A 177 = B 218–19.
o *Ibid.*, A 182–89 = B 225–32.
p *Ibid.*, A 189–95 = B 233–40.
q *Ibid.*, B 406–11.
r *Ibid.*, footnote to B 411.
s *Ibid.*, A 426 ff. = B 454 ff.
t *Ibid.*, A 466 and 468 = B 494 and 496.
u *Ibid.*, A 470–71 = B 498–99.
v *Ibid.*, A 592–602 = B 620–30.
w *Ibid.*, A 604–10 = B 632–38.
x *Ibid.*, A 623–27 = B 651–55.
y *Ibid.*, A 642–60 = B 670–88.
z *Ibid.*, A 670–86 = B 698–714.
a *Ibid.*, A 253–56 = B 306–11.
b *Ibid.*, B xxiv–xxx.
c *Ibid.*, B xxvi.

Chapter 3 / Kant: Theory of Value

a *Fundamental Principles of the Metaphysic of Morals*, translated by T. K. Abbott (Longmans Green, London, 1927), §1, pp. 9–10.

b *Ibid.*, §1, pp. 16–17.
c *Ibid.*, §2, pp. 32–33 and 35–36.
d *Ibid.*, §1, p. 18.
e This and the following passage are from *A Treatise of Human Nature,* III, ii, 1.
f *Fundamental Principles,* translated by Abbott, *op. cit.,* §2, pp. 46–47.
g K. Vorlander, *Immanuel Kant* (F. Meiner, Leipzig, 1924), Vol. II, p. 331.
h *Fundamental Principles,* translated by Abbott, *op. cit.,* §2, pp. 52–59.
i *Ibid.*, §2, p. 46.
j *Critique of Practical Reason,* translated by T. K. Abbott (Longmans Green, London, 1927), Pt. I, Bk. I, Ch. 3, pp. 188 ff.
k Compare C. D. Broad, *Five Types of Ethical Theory* (Kegan Paul, London, 1930), pp. 138–39.
l *Fundamental Principles,* translated by Abbott, *op. cit.,* §3, pp. 65–66.
m *Critique of Practical Reason,* translated by Abbott, *op. cit.,* Pt. I, Bk. II, Ch. 2, §1, p. 206.
n *Ibid.*, §5, pp. 220–22.
o *Ibid.*, §4, pp. 218–19.
p *Critique of Judgment,* translated by J. H. Bernard (Macmillan, London, 1931), §87, pp. 381–82.
q *Ibid.*, §86, pp. 372–73.
r *Religion Within the Limits of Reason Alone,* translated by T. M. Greene and H. H. Hudson (Open Court, Chicago, 1934), Bk. II, §§IA and IB, pp. 54–57.

Chapter 4   /   Reactions Against Kantianism: Hegel and Schopenhauer

a Wordsworth, *Expostulation and Reply.*
b Wordsworth, *To My Sister.*
c Keats, *What the Thrush Said.*
d Byron, *The Dream.*
e Wordsworth, *Lines composed on the beach near Calais in the autumn of 1802.*
f Wordsworth, *Ode. Intimations of Immortality from Recollections of Early Childhood.*
g Coleridge, *To a Young Ass.*
h Wordsworth, *The Prelude,* Bk. I, ll. 401–11.
i Byron, *Mont Blanc.*
j Byron, *Childe Harold,* Canto IV.
k Wordsworth, *Tintern Abbey.*
l *Faust,* translated by L. MacNeice (Oxford University Press, 1952), p. 23.
m *The Phenomenology of Mind,* translated by J. B. Baillie (Allen and Unwin, London, 1949), p. 127.
n *Ibid.*, p. 124.
o *Ibid.*, p. 125.
p *Ibid.*, pp. 80 and 113–14.
q T. S. Eliot, *The Love Song of J. Alfred Prufrock,* in *The Complete Poems and Plays* (Harcourt, Brace & World, New York, 1952), p. 7.
r *Phenomenology,* translated by Baillie, *op. cit.,* p. 68.
s *Ibid.*, p. 82.
t *Ibid.*, p. 117.
u *Ibid.*, pp. 108–10.
v *Faust,* translated by MacNeice, *op. cit.,* p. 113.
w *Phenomenology,* translated by Baillie, *op. cit.,* pp. 72–74 and 79.
x *Ibid.*, pp. 111–13.
y *Ibid.*, pp. 81–82 and 85–86.
z *Ibid.*, pp. 80–81.
a *Ibid.*, pp. 131–32 and 139–45.

b *Ibid.,* p. 70.
c *Encyclopaedia of the Philosophical Sciences,* translated by W. Wallace (Clarendon Press, Oxford, 1892), Ch. VII, §§86–88.
d *Ibid.,* Ch. VIII, §156.
e *Philosophy of Right,* translated by T. M. Knox (Clarendon Press, Oxford, 1942), §§158, 160–63, and 167–68.
f *Phenomenology,* translated by Baillie, *op. cit.,* p. 75.
g *Ibid.,* p. 89.
h *The World as Will and Idea,* translated by R. B. Haldane and J. Kemp (Kegan Paul, London, 1883), Bk. I, §6.
i *Ibid.,* Bk. I, §12.
j *Ibid.,* Bk. II, §18.
k *Ibid.,* Bk. III, §33.
l Byron, *Stanzas to the Po.*
m *The World as Will and Idea,* translated by Haldane and Kemp, *op. cit.,* Bk. III, §34.
n *Ibid.,* Bk. IV, §54.
o *Ibid.,* Bk. IV, §63.
p *Ibid.,* Bk. IV, §68.
q *Ibid.*
r Quoted in E. Caird, *Hegel* (Blackwood, London, 1903), p. 40.

Chapter 5 / Science, Scientism, and Social Philosophy

a J. Bentham, *Theory of Legislation,* translated from the French of E. Dumont by C. M. Atkinson (Clarendon Press, Oxford, 1914), Vol. I, pp. 1–5 and 42–43.
b *On Liberty,* (J. M. Dent, London, 1910), Ch. I, pp. 72–75.
c *Ibid.,* Ch. II, pp. 79–81, 95, and 102–03.
d *Ibid.,* Ch. III, p. 121.
e *Ibid.,* Ch. V, pp. 151–52.
f *Ibid.,* Ch. V, p. 154.
g *Utilitarianism* (J. M. Dent, London, 1910), Ch. IV, pp. 32–33.
h *The Positive Philosophy of Auguste Comte,* translated by H. Martineau (George Bell, London, 1896), Vol. II, pp. 151–53.
i Keats, *Lamia,* Pt. II, ll. 231–37.
j *Early Writings,* translated and edited by T. B. Bottomore (C. A. Watts, London, 1963), pp. 120–25.
k *Socialism: Utopian and Scientific,* translated by E. Aveling (Scribner's, New York, 1892) p. 43.
l *Ibid.,* pp. 51–53 and 55.
m *Ibid.,* p. 72.
n *The German Ideology,* translated by R. Pascal (International Publishers, New York, 1947), p. 22.
o *Socialism: Utopian and Scientific,* translated by Aveling, *op. cit.,* p. 82.
p *The Communist Manifesto,* edited by F. Engels (Henry Regnery, Chicago, 1954), pp. 34 and 5.
q *Ibid.,* p. 25.
r *Ibid.,* p. 35.
s "Contribution to the Critique of Hegel's Philosophy of Right," in *Early Writings,* translated by Bottomore, *op. cit.,* pp. 43–44 and 52–53.
t *Ibid.,* p. 39.
u *Ibid.,* p. 5.

v *A Contribution to the Critique of Political Economy*, translated by N. I. Stone (Charles Kerr, Chicago, 1911), pp. 11–12.

w *Socialism: Utopian and Scientific*, translated by Aveling, *op. cit.*, pp. 3–4.

x "Contribution to the Critique of Hegel's Philosophy of Right," in *Early Writings*, translated by Bottomore, *op. cit.*, p. 44.

y *Ibid.*, p. 52.

z *Socialism: Utopian and Scientific*, translated by Aveling, *op. cit.*, pp. xv–xvi.

a *Theses on Feuerbach*, in Friedrich Engels, *Ludwig Feuerbach* (International Publishers, New York, 1941), pp. 82–84.

b *The Origin of Species* (A. L. Burt, New York, n.d.), p. 17.

c *Ibid.*, p. 20.

d *Ibid.*, pp. 59–60.

e *Ibid.*, pp. 83–84.

f *Ibid.*, pp. 124–25.

g *Ibid.*, pp. 500 and 504.

h Compare G. West, *Charles Darwin* (Routledge, London, 1937), pp. 249 ff.

i *Origin of Species*, *op. cit.*, p. 505.

j *The Riddle of the Universe* (Harper & Row, New York, 1900), pp. 13–14.

k *Ibid.*, p. 349.

l *The Mechanist Conception of Life* (University of Chicago Press, 1912), p. 3.

m *Ibid.*, pp. 26–27 and 41.

n *Ibid.*, p. 31.

o *The History and Theory of Vitalism*, translated by C. K. Ogden (Macmillan, London, 1914), pp. 208–09.

p *Ibid.*, p. 204.

q *The Science and Philosophy of the Organism* (A. and C. Black, London, 1908), p. 41.

r *The Science of Mechanics*, translated by T. J. McCormack (Open Court, Chicago, 1907), p. 492.

s *Ibid.*, pp. x and 481–83.

t *Ibid.*, pp. 5–6.

u *Ibid.*, pp. 1, 4, and 489–90.

v *The Grammar of Science* (A. and C. Black, London, 1911), pp. viii, 95–96, vi, and 96.

w *Ibid.*, pp. 115–16.

x *Ibid.*, p. 73.

y *Ibid.*, pp. 15, 37, and 17.

Chapter 6 / Kierkegaard and Nietzsche

a *The Journals of Kierkegaard*, translated and edited by A. Dru (Collins, London, 1958), p. 44.

b *Ibid.*, p. 96.

c *Ibid.*, p. 54.

d *Ibid.*, p. 39.

e *Ibid.*, p. 89.

f *Ibid.*, pp. 50–51.

g *Ibid.*, p. 65.

h *Ibid.*, p. 149.

i *Ibid.*, p. 106.

j *The Point of View for My Work as an Author*, translated by W. Lowrie and edited by B. Nelson (Harper & Row, New York, 1962), p. 76.

k *Journals*, translated by Dru, *op. cit.*, p. 85.

l *Ibid.*, p. 70.

m *Ibid.*, pp. 71–72.

n *Ibid.*, p. 87.

o *Ibid.*, p. 224.

p *Point of View for My Work as an Author,* translated by Lowrie, *op. cit.*, p. 18.

q *Kierkegaard's Concluding Unscientific Postscript,* translated by D. F. Swenson with notes and introduction by W. Lowrie (Princeton University Press, 1941), p. 276.

r *Journals,* translated by Dru, *op. cit.*, p. 46.

s *Concluding Unscientific Postscript,* translated by Swenson, *op. cit.*, pp. 267, 271, and 273.

t *Ibid.*, pp. 274 and 277–81.

u *Ibid.*, pp. 302–04.

v Mark 7 : 20–21, in *The Complete Bible,* translated by J. M. Powis Smith and E. J. Goodspeed (University of Chicago Press, 1939).

w *Journals,* translated by Dru, *op. cit.*, pp. 181–82.

x *Either/Or,* translated by W. Lowrie and revised by H. A. Johnson (Doubleday, Garden City, N. Y., 1959), Vol. II, pp. 171 and 173.

y *Concluding Unscientific Postscript,* translated by Swenson, *op. cit.*, p. 180.

z *Ibid.*, p. 183.

a *Journals,* translated by Dru, *op. cit.*, p. 184.

b *Concluding Unscientific Postscript,* translated by Swenson, *op. cit.*, p. 84.

c *Either/Or,* translated by Lowrie, *op. cit.*, Vol. II, pp. 347–48 and 354.

d *Concluding Unscientific Postscript,* translated by Swenson, *op. cit.*, p. 182.

e *Fear and Trembling,* translated with notes by W. Lowrie (Doubleday, Garden City, N. Y., 1954), pp. 69–72.

f *Concluding Unscientific Postscript,* translated by Swenson, *op. cit.*, p. 431.

g *Ibid.*, p. 445.

h *Ibid.*, pp. 434–35.

i *Ibid.*, p. 178.

j *Ibid.*, p. 181.

k *Ibid.*, pp. 25–26, 29–30, and 32.

l *Ibid.*, p. 51.

m *Either/Or,* translated by Lowrie, *op. cit.*, Vol. II, p. 19; *Journals,* translated by Dru, *op. cit.*, pp. 77, 175, 214, and 191; *Concluding Unscientific Postscript,* translated by Swenson, *op. cit.*, p. 318.

n *The Genealogy of Morals,* translated by F. Golffing (Doubleday, Garden City, N. Y., 1956), p. 255; *Beyond Good and Evil,* translated by M. Cowan (Henry Regnery, Chicago, 1955), pp. 100–01.

o *Genealogy of Morals,* translated by Golffing, *op. cit.*, pp. 209–10.

p "On Truth and Lie in an Extra-Moral Sense," in *The Portable Nietzsche,* edited by W. Kaufman (Viking, New York, 1954), p. 44.

q *Genealogy of Morals,* translated by Golffing, *op. cit.*, pp. 178–79.

r *Beyond Good and Evil,* translated by Cowan, *op. cit.*, pp. 18–19.

s *Ibid.*, pp. 3–6.

t *Ibid.*, p. 15.

u *Ibid.*, pp. 24–26.

v "On Truth and Lie," in *The Portable Nietzsche, op. cit.*, pp. 42–43 and 46–47.

w *Genealogy of Morals,* translated by Golffing, *op. cit.*, pp. 217–18 and 225–26.

x "Notes, 1875," in *The Portable Nietzsche, op. cit.*, p. 50.

y *Genealogy of Morals,* translated by Golffing, *op. cit.*, p. 219.

z *Beyond Good and Evil,* translated by Cowan, *op. cit.*, pp. 42–43.

a *Ibid.*, p. 201.

b *Genealogy of Morals,* translated by Golffing, *op. cit.*, pp. 170–72.

c *Ibid.*, p. 267.

d *Ibid.*, p. 268.

e　*Ibid.,* p. 269.

f　*Ibid.,* p. 271.

g　*Ibid.,* pp. 276 and 279.

h　*Beyond Good and Evil,* translated by Cowan, *op. cit.,* pp. 70–71.

i　*Twilight of the Idols,* in *The Portable Nietzsche, op. cit.,* p. 508.

j　*Beyond Good and Evil,* translated by Cowan, *op. cit.,* p. 175.

k　"On Truth and Lie," in *The Portable Nietzsche, op. cit.,* p. 44.

l　*Collected Poems of Thomas Hardy* (Macmillan, New York, 1925), p. 7.

m　*Thus Spoke Zarathustra,* in *The Portable Nietzsche, op. cit.,* pp. 268–72.

n　"Homer's Conquest," in *The Portable Nietzsche, op. cit.,* p. 38.

o　*The Birth of Tragedy,* translated by F. Golffing (Doubleday, Garden City, N. Y., 1956), pp. 59–60.

p　"Homer's Conquest," in *The Portable Nietzsche, op. cit.,* p. 37.

q　*Twilight of the Idols,* in *The Portable Nietzsche, op. cit.,* p. 518.

r　*Thus Spoke Zarathustra,* in *The Portable Nietzsche, op. cit.,* p. 129.

s　*Twilight of the Idols,* in *The Portable Nietzsche, op. cit.,* pp. 553–54.

t　*Beyond Good and Evil,* translated by Cowan, *op. cit.,* p. 230.

u　*Genealogy of Morals,* translated by Golffing, *op. cit.,* p. 157.

Chapter 7　/　C. S. Peirce

a　*Pragmatism,* edited by Ralph Barton Perry (Cleveland, World, 1964), p. 44.

b　*Collected Papers of Charles Sanders Peirce,* edited by Charles Hartshorne and Paul Weiss (Cambridge, Harvard University Press, 1931–35), Vol. V, pp. 276–77.

c　*Ibid.,* Vol. V, pp. 274–75.

d　*Ibid.,* Vol. V, pp. 233–39 and 241.

e　*Ibid.,* Vol. V, pp. 242–43.

f　*Ibid.,* Vol. VI, pp. 6–7.

g　*Ibid.,* Vol. V, pp. 272–73 and 259–62.

h　*Ibid.,* Vol. VI, p. 331.

i　*Ibid.,* Vol. V, pp. 284–85.

j　*Ibid.,* Vol. V, pp. 417–18.

k　*Ibid.,* Vol. V, p. 182.

l　*Ibid.,* Vol. VI, pp. 356 and 358.

m　*Ibid.,* Vol. V, p. 113.

n　*Ibid.,* edited by Arthur W. Banks (Cambridge, Harvard University Press, 1958), Vol. VIII, p. 15.

o　*Ibid.,* Vol. VIII, pp. 16–18.

p　*Collected Papers,* edited by Hartshorne and Weiss, *op. cit.,* Vol. V, pp. 64 and 66–67.

q　*Charles S. Peirce's Letters to Lady Welby,* edited by Irwin C. Lieb (New Haven, Whitlock, for the Graduate Philosophy Club of Yale University, 1953), p. 39.

r　*Collected Papers,* edited by Hartshorne and Weiss, *op. cit.,* Vol. V, p. 268.

s　*Ibid.,* Vol. VI, p. 5.

t　*Ibid.,* Vol. VI, pp. 1–2 and 4–5.

u　*Ibid.,* Vol. VI, p. 12.

v　*Ibid.,* Vol. VI, pp. 26–27.

w　*Ibid.,* Vol. VI, p. 14.

x　*Ibid.,* Vol. VI, pp. 28–29.

y　*Ibid.,* Vol. VI, pp. 28 and 30.

z　*Ibid.,* Vol. VI, p. 30.

a　*Ibid.,* Vol. VI, p. 35.

b　*Ibid.,* Vol. VI, pp. 35–36.

c   *Ibid.*, Vol. VI, p. 38.
d   *Ibid.*, Vol. VI, pp. 40–42 and 45.
e   *Ibid.*, Vol. VI, p. 86.
f   *Ibid.*, Vol. VI, pp. 87–89.
g   *Ibid.*, Vol. VI, p. 109.
h   *Ibid.*, Vol. II, p. 390.
i   *Ibid.*, Vol. II, p. 395.
j   *Ibid.*, Vol. II, p. 398.
k   *Ibid.*, Vol. II, pp. 404 and 399.
l   *Ibid.*, Vol. V. pp. 258–59.
m   *Ibid.*, Vol. I, pp. 141–42.
n   *Ibid.*, Vol. I, pp. 150 and 152.
o   *Ibid.*, Vol. I, p. 153.
p   *Ibid.*, Vol. I, pp. 162–63.
q   *Ibid.*, Vol. I, p. 229.
r   *Letters to Lady Welby*, edited by Lieb, *op. cit.*, p. 10.
s   *Collected Papers*, edited by Hartshorne and Weiss, *op. cit.*, Vol. V, pp. 324–25.
t   *Ibid.*, Vol. V, pp. 326–27, 332–34, 330–31, and 341–42.
u   *Ibid.*, Vol. V, p. 335.
v   *Letters to Lady Welby*, edited by Lieb, *op. cit.*, p. 11.
w   *Ibid.*
x   *Collected Papers*, edited by Hartshorne and Weiss, *op. cit.*, Vol. V, pp. 58–59.
y   *Ibid.*, Vol. V, p. 332.
z   *Ibid.*, Vol. II, p. 134.
a   *Ibid.*, Vol. II, p. 135.
b   *Ibid.*, Vol. II, pp. 142–44.
c   *Ibid.*, Vol. I, p. 60.
d   *Letters to Lady Welby*, edited by Lieb, *op. cit.*, p. 36.
e   *Collected Papers*, edited by Hartshorne and Weiss, *op. cit.*, Vol. V, p. 334.
f   *Ibid.*, Vol. V, p. 280.
g   *Ibid.*, Vol. V, p. 296.
h   *Ibid.*, Vol. V, p. 280.
i   *Ibid.*, Vol. V, p. 289.
j   *Ibid.*, Vol. V, p. 281.
k   *Ibid.*, Vol. VI, p. 190.
l   *Ibid.*, Vol. I, p. 135.

Chapter 8   /   William James

a   *A Pluralistic Universe*, edited by Ralph Barton Perry (New York, Dutton, 1971), pp. 131–32.
b   *Pragmatism*, edited by Ralph Barton Perry (Cleveland, World, 1964), pp. 20 and 22–23.
c   *Ibid.*, pp. 23–24.
d   *Essays in Radical Empiricism*, edited by Ralph Barton Perry (New York, Dutton, 1971), pp. 24–29.
e   *Pragmatism*, *op. cit.*, p. 114.
f   *Ibid.*, pp. 126–27.
g   *Essays in Radical Empiricism*, *op. cit.*, p. 50.
h   *Ibid.*, pp. 110, 36, and 86.
i   *Pragmatism*, *op. cit.*, p. 162.
j   "Some Problems in Philosophy," in *The Moral Equivalent of War and Other Essays*, edited by John K. Roth (New York, Harper & Row, 1971), pp. 144–45.

k   *The Meaning of Truth,* edited by Ralph Barton Perry (Cleveland, World, 1964), p. 224.

l   "Some Problems in Philosophy," *op. cit.,* p. 145.

m   *Ibid.,* p. 147.

n   *Pragmatism, op. cit.,* p. 163.

o   *Essays in Radical Empiricism, op. cit.,* p. 6.

p   *Ibid.,* pp. 4–5, 8–9, and 15.

q   *Ibid.,* p. 22.

r   *Ibid.,* p. 5.

s   *Ibid.,* pp. 37–38.

t   *The Will to Believe* (New York, Dover, 1956), pp. 200–01.

u   *Ibid.,* pp. 202–03.

v   *Ibid.,* pp. 208 and 184.

w   *Ibid.,* p. 206.

x   *Ibid.,* pp. 206–07.

y   *Ibid.,* pp. 205–06.

z   *Ibid.,* p. 204.

a   *Ibid.,* p. 195.

b   *Ibid.,* p. 209.

c   *Ibid.,* p. 213.

d   "Some Problems in Philosophy," *op. cit.,* p. 164.

e   *The Will to Believe, op. cit.,* pp. 146–47.

f   *Ibid.,* p. 150.

g   *Ibid.,* pp. 175–77 and 183.

h   *Ibid.,* p. 177.

i   *The Varieties of Religious Experience* (New York, Collier, 1961), p. 17.

j   *Ibid.,* pp. 32–33.

k   *Ibid.,* p. 35.

l   *Ibid.,* pp. 143 and 91.

m   *Ibid.,* pp. 85 and 119.

n   *Ibid.,* p. 87.

o   *Ibid.,* p. 116.

p   *Ibid.,* p. 119.

q   *Ibid.,* pp. 140–41.

r   *Ibid.,* p. 189.

s   *Ibid.,* pp. 190–94.

t   *Ibid.,* p. 298.

u   *Ibid.,* p. 261.

v   *Ibid.,* pp. 264 and 271.

w   *Ibid.,* pp. 273 and 283.

x   *Ibid.,* p. 284.

y   *Ibid.,* pp. 299–300.

z   *Ibid.,* pp. 305–06.

a   *Ibid.,* pp. 397 and 398.

b   *Ibid.,* pp. 396–97.

c   *A Pluralistic Universe, op. cit.,* p. 268.

d   *The Will to Believe, op. cit.,* p. 320.

e   *The Varieties of Religious Experience, op. cit.,* p. 331.

f   *Pragmatism, op. cit.,* pp. 42–43 and 45.

g   *Essays in Radical Empiricism, op. cit.,* p. 84.

h   *Pragmatism, op. cit.,* p. 49.

i   *The Varieties of Religious Experience, op. cit.,* pp. 225, 233, and 375.

j   *Pragmatism, op. cit.,* pp. 57–58.

k *Ibid.*, pp. 133, 139–40, and 142–43.
l *The Varieties of Religious Experience, op cit.*, p. 397.
m *The Will to Believe, op. cit.*, p. 8.
n *Ibid.*, pp. 18–19.
o *The Varieties of Religious Experience, op. cit.*, p. 26.

Chapter 9 / F. H. Bradley

a Arnold, "Dover Beach."
b Arnold, "Stanzas from the Grande Chartreuse."
c *Essays on Truth and Reality* (Oxford, Clarendon Press, 1941), pp. 223–24.
d *Appearance and Reality* (Oxford, Clarendon Press, 1930), p. 120.
e *Ibid.*, p. 324.
f *Essays on Truth and Reality, op. cit.*, pp. 160–61.
g *Ibid.*, pp. 173–76.
h Wordsworth, *The Prelude*, Bk. II, 11.234 ff.
i Wordsworth, *Tintern Abbey*, 11.94 ff.
j *Essays on Truth and Reality, op. cit.*, pp. 154–55.
k *Appearance and Reality, op. cit.*, pp. 143–45.
l *Ibid.*, p. 222.
m *Ibid.*, p. 320.
n *Ibid.*, pp. 17 and 18.
o *Ibid.*, p. 517.
p *Ibid.*, pp. 520–21.
q *Essays on Truth and Reality, op. cit.*, p. 228 n.
r *Ibid.*, p. 174.
s *Appearance and Reality, op. cit.*, p. 482, n. 1.
t *Ibid.*, pp. 21 and 28.
u *Ibid.*, p. 28.
v *Ibid.*, p. 483.
w *Essays on Truth and Reality, op. cit.*, p. 219 n.
x *Ibid.*, pp. 251–53.
y *Appearance and Reality, op. cit.*, p. 169.
z *Ibid.*, pp. 397 and 429–33.
a *Ibid.*, p. 31.
b *Ibid.*, pp. 31–32.
c *Ibid.*, p. 33.
d *Ibid.*, p. 37.
e *Ibid.*, pp. 38–39.
f *Ibid.*, pp. 19 and 21.
g *Ibid.*, p. 280, n. 2.
h *Ibid.*, p. 502.
i *Ibid.*, p. 370.
j *Collected Essays* (Oxford, Clarendon Press, 1935), pp. 14–15 and 17.
k *Appearance and Reality, op. cit.*, pp. 334–35.
l *Ibid.*, p. 90.
m *Ibid.*, pp. 93–94.
n *Ibid.*, p. 103.
o *Ibid.*, pp. 356 and 362.
p *Ibid.*, pp. 362–63.
q *Ibid.*, p. 363.

r *Ibid.*, pp. 372–73.
s *Ibid.*, pp. 394–97.
t *Ibid.*, p. 123.
u *Ibid.*, p. 460.
v *Ibid.*, pp. 127–28.
w *Essays on Truth and Reality, op. cit.*, pp. 238–39 and 256.
x *Appearance and Reality, op. cit.*, pp. 130 and 139–40.
y Arnold, "Sonnet to a Friend."
z *Essays on Truth and Reality, op. cit.*, p. 221.
a *Appearance and Reality, op. cit.*, p. 459.
b *Collected Essays, op. cit.*, p. 641.
c Bertrand Russell, "Logical Atomism," in *Contemporary British Philosophy*, edited by J. H. Muirhead, (New York, Macmillan, 1924), p. 379.

Suggestions for Further Reading

The best course to pursue is to turn directly to the various great texts from which the selections in this volume have been drawn. Thus, instead of being content with the extracts given here, read more deeply in Kant's *Critique*, Hegel's *Phenomenology*, and Bradley's *Appearance and Reality*. Information concerning translations and editions will be found in the bibliographical notes section.

Beyond the masters themselves, here is a short list of books about them and their times that should help to make their theories more intelligible. I have, for the most part, chosen books that present different interpretations from my own.

KANT

L. W. Beck: *A Commentary on Kant's Critique of Practical Reason* (Chicago, 1960). Places this work "in the context of Kant's philosophy" and of eighteenth-century thought on ethics.

————: *Studies in the Philosophy of Kant* (Indianapolis, 1965). A series of papers by one of the most distinguished of living scholars on Kant.

G. Bird: *Kant's Theory of Knowledge* (London, 1965). The author points out that this book "presupposes some acquaintance with the main features of Kant's theory of knowledge."

N. Kemp Smith: *A Commentary on Kant's Critique of Pure Reason* (London, 1930). A monumental study.

S. Korner: *Kant* (Baltimore, 1966). An introduction that gives "priority to those of Kant's problems to which his approach has still a present-day interest."

B. K. Milmed: *Kant and Current Philosophical Issues* (New York, 1961). Discusses the relevance of Kant's views to contemporary disputes over "the distinction between analytical and synthetical statements" and over the presence of "a conceptual factor in all knowledge."

H. J. Paton: *The Categorical Imperative* (Chicago, 1948). Holds that "Kant contrived to say something new about morality" and that his work on moral theory is "indispensable for all who seek to lead a good life intelligently."

T. D. Weldon: *Introduction to Kant's Critique of Pure Reason* (Oxford, 1958). An excellent introduction; especially good on the background of the problem of knowledge as Kant saw it and on the complex argument of the transcendental deduction.

R. P. Wolff: *Kant's Theory of Mental Activity* (Cambridge, Mass., 1963). Seeks to establish the "analytic as a single connected argument beginning with the premise that my consciousness has a necessary unity, and concluding with the validity of the causal maxim."

HEGEL

J. N. Findlay: *Hegel: A Re-examination* (New York, 1958). Holds that Hegel was not a "transcendent metaphysician," a "subjectivist," a "manic rationalist," or a "political reactionary."

W. Kaufmann: *Hegel: Reinterpretation, Texts, and Commentary* (Garden City, N. Y., 1965). A fresh view of Hegel's development; includes a translation of the Preface to the *Phenomenology*, with helpful commentary.

A. MacIntyre (ed.): *Hegel* (Garden City, N.Y., 1972). A useful collection of critical essays.

J. M. E. McTaggart: *A Commentary on Hegel's Logic* (Cambridge, 1931). Holds that "the dialectic method is valid" and that in many cases "the categories do stand to one another in the relations in which he asserts them to stand," but that "certain errors vitiate particular stages in the process."

G. R. G. Mure: *An Introduction to Hegel* (London, 1940). A useful introduction; includes a long section on Hegel's philosophical inheritance, especially his debt to Aristotle.

MARX

I. Berlin: *Karl Marx: His Life and Environment* (New York, 1948). An interesting and readable study of Marx's life.

M. M. Bober: *Karl Marx's Interpretation of History* (Cambridge, Mass., 1927). A critical analysis of Marx's theory of economic determinism, showing its one-sidedness as well as "some logical weaknesses."

I. Fetscher: *Marx and Marxism* (London, 1971). Aims at making evident the difference between Soviet Marxism and Marx's own "critical and humanist thought."

E. Fromm: *Marx's Concept of Man* (New York, 1970). A study by the well-known psychiatrist.

G. Lichtheim: *Marxism: An Historical and Critical Study* (New York, 1961). "It is the thesis of this study that Marxism is to be understood as an historical phenomenon." Its starting point is the French Revolution and the Industrial Revolution, with their "repercussions in the theoretical sphere."

H. B. Mayo: *Introduction to Marxist Theory* (New York, 1960). Contains a useful annotated bibliography.

D. McLellan: *Marx Before Marxism* (New York, 1970). Maintains that Marx's early works "contain all the subsequent themes of Marx's thought and show them in the making."

R. C. Tucker: *Philosophy and Myth in Karl Marx* (Cambridge, 1961). Holds that Marx was less an economist than a moralist whose premise was "man's self-alienation."

KIERKEGAARD

J. Collins: *The Mind of Kierkegaard* (Chicago, 1953). This work "confines itself to the philosophical aspects of his fundamental dialectic of esthetic, ethical and religious modes of existence upon which his scale of values is founded."

M. J. Heinecken: *The Moment Before God* (Philadelphia, 1956). Maintains that Kierkegaard was right on "what it means to become and to be a Christian."

H. A. Johnson and N. Thulstrup (eds.): *A Kierkegaard Critique* (Chicago, 1962). Includes translations of essays that appeared originally in Danish, French, German, Italian, and Swedish.

W. Lowrie: *Kierkegaard* (New York, 1962). A detailed biographical study "written by a lover" of Kierkegaard, including extensive quotations from Kierkegaard's writings.

J. Thompson: *Kierkegaard* (Garden City, N.Y., 1972). "The essays in this volume have been selected so as to give the reader some sense of the shape and direction of recent Kierkegaardian criticism."

NIETZSCHE

W. Kaufmann: *Nietzsche: Philosopher, Psychologist, Antichrist* (New York, 1956). Argues that Nietzsche was not a romanticist, not a Darwinist, and not a wayward disciple of Schopenhauer's: "The will to power is the core of Nietzsche's thought but inseparable from his idea of sublimation."

A. H. J. Knight: *Some Aspects of the Life and Work of Nietzsche* (Cambridge, 1933). Emphasizes the importance of Nietzsche's Greek studies, with extensive quotations from Nietzsche's writings.

G. A. Morgan: *What Nietzsche Means* (Cambridge, Mass., 1941). A sympathetic study, holding that Nietzsche had "the courage to experience the myriad anxieties that fester the modern soul and a will to overcome them with a new vision."

PRAGMATISM

A. J. Ayer: *The Origins of Pragmatism* (San Francisco, 1968). A study of Peirce and James by a leading Logical Positivist, whose own views are discussed in this volume.

E. C. Moore: *American Pragmatism* (New York, 1961). Holds that pragmatism is "essentially a theory of meaning" and examines Peirce, James, and Dewey from this point of view.

C. Morris: *The Pragmatic Movement in America* (New York, 1970). "A work within American pragmatic philosophy, and not a book about it."

PEIRCE

J. Feibleman: *An Introduction to Peirce's Philosophy* (New York, n.d.). Undertakes to refute the contention of some writers that "Peirce's various dicta cannot be rendered consistent."

J. J. Fitzgerald: *Peirce's Theory of Signs as Foundation for Pragmatism* (The Hague, 1966). Discusses "Peirce's search for a new proof of his pragmatism subsequent to his detailed work in the theory of signs."

W. B. Gallie: *Peirce and Pragmatism* (New York, 1966). "Intended as an introduction for the general reader of philosophy."

T. A. Goudge: *The Thought of C. S. Peirce* (Toronto, 1950). Holds that there is "a deep conflict" in Peirce's thought between his naturalism and his transcendentalism.

D. Greenlee: *Peirce's Concept of Sign* (The Hague, 1973). Discusses Peirce's semiotics from the standpoint of a general theory of meaning.

M. G. Murphey: *The Development of Peirce's Philosophy* (Cambridge, Mass., 1961). Holds that Peirce was a "system builder," who aimed at "an over-all philosophic system."

M. Thompson: *The Pragmatic Philosophy of C. S. Peirce* (Chicago, 1953). Peirce's version of pragmatism "is connected with the very roots of his philosophy."

JAMES

G. W. Allen: *William James* (New York, 1967). A biographical study; holds that "James' life was a struggle to overcome crippling neuroses" and that he "kept sane by admitting his condition and fighting his symptoms."

R. B. Perry: *The Thought and Character of William James* (2 vols., Boston, 1935). Extensive selections from "the great mass of correspondence, lecture notes, diaries and other manuscripts" interwoven into "a systematic account of James' development."

J. K. Roth: *Freedom and the Moral Life* (Philadelphia, 1969). A study of James's views on ethics that holds that he deals with "problems that are very much a part of the present scene."

J. Wild: *The Radical Empiricism of William James* (Garden City, N.Y., 1969). Focuses on those "aspects of James' thought which are of special interest to phenomenologists."

B. Wilshire: *William James and Phenomenology* (Indianapolis, 1968). Brings out the relation between James's view and the phenomenological tradition.

BRADLEY

S. K. Saxena: *Studies in the Metaphysics of Bradley* (London, 1967). Maintains that Bradley's work on metaphysics is "theoretically more tenable than that of many present-day metaphysicians."

G. L. Vander Veer: *Bradley's Metaphysics and the Self* (New Haven, 1970). Argues that "Bradley's approach to metaphysics both establishes the proper character of metaphysical inquiry and leads to certain important and defensible metaphysical assertions."

R. Wollheim: *F. H. Bradley* (Baltimore, 1969). Holds that "the best approach to Bradley's thought lies through his logic."

Glossary

Short, dictionary-type definitions of philosophical terms are likely to be misleading, for philosophers use terms in many different ways and with little regard to common usage (on which, of course, dictionary definitions are based). Accordingly, many of the definitions given in this Glossary are accompanied by references to places in the text where the terms in question appear in a concrete context. For terms not defined in the Glossary, consult the Index; for fuller treatment of the terms defined here and of other philosophical terms, see *The Encyclopedia of Philosophy*, edited by P. Edwards (Free Press, New York, 1973). Also available are the *Dictionary of Philosophy*, edited by D. D. Runes (Philosophical Library, New York, 1942), and *Dictionary of Philosophy and Psychology*, edited by J. M. Baldwin (Macmillan, New York, 1925).

Absolute: A term used, in connection with the degrees-of-truth doctrine, to designate the most real thing of all. Also used, in connection with the doctrine that all finite things are parts of one infinite thing, to designate this all-inclusive whole. Hence that which is unconditioned and free from any limitations or qualifications. See pp. 131–34 and Ch. 9.

Abstraction: The power of separating, in thought, one part of a complex from the other parts and attending to it separately. Thus to consider the color of an apple in isolation from the apple's other qualities would be to abstract this quality for attention.

A priori: What is known independently of sense perception and for this reason held to be indubitable. For Kant's account of the a priori, see pp. 22–23.

Attribute: See **Substance**.

Axiom: A proposition held to be self-evidently true and so neither requiring nor indeed capable of proof. Hence a first principle from which all proofs start. Those who deny the self-evident truth of axioms hold them to be simply postulates from which such-and-such theorems can be deduced. Thus, according to this view, the axioms of one deductive system may be deduced from another set of postulates in some other deductive system.

Category: Any very general, fundamental concept used for interpreting experience. See, for instance, Peirce's use of this term (p. 283). For the meaning of "category" in Kant's philosophy, see pp. 43–45.

Conceptualism: The view that universals are neither independently existing entities nor mere names, but are concepts formed in the mind. See **Nominalism, Realism,** and **Universal**.

Contingent: That which may be and also may not be. Hence an event whose occurrence is not necessarily determined (see **Determinism**) by other events.

Cosmology: The study of the universal world process. Distinguished from ontology (see definition) chiefly by the fact that, whereas the latter asks what reality *is*, cosmology asks how reality unfolds and develops in successive stages.

Deduction: A type of inference (see definition) that yields necessary conclusions. In deduction, one or more propositions (called "premises") being assumed, another proposition (the conclusion) is seen to be entailed or implied. It is usually held that in deduction the movement of thought is from premises of greater generality to a conclusion of lesser generality (from the premises "All men are mortal" and "All Greeks are men," we deduce that "All Greeks are mortal"), but the chief mark of deduction is the necessity with which the conclusion follows from the premises.

Determinism: The theory that denies contingency (see **Contingent**) and claims that everything that happens happens necessarily and in accordance with some regular pattern or law. There are three main types, or versions, of determinism: (1) a *scientific determinism* (in which all events are determined by antecedent events in time), (2) a *logical determinism* (as with Spinoza), and (3) a *teleological determinism* (as with Augustine).

Dialectic: A widely and variously used term. Applied by Kant to the section of the *Critique of Pure Reason* devoted to exposing the claims of rationalistic metaphysics (see p. 33, n. 6); used by Hegel to designate the triadic movement of thought from thesis to antithesis to synthesis (see p. 125); and used by Marx to describe the process by which one social class replaces another (see p. 185).

Discursive: The characteristic of the human intelligence that limits it, in the main, to a step-by-step reasoning—from premises to conclusion, from this conclusion to another, and so on. Hence to be contrasted with the all-inclusive vision of the mystic, with the possible operation of a suprahuman intellect, and with the way in which, according to some writers, axioms (see **Axiom**) and other self-evident principles are comprehended by the mind.

Dualism: Any view that holds two ultimate and irreducible principles to be necessary to explain the world—as, for instance, mind and matter.

Empiricism: The view that holds sense perception to be the sole source of human knowledge.

Epistemology: From the Greek terms *episteme* (knowledge) and *logos* (theory, account). Hence the study of the origins, nature, and limitations of knowledge.

Essence: The that-about-a-thing-that-makes-it-what-it-is, in contrast to those properties that the thing may happen to possess but need not possess in order to be itself. Thus it is held (1) that we have to distinguish between those properties of Socrates that are "accidental" and so nonessential (for example, dying by hemlock) and those properties that are essential (for example, those traits of character and personality that made him the man he was). Further, it is held (2) that we have to distinguish between essence and existence (see definition): It is possible according to this view to define Socrates' essence exhaustively; yet when we have done so, the question still remains whether any such being exists. Holders of this view would maintain that there is only one object in which essence and existence are inseparable; this object is God. For Kierkegaard's attack on the notion of essence see pp. 229–31.

Eudaemonism: From the Greek term *eudaimonia*, usually translated as "happiness." Hence the view that the end of life consists in happiness, conceived of as an all-round, balanced, long-range type of well-being, in distinction from pleasure. Contrasted with hedonism (see definition).

Existence: Actuality or factuality. Contrasted with essence (see definition). For Kierkegaard's assertion of the primacy of existence over essence, see pp. 213–16.

Experiment: A situation arranged to test a hypothesis. Contrasted with "mere" observation.

Free will: The doctrine of contingency (see **Contingent**) applied specifically to human behavior; the denial that men's acts are completely determined (see **Determinism**). The question of free will is important because many philosophers hold that "ought" implies "can"—that moral judgments of approbation and disapprobation are meaningless unless the acts judged about are free, that is, under the control of the agent, who, had he so chosen, might have done otherwise. The main problems connected with free will are (1) what meaning, if any, can be attached to the notion of a free choice and (2) how the possibility of being otherwise is compatible with either (a) belief in an omnipotent and omniscient Deity or (b) the doctrine of universal causal determinism. For Kant's attempt to reconcile freedom with natural necessity, see pp. 84–88.

Hedonism: The view that pleasure is man's good. Contrasted with eudaemonism (see definition). *Ethical hedonism* holds either (1) that a man's own pleasure is the sole end worth aiming at or (2) that other people's pleasure is to be taken into account (see pp. 164–69). *Psychological hedonism* holds that, whatever men ought to aim at, they do in fact aim at pleasure.

Humanism: A variously used term. Employed (1) to describe the type of view that distinguishes man from animals on the ground that man has certain moral obligations. Also used (2) to contrast a secular type of ethics with a religious ethics. Thus Plato's and Aristotle's ethics could be called "humanistic," in contrast with the ethics of Augustine, on the ground that they hold man himself, rather than God, to be the supreme value. Also used (3) to designate a particular historical movement, beginning in the fourteenth century, that emphasized the study of classical literature and the revival of classical ideals.

Idealism: In general, any view that holds reality to be mental or "spiritual," or mind-dependent. *Subjective idealism* emphasizes the ultimate reality of the knowing subject and may either admit the existence of a plurality of such subjects or deny the existence of all save one (in which case the view is called solipsism [see definition]). *Objective idealism* denies that the distinction between subject and object, between knower and known, is ultimate and maintains that all finite knowers and their thoughts are included in an Absolute Thought (see pp. 131–34 and Chapter 9).

Induction: A type of inference (see definition) in which (in contrast to deduction [see definition]) the movement of thought is from lesser to greater generality. Thus induction begins, not from premises, but from observed particulars (for example, the observation that A, B, and C all have the property x) and seeks to establish some generalization about them (for example, that all members of the class y, of which A, B, and C are members, have the property x). The main problem connected with induction is the difficulty of determining the conditions under which we are warranted in moving from an observed "Some so-and-so's have such-and-such" to the unobserved "All so-and-so's probably have such-and-such."

Inference: The movement of thought by which we reach a conclusion from premises. Thus we speak of inductive and of deductive inference.

Intuition: Direct and immediate knowledge. To be contrasted with discursive (see definition) knowledge.

Judgment: The movement of thought by which, for example, we assert (or deny) some predicate of a subject, or, more generally, by which we connect two terms by some relation. Thus, when we say "This rose is red" or "New York is east of Chicago," we judge. Following Kant (see pp. 22–23), most philosophers distinguish between (1) *analytical judgments*, in which the predicate concept is contained in the subject concept, and (2) *synthetical judgments*, in which the predicate concept is not so contained; and also between (3) *a priori judgments*, which are universal and necessary, and (4) *a posteriori judgments*, which are not universal and necessary.

Law of nature: See **Natural law.**

Materialism: The doctrine that reality is matter. Whereas idealism (see definition) holds that matter is "really" the thought of some mind or other, materialism holds that minds and all other apparently nonmaterial things are reducible to the complex motions of material particles. For a modern version of materialism, see pp. 199–200.

Metaphysics: The study of the ultimate nature of reality, or, as some philosophers would say, the study of "being as such." To be contrasted, therefore, with physics, which studies the "being" of physical nature; with astronomy, which studies the "being" of the solar system; with biology, which studies the "being" of animate nature; and so on. By "being as such," these philosophers mean, not the special characteristics of special kinds of things (for example, living things), but the most general and pervasive characteristics of all things.

Monism: The view that everything is reducible to one kind of thing, or that one principle of explanation is sufficient to explain everything. Both Hegel and Marx, for instance, were monists; the former was an idealistic monist, the latter a materialistic monist.

Mysticism: The view that reality is ineffable and transcendent; that it is known, therefore, by some special, nonrational means; that knowledge of it is incommunicable in any precise conceptual scheme; and that it is communicable, if at all, only in poetic imagery and metaphor.

Naturalism: A variously used term. (1) In one meaning, naturalism is a view that excludes any reference to supernatural principles and holds the world to be explicable in terms of scientifically verifiable concepts. In this meaning, naturalism is roughly equivalent to secularism and, like humanism (see definition), can be contrasted with a religiously oriented view like Kierkegaard's (see pp. 213–33). (2) In another meaning, the emphasis is on the unity of behavior; any difference in kind between men and animals is denied, and human conduct and human institutions are held to be simply more complex instances of behavior patterns occurring among lower organisms.

Natural law: This term may designate (1) a pattern of regularity that holds in physical nature. Thus people talk about the "law" of gravity and hold it to be a law of nature (or a natural law) that bodies attract each other directly with their masses and inversely with the square of their distance. Those who affirm the existence of natural laws in this sense hold that these laws are necessary and universal (not merely empirical generalizations concerning observable sequences) and that they are discoverable by reason. Or the term may designate (2) a moral imperative—not a description of what actually happens in the physical world, but a description of what *ought* to happen in men's relations to one another. In this sense, too, these laws would be regarded by those who affirm their existence as being of universal application and discoverable by reason.

Nominalism: The view that only particulars are real and that universals (see **Universal**) are but observable likenesses among the particulars of sense experience.

Objective: To say that anything is "objective" is to say that it is real, that it has a public nature independent of us and of our judgments about it. Thus the question of whether or not values are objective turns on whether or not values are more than private preferences. If they are private preferences, our value judgments are subjective, and there is no more disputing about them than there is about judgments of taste: My good is what *I* prefer; yours is what *you* prefer. On the other hand, if values are objective, it follows that when we differ about them, at least one of us is mistaken.

Ontological argument: An argument for the existence of God, first formulated by St. Anselm. According to this argument, since perfection implies existence, God necessarily exists. For Kant's criticism of this argument, see pp. 55–56.

Ontology: From the Greek terms *ontos* (being) and *logos* (theory, account). For many philosophers ontology is equivalent to metaphysics (see definition). For instance, to inquire about the "ontological status" of something, say, perception, is to ask whether the objects of perception are real or illusory, and, if real, what sort of reality they possess (for example, whether they are mind-dependent or whether they exist independently of minds), and so on.

Pantheism: From the Greek terms *pan* (all) and *theos* (god). Hence the view that all things share in the divine nature, or that all things are parts of god.

Phenomenalism: A type of view that, like idealism (see definition), holds that what we know is mind-dependent, but that, unlike idealism, holds that reality itself is not mind-dependent. Hence Kant's view that we do not know reality (that is, things-in-themselves) and that our knowledge is limited to the data of inner and outer sense (that is, the sensuous manifold organized by the categories and the forms of sensibility) is a type of phenomenalism.

Positivism: A term first introduced by Comte to describe his account of the nature of knowledge (see pp. 175–76). Also used, more broadly, to characterize any view that rules out the possibility of metaphysical knowledge and that limits a priori truths to analytical statements (see, for instance, pp. 202–04).

Primary qualities: Those qualities thought to belong to bodies. To be distinguished from secondary qualities, which are held to be products of the interaction between our sense organs and the primary qualities of bodies.

Rationalism: (1) As contrasted with empiricism (see definition), rationalism means reliance on reason (that is, on deduction, on the criterion of logical consistency). (2) As contrasted with authoritarianism or mysticism (see definition), rationalism means reliance on our human powers.

Realism: (1) As contrasted with nominalism (see definition), realism holds that universals are real, and more real than the particulars of sense experience. (2) As contrasted with idealism (see definition), realism holds that the objects of our knowledge are not mind-dependent but are independently existing entities. (3) As contrasted with idealism in still another sense, realism is the point of view that interests itself in men and institutions as they are, rather than as they ought to be. In this sense, realism is almost equivalent to naturalism (see definition).

Relativism: The view that maintains our judgments to be relative to (that is, conditioned upon) certain factors such as cultural milieu or individual bias. Hence the view that we do not possess any absolute, objective (see definition) truth. The relativist need not hold that all judgments are relative; it is possible, for instance, to hold that the physical sciences yield absolute truth while maintaining that in other fields (for example, ethics and religion) there is no absolute truth.

Scepticism: The position that denies the possibility of knowledge. Here, as with relativism (see definition), it is possible either to have a total scepticism or to limit one's scepticism to certain fields.

Solipsism: From the Latin terms *solus* (alone) and *ipse* (self). Hence the view that everything other than oneself is a state of oneself.

Subjectivism: See **Objective, Relativism,** and **Scepticism.**

Substance: A variously used term. (1) In one meaning, substance is simply that which is real. Thus, because Aristotle held reality to consist of amalgams of matter and form, he called each such amalgam a "substance." (2) In another meaning, substance is about equivalent to essence (see definition). Also (3) substance is contrasted with attribute (or property, or quality) as that which *has* the attributes. Thus substance is the underlying (and unknown) ground in which properties are thought to inhere; it is that about which we are judging when we assert properties of a subject, for example, when we say, "The rose is red." Hence (4) substance is that which, unlike an attribute or property, exists in its own right and depends on nothing else.

Teleology: From the Greek terms *telos* (end, goal) and *logos* (theory, account). Hence the view that affirms the reality of purpose and holds the universe either to be consciously designed (as with the Christian doctrine of a providential God) or (as with Aristotle) to be the working out of partly conscious, partly unconscious purposes that are immanent in the developing organisms.

Universal: A universal is that which is predicable of many. Thus "man" is a universal because it is predicable of Washington, Jefferson, Hamilton, and all other individual men. The main problem about universals concerns their ontological status (see **Ontology**). Are they (1) separate entities distinct from the individuals of which they are predicable, (2) real but not separable, or (3) not real at all, but merely the names of likenesses shared by certain particulars? See **Nominalism** and **Realism**.

Verifiability principle: According to this principle, the meaning of a statement is the method of its verification. A statement that cannot be verified (for example, "God exists") is without cognitive meaning. For an early version, see p. 267.

Voluntarism: The theory that asserts the primacy of will over intellect as an explanatory principle of human behavior, of God's nature, and of the universe as a whole. See, for instance, pp. 147–50.

Index

This is primarily an index of proper names. Thus titles and principal topics of discussion are indexed under the authors. Topics that recur in the work of several philosophers are also indexed as main entries. Page numbers in *italics* refer to quotations; those in **boldface** refer to major discussions.